1987

Confusing
is not a
heroine?
Can't
speak?

Po 207

Coleridge's Imagination

Pete Laver

Nor has the rolling year twice measured,
From sign to sign, its steadfast course,
Since every mortal power of Coleridge
Was frozen at its marvellous source.

Towards the top of Grains Ghyll, where its banks begin to form a distinct gorge, walkers ascending from Seathwaite on their way to Scafell may see on their left a substantial cairn. It stands where a stream falls to the path, which here is solid rock, crosses it, and drops some sixty feet to the main beck. In winter, both falls are frozen over. Ahead is the dark face of Great End. Looking back, one can see through Borrowdale and along Derwentwater as far as Skiddaw, and below it, Coleridge's Keswick.

The cairn commemorates Pete Laver, for seven years Resident Librarian at Dove Cottage, Grasmere. On 24 August 1983 he died at this spot from a heart attack, while climbing Scafell Pike. He was thirty-six. Only a few weeks later he was to have become a Librarian to the English Faculty at Oxford. He and his wife, Mags, were in the final stages of buying a house, and their two children, Jacob and Amy, were looking forward to the move. Friends and colleagues in Grasmere were getting used to the idea of their going – sad from their own point of view, but glad about the prospects opening up for Pete and his family. Everyone assumed they would be back for the 1984 Wordsworth Summer Conference, if not before.

The contributors to this volume were indebted to Pete's knowledge of the Wordsworth Library, where he provided cheerful and indispensable help to visiting scholars. Outside the Library, he conveyed his enthusiasm for literature as a tutor for the Summer Conference, and, locally in Cumbria, by teaching for the Open University, and organizing school visits to Dove Cottage. His sensitivity and insight as a teacher were complemented by the vigorous originality of his own creative work as poet and draughtsman. His early work was published in the Newcastle journals, *Ashes* and *Iron*, and in three individual collections – *Guillotine*, *Pete Laver's Anarcho-Marxist Fun Book*, and *Water, Glass, The Toad of Guilt*.

When he died, Pete had recently completed a reading tour of northern England, where his work was becoming increasingly well known, and he had prepared a collection of his poetry for publication. He will be mourned by all the many people he reached as librarian, teacher, poet and artist. Above all, though, his gift for friendship will be missed, for it was this that gave his talent a special life. For these and many other reasons, we should like to dedicate this book to his memory.

Abbreviations

BL	S. T. Coleridge, *Biographia Literaria*, ed. J. Engell and W. Jackson Bate, *CC* VII (2 vols., 1983)
BLS	S. T. Coleridge, *Biographia Literaria*, ed. J. Shawcross (2 vols., Oxford, 1907)
BRH	*Bulletin of Research in the Humanities*
Bristol LB	George Whalley, 'The Bristol Library Borrowings of Southey and Coleridge', *Library,* IV (Sept. 1949) pp. 114–31
CC	*The Collected Works of Samuel Taylor Coleridge*, Bollingen Series LXXV, (London and New York, 1969–)
CL	*The Collected Letters of Samuel Taylor Coleridge*, ed. E. L. Griggs (6 vols., Oxford, 1956–71)
CM	S. T. Coleridge, *Marginalia*, ed. George Whalley, *CC* XII (5 vols., London and Princeton, N.J., 1980–)
CN	*The Notebooks of Samuel Taylor Coleridge*, ed. K. Coburn (6 vols., New York, 1957–73)
C&S	S. T. Coleridge, *On the Constitution of the Church and State, According to the Idea of Each*, ed. J. Colmer, *CC* X (1976)
DWJ	*The Journals of Dorothy Wordsworth*, ed. E. de Selincourt (2 vols., Oxford, 1941)
EC	*Essays in Criticism*
ELH	*English Literary History*
EOT	S. T. Coleridge, *Essays on his Times*, ed. D. V. Erdman, *CC* III (3 vols., 1978)
EY	*The Letters of William and Dorothy Wordsworth*, ed. E. de Selincourt, 2nd edn, *The Early Years, 1787–1805*, revised by C. L. Shaver (Oxford, 1967)
Friend	S. T. Coleridge, *The Friend*, ed. B. Rooke, *CC* IV (2 vols., 1969)
H Works	*The Complete Works of William Hazlitt*, ed. P. P. Howe (21 vols., 1930–4)
Lects 1795	S. T. Coleridge, *Lectures 1795 on Politics and Religion*, ed. L. Patton and P. Mann, *CC* I (1971)
LL(M)	*The Letters of Charles and Mary Lamb*, ed. E. Marrs (3 vols., New York, 1975–8).

LS	S. T. Coleridge, *Lay Sermons*, ed. R. J. White, *CC* VI (1972)
McFarland, 'SI'	Thomas McFarland, 'The Origin and Significance of Coleridge's Theory of Secondary Imagination', *New Perspectives on Coleridge and Wordsworth*, ed. Geoffrey Hartman (New York and London, 1972), pp. 195–246
Misc C	*Coleridge's Miscellaneous Criticism*, ed. T. M. Raysor (Cambridge, Mass., 1936)
MLA	Modern Language Association of America
M Phil	*Modern Philology*
N&Q	*Notes & Queries*
Norton 'Prelude'	William Wordsworth, *The Prelude, 1799, 1805, 1850*, eds. J. Wordsworth, M. H. Abrams, S. Gill (New York and London, 1979)
Oxford 'Prelude'	William Wordsworth, *The Prelude*, ed. E. de Selincourt, 2nd edn, revised by H. Darbishire (Oxford, 1959)
P Lects	*The Philosophical Lectures of Samuel Taylor Coleridge*, ed. K. Coburn (London and New York, 1949)
PMLA	*Publications of the Modern Language Association* (Baltimore, 1886–)
Prose Works	*The Prose Works of William Wordsworth*, ed. W. J. B. Owen and J. W. Smyser (3 vols., Oxford, 1974)
PW	*The Complete Poetical Works of Samuel Taylor Coleridge*, ed. E. H. Coleridge (2 vols., Oxford, 1912)
Sh C	*Coleridge's Shakespearean Criticism*, ed. T. M. Raysor (2 vols., 1930)
SIR	*Studies in Romanticism*
SM	S. T. Coleridge, *The Statesman's Manual*, ed. R. J. White, *CC* VI (1972)
TLS	*The Times Literary Supplement*
TWC	*The Wordsworth Circle*
WPW	*The Poetical Works of William Wordsworth*, ed. E. de Selincourt and H. Darbishire (5 vols., Oxford, 1940–9)

Introduction

Imagination was many things to Coleridge, and the contributors to this book have been as varied in their preoccupations and approaches as the writer himself. Thomas McFarland, in the first and most general of the essays – 'Romantic imagination, nature and the pastoral ideal' – is concerned with the origins of Romanticism in the years that followed the French Revolution, and its relation to 'the vision of a simpler existence' proffered by pastoral. Distinguishing between 'solitude of identity' and 'solitude of alienation', he takes as his texts *Alastor* and *This Lime-Tree Bower My Prison*. 'Both solitudes', he argues, 'are Romantic in that they arise from the accelerating external pressures on the ego that were determinants of Romanticism'; but only the 'solitude of identity' can find a balm in its extension of Theocritan pastoral. Shelley's poet leaves 'His cold fireside and alienated home/ To seek strange truths in distant lands', but can find no reconciliation; for the Coleridge of *This Lime-Tree Bower*, however, 'imagination's invocation of nature can serve to align Romantic solitude with the essentials of the pastoral ideal'.

Jonathan Wordsworth too is concerned with the finding of identity through an act of imagination. In 'The infinite I AM', he examines two persistent and related assumptions: that Coleridge's thinking about imagination in *Biographia Literaria* derived from German metaphysics; and that, despite his choice of words, Coleridge regarded the primary imagination as of secondary importance. Evidence is produced to show not only that Coleridge's thought is rooted in a native English tradition, but that, for all his eclectic and passionate reading, he remained broadly consistent in his beliefs throughout the twenty-year period between the first definitions of imagination in 1795, and the writing of *Biographia*. At all times Coleridge was primarily concerned not with artistic creativity (however important that might seem, or be), but with the 'Ascent of Being' – man's ability to transcend the merely human, to 'lose and find all self in God'.

Kristine Dugas and Norman Fruman lay emphasis rather on the loss, and the repression, that are implied in Coleridge's 'quest for grace'. For Dugas, in her study of the Notebooks, Coleridge is a divided being, one who 'strove for the ideal, [but] was tortured by the real'. The yearning

1

for oneness led him to suppress precisely the 'sharp and restless sensitivity' which the Notebooks suggest might have released him from lethargy and self-doubt. Fruman presents a view of the 'final, frozen recoil from the warm and vivid world of Nature and the natural man'. 'For Coleridge', he writes, 'truly human life "begins in its detachment from Nature, and is to end in union with God" '. Such life could only be of the mind – 'all else is from the bestial':

He spent the Highgate years more or less in the garb and stance of a priest, clad from head to toe in black, and declaiming against the evils of the age and the animal in us all. He was still a young man when he ceased to be a husband, father, brother, or a lover to anyone.

Meanwhile, as Molly Lefebure points out, the deserted Mrs Coleridge was leading a life that could be surprisingly lighthearted. Her brother-in-law Southey was making up for some of Coleridge's deficiencies as husband and father, and generating at Greta Hall a Shandyan atmosphere in which Sara flourished to the extent of creating a private language. 'She asks me', Southey writes affectionately in a letter of 1821,

how I can be such a Tomnoddycum (though my name, as she knows, is Robert), and calls me a detesty, a maffrum, a goffrum, a chatterpye, a sillycum, and a great mawkinfort.

In a rather different sense, as William Ruddick reminds us, Coleridge too had evolved a special language at Keswick – a highly distinctive prose capable of evoking his new-found joy in the fells: 'As I bounded down, noticed the moving stones under the soft moss, hurting my feet.' In place of the picturesque guides, and statuesque 'taking' of views, is a vivid excitement in the physical realities of the Lake District. Coleridge had come as a stranger to Wordsworth's native region, but in fact walked higher and harder than Wordsworth ever did.

Coleridge–Wordsworth relations, and the nature and effect of what Thomas McFarland has called their symbiosis, concern several contributors. Stephen Parrish, who focusses on the poems intended for *Lyrical Ballads*, advances the argument that the most revolutionary early poems of Wordsworth and Coleridge rose 'not so much out of harmonious collaboration as out of deep and unresolved conflicts of critical opinion'. In March 1801, however, writing to Godwin, Coleridge describes his imagination as no longer 'mitred with flame' but 'like a cold snuff on the circular rim of a brass candlestick'. Can we attribute Coleridge's imaginative extinction, Stephen Parrish asks, to his friend's failure to respond to an imagination more allegorical and mythic than his own?

Lucy Newlyn is also concerned with strains and complexities in the relationship. Why is it that Coleridge's detection of a 'radical difference' in their theoretical positions should belong to 1802, when Wordsworth writes his most overtly fanciful poetry, and Coleridge himself chooses to downgrade Fancy to the merely mechanical? In evolving the Fancy/Imagination definitions, she suggests, Coleridge is unconsciously pointing to a distinction between Wordsworth's literal-mindedness and his own increasingly confirmed symbolic thinking. As in *Biographia*, theoretical difference masks deeper incompatibilities. Richard Gravil, too, is concerned with antithetical imaginations, but finds Coleridge's destructively dominant over his friend's. His essay sees the friendship as marked by Coleridge's long struggle to 'totalise' Wordsworth – to make 'a perfectly congruous whole' out of a brother poet who remained, in his most characteristic work, disappointingly unregenerate.

David Erdman's 'The Otway connection' touches on similar areas of discussion, but its preoccupations are very different. The paper is a complex investigation into the relations between *The Mad Monk*, Otway's *Complaint*, Lucy, *Christabel* and *Dejection*: it would be robbed of some of its capacity to please and surprise if the reader were forewarned of its conclusions. There is a corpse, and possibly a villain; Wordsworth and Coleridge are featured as commander poet and demon power, and one's sense of their creative/destructive sparring is greatly enhanced. Nicholas Roe in taking Robespierre for his subject has the surprising task of rendering undemonic a leader who in the popular mind ranks with Caligula, Stalin and Hitler. To Coleridge, it transpires, Robespierre was an inspiration – the Man of Imagination on an heroic scale, flawed only by his lack of faith. In this respect, Roe suggests, Coleridge's idea of Robespierre corresponds to Wordsworth's account of his Godwinian self in *The Prelude*. Looking back to that time, he did not find imagination dormant: rather, it was rampant, and generative of chimaeras, having slipped the control of love, the affections, the sense of intellectual fallibility. Roe's essay not merely calls attention to the fascination Robespierre exercised upon Coleridge in this respect – as the prophet of futurity – but also points to his role as one who, prior to Wordsworth, put Coleridge on the track of imagination itself.

The book concludes with four essays on individual Coleridge poems. Robert Barth and Peter Larkin both take *Dejection* as their subject, but come to it from different directions. Barth, who is particularly concerned with the development from verse-letter to printed text, sees it as a poem about love, joy and imagination – all of them so bound together that they cannot 'stand dividually'. The word 'love', which appears twenty-one times in the *Letter to Sara*, disappears in *Dejection: an Ode*, but this merely implies that the principle itself has (as Barth puts it) 'gone underground'. *Dejection* becomes, in fact, 'a love poem in a broader and deeper sense –

now not merely the lament of a frustrated lover, but an ode to the power of love'. Peter Larkin's concerns are more abstract. He sees the relation between two different modes of Coleridge's writing (poetic and philosophical) as a difficult one, and *Dejection* itself as a fraught text. 'Which voice', he asks, 'might best name imagination?' 'Theory does not blend with poetry', in his view, 'without some liability.' And in this particular poem the cost is that 'to a philosophic eye works of imagination may always in practice stray to the fanciful'.

If Barth's Coleridge strives for wholeness, and Larkin's finds division, Anthony Harding's does both. His title, 'Mythopoesis: the unity of *Christabel*' sets up holistic expectations, but it is with fallen vision (and fragmentation) that Harding is centrally concerned. Distancing the poem from Lewis, Radcliffe and the Gothic, he takes it closer to Blake's *Visions of the Daughters of Albion* and Shelley's *Prometheus Unbound*. In this new, mythic context, *Christabel* is seen as a study of creative spirit held in thrall by nature and the natural man. If the poem reaches no conclusion, Harding argues, that is because its real subject is less a story than a state: the loss of speech, prayer, and wholeness, in an invasion of the unregenerate.

Coleridge's greatest poem of and about imagination must be *Kubla Khan*, and it is fitting that the volume should end with an essay by John Beer on the poem's 'languages'. To what extent, though passively, was Coleridge carrying forward, in the creation of *Kubla Khan*, a project already begun by Spenser, Milton, and Cowper? Why does his Abyssinian maid haunt a Tartar landscape through which there flows a Greek river? John Beer's search in Coleridge's literary haunts for comparable occurrences of rocks and rills, music and mazes, domes and dulcimers, is subsidiary here – though fascinating in itself – to a search for a way of seeing 'the effusions of unchecked libido' in significant relation to evocations of earlier 'tamers of chaos'. *Kubla Khan* is read as a ferment of competing languages which dramatise the conflicts of Coleridge's being: an imploded myth, as it were, of the tensions others of our essays have explored.

Romantic imagination, nature, and the pastoral ideal

THOMAS McFARLAND

There exists a natural and almost inevitable affinity between the Romantic and the pastoral, what in good Romantic terminology might be called a *Wahlverwandschaft*. Romanticism might be sickness, as Goethe said, but pastoral was its balm. Romanticism was frenzy, and pastoral was peace. It was the disruptive force of the French Revolution, said Hazlitt, that stirred English poetry into Romanticism and moulded its character:

> From the impulse it thus received, it rose at once from the most servile imitation and tamest common-place, to the utmost pitch of singularity and paradox. . . . There was a mighty ferment in the heads of statesmen and poets, kings and people. . . . According to the prevailing notions, all was to be natural and new. Nothing that was established was to be tolerated. . . . A striking effect produced where it was least expected, something new and original, no matter whether good, bad, or indifferent . . . was all that was aimed at. . . . The world was to be turned topsy-turvy; and poetry, by the good will of our Adam-wits, was to share its fate and begin *de novo*.

Above all, Romanticism was a convulsive response to a growing sense of perplexity and confusion with regard to received assumptions of social order, religious assurance, and economic possibility. Against this expanding complexity, pastoral proffered the vision of a simpler existence. It had muted since its Theocritan origins the eternal hurly-burly of city and court (the 'court news' of which 'poor rogues' talk has always been a matter of 'Who loses and who wins; who's in, who's out'). Now once again, though transformed in emphasis, pastoral tendered to the Romantic imagination a nostalgic invitation to a life more in harmony with nature. It was this invitation that Rousseau accepted when he abandoned Paris for the bucolic balm of the *Hermitage*:

> Although for some years I had fairly frequently gone into the country, I had hardly tasted its pleasures. Indeed my trips, generally made in the company of pretentious people and always ruined by a feeling of constraint, had merely whetted my appetite for rural delights; the closer the glimpse I got of them the more I felt the want of them. I was so tired of reception rooms, fountains, shrubberies, and flower-beds . . . I was so weary of pamphlets, clavichords . . . and great dinners, that when I spied a poor simple thorn bush, a hedge, a barn, or a meadow . . . when I heard in the distance the rustic refrain of the goat-women's song, I consigned all rouge, flounces, and perfumes to the devil.

5

To be sure, the Romantic imagination felt obliged to transform this reawakened urge to pastoral. As a classical form both artificial and conventional, pastoral to that extent seemed alien to Romanticism, which was fascinated by spontaneous overflows and effusions, by unstudied naturalness, by the rejection of imitation and the apotheosis of originality – it wanted, as Hazlitt said, to 'begin *de novo*', all had 'to be natural and new'. As Hazlitt also observed, in continuation of that passage, a characteristic of the Romantic upheaval was that 'kings and queens were dethroned from their rank and station in legitimate tragedy or epic poetry, as they were decapitated elsewhere; rhyme was looked upon as a relic of the feudal system, and regular metre was abolished along with regular government'. The tradition of formal imitation so essential to pastoral could not flourish in such an atmosphere.

But another and no less important emphasis of pastoral was precisely congruent to Hazlitt's normative specification of kings and queens being dethroned; for pastoral, as Frederick Garber has pointed out, derives much of its appeal from the fact that amid conditions of tyranny in the real world it presented an ideal world free of social and political hierarchy. The relation of the Romantic imagination and pastoral conceiving is thus inherently paradoxical, and the paradox extends along all historical lines of their convergence. Pastoral does not loom large on the surface of Romanticism; just beneath that surface it is everywhere. It is not even necessary to rely wholly on Empson's recognition of transformations of the pastoral impulse to document this perception. On the contrary, though pastoral awareness was relegated to the background by the Romantic emphasis on originality, it was widely diffused in that background and again and again emerges briefly to view. 'I envy you the first reading of Theocritus', wrote Shelley to John Gisborne; and elsewhere Mary Shelley notes of 'a record of the books that Shelley read' during the years 1814 and 1815, that it 'includes, in Greek, Homer, Hesiod, Theocritus, the histories of Thucydides and Herodotus, and Diogenes Laertius'; for 1816 she finds 'in Greek, Theocritus, the *Prometheus* of Aeschylus, several of Plutarch's *Lives*, and the works of Lucian'. 'Every ten lines almost' of Theocritus, wrote Coleridge, 'furnish one or more instances of Greek words, whose specific meaning is not to be found in the best Lexicons', and he then gives examples.

Shelley and Coleridge perhaps knew Greek better than the other English Romantics, but there was a corollary Latin tradition stemming from Virgil, and from this almost all the Romantic writers could claim edification. Wordsworth was of course an excellent Latinist, and his *Michael* is not merely a pastoral poem by grace of the Empsonian formula, but is in fact firmly subtitled *A Pastoral Poem* by Wordsworth himself.

Again, the youthful De Quincey (who boasted of his prowess in both Latin and Greek) notes offhandedly, but significantly in terms of the lurking presence of specifically classical awarenesses, that 'there is no good pastoral in the world but Wordsworth's *Brothers*'.

Still again, the seacoast idyll of Juan and Haidée in the second canto of *Don Juan* seems a version of pastoral by way of a tradition running from Virgil through Sannazaro. Byron was of course well versed in Italian literature, and that specific pastoralism was present to his mind is attested by his sardonic reflections in the first canto on Juan's 'classic studies', where he says that 'Virgil's songs are pure, except that horrid one/ Beginning "Formosum Pastor Corydon" '. But it was not merely the Second Eclogue that came to Byron's notice; he seems to have been virtually saturated in the *Eclogues*. He quotes the Third Eclogue to Hobhouse in 1811, quotes it again in his journal in 1813, and once again to Moore in 1814. To Moore in that same year he quotes the Seventh Eclogue, as he does to Hobhouse in 1820 and to Murray in 1822. Rousseau, too, who quit urban society for the bucolic *otium* of the country ('I felt that I was born for retirement and the country; it was impossible for me to live happily anywhere else') was conditioned by Virgilian awareness: 'I must have learned and re-learned Virgil's *Eclogues* a good twenty times', he recalls.

How specific, and how firmly based in knowledge of Greek and Latin texts, was the knowledge of pastoral that underlay Romanticism's love of the natural has been somewhat obscured by their dislike of imitation and imposed form. *Mont Blanc*, said Shelley himself, was 'an undisciplined overflowing of the soul.' Yet Shelley translated fragments of Bion's *Death of Adonis* and of the *Death of Bion* attributed to Moschus, and he also translated a fragment from the Latin of Virgil's Tenth Eclogue. Moreover, there are places where all the elements of pastoral are present, although the poem itself is not formally of that genre. An example is provided by his *Hymn to Pan*, which runs in part:

> From the forests and highlands
>> We come, we come;
> From the river-girt islands,
>> Where loud waves are dumb
>>> Listening to my sweet pipings.
> The wind in the reeds and the rushes,
>> The bees on the bells of thyme,
> The birds on the myrtle bushes,
>> The cicade above in the lime,
> And the lizards below in the grass,
> Were as silent as ever old Tmolus was,
>> Listening to my sweet pipings.

II

> Liquid Peneus was flowing,
>   And all dark Tempe lay
> In Pelion's shadow, outgrowing
>   The light of the dying day,
>   Speeded by my sweet pipings.

Bees are especially important in Theocritus; lizards figure prominently in both Theocritus and Virgil; and Pan himself, as Bruno Snell points out in *The Discovery of the Mind: The Greek Origins of European Thought*, was part of the reason for Virgil's transfer of the pastoral locale from Theocritan Sicily to Arcadia:

> Polybius who came from the humdrum Arcadia cherished a great affection for his country. Although there was not much of interest to be related of this land behind the hills, he could at least report (4.20) that the Arcadians were, from the days of their infancy onwards, accustomed to practice the art of singing, and that they displayed much eagerness in organizing musical contests. Virgil came across this passage when he was composing his shepherd songs, the *Eclogues*, and at once understood it to refer to the Arcadian shepherds; for Arcadia was shepherds' country and the home of Pan, the god of the herdsmen, inventor of the syrinx.

Shelley's great formal effort, *Adonais*, is prefixed by a Greek passage from the *Epitaphios Bionos*, and in *Adonais* itself the pastoral conventions are activated in a dazzlingly effective manner. This mighty poem is atypical, however, not only for Romanticism in general, but even for Shelley himself. Nothing else in his canon has such rhetorical splendor, slow-paced dignity, *decorum* and *gravitas*. For the most part – the truth deserves reiteration – the reaching for spontaneity (perhaps the most descriptive term for the rise of this new element is provided by the rubric of Wackenroder, *Herzensergiessungen* . . . – outpourings of the heart) occluded the sophisticated infrastructure of Romantic pastoralism. In most situations, as his wife recalls and as was stressed above in his own words, Shelley 'wrote because his mind overflowed'.

One place where the infrastructure is not occluded, though, is in the common emphasis of the two traditions upon external nature. Of the various criteria for Romanticism, complexly interwoven into an almost seamless cultural texture, first one, then another is put forward by commentators as the ruling passion of that sensibility: imagination, organicism, medievalism, subjectivism. But the most constant of all defining factors is nature. It was as though literature in the neo-classic age had been enclosed, and Romanticism opened a door and stepped outside to bathe in a new reality. 'My imagination', said Rousseau, 'languishes and dies in a room beneath the rafters of a ceiling'; it 'only thrives in the country and under the trees'. 'Come forth into the light of things', counseled Wordsworth, 'Let Nature be your Teacher.' In his very first statement, Goethe's Werther complains that 'the city itself is unpleasant; but then, all around it, nature is inexpressibly beautiful'; and in the next letter he is in rapture:

When the lovely valley teems with mist around me, and the high sun strikes the impenetrable foliage of my forest, and but a few rays steal into the inner sanctuary, I lie in the tall grass by the trickling brook and notice a thousand familiar things: when I hear the humming of the little world among the stalks, and am near the countless indescribable forms of the worms and insects, then I feel the presence of the Almighty . . .

Wordsworth, again, laments that

> The world is too much with us; late and soon,
> Getting and spending, we lay waste our powers:
> Little we see in Nature that is ours . . .
> This Sea that bares her bosom to the moon;
> The winds that will be howling at all hours . . . .
> For this, for every thing, we are out of tune; . . .

Still again, Keats in his youthful *Sleep and Poetry* attacked his neo-classic predecessors as men who 'sway'd about on a rocking horse,/And thought it Pegasus'. 'Ah dismal soul'd!', he continues,

> The winds of heaven blew, the ocean roll'd
> Its gathering waves – ye felt it not. The blue
> Bared its eternal bosom, and the dew
> Of summer nights collected still to make
> The morning precious: beauty was awake!
> Why were ye not awake? But ye were dead
> To things ye knew not of . . .

But Romanticism was not dead to these wonders. 'To every natural form, rock, fruit or flower', said Wordsworth,

> Even the loose stones that cover the highway,
> I gave a moral life: I saw them feel,
> Or linked them to some feeling: the great mass
> Lay bedded in a quickening soul, and all
> That I beheld respired with inward meaning.

In short, one must in the main agree with Paul de Man that

An abundant imagery coinciding with an equally abundant quantity of natural objects, the theme of imagination linked closely to the theme of nature, such is the fundamental ambiguity that characterizes the poetics of romanticism.

The primacy of nature must be stressed, because even in de Man's passage, and much more so in certain emphases of Geoffrey Hartman and Harold Bloom, the role of nature in the Romantic sensibility is misconceived or diminished. Bloom, for instance, sees the 'context of nature as a trap for the mature imagination'. 'The internalization of quest-romance', he says again, 'made of the poet-hero a seeker not after nature but after his own mature powers, and so the Romantic poet turned away, not from society to nature, but from nature to what was more integral than nature, within himself.' Hartman, for his part, speaks of 'the deeply paradoxical character of Wordsworth's dealings with nature' and suggests that what Wordsworth calls imagination 'may be *intrinsically* opposed to Nature'. Hartman goes on to make extended play with an 'unresolved opposition between Imagination and Nature' that he posits for Wordsworth.

These views, which are versions of Blake's idiosyncratic position that 'Natural objects always did & now do Weaken deaden & obliterate Imagination in Me', cannot it seems to me be maintained either for Wordsworth or for Romanticism as such except by disregarding overwhelming evidence to the contrary. Nature was not in opposition to Wordsworth's imagination; the vision of nature was itself the richest fulfillment of that imagination. The irreducible truth about Wordsworth is the one presented in Shelley's apostrophe to him: 'Poet of Nature, thou hast wept to know/ That things depart which never may return.' Mary Shelley says that 'The love and knowledge of Nature developed by Wordsworth' composed part of Shelley's 'favourite reading'; and she also reports of her husband that 'Mountain and lake and forest were his home; the phenomena of Nature were his favourite study.' She testifies again that Shelley 'loved to shelter himself' in 'such imaginations as borrowed their hues from sunrise or sunset, from the yellow moonshine or paly twilight, from the aspect of the far ocean or the shadows of the woods, – which celebrated the singing of the winds among the pines, the flow of a murmuring stream, and the thousand harmonious sounds which Nature creates in her solitudes'.

Wordsworth's witness is still more unequivocal. His highest vision of what he and Coleridge were trying to do was to preach the gospel of nature. They were to be 'joint labourers' in the work of men's 'deliverance'; they were, in fact, to be 'Prophets of Nature':

> Prophets of Nature, we to them will speak
> A lasting inspiration, sanctified
> By reason, blest by faith: what we have loved,
> Others will love, and we will teach them how . . .

To say that Wordsworth merely approved of nature would be radically to understate the situation. He recognized

> In nature and the language of the sense,
> The anchor of my purest thoughts, the nurse,
> The guide, the guardian of my heart, and soul
> Of all my moral being.

If he still retains a faith

> That fails not, in all sorrow my support,
> The blessing of my life; the gift is yours,
> Ye mountains! Thine, O Nature! Thou hast fed
> My lofty speculations; and in thee,
> For this uneasy heart of ours, I find
> A never-failing principle of joy
> And purest passion.

From 'Nature and her overflowing soul', he says,

> I had received so much, that all my thoughts
> Were steeped in feeling

and he speaks of 'That spirit of religious love in which/I walked with Nature'. The chief memory he bequested to his sister was

> That on the banks of this delightful stream
> We stood together; and that I, so long
> A worshipper of Nature, hither came
> Unwearied in that service; . . .

Similarly, Keats's earliest poetry is replete with a kind of intoxication with nature. 'What has made the sage or poet write', he asks, 'But the fair paradise of Nature's light?' The same intensity is maintained in Hölderlin's impassioned statement that 'to re-establish the peace above all peace, which passeth all understanding, to unite ourselves with Nature, into one infinite entity, that is the aim of all our aspiration'. 'He is made one with Nature', confirms Shelley in elegy of the dead Keats, there is heard

> His voice in all her music, from the moan
> Of thunder, to the song of night's sweet bird . . .

Pastoral too is preoccupied with nature, to an extent indeed only marginally less insistent than in the Romantic upheaval. Green grass, shading trees, humming bees, and purling brooks are indispensable to the pastoral vision, however the details of that vision may vary in other respects. As Renato Poggioli emphasizes, in *The Oaten Flute: Essays on Pastoral Poetry and the Pastoral Ideal*, 'When the poet is unable to escape into Arcadia, pastoral strategy requires that he retreat at least into an orchard or a park.' Ellen Zetzel Lambert, again, in her book called *Placing Sorrow: A Study of the Pastoral Convention from Theocritus to Milton*, notes that 'Pastoral consoles us by enfolding us in nature's sympathies.'

In high pastoralism the invocation of nature's richness and benignity can become extraordinarily intense. It is no accident that Milton, whose imagination was so profoundly moved by pastoral implication, described the Garden of Eden itself as a pastoral landscape. And no evocation of nature's texture could be more rich than that summoned by Theocritus in his Seventh Idyll:

Many an aspen, many an elm bowed and rustled overhead, and near by, the hallowed water gushed purling from a cave of the nymphs, while the brown cricket chirped busily amid the shady leafage, and the tree-frog murmured aloof in the dense thornbrake. Lark and goldfinch sang and turtledove moaned, and about the spring the bees hummed and hovered to and fro. All nature smelled of the opulent summertime, smelled of the season of fruit. Pears lay at our feet, apples on either side, rolling abundantly, and the young branches lay splayed upon the ground because of the weight of their damsons.

How readily this opulent vision coincides with the Romantic imagination's apprehension of nature can be illustrated from Keats's apprentice poem, *I Stood Tiptoe*, where the poet focuses the Romantic awareness of nature by his own untrained but intuitively prescient Hellenism. In a context of 'Fauns, and Dryades' and 'Arcadian Pan', Keats invokes

> A bush of May flowers with the bees about them;
> Ah, sure no tasteful nook would be without them;
> And let a lush laburnum oversweep them,
> And let long grass grow round the roots to keep them
> Moist, cool and green; and shade the violets,
> That they may bind the moss in leafy nets.

Again, Rousseau's very statement, 'my imagination, which only thrives in the country and under trees, languishes and dies in a room beneath the rafters of the ceiling', which was adduced above as normative of the Romantic discovery of nature, is immediately followed by a sentence from the realm of pure pastoral: 'J'ai souvent regretté qu'il n'existât pas des Dryades; c'eut infailliblement été parmi elles que j'aurois fixé mon attachement' – I often have regretted that dryads do not exist; for among them I should assuredly have found an object for my love. A few paragraphs later, Rousseau again connects the real landscape of Romantic discovery with the imaginary landscape of pastoral: 'I found no woodland fresh enough, no countryside moving enough, to suit me. The valleys of Thessaly would have satisfied me, if I had seen them; but my imagination was tired of inventing, and wanted some real locality to serve as a basis.'

Nevertheless, though pastoral nature and Romantic nature can be virtually identical presentations, a certain specific element, present in Romanticism but absent in the pastoral, makes the Romantic form at best a problematic version of pastoral and possibly one that in some instances should not even be called a version of pastoral at all. The uncertainty of the relationship is correlate with an uncertainty in defining pastoral as such. For there exists alongside a primary vision of the pastoral what one might call a laminated vision of pastoral. Both are important for pastoral meaning, and both are historically valid.

The primary vision is simply the sum of those factors to be found in Theocritus's idylls. The laminated vision, however, bonds to the primary vision certain historical accretions that fulfill the implication of the primary vision even though they were not present in it. A notable example is the idea of the 'golden age'. This conception does not occur in Theocritus; it stems rather from the earlier source of Hesiod, who speaks of a 'golden race' of men. Ovid, in the *Metamorphoses*, invokes a 'golden age' (*aurea aetas*), and Virgil, in his Fourth Eclogue, takes the conception into the realm of pastoral, forecasting that there will spring up a 'golden race' (*gens aurea*) throughout the world. By the time of the Renaissance, the golden age was incessantly invoked, by Tasso, by Guarini, by Ronsard, by Shakespeare, among others, and by 1659 Rapin, in his *Dissertatio de carmine pastorali*, theoretically bonded golden age and pastoral by saying that 'pastoral belongs properly to the golden age'. By Pope's *A Discourse on Pastoral Poetry*, published in 1717 but possibly written as early as 1704, the lamination was complete, because Pope there says that 'pastoral is an image of what they call the Golden age', while he still recognizes that '*Theocritus* excells all others in nature and simplicity. The subjects of his *Idyllia* are purely pastoral . . . . all others learn'd their excellencies from him'.

Another lamination occurred by the joining of the motifs of Virgil's *Georgics* to those of his *Eclogues*. Indeed, a fine example of the discrimination of laminated pastoral and primary pastoral is afforded by two examples noted earlier: that Wordsworth's *Michael* is subtitled *A Pastoral Poem*, while De Quincey chooses not *Michael* but *The Brothers* as his example of 'good pastoral'. The choice is significant, for *Michael* and *The Brothers* are closely linked in tone, diction, and theme, and in fact these two poems were the ones Wordsworth sent to the statesman Charles James Fox as co-operatively honoring the domestic affections. *Michael*, however, has laminated to its pastoralism the tradition of the *Georgics*. Its shepherd is not in a state of pastoral *otium*, but instead labors. 'I have been toiling more than seventy years', says Michael, thereby activating the principle of toil that rules the world of the *Georgics*, where '*labor omnia vicit'*. On the other hand, *The Brothers* incorporates no such rejection of *otium* and accordingly exhibits the characteristics of primary pastoral.

De Quincey's classical sophistication appears to advantage in his choice of *The Brothers* as 'good pastoral'. But Wordsworth, too, it must be stressed, knew exactly what he was doing in pastoral matters. Paul Alpers has recently praised lines from *The Prelude*'s eighth book as revealing Wordsworth's clear understanding of the pastoral tradition, and earlier critics such as Herbert Lindenberger, Stephen Parrish, and I myself have discussed the topic as well, not to mention Leslie Broughton's volume of 1920 called *The Theocritan Element in the Works of William Wordsworth*.

Yet, though both *Michael* and *The Brothers* can properly be termed pastorals, many Romantic invocations of nature perhaps cannot, even by the conception of laminated pastoral, be seen as according with pastoral implication. The possible rupture occurs not in the view of nature as such, but in the view of the relation of man to nature. A certain social interaction is necessary to pastoral; the natural landscape is merely the arena for the interplay of a group. Alpers, indeed, in the same article in which he praises Wordsworth's knowledge of pastoral ('What is Pastoral?', *Critical Inquiry*, 8 (Spring, 1982), pp. 437–60), argues that the 'representative anecdote' of pastoral (he is using a conception from Kenneth Burke) is the lives of the shepherds within the landscape, rather than the landscape itself. 'Whatever the specific features and emphases', he says, 'it is the representative anecdote of shepherds' lives that makes certain landscapes pastoral.'

Romantic nature, on the other hand, is customarily not the arena for social interaction, but for solitude. The 'representative anecdote' in this case may be indicated by Tieck's 'Waldeinsamkeit' – forest loneliness – the 'wondrous song' in *Der blonde Eckbert* that resounded throughout German Romanticism. Nature, in this instance the forest, is linked inextricably to solitude. We need only think of Thoreau at Walden Pond. Or consider Werther's comment in his first letter: 'Die Einsamkeit ist meinem Herzen köstlicher Balsam in dieser paradiesischen Gegend' – loneliness is precious balm to my heart in this paradisal region; and he immediately specifies the paradisal region: 'Every tree, every bush is a bouquet of flowers, and one might wish to be a spring beetle, to float about in this ocean of fragrance and therein find all his nourishment.' Chateaubriand, again, links Romantic nature not only to solitude but also to the further Romantic criterion of freedom:

Primitive liberty, I regain thee at last! I pass as this bird that flies before me, directed by chance and only encumbered by the choice of shades. Here I am, as the All-Powerful created me, sovereign of nature. . . . Is it on the brow of the man of society, or on mine, that the immortal seal of our origin is set? Go, shut yourself in your cities, obey your petty laws . . . while I go wandering through my solitudes.

In a different kind of expression, Wordsworth presents the bonding of solitude to Romantic nature through a memorable salute to Coleridge:

> For thou hast sought
> The truth in solitude, and thou art one,
> The most intense of Nature's worshippers;
> In many things my brother, chiefly here
> In this my deep devotion.

Now Romantic solitude is a topic of such depth and complexity that it would rather require a treatise for its elucidation than the fleeting remarks that can be accorded it here. Suffice it to say that the invocation of solitude occurs in the most diverse contexts, and that solitude has its own subsistence; that is to say, though it is frequently, it is not necessarily, bonded to nature. In this noteworthy evocation by De Quincey, for instance, it is bonded to another Romantic criterion, that of childhood:

. . . in solitude, above all things . . . God holds 'communion undisturbed' with children. Solitude, though silent as light, is, like light, the mightiest of agencies, for solitude is essential to man. All men come into this world *alone*; all leave it *alone* . . . . The solitude, therefore, which in this world appalls or fascinates a child's heart is but the echo of a far deeper solitude through which he already has passed, and of another solitude, deeper still through which he *has* to pass: reflex of one solitude – prefiguration of another.

O burden of solitude, that cleavest to man through every stage of his being! In his birth, which *has* been, in his life, which *is*, in his death, which *shall* be – mighty and essential solitude that wast, and art, and art to be, thou broodest like the spirit of God moving upon the surface of the deeps, over every heart that sleeps in the nurseries of Christendom.

Solitude, in truth, is so fundamental to the Romantic complex that we may even take as the representative anecdote of the passage from neo-classic sensibility to that of Romanticism the breakdown of the friendship of Diderot and Rousseau over that single conception. As Cassirer remarks, Diderot

regarded Rousseau's untamable urge for solitude merely as a singular quirk. For Diderot needed social intercourse not only as the essential medium for his activity but also as the spiritual fluid in which alone he was capable of thinking. The will to solitude accordingly appeared to him as nothing less than spiritual and moral aberration. It is well known that Diderot's phrase in the postscript to the *Fils naturel*, that only an evil man loves solitude – a phrase that Rousseau immediately applied to himself and for which he took Diderot to task, gave the first impetus to their break. After this break, Diderot's feeling of something uncanny in Rousseau's nature rose until it became almost intolerable.

To be sure, the Romantics talked of solitude more frequently than they practiced it. Rousseau's *Hermitage* was actually a cottage for three on the estate of Mme d'Épinay, a dozen miles from Paris. His island retreat, to which he looked forward with such anticipation of pastoral *otium* ('I meant at last to carry out my great scheme for a life of idleness'), was blessed by the repeated presence of Thérèse Levasseur. Wordsworth, too, was in fact almost never alone throughout his adult life, and as Robert Langbaum has pointed out, poems wherein he presents himself as being solitary again and again distort the actual situation. For instance, 'the bliss of solitude' is a phrase in his poem that begins 'I wandered lonely as a cloud'; but we know from Dorothy's journal, where the same daffodils are described, that the situation might more truly be described as '*We* wandered *companionably* as *two* clouds'. Likewise, the solitary 'I' who was 'a Traveller . . . upon the moor' when he encountered the old leech-gatherer was, as we also know from Dorothy's journal, really a 'we', while the leech-gatherer himself, who in the poem surpasses even the 'vast solitude' of the Old Cumberland Beggar, had fathered ten children.

But the discrepancy between the practice of solitude and its ideal actually strengthens rather than weakens the special force of that ideal. However much company he may have had as man walking, Rousseau as reveristic 'promeneur' was ineluctably 'solitaire'.

It is in the defining origins of Romantic solitude, I suggest and will try to illustrate in the remainder of this essay, that there is contained the ambivalence of whether or not its bonding to nature can be considered a valid extension of pastoral. Ultimately, I suppose, it is not some mechanical formula but our intuitive sense of whether or not a representation fits the rest of the tradition that determines our willingness to think of it as pastoral. As Charles Segal says, in his *Poetry and Myth in Ancient Pastoral*, 'the homogeneity of the pastoral landscape and the generality of the pastoral characters, whether in Theocritus or Milton, in Tasso or Pope, contribute to [the] sense of the simultaneous and visible coexistence of all the parts of the tradition, the latest developments with the first beginnings'.

In this context, I should argue that one aspect of Romanticism's bonding of nature and solitude does fit into the pastoral tradition, while a second does not. The two versions are both representations of solitude, but they take their origin from different situations. The first is what I may provisionally call *solitude of identity* and the second *solitude of alienation*. The first is amenable to the pastoral tradition, the second is not; and I shall try to illustrate the one by reference to Coleridge's *This Lime-Tree Bower my Prison* and the other by reference to Shelley's *Alastor*.

Both solitudes are Romantic in that they arise from the accelerating external pressures on the ego that were determinants of Romanticism. Fichte's apotheosis of the ego as the font of all reality, for instance, seems more a reaction formation occasioned by the ego's increasing beleaguerment than a maintainable scientific hypothesis. Likewise, Romantic suicide and Romantic madness both seem to be symptoms of increasing constriction: 'Ach diese Lücke!', exclaims Werther, 'diese entsetzliche Lücke, die ich hier in meinem Busen fühle' – Ah, this void, this terrible void that I feel here in my breast. *Solitude of alienation*, I suggest, is a variant of this awareness; it is the unhappy consciousness carried to exponential urgency. As such, it constitutes virtually an eviction of being, as in the solitude of Mary Shelley's Frankenstein creature or in the many Romantic avatars of the Wandering Jew. 'When early youth had passed', says Shelley in *Alastor*, the poet 'left/His cold fireside and alienated home/ To seek strange truths in undiscovered lands'.

Solitude of identity, on the other hand, seems to be the pastoral retreat from the city pushed one step further in the same line by the pressures of Romanticism. All pastoral prefers the country to the city. In Romanticism, however, the city, swollen and polluted by the industrial revolution, became increasingly malign. 'Hell', said Shelley, 'is a city much like London.' A. J. George, in a study of French Romanticism that sees the industrial revolution as one of its prime sources, notes that under industrialism's disruptive impact – which, as we might remember, was the subject of Wordsworth's pastoral letter to Fox – the 'urban population' of Paris 'jumped from 588,000 in 1801 to 890,000 in 1826'. The Malthusian spectre was rearing its head, and Malthus himself, we must not forget, was Wordsworth's contemporary. To Wordsworth, London was a 'monstrous ant-hill on the plain/ Of a too busy world'. 'What a shock/ For eyes and ears! what anarchy and din,/ Barbarian and infernal', he says of London's epitome, Bartholomew Fair:

> Oh blank confusion! true epitome
> Of what the mighty City is herself
> To thousands upon thousands of her sons.
> Living amid the same perpetual whirl
> Of trivial objects, melted and reduced
> To one identity. . .

It was to counter the city's threat of melting and reducing by restoring the identity of the individual that solitude became an ideal. Other people were the threat, and so other people were discarded until the individual identity could re-establish itself.

In any event, *solitude of identity* is marked by joy and fullness of being. Tieck's 'Waldeinsamkeit' is such a solitude, and it resonates with rejoicing:

> Waldeinsamkeit,
> Die mich erfreut,
> So morgen wie heut,
> In ew'ger Zeit,
> O wie mich freut
> Waldeinsamkeit.

Later, the forest loneliness is hailed as the 'only joy', and still later it 'Von neuem mich freut'. Wordsworth found in solitude 'Sublimer joy':

> . . . for I would walk alone,
> In storm and tempest, or in starlight nights
> Beneath the quiet heavens, and at that time
> Have felt whate'er there is of power in sound
> To breathe an elevated mood, by form
> Or image unprofaned; and I would stand,
> Beneath some rock, listening to sounds that are
> The ghostly language of the ancient earth,
> Or make their dim abode in distant winds.
> Thence did I drink the visionary power.

Chateaubriand, who contemptuously rejected the society of the city for solitude ('Go, shut yourself in your cities, obey your petty laws . . . while I go wandering through my solitudes'), drank the visionary power, too, and exulted in his isolation:

Not a single beat of my heart shall be constrained, not a single one of my thoughts shall be enchained; I shall be as free as nature; I shall recognize as sovereign only him who kindled the flame of the suns, and with one stroke of his hand set all the worlds rolling.

Solitude of alienation, on the other hand, looks into the abyss. 'To transform the world, to recreate it afresh', says the mysterious visitor to Father Zossima in *The Brothers Karamazov*, 'men must turn into another path psychologically':

'You ask when it will come to pass; it will come to pass, but first we have to go through the period of isolation.'
  'What do you mean by isolation?' I asked him.
  'Why, the isolation that prevails everywhere, above all in our age. . . . For every one strives to keep his individuality as apart as possible, wishes to secure the greatest possible fulness of life for himself; but meantime all his efforts result not in attaining fulness of life but self-destruction, for instead of self-realisation he ends by arriving at complete solitude. All mankind in our age have split up into units, they all keep apart, each in his own groove; each one holds aloof, hides himself and hides what he has, from the rest, and he ends by being repelled by others and repelling them. . . . For he is accustomed to rely upon himself alone and to cut himself off from the whole. . . . Everywhere in these days men have, in their mockery, ceased to understand that the true security is to be found in social solidarity rather than in isolated individual effort. But this terrible individualism must inevitably have an end, and all will suddenly understand how unnaturally they are separated from one another. . . . Sometimes even if he has to do it alone, and his conduct seems crazy, a man must set an example, and so draw men's souls out of their solitude, and spur them to some act of brotherly love, that the great idea may not die.'

Now pastoral as such tends to thin out the populace into what I have elsewhere called a 'significant group' rather than to deny it altogether. This is precisely what Wordsworth does in both *Michael* and *The Brothers*. Even what Coleridge censured as a flaw in Wordsworth's poetic practice, that is, his 'undue predilection for the *dramatic* form in certain poems', can be seen as a subliminal loyalty to pastoral groupings. Indeed, Wordsworth's own theoretical propensity for solitude is cast into pastoral reference: 'Hitherto I had stood/ In my own mind remote from social life/...Like a lone shepherd on a promontory'. But though Wordsworth holds to *solitude of identity*, he repeatedly warns against *solitude of alienation*, as in the character of Vaudracour or the man in *Lines Left Upon a Seat in a Yew-Tree*, who 'turned himself away,/ And with the food of pride sustained his soul in solitude'. Such a person is a 'lost Man!'.

The representative anecdote for this kind of figure is supplied by Shelley's *Alastor, or, the Spirit of Solitude*. Shelley's awesomely despairing poem is surely one of literature's most painful testaments to wretchedness, a wretchedness so frantic, so alienated, and so alone that it burdens the heart. The melancholy is compounded by Mrs Shelley's testimony that 'None of Shelley's poems is more characteristic than this', though Shelley himself sees the poem as an *exemplum*:

The picture is not barren of instruction to actual men. The Poet's self-centered seclusion was avenged by the furies of an irresistible passion pursuing him to speedy ruin. . . .They who . . . keep aloof from sympathies with their kind, rejoicing neither in human joy nor mourning with human grief; these, and such as they, have their apportioned curse. They languish, because none feel with them their common nature. They are morally dead. . . .Those who love not their fellow-beings live unfruitful lives, and prepare for their old age a miserable grave.

Nature, in high Romantic fashion, figures importantly. 'The magnificence and beauty of the external world', says the Preface, 'sinks profoundly into the youth's conceptions.' In the poem itself Shelley writes of 'the Poet's blood/ That ever beat in mystic sympathy/ With nature's ebb and flow'. But nature here is nightmarish and alien:

> At length upon the lone Chorasmian shore
> He paused, a wide and melancholy waste
> Of putrid marshes.

The setting is blasted, but it is co-ordinate with the frantic protagonist himself: 'A gloomy smile/ Of desperate hope wrinkled his quivering lips.' In other words, to cut discussion to the bone, the *solitude of alienation* is here not redeemed by nature; rather nature, or at least any pastoral possibility of nature, is itself disfigured.

Coleridge's exquisite *This Lime-Tree Bower my Prison*, on the other hand, constitutes, among other things, a careful progress, a *manuductio*, so to speak, from a social group in the setting of pastoral to the *solitude of identity* also in the setting of pastoral. The poem, we will remember, is about some friends taking a walk in nature, but the poet, Coleridge, must stay behind because of an injury to his foot. So he imagines them on their walk – first in umbrageous Theocritan recesses, where they

> Wander in gladness, and wind down, perchance
> To that still roaring dell,
>   ...o'erwooded, narrow, deep
> And only speckled by the mid-day sun...

Then Coleridge imagines his friends coming onto high ground, with a view

> Of hilly fields and meadows, and the sea...
>   Yes! they wander on
> In gladness all; but thou, methinks, most glad,
> My gentle-hearted Charles! for thou hast pined
> And hunger'd after Nature, many a year,
> In the great City pent...

The passage, even after it has left the Theocritan dell, maintains its pastoralism by invocation of the tension between city and country; then, however, the pastoral tone changes to the heroic:

>   Ah! slowly sink
> Behind the western ridge, thou glorious Sun!
> Shine in the slant beams of the sinking orb,
> Ye purple heath-flowers! richlier burn, ye clouds!
> Live in the yellow light, ye distant groves!
> And kindle, thou blue Ocean!

But even here a Theocritan propriety is maintained, for as Segal points out, an

elusive . . . aspect of the bucolic world is closely associated with . . . sea and mountains. Played off against the shady trees, soft grass, cool water, and the soothing sounds of bees, cicadas, or birds, sea and mountain help shape that inner rhythm of closed and open, finite and infinite, which is so fundamental a part of the inner dynamics of Theocritan bucolic.

Having established the pastoral credentials of his group, as it were, Coleridge then transfers the mood to his own solitude, which is also carefully placed in the pastoral matrix:

>   A delight
> Comes sudden on my heart, and I am glad
> As I myself were there! Nor in this bower,
> This little lime-tree bower, have I not mark'd
> Much that has sooth'd me. Pale beneath the blaze
> Hung the transparent foliage; and I watch'd

> Some broad and sunny leaf, and lov'd to see
> The shadow of the leaf and stem above
> Dappling its sunshine!
>   . . . and though now the bat
> Wheels by, and not a swallow twitters,
> Yet still the solitary humble-bee
> Sings in the bean-flower!

The delight in the passage is characteristic of the *solitude of identity*. The invocation of 'the humble-bee' points to Theocritus, for the humming of bees is one of the chief evocations of his most characteristic moment.

Yet the humble-bee here is as 'solitary' as the poet himself. In the passage from the Seventh Idyll quoted above, 'the bees hummed to and fro' about the spring; in the Fifth Idyll there are 'bees humming bravely at the hives'; here the solitary humble-bee 'Sings in the bean-flower'. The delicacy of the single bee, symbolizing in the same way as its Theocritan plural, points the path for the solitary poet to rejoin a pastoral society, and the bonding of his solitariness to his friends' socialness is supplied by the agency of nature:

> Henceforth I shall know
> That Nature ne'er deserts the wise and pure;
> No plot so narrow, be but Nature there . . .

So we may conclude that in this kind of instance imagination's invocation of nature can serve to align Romantic solitude with the essentials of the pastoral ideal.

The Infinite I AM:
Coleridge and the Ascent of Being

JONATHAN WORDSWORTH

The main sections of *Biographia Literaria* were written – in fact largely dictated – in the summer of 1815. Within three years Coleridge was looking back on the work, and rejecting it as pantheist. His letter to J. H. Green of September 1818 lies about how much Schelling he had known at the time of writing, but makes the very interesting statement:

I was myself *taken in* by his system, retrograding from my own prior and better lights, and adopted it in the metaphysical chapters of my Literary Life ... (*CL*, IV, p. 874)

Two months later he commented to C. A. Tulk about Schelling:

as a *System* it is little more than Behmenism, translated from visions into Logic and a sort of commanding eloquence: and like Behmen's it is reduced at last to a mere Pantheism ... (*CL*, IV, p. 883)[1]

The presence of Schelling in the metaphysical chapters of *Biographia* is well attested. Coleridge might choose to tell Green that he had known 'little or nothing of any of his works, excepting his Transcendental Idealism' (*CL*, IV, p. 874), but scholars concerned with the issue of plagiarism – the poet's nephew and daughter among the first, in 1847 – have listed up to a dozen Schelling volumes and individual tracts on which he drew. Norman Fruman in *The Damaged Archangel* (1971) not only brought out the extent of these unacknowledged borrowings – often running to several pages of verbatim translation – but revealed to a queasy Coleridge establishment the pains taken to deceive the reader into believing the material was original.[2] More recently, James Engell in the new Bollingen edition of *Biographia* has categorized the ways in which Schelling and others have been introduced into the text, and even tabulated the borrowings. Among other things to emerge is the fact that the concentration of Schelling as Coleridge builds up to the definitions of imagination and fancy at the end of Chapter 13 is especially heavy.

Those who do not know *Biographia* well might easily think that it was the critics who have given the imagination definitions their prominence; but there can't be many passages in English prose that have been so deliberately and skilfully thrown into relief by their author. As the final page and a half of Volume One, the definitions are right at the centre of the work, and it is clear that Coleridge gave thought to their placing. Not only do they form a conclusion to the metaphysical section of *Biographia*; they are prepared for in the matter of the preceding chapters, in their arrangement, and in the very typography – again something that Coleridge cared about a great deal. The spoof letter from a friend advising against an unwritten further chapter on imagination, both implies (whimsically, but impressively) that the definitions concentrate material that might normally have taken 100 pages, and at the same time has the effect of marking them out visually. The letter is printed in italics, and the definitions comprise the final roman paragraphs of the volume.

Coleridge staked a great deal on these paragraphs, and, though there was no second edition of *Biographia* until Henry Nelson and Sara Coleridge's act of piety in 1847, the attention they have received in this century surely justifies his faith. Since the Oxford edition of Shawcross in 1907 an orthodoxy has grown up among scholars which holds that the secondary imagination, despite the usual force of the words, was more important to Coleridge than the primary. 'The distinction appears to be this', Shawcross writes, perhaps a little hesitantly:

The primary imagination is the organ of common perception, the faculty by which we have experience of an actual world of phenomena. The secondary imagination is the same power in a heightened degree, which enables its possessor to see the world of our common experience in its real significance. (*BLS*, I, p. 272)

According to I. A. Richards in 1934:

The primary imagination is normal perception that produces the usual world of the senses,
>   That inanimate cold world allowed
>   To the poor loveless ever-anxious crowd
the world of motor-buses, beef-steaks and acquaintances . . .

The secondary imagination, by re-forming these banal perceptions,

gives us not only poetry – in the limited sense . . . – but every aspect of the routine world in which it is invested with other values than those necessary for our bare continuance as living beings . . .[3]

Engell in the most recent statement of this position puts it in more philosophical terms:

The primary imagination is spontaneous, involuntary.... It is a reflex or instinct of the mind and what Kant calls an empirical – as distinct from a transcendental – degree of the imagination. It 'unifies' by bringing together sensory data into larger units of understanding . . .   (*BL*, I, p. lxxxix)

It is Jackson Bate, a silent presence as Engell's co-editor of the Bollingen volumes, who in 1950 was the first to put the alternative point of view. 'The entire direction of Coleridge's criticism', he writes,

is opposed to the belief that he regarded the poetic imagination as merely an 'echo' of a capacity common to us all. The primary imagination is rather the highest exertion of the imagination that the 'finite mind' has to offer; and its scope . . . necessarily includes universals which lie beyond the restricted field of the 'secondary' imagination. For the appointed task of the 'secondary' imagination is to 'idealize and unify' its objects; and it can hardly 'unify' the universals.[4]

As Coleridge is credited with inventing the term, and as Richards strangely failed to apply the method he himself had patented, one might pause for a little Practical Criticism.[5] Sentence One of Coleridge's definition is brisk and to the point: 'The IMAGINATION then I consider either as primary, or secondary.' One's expectations at this stage are surely that the primary will be more important? Under 'secondary' the *NED* does of course permit 'Belonging to the second phase in a process or temporal sequence', but its first definition – the primary meaning of 'secondary' – is quite unequivocal:

Belonging to the second class in respect of dignity or importance; entitled to consideration only in the second place.[6]

Sentence Two of the *Biographia* definition is so famous that it is embarrassing to quote – which does not mean that it has always received the detailed attention that it needs:

The primary IMAGINATION I hold to be the living Power and prime Agent of all human Perception, and as a repetition in the finite mind of the eternal act of creation in the infinite I AM.

By side-reference it can, I believe, be shown that Coleridge is being entirely precise in his use of language, but for the practical critic it is the grandeur that is most impressive. The sentence is magnificently affirmative. Stress in both halves falls on the adjectives. Those in the first could hardly be more positive: '*living* Power', '*prime* Agent', '*all* human Perception'; while in the second there is an escalation, 'finite' – 'eternal' – 'infinite', that speaks for itself. Whatever its purpose, the prose exultantly proclaims an incarnation of the eternal in the finite, a personal reenactment of God's original, and endlessly continuous, moment of self-naming.

The tone of Sentence Three is by comparison business-like, even a little flat:

The secondary I consider as an echo of the former, co-existing with the conscious will, yet still as identical with the primary in the *kind* of its agency, and differing only in *degree*, and in the *mode* of its operation.

Grandiloquence, swelling rhythm, vaunting of scriptural authority, have
been replaced by a prose dependent on logical and painstaking opposi-
tions. Because it can be directed consciously, the secondary imagination
might be expected to be different in kind from the spontaneous primary,
but we are told that in fact the two shade into each other – are different
merely in degree and mode. If one asks the question which imagination
is meant to seem more impressive, the drop in style, the common associations of 'secondary', the diminishment implied by the word 'echo', all
point to the same conclusion. Only the phrase 'coinciding with the conscious will' for a moment seems to imply that the secondary might be
valued as a special human achievement; and here the tones of the qualifying clause ('yet still as identical with the primary . . .') counteract any
suggestion that in such a context deliberation could be important.[7] 'It
dissolves', Coleridge goes on in Sentence Four, defining more precisely
the way in which the secondary works –

It dissolves, diffuses, dissipates, in order to re-create; or where this process is
rendered impossible, yet still at all events it struggles to idealize and to unify.

With the primary imagination there had been no uncertainty, no en-
visaging of failure: the finite human mind had been said categorically to
be capable of its godlike act of creative perception. The feebleness of
struggling 'at all events . . . to idealize' replaces a process that had been
clearly and unwaveringly ideal. As Bate pointed out, the secondary imagination must inevitably be restricted in scope if it deals with materials
that the human mind is able to unify. One cannot unify the universals.

Sentence Five – the last of this paragraph – seems concerned mainly
to set up the comparison that is to follow between imagination and fancy: 'It [the secondary imagination] is essentially *vital*, even as all objects
(*as* objects) are essentially fixed and dead.' In a tacit reference back to 'the
living Power' of the primary, Coleridge first reaffirms the link between
the two degrees of imagination, and then moves on to oppose the vitality found in both to the mechanical nature of fancy, which can do no more
than 'play with . . . fixities and definites'. With the primary imagination
man unknowingly reenacts God's original and eternal creative moment;
with the secondary he consciously vitalizes an object-world that would
otherwise be dead; with the fancy he plays unvital games, dependent
upon choice and the laws of association. There can be no doubt whatever
that the least of the three powers is fancy; looking merely at the words on
the page, one would surely conclude that Coleridge was
scaling from the godlike primary at the top, downwards through its secondary echo, to the merely mechanical at the bottom?

Why then the consensus that reads the secondary as coming first? The answer must lie not in the definitions themselves, but in the preconceptions with which they have been approached. One is taken back at once to the relationship of Coleridge and German philosophy. The material that leads up to the definitions is almost all borrowed – stolen would be more accurate – and it seems reasonable to assume that they too will have a German source. The two most impressive recent accounts of Coleridge in terms of German thinking, Thomas McFarland's essay in *New Perspectives on Coleridge and Wordsworth* (1972) and Engell's *Creative Imagination* (1981), both make play with the origins of Coleridge's three-fold scheme. McFarland claims that in the *Philosophische Versuche* (1777) of Kant's older contemporary Tetens, is to be found

not only the formulation of the theory of secondary imagination, but also the entire threefold division of the imaginative faculty that (Coleridge) deposits at the end of the thirteenth chapter of the *Biographia Literaria*. (McFarland, 'SI', p. 208)

His case that Tetens' *Dichtungsvermögen* is the basis of the secondary imagination is very persuasive, but he then goes on to list the three components of Tetens' overall scheme, glossing them as perception, fancy, imagination; and quietly on the following page reorders them so that fancy shall come last, and the pattern shall correspond more closely to Coleridge. The fact that has to be sidestepped in this account is that Tetens' *Phantasie*, though it can obviously be translated as fancy, is an ordinary thinking process that necessarily follows the initial perception, and which is replaced only in the favoured few by the creative Dichtungsvermögen. For Coleridge, of course, fancy has no inevitable part to play. It is an unvital alternative; by implication the fully imaginative mind would have nothing to do with it.[8]

Engell exchanges Tetens for Schelling, but also has a threefold scheme to offer. Again the 'erste Potenz' is sense perception; the 'zweite Potenz' is the mind's building up of a comprehensible picture of the external world (Engell, *CI*, p. 307); and the 'höchste Potenz', or highest power, is art. It is not clear how far the two intermediate powers coincide, but if Coleridge came to Schelling after Tetens he would have found little to surprise him: the two schemes are broadly alike. Three things will follow from approaching *Biographia* with either of them – or with any related system – in one's mind. It will seem that for all the grandeur of Coleridge's language he can mean nothing more by the primary imagination than mere sense perception. It will seem that despite the normal connotations of the word (and his own usage at other times in *Biographia* and elsewhere), Coleridge must have intended 'secondary' to be read as 'more important'. Finally, it will seem that for Coleridge as for Tetens, and still more emphatically for Schelling, man's highest achievement is art.

This last position is quite untenable. As Engell points out, Schelling defines the human creative genius as 'the indwelling divinity in man . . . so to speak, a portion of the absolute nature of God' (Engell, *CI*, p. 320). Coleridge was undoubtedly aware of these views, and he adopted them three years later in his 1818 Lecture, *Poesy or Art*, which is borrowed wholly from Schelling, and proclaims that '*Art* is the mediatress and reconciliator of Man and Nature' (*Misc C*, p. 205). The metaphysical chapters of *Biographia*, however, though they draw from many different parts of Schelling, are preoccupied with his Nature-philosophy, not his theory of art.[9] Added to which there is the evidence of the letters quoted at the beginning of this essay that Coleridge regarded Schelling as having seduced him to Behmenism. Jacob Boehme had no interest in art or human creativity; he was an early seventeenth-century Lutheran mystic. The views of Schelling that depend upon him, or are closest to him, are pantheist statements of oneness with the God in Nature.

Coleridge in his 1818 letters was putting the blame on Schelling for the continuation in his own thinking of the pantheism that had been his faith in the mid-1790s before he ever read the Germans. He was also of course regarding pantheism as central to *Biographia* although it is present neither in his definition of the secondary imagination (which, be it said, is notably unlike Schelling's exalted claims), nor in the commonly accepted reading of the primary. It seems that a rather more complex view may have to be taken of the definitions. May they be doing more than one thing at once? Does not their consciously evocative language in fact invite us to read associatively and with an awareness of differing possibilities? There can be no doubt that the primary is, as Engell terms it, the 'necessary imagination' – the power that enables us to interpret the evidence of the senses, make the other kind of sense of our surroundings. But does it do merely that? May not 'the supreme Power and prime Agent of *all* human Perception' enable us to perceive God as well as 'the routine world . . . [of] our bare continuance as living beings' (Richards)? There had certainly been a time when Coleridge thought so. And what of the human repetition of God's self-naming? Might it not be expected to lead to a self-awareness rather more impressive than the ability to deduce one's own existence from the presence of an object-world? Are we to ignore the pointers towards a pantheist reading that are so frequent in preceding chapters? What for instance of the great assertion in Chapter 12: 'We begin with the I KNOW MYSELF, in order to end with the absolute I AM. We proceed from the SELF, in order to lose and find all self in GOD' (*BL*, I, p. 283).

It may be significant that those who view the primary imagination as secondary seem never to have approached the definitions by way of the period in which Coleridge's thinking was originally formed. They come via the Germans who Coleridge was scarcely aware of until the end of 1798, and whom he made no attempt to come to terms with until 1801. Because German metaphysics supplied so much copy for the later Coleridge, and so many of the niceties of his thinking, they assume that everything is there – or at least, everything of importance. To go to the opposite extreme would be ridiculous, but I am not very far from believing that Coleridge was telling the truth when he said in *Biographia* that 'all the main and fundamental ideas were born and matured in [his] mind before [he] had ever seen a single page' of Schelling.[10] The 'main and fundamental ideas' were not of course 'born' in Coleridge's mind at all, in the sense of originating there, but they derive from a native English tradition, not a German one. For an understanding of his later positions, and especially of the language and preoccupations of *Biographia* Chapters 12 and 13, it is essential to go back to the 1790s. One might for a start turn to the *Lecture on the Slave Trade* of June 1795:

To develope the powers of the Creator is our proper employment – and to imitate Creativeness by combination our most exalted and self-satisfying Delight. But we are progressive and must not rest content with present blessings. Our Almighty Parent hath therefore given to us Imagination . . . (*Lects 1795*, p. 235)

Already, twenty years before *Biographia*, imagination is associated with fulfilment of the self through the attainment of godlike power: 'To develope the powers of the Creator is our proper employment.' The stress on progressiveness is especially important. Coleridge's source is Akenside, *Pleasures of Imagination* (1744), and behind him lie Addison, and the Milton of *Paradise Lost*, Book v. 'Imagination', Coleridge goes on, extending the metaphor of mountain-climbing that will appear again and again in his and Wordsworth's poetry:

stimulates to the attainment of *real* excellence by the contemplation of splendid Possibilities that still revivifies the dying motive within us; and, fixing our eye on the glittering Summits that rise one above the other in Alpine endlessness, still urges us up the ascent of Being . . .   (*ibid.*)

Notes in the beautifully edited Bollingen volume of the 1795 *Lectures* point us both to *Pleasures of Imagination*, Book II –

> To climb th' ascent of being, and approach
> For ever nearer to the life divine . . .   (ll. 362–3)

and to the similar passage in Book I, where God has ordained that the soul

> Thro' all th' ascent of things inlarge her view,
> Till every bound at length should disappear,
> And infinite perfection close the scene. (ll. 219–21)

Progressiveness had of course its political, or millenarian, aspect for the Coleridge of 1795. To use Wordsworth's phrase from the Prospectus to *The Recluse*, he was concerned with 'the progressive powers . . . Of the whole species'[11] – and concerned especially to present them in Christian, Hartleyan terms, in opposition to the atheist rationalism of Godwin. The theological fragment that lies behind the *Lecture on the Slave Trade*, however, confirms that in this context the Ascent of Being is that of the individual soul to God. 'The noblest gift of Imagination', Coleridge writes, in words that explain one important aspect of the primary in *Biographia*, 'is the power of discerning the *Cause* in the *Effect*.' The power, that is, of perceiving God in His creation. 'We see our God everywhere', Coleridge adds in the next sentence, 'the Universe in the most literal Sense is his written Language' (*Lects 1795*, pp. 338–9). In May 1795, a month before the Slave Trade lecture, Coleridge had told his Bristol audience in the first of the series on Revealed Religion:

The existence of the Deity, and his Power and his Intelligence are manifested . . . The Omnipotent has unfolded to us the Volume of the World, and there we may read the Transcript of himself. (*ibid.*, p. 94)

Again the source is Akenside –

> To these the sire omnipotent unfolds
> The world's harmonious volume, there to read
> A transcript of himself . . .
> (*Pleasures of Imagination*, I, 99-101)

– but these were views that may already have been associated in Coleridge's mind with Bishop Berkeley. Akenside merged into Berkeley, and to some extent Berkeley himself later merged into German transcendentalism. But this was never wholly the case. He was strong enough to keep his own identity, and references to his thinking occur throughout Coleridge's writings. However facetious the context, it is interesting that one should appear in *Biographia* less than a page before the imagination definitions of Chapter 13. 'Be assured', writes the spurious Friend in his letter,

if you do publish this Chapter in the present work, you will be reminded of Bishop Berkley's Siris, announced as an Essay on Tar-water, which beginning with Tar ends with the Trinity . . . (*BL*, I, p. 303)

The laughable progression from tar-water to the Trinity is indeed to be found in *Siris*, but there is also a subtler version of the Ascent of Being that Coleridge undoubtedly read in 1796, and that could not fail to be of interest to him in the period when he was formulating his views of a transcendental human power. 'The perceptions of sense are gross', writes Berkeley towards the end of the work,

but even in the senses there is a difference . . . and from them, whether by gradual evolution, or ascent, we arrive at the highest. Sense supplies images to memory. These become subjects for fancy to work upon. Reason considers and judges of the imaginations. And these acts of reason become new objects to the understanding. In this scale, each lower faculty is a step that leads to the one above it. And the uppermost naturally leads to the deity . . .[12]

Berkeley's terms are not identical to Coleridge's – imagination is still a comparatively low faculty, and of course it is not as yet distinguished from the fancy – but his assumptions, and his upward scale, are very similar. In both thinkers we see imagination playing its part in a mental process, or progression (not, incidentally, at all unlike those of Tetens and Schelling), and in both, the 'uppermost' human faculty 'naturally leads to the deity'.

It also, as Coleridge recognizes in *Religious Musings* (in lines that date from the end of 1794, or very early '95) leads to the loss of self – the loss, that is, of all the merely human faculties. Moving in a progression from hope to faith, the spirit becomes at last absorbed in perfect love,

> and center'd there
> God only to behold, and know, and feel,
> Till by exclusive consciousness of GOD
> All self-annihilated, it shall make
> God it's Identity: God all in all!
> We and our Father ONE![13]

The source this time is Hartley, and such is his proselytizing zeal that Coleridge, so far from covering his tracks, adds chapter and verse in the footnote of 1797:

See this *demonstrated* by Hartley, vol. 1, p. 114, and vol. 2, p. 329. See it likewise proved, and freed from the charge of Mysticism, by Pistorius in his Notes and Additions . . .

Hartley's demonstration – needlessly elaborated in the 1791 edition by Hermann Pistorius – proves to be an Ascent of Being logically deduced from the principle of association:

Since God is the source of all good, and consequently must at last appear to be so, *i.e.* be associated with all our pleasures, it seems to follow . . . that the idea of God . . . must, at last, take place of, and absorb all other ideas, and HE become, according to the language of the scriptures, *all in all*.[14]

Coleridge, who reads Hartley in terms of Priestley's Unitarian pantheism, in fact goes a lot further. The concept of God's becoming all in all is replaced by an active power in the human spirit to '*make*/GOD it's

Identity'; and the final half-line, 'We and our Father ONE', is quite un-equivocal. Man can ascend to godhead, arrive there by his own endeavours. There follows in *Religious Musings* a vision of the Priestleyan elect treading 'all visible things' of the world beneath them, treating them as steps that in a Miltonic pun 'lead gradual' to the throne of God:

> And blest are they,
> Who in this fleshly World, the elect of Heaven . . .
> Adore with stedfast unpresuming gaze
> Him, Nature's Essence, Mind, and Energy!
> And gazing, trembling, patiently ascend
> Treading beneath their feet all visible things
> As steps, that upward to their Father's Throne
> Lead gradual . . .   (ll. 51–9)

In this early period Coleridge himself does not often refer to the up-permost human faculty as imagination. In fact he doesn't usually iden-tify it at all; he evokes its powers, shows supreme confidence in its achievements, and feels no need to give it a name. As it leads to a merg-ing in the godhead it can be associated with any of the attributes of God himself. It is an ultimate stage of love, or consciousness, or perception. At the opening of *The Destiny of Nations* (written for Southey's *Joan of Arc* in June–July 1795), emphasis is placed on vision, the ability to part the substance from the shadow, see through the clouds that veil the blaze of the sun. God is 'Great Father', 'Rightful King', 'Eternal Father', 'King Omnipotent' – all of which is much to be expected – but he is also

> the Will Absolute, the One, the Good!
> The I AM, the Word, the Life, the Living God!   (ll. 5–6)

All these names have their later implications; but 'the I AM', with its capital letters, leaps out from the page. Forty lines later one comes across a specific reference to God's self-naming: 'His one eternal self-affirming act' which, as if to mark Coleridge's new reading of Berkeley, occurs 'with absolute ubiquity of thought' (ll. 45 – 6). He might not have put it to himself in exactly the terms that he was to use in Chapter 12 of *Biographia*, but already Coleridge believes that

in the very first revelation of his absolute being ['And God said unto Moses I AM THAT I AM'] Jehovah at the same time revealed the fundamental truth of all philosophy, which must either commence with the absolute or have no fixed com-mencement; i.e. cease to be philosophy.   (*BL*, I, p. 275)

'True metaphysics', as he commented at the end of Chapter 12, 'are nothing else but true divinity' (*ibid.*, p. 291).

Coleridge is at all times a Christian thinker. Philosophy is not a pastime, or an intellectual pursuit; it is a means of understanding the nature of God, and the nature of man's relation to God. 'For what is Freedom', he asks in *The Destiny of Nations*,

> But the unfettered use
> Of all the powers that God for use has given?

To which predictably he adds:

> *But chiefly this*, him First, him Last to view
> Through meaner powers and secondary things
> Effulgent, as through clouds that veil his blaze.(11. 13–17)

'If the doors of perception were cleansed', Blake had remarked only five years before, 'everything would appear to man as it is, infinite.'[15] There might well have been agreement too about the 'meaner powers and secondary things' that dim the imagination, stand in the way of perception. For both poets 'the sublime of man,/ Our noontide Majesty', was 'to know ourselves/ Parts and proportions of one wond'rous whole' (*Religious Musings*, 135–7). And both would have named selfhood as the great impediment to such knowledge. 'A sordid solitary thing', Coleridge writes a few lines further on in *Religious Musings*,

> Mid countless brethren with a lonely heart
> Thro' courts and cities the smooth Savage roams
> Feeling himself, his own low Self the whole
> When he by sacred sympathy might make
> The whole ONE SELF! SELF, that no alien knows!
> SELF, far diffus'd as Fancy's wing can travel!
> SELF, spreading still! Oblivious of it's own
> Yet all of all possessing!   (ll.163–71)

Coleridge scarcely needs to add,

> This is FAITH!
> This the MESSIAH'S destin'd victory!   (ll.171–2)

to tell us that his lines are a moment of personal apocalypse, an account of imaginative transcendence in which the individual loses and finds all self in God. It is interesting to look briefly at the language used. Fancy is still merely a synonym for imagination (and will be for another five years, or so), but 'sacred sympathy' and 'faith' lead straight through to later definitions. In *The Friend*, for instance, 'faith is a *total* act of the soul: it is the *whole* state of the mind, or it is not at all'(*Friend*, I. 315). And in *The Statesman's Manual* this losing of selfhood is evoked in terms that are still closer to those of *Religious Musings* twenty years before. 'Self', Coleridge writes,

which then only *is*, when *for itself* it hath ceased to be. Even so doth Religion finitely express the *unity* of the infinite Spirit by being a total act of the soul.(*SM*, p. 90)

For all the prominence he gives to it , Coleridge uses the term 'primary imagination' only once. It is difficult, however, not to think that the power that enables the human being finitely to 'express the *unity* of the infinite spirit by . . . a total act of the soul' is not also a total act of imagination – 'a repetition in the finite mind of the eternal act of creation'. And it is difficult not to think that Coleridge was evoking precisely the same perceptive – creative power of achieving union with God in the Slave Trade lecture, *Religious Musings* and *The Destiny of the Nations*.

These early definitions, or invokings, of primary imagination are not of course restricted to the years 1794–6 – the Berkeleyan readings of the eternal language of God in *This Lime-Tree Bower My Prison* (July 1797) and *Frost at Midnight* (February 1798) are sufficiently well known – but from 1798 there are several new factors to be taken into account. Coleridge begins to write less poetry himself, and to use Wordsworth as spokesman for the more serious thinking that the poetry has tended to examine.[16] He forms at least an acquaintance with German philosophy in 1798–9, and starts to read it seriously in 1801. And at some stage, about which it is impossible to be clear, he begins to argue himself out of his Unitarianism. And in addition to all this, there is the fact that in the period following the 1798 *Lyrical Ballads* both Coleridge and Wordsworth come to be interested in literary criticism – the theory of what they have been doing as poets. Definitions of the secondary imagination begin to appear; and as a corollary it now becomes useful to separate imagination and fancy. The 1800 note to *The Thorn* suggests that Wordsworth from the first was rather more positive about fancy; but for Coleridge the distinction was effectively between good and bad poetry – 'good' meaning something akin to 'prophetic', 'having as its object a true understanding of the individual's relationship to God'.

Coleridge's first pronouncement on the subject of imagination and fancy, in September 1802, exactly parallels Blake's distinction in the Preface to *Milton*, between literary works that are 'Daughters of Inspiration', and those that are merely 'Daughters of Memory'. The first are associated by Blake with imagination, 'the Sublime of the Bible', truth, justice and eternity; the second with artifice, imitation, classical poetry and philosophy, and also war (seen as the conflict between parts that ought to be in harmony). Coleridge, writing very possibly in the same year, is con cerned for a start with the errors of Greek polytheism (as indeed Blake had been in *Marriage of Heaven and Hell*, Plate 11). 'It must occur to every Reader', he writes

that the Greeks in their religious poems address always the Numina Loci, the Genii, the Dryads, the Naiads, etc. etc. All natural Objects were *dead* – mere hollow Statues – but there was a Godkin or Goddessling *included* in each.

'In the Hebrew Poetry', he goes on,

you find nothing of this poor Stuff – as poor in genuine Imagination, as it is mean in Intellect. At best, it is but Fancy, or the aggregating Faculty of the mind – not *Imagination*, or the modifying, and *co-adunating* Faculty. (*CL*, II, 856–6)

'Co-adunating', as one might expect, comes from Latin 'co-adunare', 'to join into one'. Fancy is cumulative – and her works are the Daughters of Memory: imagination modifies, and by recreating the materials of experience produces the oneness that for Coleridge, as for Blake, is ultimate truth. 'In the Hebrew Poets', the letter continues,

each Thing has a Life of it's own, & yet they are all one Life. In God they move & live, & *have* their Being – not *had,* as the cold System of Newtonian Theology represents, but *have.*   (*ibid.*, p. 866)

One recalls that in *Jerusalem* – the poem in which the parts of Blake's fallen, or vegetable, world come finally together – there are prefaces addressed respectively to The Deists and The Christians. Deism is 'the cold System of Newtonian Theology', according to which God in the beginning started the world going and left it. Christianity (in this context, at least) is the universe pervaded by a God who is eternally present in his Creation. There is no reason to think that Coleridge would at this period have dissented from the gigantic claims made by Blake in *Jerusalem*, Plate 77:

I know of no other Christianity and of no other Gospel than the liberty both of body and mind to exercise the Divine Arts of Imagination – Imagination, the real & eternal World of which this Vegetable Universe is but a faint shadow, & in which we shall live in our Eternal or Imaginative Bodies when these Vegetable Mortal Bodies are no more.

Imagination is that which is eternal within the individual human being, and thus 'a portion of eternity' itself. To put it in Coleridge's terms, 'In God [we] move & live & *have* [our] Being'. Though by this stage one might expect him to be moving towards Trinitarian ways of thinking, the Hebrew poets are still for Coleridge prophets of Unitarian pantheism. Earlier in his letter he had commented:

Nature has her proper interest; & he will know what it is, who believes & feels, that every Thing has a Life of it's own, & that we are all *one Life*.(*CL*, II, p. 864)

The proper interest of Nature lies in its being permeated by the One Life – 'tis God/Diffused through all, that doth make all one whole' (*Religious Musings*, ll. 139–40) – and in its being, in Blake's words, 'a faint shadow' of 'the real & eternal World'. The proper function of the poet is to proclaim the One Life, and to reveal the faint shadow as consisting of clouds that veil the Almighty from the gaze of fallen man.[17]

Needless to say, the poet whom Coleridge thinks capable of achieving this task is Wordsworth:

the only man who has effected a compleat and constant synthesis of Thought &
Feeling and combined them with Poetic Forms, with the music of pleasurable passion and with Imagination, or the modifying Power, in that highest sense of the
word in which I have ventured to oppose it to Fancy, or the *aggregating* power . . .
                                                                    (*CL*, II, p. 1034)

The date now is January 1804. Coleridge, who has just spent a month
in Grasmere on his way south to London and the Mediterranean, goes
on to explain what he means by 'the highest sense of the word' imagination. It is 'that sense in which it is a dim Analogue of Creation, not all that
we can *believe*, but all that we can *conceive* of creation' (*ibid.*). The context
is literary, and in terms of *Biographia* Coleridge is discussing the secondary imagination; yet in so doing he anticipates the language, and the
transcendental implication, of his primary definition. Already there is
the tacit assumption of different levels of importance – imaginative
modes that differ not in kind, but in degree. Context will establish which
it is that is being referred to in a given case, but the theological must
always have priority. In the *Letter to Sara Hutchinson*, for instance, one may
suspect that 'My shaping Spirit of Imagination', at line 242, is a reference
to creativity as a writer, but the great poetry –

> Ah! from the soul itself must issue forth
> A Light, a Glory, and a luminous Cloud
> Enveloping the Earth!   (ll. 302–4)

– is the celebration of a power,

> That, wedding Nature to us, gives in Dower
> A new Earth & new Heaven . . .   (ll. 316–17)

Coleridge may feel that he has lost the power himself, but there can be
no doubt of the fervour with which he continues to believe in its existence
– and with which he confers it upon Sara:

> O pure of Heart! thou needst not ask of me
> What this strong music in the Soul may be,
> What, & wherein it doth exist,
> This Light, this Glory, this fair luminous Mist,
> This beautiful & beauty-making Power!
> JOY, innocent Sara! Joy, that ne'er was given
> Save to the Pure, & in their purest Hour . . .   (ll. 308–14)

In many ways the *Letter* is a retrospective poem, looking back to the
companionship and confidence of Alfoxden, when for both Coleridge and
Wordsworth joy had been a name given to the pantheist life-force: 'In
all things / He saw one life, and felt that it was joy' (*Pedlar*, 217–18). But
Coleridge's pantheism does not disappear with his new reading of German philosophy. When the *Letter* was written in April 1802, the 'abstruse
Research' had been going on for well over a year, but he was still able to

comment that 'we are all *one Life*' when writing to Sotheby six months later. The first fruits of his research had been the four letters reexamining Locke, that were written for Josiah Wedgwood in February 1801, and summed up for Thomas Poole the following month:

If the mind be not *passive*, if it be indeed made in God's Image, & that too in the sublimest sense – the Image of the *Creator* – there is ground for suspicion, that any system built on the passiveness of the mind must be false, as a system.

(*CL*, II, p. 709)

How much had Coleridge really changed since the *Lecture on the Slave Trade* in '95?

To develope the powers of the Creator is our proper employment . . . Our Almighty Parent hath therefore given to us Imagination.

How much indeed – for all the reading of Kant and Fichte, Tetens, Leibnitz, Schelling, and others – did his most deeply held beliefs ever change, until the period of rethinking, in about 1818, that follows *Biographia*?[18]

What is certain is that for Coleridge 'the sublime of man' continued, despite his new interest in the poetic imagination and the fancy, to be a transcendental power analogous to divine creativity. After the *Letter to Sara Hutchinson* in 1802 the poetry that celebrates this power ceases to be written by Coleridge; but there can be no doubt that the higher imagination that comes to dominate the later stages of *The Prelude* depends upon his thinking. The Climbing of Snowdon of February 1804 presents us with an equation of soul and imagination ('had Nature lodged / The soul, the imagination of the whole' (1805 *Prelude* XIII, 64–5)). The central lines of Book VI, written the following month, show imagination coming 'athwart' the poet 'in all the might of its endowments'; at which he turns grandly to his soul and says, 'I recognize thy glory' (ll. 525–32). A year later, the Snowdon gloss produces yet another version of the creative/perceptive human mind made in the image of God:

> it appeared to me
> The perfect image of a mighty mind,
> Of one that feeds upon infinity,
> That is exalted by an under-presence,
> The sense of God, or whatsoe'er is dim
> Or vast in its own being . . .   (XIII, 69–74)

And as he brings his poem to a close, Wordsworth not only comes to think of imagination as having provided a structural principle (XIII, 171–84), but offers an amazing list of its 'endowments':

> imagination, which in truth
> Is but another name for absolute strength
> And clearest insight, amplitude of mind,
> And reason in her most exalted mood.   (XIII, 167–70)

It is certainly one of Wordsworth's most exalted statements. As with the primary definition in *Biographia*, one is confronted by superlatives that easily seem hyperbolical, but which are capable of very precise meaning. It is the last line that is most important. 'Reason in her most exalted mood' is no doubt to be related to the Kantian 'vernunft', but Kant had not been the first to distinguish pure reason from understanding ('verstandt'). Though it was a little disingenuous to parade his own achievement, and to leave Kant out of the question, Coleridge was broadly telling the truth when he wrote in *Biographia* Chapter 10,

I have cautiously discriminated the terms, the REASON, and the UNDERSTANDING, encouraged and confirmed by the authority of our genuine divines, and philosophers, before the revolution [of 1688].

(*BL*, I, p. 173)

And for those who wish to understand what is meant by the primary imagination nothing is of greater importance than the passage he then goes on to quote from *Paradise Lost*. Raphael is explaining to Adam in Book V the doctrine of perfectibility – how the different orders of Creation not only become more spiritual as they come closer to God, but have each the power to climb the next rung of the ladder. Because of the difficulty of breaking into Milton's syntax, Coleridge's quotation begins rather awkwardly:

> – both life, and sense,
> Fancy, and *understanding*: whence the soul
> *Reason* receives, and REASON is her *being*,
> DISCURSIVE or INTUITIVE.

'Discourse', Raphael continues, talking down from his angelic rung,

> Is oftest your's, the latter most is our's,
> Differing but in *degree*, in *kind* the same.　　(*ibid.*, ll. 173–4)

Angels for most of the time are intuitive reasoners, men are chiefly restricted to the level of understanding; but because the soul is reason's being, man has the capacity to become angelic. Engell in the Bollingen footnote remarks, 'The lines probably encouraged [Coleridge] in one of his favourite qualifications: differing in degree but not in kind.' There can't be much doubt that this is true; but it hardly explains why Coleridge should return to the passage again and again, and it surely underplays the importance to him of the Ascent of Being. In *The Statesman's Manual* (published in 1816, the year before *Biographia*) he first comments that 'Milton opposes the discursive to the intuitive, as the lower to the higher', then quotes 'Differing but in degree, in *kind* the same', and finally goes on to say damningly that understanding 'contemplates the unity of things in their *limits* only, and is consequently a knowledge of superficies without substance'. Reason, by contrast, is 'the integral spirit of the regenerated man . . . substantiated and vital'. In the words of the Wisdom of

Solomon, it is 'the breath of the power of God, and a pure influence from the glory of the Almighty' (*SM*, p. 69).

If it is possible to go further than this in equating reason with godhead, then Coleridge does so in a famous passage in the 1818 *Friend* where the argument is in fact clinched in Milton's words:

I should have no objection to define Reason with Jacobi . . . as an organ bearing the same relation to spiritual objects, the Universal, the Eternal, and the Necessary, as the eye bears to material and contingent phaenomena.

'But then it must be added', Coleridge goes on, in terms that are unambiguously pantheist:

that it is an organ identical with its appropriate objects. Thus, God, the Soul, eternal Truth, etc. are the objects of Reason; but they themselves are *reason*. We name God the Supreme Reason; and Milton says, 'Whence the Soul *Reason* receives, and Reason is her Being.'   (*Friend*, II, pp. 155–6)

To say that for Coleridge 'reason in her most exalted mood' *is* imagination would take a little qualifying. In *The Statesman's Manual*, for instance, imagination, though clearly akin, is defined as separate. It is the 'completing power' that *creates* reason by 'impregnating' the understanding (*SM*, p. 69). To the case that I am making, however, such distinctions are irrelevant. What we have in Coleridge is a lasting preoccupation with 'the sublime of man' – the power that enables him to become all spirit, to 'lose and find all self in God'. Whether he calls this power love, or joy, or imagination, or reason, doesn't matter in itself.

References to the divine reason in the years just before and just after *Biographia* have an especial importance because they draw attention to higher and lower powers that are linked in the Ascent of Being, and resemble the primary and secondary imagination. They are important too because they suggest that Coleridge is trying to tell us something when he chooses to quote Raphael's words to Adam at length as the first of three epigraphs to *Biographia*, Chapter 13:

> O Adam! one Almighty is, from whom
> All things proceed, and up to him return
> If not depraved from good: created all
> Such to perfection, one first nature all
> Indued with various forms, various degrees
> Of substance, and, more spiritous and pure,
> As nearer to him plac'd or nearer tending,
> Each in their several active spheres assigned,
> Till body up to spirit work, in bounds
> Proportion'd to each kind.   (*BL*, I, p. 295)

Even flowers and fruit, in this Ascent, have their 'sublime'. They cannot, like men, know themselves 'Parts and proportions of one wond'rous whole' (*Religious Musings*, 137), but in providing man's nourishment, they too are 'by gradual scale sublim'd'. They aspire in turn 'To vital spirits', then 'to animal', and finally 'to intellectual' (the realm of ultimate purity). En route they give to man

> both life and sense,
> Fancy and understanding: whence the soul
> REASON receives.   (*BL*, I, p. 295)

On this occasion Coleridge cuts short his quotation with the words 'And reason is her *being*,/Discursive or intuitive'. There was little need to go further. The fuller distinction between understanding and reason had been made in Chapter 10; and in the new context Coleridge wished rather to stress that reason was the being of the soul – the principle that enabled her to climb the ladder back to God. More significant is the misquotation – strictly, perhaps, the emendation – of *Paradise Lost*. Milton, in keeping with his argument in *De Doctrina Christiana*, had written that all things proceed from God, created out of 'one first *matter* all': Coleridge quietly changes 'matter' to 'nature'. The universe that is to us the 'natural' world is created not from preexisting matter, but out of the spiritual 'nature' of God.[19] The second epigraph to *Biographia*, Chapter 13, is again of great importance, and again subject to careful emendation by Coleridge. Quotations from two separate works by Leibnitz have been welded together to form a whole that argues for the existence of a spiritual principle in matter. The train of Coleridge's thought is obvious – and confirmed by the choice as his third epigraph of lines from Synesius, the fifth-century bishop who had been cited in a footnote to Chapter 12 as evidence that pantheism is 'not necessarily irreligious or heretical' (*BL*, I, 246–7). The appearance of Leibnitz at this moment just before the imagination definitions is significant. He forms a particularly strong connection with Coleridge's early thinking, and has a good claim to have been the first of the Germans to make an impression. On seeing his bust at Hanover in March 1799, Coleridge writes: 'It is the face of a God! & Leibnitz *was* almost more than a man in the wonderful capaciousness of his Judgment & Imagination' (*CL*, I, p. 472).

By June 1800, Coleridge is looking forward to settling at Keswick so that he can read Spinoza and Leibnitz, and asking Humphry Davy how his own thinking differs from theirs (*CL*, II, p. 590). On 13 February 1801 he is still reading Leibnitz, but Spinoza has been replaced by Kant (*CL*, II, p. 676). Five days later Coleridge writes the first of the letters to Wedgwood that are designed to overthrow the 'sandy Sophisms of Locke' and to establish both his own position as philosopher and that of Wordsworth as author of *The Recluse*. It is Leibnitz who, in the *Nouveau Essai sur L'Entendement* (not published till 1765, fifty years after his death) provides the means of countering Locke's insistence on the mind as *tabula rasa*. 'There are some ideas and principles', he writes,

which do not come to us from the senses, and which we find in ourselves without forming them, although the senses give us occasion to perceive them.

McFarland draws attention to the passage in his essay on the secondary imagination, and goes on to relate this belief in innate ideas to the doctrine of the monad for which Leibnitz is chiefly famous (McFarland, 'SI', p. 219). Anyone who chooses to look up 'Monads and Monadology' in the *Encyclopedia of Philosophy* will find that the topic is taken a good deal more seriously than might be supposed. There are philosophers who put their trust in monads before Plato, and there are philosophers who put their trust in monads in the twentieth century. Basically, a monad is an irreducible unit of life, or power, held to be present in the different organisms of the material world. In its spiritual oneness the monad is analogous to the human mind, and also to God. According to one view each monad is a microcosm of the universe – Blake's 'world in a grain of sand' – and yet entirely separate. According to another, which is of course pantheist, the sum total of the monads in existence is God. Leibnitz held to the first view,[20] but this does not prevent his making frequent statements that have a pantheist implication.

The epigraph to *Biographia* 13 is a case in point:

If indeed corporeal things contained nothing but matter they might truly be said to consist in flux and to have no substance, as the Platonists once rightly recognized ... I have come to the conclusion that certain metaphysical elements perceptible to the mind alone should be admitted, and that some higher and, so to speak, *formal principle* should be added to the material mass ... It does not matter whether we call this principle of things an entelechy or a power so long as we remember that it is intelligibly to be explained only by the idea of *powers*. (*BL*, I, p. 296)

'Entelechy' is another word for monad, and the point of this last sentence may be to warn those who prefer the concept of a life-force that they should regard it as consisting of separate powers, not the pantheist totality that is God. It is important, however, that 'metaphysical elements' in the material world are said to be perceptible to the human mind. And it is interesting that 'this principle of things', the phrase that so strongly recalls *Tintern Abbey*, should be another Coleridge emendation. Leibnitz is being read, and presented, in terms of Wordsworth's 'see[ing] into the life of things', his evoking of the 'something far more deeply interfused' that is both motion and spirit, and

> impels
> All thinking things, all objects of all thought,
> And rolls through all things.   (*Tintern Abbey*, 101–3)

The pattern becomes still clearer when one recollects that the source of Wordsworth's lines is an address that Coleridge himself had written at the end of *Religious Musings* to spirits of 'plastic', or creative, power

> that interfus'd
> Roll thro' the grosser and material mass
> In organizing surge!

'Holies of God', he had called them and added the parenthesis, 'And what if Monads of the infinite mind' (ll. 423–6).

Coleridge's own source in 1796 had been not Leibnitz but Cudworth, the slightly earlier English neo-Platonist under whose influence he had written the *Lectures on Revealed Religion* in the previous year. Cudworth's immense, and immensely learned book, *The True Intellectual System of the Universe*, is an attack on 'hylozoic atheism' – the belief that matter has life. Like Leibnitz he had dealt in terms of separate plastic powers; as a Unitarian, however, Coleridge had joined them up, turned them into component parts of the mind of God. It is this kind of thinking that lies behind the *Biographia* definitions. *The Destiny of Nations* beautifully explains how it is that the primary imagination in its highest power is 'a repetition in the finite mind of the infinite I AM'. 'Properties', Coleridge announces categorically,

> are God: the naked mass
> (If mass there be, fantastic guess or ghost)
> Acts only by its inactivity. (ll. 36–8)

God is not matter (which is Spinoza's view, attacked by Cudworth, and at no point accepted by Coleridge); He is the sum total of 'properties', individual attributes, within the world of His creation. The playful reference to mass as 'fantastic guess or ghost' makes the point that Coleridge's position is not altered if one adopts an immaterialist view; indeed he is half inclined to do so himself. After a moment of not unbogus humility, he continues to speculate:

> Here we pause humbly. Others boldlier think
> That as one body seems the aggregate
> Of atoms numberless, each organized;
> So by a strange and dim similitude
> Infinite myriads of self-conscious minds
> Are one all-conscious Spirit, which informs
> With absolute ubiquity of thought
> (His one eternal self-affirming act!)
> All his involvéd Monads . . . (ll. 39–47)

Monads are the expression of the divine imagination. Each has his individuality and separate job, as together they 'Evolve the process of eternal good' (l. 59); but they are informed, empowered, interfused, by the 'eternal self-affirming act' of God – 'the infinite I AM' – which already in the Slave Trade lecture Coleridge has said it is man's primary duty to imitate.

Leibnitz must have seemed to take up where Cudworth left off; but before coming across him in the winter of 1798–9, Coleridge had assimilated the later, pantheist, thinking of Berkeley's *Siris*, with its emphasis on human creativity and the Ascent of Being. 'In this scale', Berkeley had written, in words already quoted,

each lower faculty is a step that leads to the one above it. And the uppermost naturally leads to the deity.

It was Leibnitz who above all enabled Coleridge to carry this central faith of the early period into the years leading up to *Biographia*. Thinking of Wordsworth, and of their shared aims, Coleridge made a note during his voyage to Malta,

To write to the Recluse that he may insert something concerning *Ego/* its metaphysical Sublimity – & intimate Synthesis with the principle of Co-adunation . . .   (*CN*, II, 2057)

Quoting the passage in his essay, McFarland comments with surprise:

Although the 'principle of Co-adunation' here invoked is clearly the secondary imagination or *Dichtkraft*, the phrase about the ego's 'metaphysical Sublimity' can refer neither to poetry nor to psychology, but only to metaphysics – that is, not to Tetens, but to Leibnitz.

There could be no clearer example of approaching Coleridge with set philosophical assumptions. Because he is determined that the primary imagination is no more than sense-perception, McFarland is forced to use the term 'secondary' in an instance that he knows to be inappropriate. The last page-and-a-half of his essay produces in fact all the evidence that is needed to distinguish a secondary imagination dependent on Tetens from a transcendental primary going back through Leibnitz to Plato. It is even suggested in a footnote that the *vis primitiva* of Leibnitz (the essential force that empowers the monads) may have given the primary its name.

Before returning one last time to the definitions, it may be worth pausing to ask why the Coleridge of 1818 thought his dependence on Schelling in *Biographia* had been a case of 'retrograding from . . . prior and better lights'. Pantheism for the early Coleridge, though it drew support from many different sources (some of them incongruous), had consisted basically of Priestleyan Unitarianism; the question to be asked is therefore whether Coleridge at any time in the intervening period

established a settled Trinitarian faith. From March 1796 onwards there
are criticisms of Priestley in the letters and notebooks that sound as if they
should be final, but then seem not to have been.[21] When definitions of
the Trinity begin to appear, they show Coleridge arguing himself into
a metaphysical position, yet conscious that his underlying beliefs have
failed to change. On 12 February 1805 it burst upon him as 'an awful
Truth' that 'No Christ, No God!' – that the Trinity is necessary to his
conception of God, and that 'Unitarianism in all its Forms is Idolatory'.
'O that this Conviction may work upon me and in me', he pleads,

and that my mind may be made up as to the character of Jesus, and of, historical
Christianity, as clearly as it is of the Logos and intellectual or spiritual Christianity.   (*CN*, II, 2448)

Coleridge's intellectual Christianity is very intellectual indeed. Three
notes earlier, he had written: 'the moment we conceive the divine energy,
that moment we co-conceive the Logos' (*ibid.*, 2445). His position is not
in fact unorthodox, but the emphasis on metaphysical proof is significant.
The Unitarian Jesus, who is a human being and the son of Joseph, has
been replaced in Coleridge's thinking not by Christ as the incarnate Son
of God, but by the satisfyingly abstract concept of the Word. God in his
self-naming – I AM – creates himself as both subject and object, and,
in Coleridge's later explanation,

becometh God the Father, self-originant and self-subsistent, even as the Logos
or Supreme Idea is the co-eternal Son, self-subsistent but begotten by the Father
. . .   (*SM*, p. 694)

Instead of informing 'all his involvéd Monads', God's 'one eternal self-
affirming act' begets the Son (the portion of himself that, in Berkeley's
term, has 'outness'). Two months later, on 14 April 1805, Coleridge
wrote his now famous note on the Word as symbolic language:

In looking at objects of Nature while I am thinking, as at yonder moon dim- glimmering thro' the dewy window-pane, I seem rather to be seeking, as it were *asking*, a symbolical language for something within me that already and forever exists, than observing anything new. Even when that latter is the case, yet still I have
always an obscure feeling as if the new phaenomenon were the dim Awaking of
a forgotten or hidden Truth of my inner Nature. It is still [i.e. always] interesting
as a Word, a Symbol! It is *Logos*, the Creator!   (*CN*, II, 2546).

The Logos, or Creator, or Christ, within man, offers a symbolic correspondence *that forever exists* between man and the natural world. Clearly
it is another definition of the primary imagination; and clearly the new
abstract Trinitarianism has not prevented Coleridge's pantheist yearnings for oneness with the God in Nature from finding expression. Nor,
be it said, did his new views alter the pattern of his reading. Those who

portray Coleridge either as by this stage safely orthodox, or as moving away from Unitarianism because he was frightened by pantheism, have to explain why in the period between his return from Malta and the writing of *Biographia* he should have taken pains to procure ten different works of Schelling – all of them pantheist. And they have to explain how it is that to the years 1808–10 belongs Coleridge's most committed reading of Jacob Boehme.

Coleridge claims to have read Boehme at school, and seems to have been aware of him at different times in the 1790s,[22] but he was actually given the four-volume 'Law' edition by De Quincey in February 1808. Some of his notes, according to George Whalley in Volume One of the Bollingen *Marginalia*, belong to this early period; but most look back upon it from the vantage-point of 1817–18. To the Coleridge of these later notes – the man who thinks of *Biographia* as pantheist and Behmenite – Boehme's chief fault can be readily identified. It is

the confusion of the creaturely spirit in the great moments of its renascence . . . thro' the Breath and Word of Comforter and Restorer, for the deific energies in Deity itself.   (*CM*, I, 602)

The confusion had of course been shared by the Coleridge who could write, 'the moment we conceive the divine energy, that moment we co-conceive the Logos', or who, looking out at the dim-glimmering Maltese moon, could feel the Logos as a hidden truth of his inner nature. Boehme had enabled Coleridge to go on believing that the experiences of spiritual transcendence celebrated in his own and Wordsworth's earlier poetry had been a losing and finding of the self in God. Such moments are no less important to the Coleridge of 1818, but he sees them as visitings of the Holy Spirit bestowed by God upon his creature man. Deific energy in man himself, variously defined as love, joy, the pure reason, the primary imagination, is now denied. Or, to put it another way, the soul loses its status as a monad of the infinite mind. Aspiration goes, to be replaced by duty. The ladder that has offered an Ascent of Being is pulled away.

All this, however, takes place not in *Biographia*, but just after it. *Biographia* itself, as Coleridge so soon realized, is a pantheist work, dependent upon Schelling, who in turn both derives from Boehme and closely resembles him. But there were two sides to Schelling: the early Nature-philosopher, and the thinker who came to regard art as an expression of the 'indwelling divinity in man'. It is the philosopher of art whom Engell, in *The Creative Imagination*, takes to be central to *Biographia*. 'No other romantic thinker', he writes of Schelling, more cogently backed his plea for the divine nature of imagination and art. It was not a new idea, but Schelling's claim has an added dimension: for him, art is the pursuit of objectivity. . . Art solves the dilemma of philosophy, the split between man and nature, the riddle of creation and its relationship to the individual mind.

(pp. 320–1)

This exalted power hardly sounds like the faculty that in *Biographia* 'struggles at all events to idealize and to unify', but Engell never doubts either that Schelling is behind the secondary imagination, or that the secondary is for Coleridge more important than the primary. The two assumptions depend above all on a belief that the *Biographia* definitions coincide with Schelling's three-fold account of mental process; but they receive a further support from Engell's shaping of his book. Hazlitt, Shelley, Wordsworth, Keats are taken out of chronological sequence so that the last two chapters of *The Creative Imagination* can be given, respectively, to Schelling and Coleridge. Schelling's philosophy of art is dwelt upon at length, and there is an implication – as indeed there has been throughout the book – that we are leading up to a final assessment of *Biographia*. In Coleridge's chapter, however – the long-expected climax – Schelling plays no part. This despite the fact that Chapter 12 of *Biographia* consists largely of verbatim transcriptions from his Nature-philosophy. At some level, it would seem, Engell himself is aware that the tendency of the Schelling borrowings is to exalt the primary imagination in its transcendental role, and thus to emphasize that for Coleridge the imagination of the artist is not of comparable importance.

The notes that Engell produces wearing his other hat as editor of *Biographia* are exemplary. Full translations are presented of the Schelling plagiarisms, and attention is drawn also to the interpolations that Coleridge made en route. These have a particular importance as they cannot have been incorporated for convenience, or by mistake. As one might expect they show Coleridge preparing the way for his final definitions. One insertion in Chapter 12 stands out especially. 'The theory of natural philosophy', Schelling and Coleridge write,

would then be completed, when all nature was demonstrated to be identical in essence with that which in its highest known power exists in man as intelligence and self-consciousness . . .

to which Coleridge on his own has added:

when the heavens and the earth shall declare not only the power of their maker, but the glory and the presence of their God, even as he appeared to the great prophet during the vision of the mount in the skirts of his divinity. (*BL*, I, p. 256)

The skirts of God's divinity are the clouds that shielded the Israelites from the glory and presence of Jehovah as Moses went up alone to receive the tablets on Mount Sinai. In the portion of his sentence drawn from Schelling, Coleridge looks forward to the fulfilment of natural philosophy when it can demonstrate the pantheist assumption (seen for instance in *Tintern Abbey*) that Nature and 'the mind of man' are in essence the same. In the portion that he adds, Coleridge looks forward to the time when Creation as a whole will be able to perceive the glory and presence of God as it was perceived uniquely by Moses.

It is in the last paragraph of Chapter 13, before he breaks off for his spoof letter, that Coleridge himself accepts the challenge to prove Nature and the mind consubstantial. In a passage that shows awareness of Kant and Fichte as well as Schelling, but draws its conclusion from none of them, he affirms that in the reconciliation of subject and object, the I and the not-I: 'no other conception is possible, but that the product must be a tertium aliquid, or finite generation'. To which he adds the all-important words: 'Now this tertium aliquid can be no other than an interpenetration of the counteracting powers, partaking of both' (*BL*, I, p. 300). McFarland's comment, as he strives to maintain the primacy of the secondary imagination, seems a little desperate:

The tertium aliquid would metaphysically have to be God, so the solution would be pantheistic. I suspect, however, that Coleridge did not see this until the last moment because his mind was set on the poetic imagination.
(McFarland, 'SI', p. 227)

If Coleridge's mind had been set on the poetic imagination – apart from the fact that he would probably have made his definition a little more impressive – he would in Chapters 12 and 13 have been translating from Schelling the philosopher of art, not the Nature-philosopher. And if at the climax of the metaphysical section of *Biographia* he was truly surprised by the pantheist tendency of his own thinking, he must have been writing in his sleep since 1795.

It is not Coleridge but his critics who have been preoccupied with the poetic imagination. The game of Pick-your-own-German-philosopher has led to Kant, Fichte, Tetens, Schelling being ridden like hobby-horses through the pages of *Biographia*, and has distracted attention from the fact that imagination is for Coleridge an act of faith. In Chapter 9, though he is not too truthful about the number of Schelling's works he possesses,[33] Coleridge gives an account of his own sources and intentions that is basically accurate. Schelling is praised as

the founder of the PHILOSOPHY OF NATURE, and as the most successful improver of the Dynamic System which, begun by Bruno, was reintroduced . . . by KANT.

'With the exception of one or two fundamental ideas which cannot be withheld from FICHTE', Coleridge continues, 'to SCHELLING we owe the completion . . . of this revolution of philosophy.' Having established this pantheist succession,[24] and made clear that Schelling is to him the Nature-philosopher, not the philosopher of art, Coleridge states his own position. The tones are unctuous, but the meaning is not in doubt:

To me it will be happiness and honor enough, should I succeed in rendering the system itself intelligible to my countrymen, and in the application of it to the most awful of subjects, for the most important of purposes.   (BL, I, pp. 162–4)

'By this', Engell writes, with comic incredulity, 'C[oleridge] apparently means religion'. Then, fearing that he has gone too far, he takes it back again: 'or a point where philosophy, art and religion become one' (ibid.). Art has been inserted not because of anything Coleridge himself has said, but because it is the preoccupation of the editor. Again and again it is clear that Engell cannot take seriously the fact that Coleridge's religion is the centre of his life. The Dynamic System, begun by Giordano Bruno, 'completed' by Schelling, is the pantheist alternative to the dead world of Newton, Locke, and 'the Mechanic Dogmatists' (CL, IV, 574). The histories and political economy of the present and preceding century', writes Coleridge in The Statesman's Manual, 'partake in the general contagion of its mechanic philosophy.' If, by contrast, we go back to the histories of the Bible,

they are the educts of the Imagination, of that reconciling and mediatory power, which . . . gives birth to a system of symbols, harmonious in themselves, and consubstantial with the truths of which they are the conductors.   (SM, pp. 28–9)

'Consubstantial', Robert Barth reminds us, in a book that goes to the heart of Coleridge's religious thinking, is 'the privileged word canonized by the Council of Nicea in A.D. 325 to express the relationship of the Son to the Father in the Trinity.' 'The Son', he continues, 'truly "symbolizes" the Father; he "images him forth"', at the same time partaking in the most perfect possible way of the inner reality of the Father.'[25] In giving birth to symbols 'consubstantial with the truths of which they are the conductors', the imagination is inevitably divine. In reading the symbol-language of God, man in his turn is enabled to partake of the inner reality that is the Logos.

What then of the Biographia definitions? As 'the prime Agent of all human perception', the primary imagination does have to include sense-perceptions – or at least the faculty that orders them. Logically, therefore, we have another triple process (though not one that is akin to

Tetens or Schelling). The Ascent begins with the lower power of the primary, and mounts thence through the poetic secondary to the sublime of the primary at its highest. It can be argued that Coleridge, who by 1815 was concerned not to be thought unorthodox, allowed for the possibility that the pantheist third stage in the process might not be perceived.[26] But is it seriously to be thought that the man who had earlier linked God's 'one eternal self-affirming act' with a view that

> Infinite myriads of self-conscious minds
> Are one all-conscious Spirit . . .
> *(Destiny of Nations*, ll. 43–4)

– who in *Biographia* itself had considered Jehovah's self-naming to reveal 'the fundamental truth of all philosophy'*(BL*, I, p. 275), and gone on to claim that 'true metaphysics are nothing else but true divinity' *(ibid.*, p. 291), should bring the philosophical section of his great work to a close by claiming that sense-perception (of all things) is 'a repetition in the finite mind of the eternal act of creation'? Few people have rated the evidence of their senses lower than Coleridge, or would have been less inclined to celebrate it in exalted biblical language. In his definitions he scaled downwards from the primary at the top to the fancy at the bottom because he was thinking in terms of human achievement, and the primary in its full potential showed man at his closest to God. The primary definition is a statement of faith. It may be that Coleridge did not intend it easily to be understood, but by comparison with some of the material he incorporated from Schelling and others it is by no means difficult.

So far from betraying himself unwittingly into the trap of pantheism, Coleridge in his definition of the 'tertium aliquid' – the 'third something' that is an inter-penetration of counteracting powers – is telling his readers firmly, and not for the first time, how the primary imagination should be interpreted.[27] Chapter 13 is brief, and argues its way step by step from the epigraphs at the opening, through to the pantheist assertion which they so clearly predict. The tertium aliquid is the angelic reason in man that will enable him to climb the next rung in Milton's Ascent of Being; it is the 'principle of things' in Coleridge's Wordsworthian emendation of Leibnitz; it is the pantheism of Synesius that is 'not necessarily irreligious or heretical' (though it may be so in the teaching of others). The inter-penetration of subject and object, mind and the external world, can logically take place only in the self-assertion of God. Here alone are the conditions under which the ground of existence, and the ground of the knowledge of existence, are the same. Coleridge spells this out carefully in Chapter 12, and his position is also made clear in a marginal comment to *Omniana* that is footnoted by Engell. Southey had wished that Jehovah's 'I AM THAT I AM' should be translated, 'I am he who am', and Coleridge writes emphatically:

No! the sense of *that* is because, or in that – I am in that I am! meaning I affirm myself, [and] affirming myself to be, I am. Causa Sui. My own act is the ground of my own existence. (*BL*, I, p. 275).

A repetition of this eternal act in the finite mind is possible only in that the tertium aliquid is God. It is the 'something far more deeply interfused', the 'motion and . . . spirit' that is present at once in the round ocean, the living air, the blue sky, and *in the mind of man* (*Tintern Abbey*, 97–101).

The spirit is of course no less present in the minds of uncomprehending men, but its potential – 'the sublime of man' – is realized only in those who have the imaginative capacity to 'see into the life of things', to lose their individuality and find in God the oneness that is the true self. It is for this reason that the higher role of the primary is at times referred to as the 'philosophic imagination'. Quoting Plotinus (but with Milton, and his own approaching definitions in mind), Coleridge in Chapter 12 describes this power as 'the highest and intuitive knowledge, as distinguished from the discursive' (*BL*, I, p. 241). It is 'the sacred power of self-intuition', comprehensible to those

who within themselves can interpret and understand the symbol, that the wings of the air-sylph are forming within the skin of the caterpillar . . . (*ibid.*, pp. 241–2)

Coleridge might, one feels, have allegorized the butterfly as Psyche, or the Soul; instead he comments simply that those who possess the philosophic imagination 'know and feel' the potential that is working within them. Self-intuition is intuition not of the limited temporal self, but of future totality: 'We begin with the I KNOW MYSELF in order to end with the absolute I AM' (*ibid.*, p. 283).[28]

Coleridge, as he would soon recognize, was at this moment a Behmenite. The primary imagination in its highest power is one with 'the deific energies in Deity itself' (*CM*, I, p. 602). By comparison, the secondary can only be inferior: it is a merely human faculty, not an interpenetration of the divine. In the circumstances, however, Coleridge's statement that the secondary is not different in kind is an astonishing claim. Schelling came for a time to think of art as reconciling man and Nature; Coleridge never adopts this position in *Biographia*, but the fact that the creative imagination could merge into the primary gives to the poet a special position in the Ascent of Being. His work is limited because it 'coincid[es] with the conscious will', and true self-consciousness – the losing and finding of self – is a spontaneous act of love, or blessing, or imagination, which cannot be deliberately achieved. No bounds are set, however, on the poet's Ascent. His vision has an almost Blakean power. He

contemplate [s] the ANCIENT of Days and all his works with feelings as fresh, as if all had then sprang forth at the first creative Fiat . . .

He has a 'mind that feels the riddle of the world, and may help to unravel it' (*BL*, I, p. 80). The primary imagination at its highest is the supreme human achievement of oneness with God; the secondary, though limited by comparison, contains the hope that *in the act of writing* the poet may attain to a similar power.

Notes

1 For Coleridge's reading of Jacob Boehme (Behmen), and Boehme's relation to Schelling, see p. 44, below.

2 Fruman, pp. 80–3, and *passim*.

3 I. A. Richards, *Coleridge on Imagination* (1934), p. 58.

4 W. Jackson Bate, 'Coleridge on the Function of Art', *Perspectives of Criticism*, XX (Cambridge, Mass., 1950), p. 145. Bate's definitions are cited approvingly by James Volant Baker, *The Sacred River: Coleridge's Theory of The Imagination* (Louisiana, 1957), p. 121, but have not been widely accepted.

5 See *BL*, II, p. 15 and I. A. Richards, *Practical Criticism* (1929).

6 The first recorded usage of the phrase 'secondary education', at which critics tend to clutch at this point in the discussion, is by Matthew Arnold in 1861. The use of 'primary' to mean earlier, primal, is not uncommon (it occurs in Coleridge himself, for instance, at *Misc C*, p. 205); the use of 'secondary' to imply greater importance is decidedly rare. I have not found a clear example in Coleridge.

7 It should be stressed that Coleridge follows Schelling (see *BL*, I, pp. 279–80) in defining the will as the highest act of self-consciousness, but yet spontaneous. The Mariner blesses the water-snakes 'unawares', but his doing so is an expression of will. The 'conscious will' – will under control of the conscious mind – is not different in kind, but inevitably lesser in degree.

8 McFarland's essay has the support of Kathleen M. Wheeler, *Sources, Processes and Methods in Coleridge's 'Biographia Literaria'* (Cambridge, 1980), p. 127 and n.

9 At one point, just before the Theses of Chapter 12, Coleridge says that in the following Chapter the results of his enquiry 'will be applied to the deduction of imagination, and with it the principles of production and of genial criticism in the fine arts' (*BL*, I, p. 264). It doesn't happen – or, at least, it doesn't happen until Volume Two, after the transcendental implications have first been drawn in Chapter 13.

10 For a more sceptical view, see Fruman, pp. 85–6. Coleridge's claim to have had the ideas before Schelling ever *wrote* them, is not defensible.

11 *Home at Grasmere*, 1007–8.

12 Paragraph 303; *Works of George Berkeley, D. D.* (2 vols., 1784), II, p. 600.

13 *Religious Musings*, 46–50; Coleridge's poetry in this essay is quoted from *Poems*, selected and ed. John Beer, revised edition 1974.

¹⁴ David Hartley, *Observations on Man*, reissued with Notes by H. Pistorius (3 vols., 1791), I, p. 114.

¹⁵ *The Marriage of Heaven and Hell*, Plate 14; Blake quotations are drawn from *Poetry and Prose*, ed. David V. Erdman and Harold Bloom (New York, 1965).

¹⁶ 'Why so violent against *metaphysics* in poetry?' Coleridge wrote to Thelwall in May 1796, and added, 'Is not Akenside's a metaphysical poem?' Wordsworth is cited later in the same letter as liking best the most exalted philosophical sequences in *Religious Musings* (*CL*, I, pp. 215–16). To Lamb it seemed that *Religious Musings* was second only to *Paradise Lost*, and in some respects greater still in that Milton did not contain 'Such grand truths' (*LL*, I, p. 95).

¹⁷ As in *Destiny of Nations*, 15–26, *Religious Musings*, 413–19, *This Lime Tree Bower My Prison*, 37–43.

¹⁸ Rethinking in 1818 is associated with the Philosophical Lectures and with the new version of *The Friend*; Coleridge did not, however, cease to make statements that imply his earlier pantheist views. See, for instance, the note of 1827 quoted by Henry Nelson in the 1839 edition of *The Statesman's Manual*: 'By reason we know that god is: but God is himself the Supreme Reason ... the organs of spiritual apprehension having objects consubstantial with themselves' (*SM*, p. 68n). Cf. *SM*, pp. 28–9 (quoted above, p. 47) and, for the rethinking of 1818, n26 below.

¹⁹ It is tempting to say that Coleridge's reading is pantheist, Milton's is not; but *De Doctrina* (not published until 1825) shows Milton arguing for *creatio ex Deo*, the Platonist belief held by Plotinus among others that the preexisting matter from which the world was fashioned had itself been created out of the Godhead; see *Complete Prose Works of John Milton* (New Haven and London, 8 vols., 1953–82), VI, pp. 305–9. Coleridge's reading serves to emphasize that the material universe derives from the spiritual existence of God.

²⁰ In February 1805 Coleridge notes the 'instructive Truth of the presence of all meanings in every meaning, as Leibnitz felt and layed [down] as the foundation of metaphysics in his representative Monads' (*CN*, II, 2442).

²¹ See for example March 1796, 'How is it that Dr. Priestley is not an atheist . . .' (*CL*, I, p. 192); April 1799, 'the more I think, the more I am discontented with the doctrines of Priestly' (*ibid.*, p. 482); July 1802, 'neither do I conceive Christianity to be tenable on the Priestleyan Hypothesis' (*CL*, II, p. 821). Priestley's 'impious and pernicious tenets' are denounced in *Biographia* (*BL*, I, p. 291), and a public attack is made on Unitarianism in the *Lay Sermon* (1816), *SM*, p. 176.

²² The claim to have '*conjured over*' Boehme at school is made, *CL*, IV, p. 751. It is tempting to see Boehme's influence in *The Aeolian Harp* (autumn 1795), and in 1795–6 he features in a notebook list of possible projects (*CN*, I, 174). In August 1808, Coleridge notes: 'W. Law's Scheme of Religion founded on J. Boëmen is that which is most convincing to my Judgement' (*CN*, III, 3354).

²³ Concerned that he 'be not charged ... [with] ungenerous concealment, or intentional plagiarism', Coleridge writes, 'I have not indeed (eheu res angusta domi!) been hitherto able to procure more than two of his books (*BL*, I, p. 164). Ownership is difficult to prove, but five would probably be an underestimate.

²⁴ The sense in which Kant may be said to have reintroduced the dynamic

Platonism of Bruno is defined at the beginning of Chapter 8; see *BL*, I, p. 129 and n3.

25 J. Robert Barth, S.J., *The Symbolic Imagination* (Princeton, 1977), p. 11. Professor Barth sees Coleridge's symbolic vision as 'profoundly sacramental': 'It is God reaching out to man, man reaching out to God – "through and in the Temporal" – and encountering each other in the joy of the symbolic act' (*ibid.*, p. 21). My only reservation would be that such a description takes no account of joy as 'the One Life within us and abroad' (line added to *The Aeolian Harp* (1795) before republication in *Sybilline Leaves*, 1817).

26 A number of critics, McFarland and J. A. Appleyard (*Coleridge's Philosophy of Literature*, Cambridge, Mass., 1965) among them, have seen the Coleridge of *Biographia* as frightened by pantheism. Even at the time of the 1818 *Friend*, however, he seems to have been very divided on the issue, first referring (in Essay XI) to 'the intellectual re-union of the all in one, in that eternal reason whose fulness hath no opacity, whose transparency hath no vacuum' (*Friend*, I, p. 522), and then claiming to his correspondents that a paragraph had been 'unfortunately omitted – it's object being to preclude all suspicion of any leaning towards Pantheism, in any of it's forms'. 'I adore the living and personal God . . .' he continues uneasily (*CL*, IV, p. 894).

27 The tertium aliquid itself is anticipated in the account of the water-insect in Chapter 7, which is an emblem of the mind's active and passive faculties being reconciled by the intermediate imagination. 'In common language', he writes, 'and especially on the subject of poetry, we appropriate the name [imagination] to a superior degree of the faculty, joined to a superior voluntary control over it' (*BL*, I, p. 125). The references to poetry and voluntary control establish that Coleridge has the secondary in mind (it is 'superior' merely 'in common language'). In its reconciling power, it is not different in kind from the tertium aliquid.

28 Paul Hamilton in *Coleridge's Poetics* (Oxford, 1983) has argued that *Biographia*, 'the most famous self-professed attempt in English literature to exhibit the relation of philosophy to poetry', disintegrates because 'in Coleridge's own admission' the central definitions are 'not conclusions drawn from a preceding line of reasoning' (p. 8). Much of what he has to say is admirable and to the point, but he wants Coleridge to be a common-sense philosopher, and has no truck with 'the sacred power of self-intuition'. The unity of *Biographia* lies not in sustained argument, but in Coleridge's apprehension of man in his relationship to God.

Struggling with the contingent: self-conscious imagination in Coleridge's notebooks

K. DUGAS

I

Coleridge was an explorer of self-consciousness, but an explorer bogged down in a morass of his own making. His loneliness, his prodigious curiosity, and his voracious reading led him to keep journals as a virtual necessity. Beyond offering a means of probing his experience, his notebooks gave him the chance to fix a habit of speculative thinking whose momentum might fuel itself, to sustain him over stretches of creative frustration. They fulfilled in part his need for companionship, and for self-analysis. Accommodating the insights of the moment, journal-keeping became his way to make connections otherwise unavailable, and to produce what he hoped might deliver him from lethargy and self-doubt.

But if Coleridge's works record a mind fascinated by both the generalizing power of science and the sensuous minutiae of lived experience, they also record the strains inherent in these means of approaching experience. They testify to the conflicts of a mind driven at times to moralize, yet painfully conscious of private dissipations. If he strove for the ideal, he was tortured by the real. He benefited by crossbreeding his ideas, by adapting concepts from widely varying sources, yet the magnitude of conceptual possibilities, sources of metaphor, and disciplines of knowledge often paralyzed his ability to shape ideas into literary forms. The record (some might say wreckage) of his plans, his literary schemes, his publications, marginalia, and notebooks show that writing was for him endlessly speculative. He could not carry enough of his ideas to completion; he was always beginning some new production. It was as if thinking or writing – about anything – was an end in itself. If individual ideas were no more than temporary fixatives of relations yet to be fully determined, they were also imaginatively seductive as ends in themselves. Although a determination of its fuller relations could save an idea from the oblivion facing an isolated thought, it also required a rigorous selectivity, the imposition of limits which Coleridge's polymathic reading seemed designed to circumvent.

Coleridge did not find this situation easily resolvable. Despite his prodigious curiosity, he voiced doubts about the dispersion of his powers. Could he make anything of his separate formulations? Could he generalize his insights into some pattern or plan? His experience was one of frustration and doubt, of proliferation more lateral than he had hoped, expressed in literary forms – the conversation poems, the essays, even the notebooks themselves – which he did not wholly respect, his work littered throughout by marks of incompleteness. Thus Coleridge's work inhabits, perhaps more than that of any other writer, the intermediary zone between thought 'merely' articulated in words and formalized literary production. From essays and notebooks and marginalia, from published papers and poems to manuscript drafts of articles, economic and philosophical analyses, literary criticism and plays, Coleridge lived, thought, and wrote in a margin, inhabiting the space between experience and literature, and between literature and ideas – a space which each of these things borders on, intermingles with, and shares.

In this essay I will investigate some of the reasons for that marginality as they are revealed in notebook entries written at the time when Coleridge first began to analyze his dispersion of imaginative power. In the notebooks I hope to discover the way Coleridge thought – in the moment of composition and as he faced his own inner struggles and intellectual perplexities. My method thus parallels the practical methodology for Coleridge studies that Lawrence Lockridge has recently set forth. By turning to the early notebooks, I hope to reveal, as Lockridge has put it, 'the continuities of an internal dialogue' rather than any 'total consistency in doctrine or steady development toward some settled point of view'.[1]

II

It is 1803, in October – some nine years after Coleridge first began journal-keeping, but these nine years (and one more) fit into a single volume in the Coburn series. It was at this time that Coleridge began treating his writing in the notebooks as an activity for sustained, self-conscious reflection, and as a place to work through ideas drawn from the range of his readings. In a few simple lines, he writes what is not just a statement of intention, but rather more, a portent of his later fate:

Seem to have made up my mind to write my metaphysical works, as *my Life*, & *in* my Life – intermixed with all the other events/or history of the mind & fortunes of S. T. Coleridge.   (*CN*, I, 1515)

Though this articulation is often cited as early evidence of his intention to write what would become the *Biographia Literaria*, we would be
wrong to think it fulfilled in that work. Why would Coleridge need to state
in his conclusion to the *Biographia* that he still felt he needed to write 'my
history'? Why would he need to apologize in the first chapter, to explain
that what narrative there was was less an instrinsic part of his conception
than a structure which existed 'chiefly for the purpose of giving a continuity to the work, in part for the sake of miscellaneous reflections . . .
but still more as introductory to the statement of my principles in Politics,
Religion, and Philosophy' (*BL*, I, p. 5)? Even less synthetically, the narrative was an introduction to 'the application of the rules, deduced from
philosophical principles, to poetry and criticism' (*BL*, I, p. 5). Whatever
his original intention, in its published form the *Biographia Literaria*, a work
of literary criticism and critical metaphysics, did not successfully 'inter-
mix' events and history with metaphysics and mind. Nor do formal
statements of principles reflect the evolutionary development we would
expect from the words 'as *my Life*, & *in* my Life'. The more ambitious
claim made in the notebook has no formal equivalent; it is, rather, a
description of the way Coleridge came to write his notebooks.

But the central problem for a writer trying to achieve the systematic
completeness Coleridge desired and yet finding himself so attuned to
possibilities observed in the moment, possibilities which could frustrate
and challenge that completeness, arose from the experience which
resulted: that of being pulled in opposing intellectual and emotional
directions. On the one hand, philosophical completeness produced a
closed form, implied an end to speculation and an arrogation of finality,
with which Coleridge, as perhaps the most systematic English Romantic
articulator of the idea of process, would have nothing to do: the idea of
an end or limit to knowledge embodied in closed forms was the target of
Coleridge's attacks on controversies in scriptural interpretation and the
sciences, and contradicted what in Coleridge's terms we know as 'polar
logic'. On the other hand, the infinite possibilities of the moment were
threatening because they stood in the way of completing anything. The
same threat attended Coleridge's practice of giving himself over to the
moment in search of the lucid impression. I want to suggest that the latter was a problem for Coleridge not so much because of what he claimed
(that he had no pleasure in temporal impressions) but rather, because he
was so good at articulating momentary impressions, and because it was
this very sensitivity that he felt he had to suppress rather than
acknowledge.

We might expect the notebooks to be ultimately revealing of the tensions in Coleridge – and they are. If at one moment he writes, 'Of all

men I ever knew, Wordsworth himself not excepted, I have the faintest pleasure in things contingent & transitory . . . to a disease in me' (*CN*, II, 2026), at another he will claim 'I feel too intensely the omnipresence of all in each, . . . tho' [my brain] perceives the *difference* of things, yet [it] is eternally pursuing the likenesses' (*CN*, II, 2372). We will have to consider in what way Coleridge's antipathy for the individual and the transitory, along with its corollary desire for unifying 'affinit[ies]' or 'likenesses', suggests tension. Is it this antipathy, or some confusion between the critical distinction of what it is to feel versus what it is to see, that poses a problem? It may be that Coleridge's marginality is only explicable by understanding the interrelation between his susceptibility to the transitory and the feelings (as opposed to the knowledge) arising from the practice of self-analysis itself.

Answers can be found in the notebook entries around this time. I have observed that it was around October 1803 that Coleridge begins journal-writing in earnest. The writing begins to modulate away from singly entered aphorisms, foreign quotations, and lists – of daily purchases, German or botanical vocabularies, literary schemes (to be read and to be written), outlines for poems, intricate distinctions among meters. It shifts towards longer entries spanning a wider range of interests: metaphysical and moral speculations, usually arising out of personal events; observations of the behavior of children, particularly of the ways in which they try to understand their experience of the world; a wide variety of visual illusions and *trompes-l'oeil*, in which the pleasures of the mind in such illusions figure strongly. Before this time, the longer notebook entries are almost exclusively descriptions of natural phenomena, usually mountain landscapes. While Coleridge continues to write this kind of entry, their relative frequency as extended subjects decreases. Many more of the later natural observations concern animal behaviour, and they typically read as if they were themselves originally gleaned from popular scientific journals; most often Coleridge uses them as the basis for an analogy about human behavior or an abstraction from animal behavior to natural law or aesthetic principle. What replaces these descriptions are Coleridge's increasingly self-conscious analyses of his own behavior, sometimes generalized as human experience, sometimes pertaining specifically to his own psychology.

Between October 1803 and December 1804, and following what Coleridge had called a 'freezing' of his poetic powers, is a fitfully extended examination of the apparent contradiction between multiplicity and singularity in nature. This contradiction arises from the coexistence of difference with sameness and form with resistance to form. The same contradiction can be found in Coleridge's dialectically opposed categories of thought, which also include temporal and eternal, material and spiritual, particular and general. Coleridge would eventually call his practice of dialectical thinking 'the universal Law of Polarity', the process by which 'EVERY POWER IN NATURE AND IN SPIRIT . . . *evolve*[*s*] *an opposite, as the sole means and condition of its manifestation*' (*Friend*, I, p. 94n). The 'essence of polarity' is, as Owen Barfield has described it, the '*dynamic* conflict between coinciding opposites';[2] it is 'no proper opposition but between the two polar forces of one and the same power' (*Friend*, I, p. 94). Coleridge was to study well-developed articulations of dialectical thinking in his readings of Schelling, Goethe, Oken, and Kant (among others), as Thomas McFarland has recently so well documented.[3] But if Coleridge wrote in April 1820:

In all subjects of deep and lasting Interest you will detect a struggle between two opposites, two polar Forces, both of which are alike necessary to our human Well-being, & necessary each to the continued existence of the other,[4]

in December 1803, Coleridge merely identifies the process as 'EX-TREMES MEET' (*CN*, I, 1725). So definitive a statement as the one in 1820 seems incontrovertible as a declaration of method, but we might wonder how rigorously Coleridge carried this method out. For Coleridge persistently privileged one polar opposite over the other, giving his dialectical practice a hierarchical, and often a moralistic, charge – which was usually self-condemnatory and which complicated, rather than contributed to, his 'Well-being'. In this way his failure to carry out his dialectical method lay beneath his despair. For what we find in the notebooks is a peculiar set of contradictory relations: one, between his oppressive dissatisfaction with himself and his speculative, inward vigor; another, between his desire for unity and the experience of self-division which arose out of his practice of self-conscious reflection. For Coleridge, the combination seems to have resulted in an informal literary production which strangely belied much of its subject. It forms a set of opposing effects which are themselves ironically expressive of the problems that plagued their author.

One of the first instances of tensi.n appears in October 1803. It surfaces in the context of a desire to write a poem on 'Spirit, – or on Spinoza', an early practitioner of the dialectic. Could he understand

how the *one can be many!* . . . It seems as if it were impossible; yet it *is* – & it is every where! – It is indeed a contradiction *in Terms*: and only in Terms! – It is the co presence of Feeling & Life, limitless by their very essence, with Form, by its very essence limited – determinate – definite.   (*CN*, I, 1561)

To readers of Coleridge, this is familiar enough. It is the 'irreducible contradiction . . . at once the most unacceptable and the most important truth he had to deliver'.[5] For the two 'conflicting principles of FREE LIFE, and of the confining FORM'[6] are 'the primary forces from which the conditions of all possible directions are derivative' (*BL*, I, p. 197). The co presence of formlessness (of feeling and life) with form (with definitive ideas) is exactly the condition of Romantic process. If the problem is one of the inadequacy of human understanding and human language to encompass a 'given' which is assumed to exist beyond both, what blocks Coleridge's recognition of it? We will find the answer both in the conflict of his feelings and in his habits of thinking – particularly of organizing the terms of his experience into hierarchies of time and sometimes of language. In these hierarchies, the categories of eternal and spiritual are valued over those of temporal and material. Later, Coleridge will base the very foundations of imagination and reason on a related hierarchy – that of a unity which encompasses division while still remaining a unity. The very direction of his dialectic will always be towards 'restoring, or rather renewing, the original unity, from which it springs'.[7] For now, of his feelings Coleridge writes some entries later:

Nothing affects me much at the moment it happens – it either stupifies me, and I perhaps look at a merry-make & dance the hay of Flies, or listen entirely to the loud Click of the great Clock/or I am simply indifferent, not without some sense of philosophic Self-complacency. – For a Thing at the moment is but a Thing of the moment/it must be taken up into the mind, diffuse itself thro' the whole multitude of Shapes & Thoughts, not one of which it leaves untinged – between w/ch & it some new Thought is not engendered/this a work of Time/but the Body feels it quicken with me – .   (*CN*, I, 1597)

The claim is that new thoughts, rather than being capable of arising immediately out of the moment, must instead be the result of the gradual (for Coleridge, the endlessly deferrable) work of time, and yet such a claim must be at least in part a falsification, as the fact that his body 'feels it quicken' within him suggests. Compare this entry with one written in December:

. . . but overpowered with the [?] Phaenomena I arose, lit my Candle, & wrote – of figures, even with open eyes/of squares, &   & of various colours, & I know not what/

How in a few minutes I forgot such an Assemblage of distinct Impressions, ebullitions & piles of golden colour & thence to think of the Nature of Memory. So intense/& yet in one Minute forgotten! the same is in Dreams/ *Think of this*/if, *perchance*, thou *livest* – ALAS!

Of the necessity of writing & indeed of all other m[otion] IN LARGE, whenever.
                    (*CN*, I, 1750)

If such an entry (I could have chosen others) shows that Coleridge, powerfully motivated by immediate sensations, was capable of a response other than stupefaction or indifference, his directives to '*Think of this*/if, *perchance*, thou *livest*' suggest self-condemnation, disgust turned toward himself, for certain inevitable moments of failure in the writing process. He could be stupified by the sensual, and transfixedly look or listen without the slightest impulse towards self-expression, feeling self-complacently indifferent to any significance the moment might possess; he could simply be unable to remember the shape of an inspiration or make good the rush of emotion which comes with it. Any one of these responses is characteristic of the experience of writing, where fallowness, indulgent play, stupefaction, and inspiration are matters of course affecting the mood of their author. Thus when Coleridge describes the diffusion of things of the moment into the multitude of preexisting thoughts, he produces a slanted and emotionally colored description of the experience of writing. For his claim that stupefaction was consummately characteristic of his practice is not corroborated by the evidence of the notebooks, which show his amazing facility for articulating ideas in the moment just as much as they show his habit of endlessly deferring the use of those very ideas. It seems clear that in these passages he is undertaking something other than merely understanding his experience. There is an excess of emotion here, and it seems directed against some part of himself which apparently he feels he must control – by denigrating it. This excess, with its exhortations, can only put his analysis in a different, and a shiftier, light.

But shifty in what way? First, the phrase 'is but a Thing of the moment' suggests that Coleridge here prefers the eternal to the transitory, a privileging which introduces a hierarchical distinction between these terms rather than values both as functional parts of a working dialectic. But because to arrive at 'the eternal' requires many transitory moments, any eternal formulation is always only a transition towards another formulation. It is in this sense that the transitory is necessary to that dialectic: as old forms are continually being superseded by new ones, the evolution of new ideas makes for a succession of such eternally transitory moments of thought. Second, the absolutism in Coleridge's proclaiming both his own stupefaction and his need to diffuse the singular moment into all other moments (and thus by extension, into all other ideas) for 'thought' to be engendered suggests that he is attempting here to hide his habit of endlessly deferring closure even as he tries to expose it – or perhaps, to break it. For neither the claim to be stupefied nor the need to diffuse is borne out in his notebooks. What this lack of corroboration suggests is that Coleridge here silences the voices within him which correspond to a set of alternate realities in order to support apparently more important claims. That is, Coleridge 'adjusts' his experience of writing in calling upon it to support convictions that he has clearly some stake in, when the same experience, interpreted differently, could as easily have subverted those very convictions.

Given Coleridge's stated reasons for his stalled productivity, his interpretation of the experience of writing cannot be taken innocently. Instead, it seems to represent a destructively exaggerated concentration of emotional energy upon himself. Coleridge's recurrent perception, despite the variety and fertility of ideas in his Malta journals, was that 'I have done nothing; not even layed up any material, any inward stores.' Other entries show that he did not always consider such imaginative indolence to be self-representative, for at times he felt his mind – 'so populous, so active, so full of noble schemes, so capable of realizing them' – to be a 'deep reservoir into which all these streams & currents of lovely forms flow' (*CN*, I, 1577). But such moments are rare, and most often work out of negation in that they, too, arise out of despair, in this case, despair because of the absence 'for years . . . [of] one pure & sincere pleasure! one full Joy!' That is, positive assertions of being capable of mental activity are elaborate sighs made in response to the pervasive feeling that pleasures were invariably 'cracked', found 'dull with base Alloy' (*CN*, I, 1577).

But it is here that we need to ask certain questions. What is the relation between Coleridge's professed need to experience single emotions and his disgust for the momentary, which seems so allied to his disgust for himself? What is the reason for the disparity between his interpretation of his experience of writing and his apparent practice? What is it that may be blocking not so much the action of his creative powers as his perception of those powers, especially his ability to formalize related ideas into larger if inevitably incomplete wholes? Coleridge would come to attribute his dwindling capacity to a 'lack of will', but it is less simple than that. To rest with such an explanation would be to accept the writer's own most pitilessly (de-)moralizing self-negation. What is clear is that for Coleridge, the possibility for understanding the root of his own despair seems paradoxically to recede under the lens of the increasingly powerful activity of self-conscious reflection which he so rigorously practiced after 1803.

III

To begin to appreciate the complexity of this problem, we have first to turn to the earliest form of *Dejection: an Ode*, the *Letter to Asra*.[8] In it Coleridge claims that the loss of his capacity to *feel* joy 'Suspends what Nature gave me at my Birth,/My shaping Spirit of Imagination'. Since the capacity to shape ideas is a form of the ability to formalize perceptions, the claim is that feeling is necessary for imaginative shaping or formative closure. His 'sole Resource' against its suspension is 'not to think of what I needs must feel' but patiently 'by abstruse Research to steal/From my own Nature all the Natural Man'. As this stealing became habitual, his original (and he would say, natural) 'birthright' seemed more and more unavailable, and the solution he had chosen came to be to him not a solution but a disease, spreading with the power of an infection.

Here comparison with Wordsworth is fruitful. Where Wordsworth steals, he appears to steal from nature, as he does in the second book of *The Prelude*. Although nature derives its power from his own projections, this fact is veiled in the action and the metaphor of the poem. The actual coming to terms with this reality is reserved for the final book, for the ascent of Snowdon. It is the very veiling of the theft that makes the *Prelude* possible, for this unveiling is the poem, is the discovery of unmediated power, and guarantees the celebratory final vision. The veiling and the deferral of the unveiling thus work, structurally and emotionally, *for* Wordsworth. Because he only approaches self-consciousness in his narrative rather than takes self-consciousness as his point of departure, he does not directly experience it as a threat.

But in the *Letter to Asra* Coleridge expresses the same theft without mediation. He steals from himself, in the workings of self-consciousness, and knows it, by the workings of self-consciousness. This is one element of the 'abstruse research', his only other 'plan'. In addition to self-consciousness, this 'research' encompassed his readings in a range of scientific, psychological, and philosophical disciplines which he pursued far more voraciously (and more desperately) than Wordsworth. The attempt to use self-consciousness and scientific rigor to regain the 'natural man', here synecdochical for the desired experience of sincerity and joy, boomeranged. The failure is experienced both as a deadening or blank void and as an internal storm, a Wordsworthian formulation of a mind 'vexed by its own creation'. This dual choice of metaphors reflects the complex situation in which powers felt to be frozen or suspended exist simultaneously with a vital creativity which persists but which has no outlet except to rage destructively about itself. These metaphors and the metaphor of infection emerge out of the experience of self-consciousness. They can be found in other writers, Romantic and post-Romantic, who employ similar self-reflective techniques. Such writers typically share as well a particular sense of regret and loss, depression and despair; they articulate correspondent desires which are versions of a longing for a wholeness now unavailable.

If Coleridge's 'natural man' could somehow exist *a priori* and were not just a human construct, then Coleridge could indeed have 'lost' his birthright. But what can this edenic formulation of the 'natural man' mean to a poet committed to self-consciousness? And what kind of joy is this, that only the pure can partake of it? In structuring the poem, Coleridge places Sara Hutchinson in the same position relative to himself as that in which William Wordsworth placed his sister years before in *Tintern Abbey*. Each woman stands for some quality of wholeness lost and impossible to regain, but each poet is made a poet by the very fact that he cannot regain what is lost. Moreover, each poet is made a poet by his implicit realization that what was said to be lost was in fact never there. The emotion of which each poet speaks is thus not merely unavailable to the speaker in the moment of speaking; it is a chimera which never was, an indulgent fiction which the speaker himself gave up long ago, even though it is only in the poem that he records the sacrifice. The loss of joy experienced is the 'disease' of consciousness, indicative of the alienating power of the knowledge which comes from self-analysis itself, which destroys faith in beliefs one would like to hold on to even as it liberates the mind to pursue ever subsequent ones.

I want to relate, then, Coleridge's involvement with self-conscious analysis and dialectical thinking to the principal feature of his experience of creative despair: the necessity he felt for feeling pleasure 'pure' and 'unalloyed', or in a related formulation, for experiencing a 'unity of feeling'. This need is a primary focus of the notebooks after October 1803, during the period after Coleridge completed the *Letter to Asra*. His explorations in the notebooks represent refinements of what he expressed in that poem, as well as further probings into his responses, as if he were unsatisfied with that earlier understanding of the reasons for his continued despair. While the loss of an ability 'to feel' still plays a large part, the notebook entries themselves testify to a more complicated struggle, involving the tensions I have been positing throughout this essay. His claim that he took no pleasure in things transitory – to the point of devaluing, even almost refusing to recognize, the conceptions the individual moment inspired – conflicted both with the reality of his practice and with his baffled appreciation for 'the co presence' of form with formlessness, of unity with diversity. Despite his recognition of co presence, he could not free himself from thinking in the hierarchies which led him at various times to privilege permanent over transitory, form over formlessness, unity over diversity. Nor could he resist buttressing those hierarchies by resorting to absolutes on which he could ground his whole mode of thinking. The conflicts which resulted, rather than actually causing the freezing up of his poetic powers, instead reveal to us the considerable practical and theoretical problems which a commitment to self-analytical and dialectical processes poses for the action of fixing and limiting ideas, an action which makes possible the finishing of any formal literary, critical, or philosophical work. Thus I want to suggest that, despite his claims to the contrary, the *feeling* (rather than the actuality) that his creative powers were frozen arose from the conflict between the philosophical skepticism generated by the action of his self-conscious reflections and his longing for the absolutes lost by these very advances – a conflict which operated at two levels, one formal and theoretical, the other personal and experiential.

IV

In the journals, we find some contradictory responses to transitory phenomena, as if Coleridge were indeed being pulled in more than one direction. These responses represent a fault-line or fracture within his thinking and his psyche. In the entry which follows, both pleasure and unmitigated delight are salient characteristics of Coleridge's extended description, and this is true despite his typical disavowals of being able to experience either.

Delightful weather, motion, relation of the convoy to each other, all exquisite/ – and I particularly watched the beautiful Surface of the Sea in this gentle Breeze! every form so transitory, so for the instant, & yet for that instant so substantial in all its sharp lines, steep surfaces, & hair-deep indentures, just as if it were cut glass, glass cut into ten thousand varieties/& then the network of the wavelets, & the rude circle hole network of the Foam/

And on the gliding Vessel Heaven & Ocean smil'd!   (*CN*, II, 1999)

Here Coleridge has given himself over to the sense of forward motion in the gliding vessel; to his perception of individual interrelation to the whole in the 'relation of [each single member of] the convoy' to the others, and in the networks of wavelets and foam; and finally, to his acknowledgement of elemental accord in the context of an infinite diversity of form, signified by the approbation in the very last phrase. The observed totality is exquisite for the very reason that a transitory fecundity is the main part of that essential forward motion, that definition and accord. The passage reflects his admission that the transitory was both substantial and imaginatively provocative, and appeared to share enduring qualities of permanence and form. Unity of feeling has been achieved, though the implied surprise of that achievement is only part of the pleasure. But almost predictably, the entry immediately following this one is filled with longing:

Why an't you here? This for ever/I have no rooted thorough thro' feeling – &
never exist wholly present to any Sight, to any Sound, to any Emotion, to any
series of Thoughts received or produced/always a feeling of yearning, that at times
passes into Sickness of Heart.   (*CN*, II, 2000)

The achieved *feeling* of unity cannot be sustained, but it is not the idea
of being able to sustain such a unity that is questioned, but the transitory
itself which is deemed the source of his failure, regardless of the original
potency of the perception and despite the fact that what Coleridge is dealing with here is feeling, not ratiocination. It is this sliding of categories
which insures that his idea of a unity of feeling as a desirable outcome remains unchallenged. Further, in the entries above, it is the momentary
success of transitory phenomena in creating a unity of feeling which actually provokes Coleridge to articulate the contrary feeling – desire,
hence (for him) the lack of such unity. This was perhaps in part because
to attain the valued absolute, he had to exclude, conceptually and experientially, what was undesirable, and this contrived absence of the
thing which would break the desired wholeness functioned instead as a
potently disruptive presence. Paradoxically, then, unity of feeling as
generated by temporal phenomena is made a passing experience, giving
rise to an irony which, since Coleridge did not consciously articulate it,
must have entered the substratum of contradiction and conflict within
his writing. Needless to say, this current of opposing internal energy complicated Coleridge's very perception of the feelings which here served as
sole judge and jury too.

What makes the exploration of joylessness in these journal entries different from that in *Dejection: an Ode*, with its explanation for the freezing
of the fountains within? In the poem, unspecified 'afflictions' rob Coleridge of joy which, with or without the pun on 'genial', is identified with
his shaping power. But the loss of joy is itself an affliction, hence the viper
imagery as the thing turns back on itself, to be both an effect and a cause
of the dead, emotionless center. In the first version of the poem, the *Letter to Asra*, these connections are more oblique. The afflictions include his
unsuccessful marriage, his mixed feelings for his children, the awareness
that he continually causes Sara pain, his frustration at not being able to
comfort her, his overwhelming sense of ultimately not belonging to the
Wordsworths' circle. But the last three afflictions stem from something
deeper – an inner 'change' which troubles him 'with pangs untold' and
with a deadening feeling of estrangement from nature.

It is when Coleridge begins to probe further into the reasons for his inability to feel unity that permanence and transience really enter the picture. But instead of questioning the idea of this unity itself – its purposes,
its value, its unreality – he assumes first that it is and second that it is

good. And yet how can anyone, once he has discovered the practice of self-conscious reflection, ever hope to experience the feeling of unity? And, on a symbolic level, how can anyone committed to the notion of process devalue the perpetual dissatisfaction which guarantees forward movement? Yet this is exactly what Coleridge does. Self-consciousness makes unity of feeling impossible; process requires dissatisfaction – these two experiences are inevitable, although Coleridge wishes them not to be. In the notebook entries above, he first sees and describes the apparently unified and harmonized world; then, he self-consciously thinks of himself, and perceives his division, his yearning. He attributes this yearning in part to the lack of an other – a Sara, who synecdochically embodies wholeness and joy. But he does not seem to carry through with the implications of his distinction between feeling and seeing; and because he does not, he cannot question the possibility that seeing is potentially suspect as well. The state in which he finds himself is one he views as aberrant, not as inevitable. And so some reason for it must be found elsewhere than in the practice of meditation itself which, unlike its pre-enlightenment religious precursors, does not promise ever greater wholeness and vision. Thus the mere sight of the transitory functions as a sign for his incompleteness and loss; it bears the full weight of the blame, taking responsibility for the feeling of lost unity which it shares with what endures – and what endures is his desire.

One could thus say that Coleridge's fixing on the transitory as the thing which disrupts unity resulted in a displacement of his desire. Unconsciously, this displacement is designed to preserve those values and *a priori* categories which were undermined by the corrosive power of dialectical and self-conscious analysis (as well as the utter subjectivity of the mind which seemed their corollary). For although the problems of despair, of lack of unity and joy, of persistent yearning, of his antipathy for transitory phenomena and for things of the moment, recur – invariably in close proximity to each other – and although parts of the analysis belonging to any particular one of these problems keep turning up in the analyses of any combination of its counterparts, Coleridge does not ever confront the problem of the permanency of his desire with his professed devaluing of the transitory – even when the two lie side by side. It is only years later, in a handful of poems – *What is life?*, *To Nature*, *Fragment: the Body*, *Limbo*, and *Ne Plus Ultra* – that some of these interrelations are examined. Even though the idea of transitory phenomena is implicit in the experience of permanent yearning, since rootlessness of feeling conceptually and experientially is a thing of flux, Coleridge continues to prefer the permanent to the transitory. The consequences affected not just his perception of his lack of will, but confidence in his shaping power of imagination. And they affected his attitude toward his experience of self-conscious reflection — causing him to blame himself when that experience seemed to twist and darken, vex and undercut.

V

If Coleridge muted his multiplicity of voices, and moreover, could not sustain an inner philosophical composure, the evolution of the *Dejection: an Ode* through its various versions (the *Letter to Asra* written in April 1802, the short form published in the *Morning Post* in October 1802, the *Ode* proper published in *Sibylline Leaves* in 1817) shows his increasingly clear consciousness of the need to separate external or local afflictions from a dejection born out of formal and epistemological tensions. Yet such realizations were cripplingly incomplete: Coleridge too readily, too humorlessly attributed to himself the feeling of a lack of unity and the inability to resist despair which were generated by difficult philosophical problems and uneasily resolvable dilemmas of process, with its appropriately dynamic form. Coleridge's desire for unity was as much an attempt to preserve hierarchies of his own constructing as it was an attempt to heal Cartesian dualisms and to develop a counter to the associationist universe of death. Although his attempt to devalue the transitory impressions of the moment was an attempt to spur himself to finalize his thoughts, this devaluation allows him to shift the blame for his experience of a lack of another unity — a unity of feeling — onto the transitory at the same time that it allows him to indulge in self-flagellation for his deferrals of closure. Ultimately, such self-flagellation was unproductive because it confirmed his hierarchy of values rather than overthrowing it, and without restoring his poetic self-confidence. If such an overthrow would have offered less of a reconciling or transforming vision, it could not have tormented him with utopian hopes he could never attain. As it was, the purpose of Coleridge's dialectic was to achieve 'the true *Atonement* — /i.e. to reconcile the struggles of the infinitely various Finite within the *Permanent*' (*CN*, II, 2208). His loaded language suggests that he desires both spiritual regeneration (the atoning for past sins) and the unification of subject with object, many with one. Here we see how intimately Coleridge's way of thinking, with its formal problems, interpenetrates his way of being, with its psychological ones. For Coleridge, 'intelligence and being are reciprocally each other's Substrate' (*BL*, I, p. 143). It is indeed true that 'in the Coleridgean world everything is connected to everything else'.[9]

Thus Coleridge's feeling of lost wholeness, aggravated by his self-

conscious practice, joined with his self-denigrations, even though his feelings of indolence were partly generated by the overabundance of thoughts
in his restless mind. He came to believe he simply lacked the will to finish
projects, even though inherent in his commitment to Romantic process
was a program of delayed foreclosure. Add to this his fear of subjectivity itself, and it becomes clear that these potentially revealing aspects of
his ways of thinking contributed to his despair because he remained
oblivious to their inevitability. It is this very obliviousness which made
it difficult for him to realize that what he felt as the freezing of his poetic
powers was instead complexly multivalent, that in fact those powers
themselves remained vital – even when those feelings which were
grounded in his beliefs changed. And change they had to: as the under-
pinnings of the epistemology of a period or culture gradually shift beneath
one, so must the feelings which arise from them. Yet feeling almost always
lags behind new conceptions; the experience of revolutions in thought
is never accomplished overnight. If every cultural moment is an interim,
the feelings that belong to it look back towards the past of which they are
no longer a·part, even as they belong to the present and the future.

Coleridge's expectation that the practice of self-conscious reflection
could only work toward his good made it difficult for him to question his
most paralyzing feelings and his most debilitating self-denigrations. The
experiences which were partially the result of his hierarchically loaded
thinking were more divisive than he realized, the problems they created
more enduring. Ultimately, Coleridge was undercut by this very sensitivity, which allowed him to intuit the substance of these inconsistencies even if he had not the analytical means (or emotional disinvestment)
to see them for all their persistently divisive complexity. If it was this
aspect of Coleridge, this sharp and restless sensitivity, which made up,
as Coburn has put it, his 'inquiring spirit', it was also what made him,
in Shelley's words, 'a hooded eagle among blinking owls'.

Notes

[1] Lawrence S. Lockridge, 'Explaining Coleridge's Explanation: Toward a
Practical Methodology for Coleridge Studies', in *Reading Coleridge: Approaches
and Applications*, ed. Walter B. Crawford (Ithaca, Cornell University Press,
1979), p. 48 (cited hereafter as Crawford).

[2] Owen Barfield, *What Coleridge Thought* (Middletown, Conn., Wesleyan
University Press, 1971), p. 187 (cited hereafter as Barfield).

[3] Thomas McFarland, 'A Complex Dialogue: Coleridge's Doctrine of
Polarity and Its European Contexts', in Crawford.

[4] *Ibid.*, p. 56, citing *CL*, v, p. 35.

[5] Barfield, p. 106.
[6] *On the Principles of Genial Criticism*, in *BLS*, II, p. 235.
[7] Barfield, p. 53.
[8] In *Coleridge and Sara Hutchinson and the Asra Poems*, George Whalley (Toronto, University of Toronto Press, 1955), pp. 155–68.
[9] L. C. Knights, *The New York Review of Books*, XVI (22 April 1971), p. 55.

Coleridge's rejection of nature
and the natural man

NORMAN FRUMAN

The subject of Coleridge and the 'natural' seems to divide itself naturally into two parts: Coleridge and the inner world of human nature, and Coleridge on the external world, physical nature. His views on both subjects, which are deeply connected, developed and changed dramatically, and his final thoughts are sometimes startlingly at odds with the Coleridge familiar in anthology selections.

'Nature' and 'natural' are words too common in familiar usage to expect that Coleridge, or anybody else, would always employ them in a precise or consistent way. Just as our spontaneous oaths and damnations are usually bare of theological implication, despite the actual meaning of the words we use, so Coleridge had no theory of human nature in mind when, in an early Preface, he announced that 'By a law of our Nature, he who labors under strong feeling, is impelled to seek for sympathy' (*PW*, ii, p. 1144), or when in a late newspaper essay he marvelled at 'those prudent youths, in whom money is an innate idea, and the dull shrewdness by which it is amassed, an instinct of nature' (*EOT*, ii, p. 469), or when he later said that 'instead of human nature', materialistic philosophy was giving us 'a French nature' (*P Lects*, p. 349).

At twenty-five he recalled that as a young child his 'memory and understanding [had been] forced into an almost unnatural ripeness', and he remarked of Wordsworth, 'It is his practice and almost his nature to convey all the truth he knows without any attack on what he supposes falsehood' (*CL*, i, pp. 347–8, 410). Coleridge never wholly abandoned this familiar sense of 'natural' and its cognates either in letters, notebooks, or essays, and it is important not to confuse these essentially casual uses from those where he is specifically focusing on the concept. The first category shelters a vast number of such references. We should understand that Coleridge was not on philosophical oath when he wrote casually of 'the common instincts of human nature' (*EOT*, i, p. 51), 'our imperfect nature' (*EOT*, i, p. 87), 'natural emotions' (*CL*, i, p. 333), 'natural vanity' (*EOT*, ii, p. 422), or 'the light of natural conscience'

(*CL*, II, p. 1192), and he expected to be understood without learned gloss when he drew the following comparison for his quick-tempered wife, 'Permit me, my dear Sara! without offence to you [to say] that in sex, acquirements, and in the quantity and quality of natural endowments whether of Feeling, or of Intellect, you are the Inferior' (*CL*, II, p. 888), and it was only natural that she was not pleased.

What educated people toward the close of the eighteenth century understood by the term 'human nature' cannot be safely summarized in a page, or a book, any more than contemporary views can. Nevertheless, it is on the whole true to say that man was thought to come into the world with few if any instincts and with free will. The contents of the mind, originally a *tabula rasa*, were built up from the 'notices derived from the senses', and the extent to which the mind was an active participant in this process – that is to say, how much of what we perceived was the consequence of the way our minds worked – was a central problem of philosophy. We see this in Young's *Night Thoughts*:

> And half create the wondrous world they see.
> Our senses, as our reason, are divine   (VI, ll. 424–5)

– lines which Wordsworth cited in connection with his own

> mighty world
> Of eye, and ear, – both what they half create,
> And what perceive . . .   (*Tintern Abbey*, ll. 105–7)

The young Coleridge, so far as I know, never identified what he thought natural in human nature,[1] but his many passing comments reveal opinions common among his contemporaries and familiar enough now. Man's nature was imperfect, or fallen, and embraced a broad range of impulses, tendencies, or imperatives that were innate, not learned. *The Prelude* was 'a sweet continuous lay, / Not learned, but native, her own natural notes!' (*To William Wordsworth*, ll. 59–60). Somewhat surprisingly, the word 'natural' seems not to appear in his poetry until the play *Osorio* (1797): 'Men think it natural to hate their rivals' (II, 266). 'Fears in Solitude', a year later, speaks of 'All bonds of natural love' (l. 180).

Now none of this tells us much of compelling interest. In *Dejection: an Ode*, however, both 'nature' and 'natural' function in a context of central importance, and because the meanings are uncertain, an enduring interpretive problem has resulted. We read that 'in our life alone does Nature live: / Ours is her wedding garment, ours her shroud!' (ll. 48–9), lines which memorably capture one momentous resting place in the unsteady arc of Coleridge's feelings about nature. The speaker in this poem is bowed down with afflictions, his grief 'finds no natural outlet, no relief, / In words, or sigh, or tear', and he turns to 'abstruse research to steal / From my own nature all the natural man'. But what is the natural man? Here he would appear to be the man who weeps when he suffers, and pays a heavy price to banish thoughts of a beloved but tabooed woman from his mind. Suppression of so powerful an impulse, in fact, can 'infect' and desensitize the entire range of natural sensibilities.

At twenty-three, Coleridge condemned Erasmus Darwin for deciding too quickly whether we are 'the outcasts of a blind idiot called Nature, or the children of an all-wise and infinitely good God' (*CL*, I, p. 177). Next year, just four months after the joyous celebration of the visual and spiritual glories of the no-longer-blind idiot in *This Lime-Tree Bower My Prison*, Coleridge wrote John Thelwall, 'I can *at times* feel strongly the beauties, you describe . . . in themselves, and for themselves – but more frequently *all things* appear little . . . the universe itself – what but an immense heap of *little* things? . . . My mind feels as if it ached to behold and know something *great* – something *one and individual* – and it is only in the faith of this that rocks or waterfalls, mountains or caverns give me the sense of sublimity or majesty!' (*CL*, I, p. 349). This is essentially the detachment that informs the *Lines Written in the Album at Elbingerode* and *Dejection: an Ode*. It is notable that at the very zenith of his poetical powers, possibly only a few days after he had written *Kubla Khan*, Coleridge could declare that *only* in the faith of 'something one and indivisible' could nature give him a sense of sublimity and majesty.

And yet *Fears in Solitude* describes him as 'All adoration of the God in Nature' (l. 182), the characteristic stance of almost all the poetry of the *annus mirabilis*. In his letters he wrote of the 'divine Prospects' outside his window, which distracted him while shaving, so that 'I offer up soap and blood daily, as an Eye-servant of the Goddess Nature' (*CL*, II, p. 658), and the rather humble mountains around his home in Nether Stowey were perceived as 'that visible God Almighty that looks in at all my windows' (*CL*, II, p. 714).

This ambivalence is probably far more representative of the generality of thinking mankind than Wordsworth's extraordinary standpoint. It is well to remember that Coleridge could regard nature with fitful scepticism between the awed, pantheistic reverences of *This Lime-Tree Bower* and *Frost at Midnight*. And barely a year after seeing and hearing in nature

> The lovely shapes and sounds intelligible
> Of that eternal language, which thy God
> Utters . . .

he could in a 'low and languid mood' (while travelling in Germany) look upon even the loftiest of 'outward forms' and find them only 'fair cyphers', 'of import vague', unless they took their significance from the 'Life within' (*Elbingerode*, ll. 16–19).

Although the young Coleridge usually speaks of human nature, as I have said, in a way characteristic of his age, he would not be Coleridge if there were not powerful cross currents:

> . . . I believe most steadfastly in original Sin [he wrote in 1798]; that from our mothers' wombs our understandings are darkened; and even where our understandings are in the Light, that our organization is depraved, and our volitions imperfect; and we sometimes see the good without *wishing* to attain it, and oftener wish it without the energy that wills and performs – And for this *inherent depravity* [my emphasis], I believe, that the Spirit of the Gospel is the sole Cure – .
>
> (*CL*, I, p. 396)

Coleridge was here writing to his parson brother, George, but that this represents a deep conviction is underscored by his much later *Confessio Fidei*: 'I am a fallen creature . . . capable of moral evil, but not of myself capable of moral good [and only by the grace of God can I be] restored from my natural inheritance of Sin and Condemnation' (*CN*, III, 4005).

The 'inherent depravity' of human nature reveals a deepening gloom, and in the last decade of his life he would pounce upon Sir Walter Scott's innocuous reference to 'feelings of natural humanity' and tear it to shreds, declaring the phrase '*natural* humanity . . . almost as inconsistent as a round square' (*Misc C*, p. 326). Yet in a notebook passage of 1803 (*CN*, I, 1710) dealing with Kant, Coleridge focussed on 'Man's double nature . . . as Man and God', and henceforth that portion of man's nature and consciousness which derives from the senses is uniformly the 'lower' or 'brutal' part. 'Man must not be, man cannot be, on a level with the beast . . . either above them beyond all measure, or deplorably below them . . . ' (*P Lects*, p. 212).[2]

Now Coleridge had always been uneasy about the body, and its fleshy appetites and urgencies were to be kept under taut reins. 'Sensual' is typically a damning word: 'sensual France, a natural slave' (*Ode to Tranquillity, app. crit.*); 'The sensual and dark rebel in vain' (*France: An Ode*, l. 85); 'I do consider Mr. Godwin's book as a Pander to Sensuality' (*CL*, I, p. 199), and so forth. Among the many 'moral uses of Marriage', Coleridge identified the confining of the 'appetites to one object', so that they are 'swallowed up in affection' (*CL*, I, pp. 213–14). In his often-quoted letter to Southey dealing with his languid appetite for the woman he had engaged himself to, he wrote, 'Love makes all things pure and heavenly like itself – but to marry a woman I do *not* love – to degrade her, whom I call my Wife, by making her the Instrument of low Desire – ' (*CL*, I, p. 145). The thought sickens him.

His debilitating struggle with *le diable au corps* intensified during his long torment over Sara Hutchinson. A notebook entry of 1802 captures, I think, one of the last moments during which his intellect and instinctive life were in reasonably healthy equipoise. 'The great business of real unostentatious Virtue', he wrote, 'is not to eradicate any genuine instinct or appetite of human nature; but to establish a concord and unity betwixt all parts of our nature, to give a Feeling and a Passion to our purer Intellect, and to intellectualize our feelings and passions.'[3] The 'concord and unity betwixt all parts of our nature', here cherished in such lovely phrases, clashes sharply with his austere later conviction that 'all that is fully human must come from within' (*P Lects*, p. 226).[4] What was not 'fully human' was sensual experience, which fallen man ignominiously shares with the swarming generations of animal life.

A deepening distrust of all the pleasures that derive from the senses contributes, of course, to the erosion of his spontaneous joy in the natural world. In the privacy of an 1803 journal he had admonished Wordsworth that 'always to look at the superficies of Objects for the purpose of taking Delight in their Beauty, and sympathy with their real or imagined Life, is . . . deleterious to the Health and manhood of Intellect' (*CN*, I, 1616). A month later he cited strong affections between people as 'a glorious fact of human Nature', and discerned other 'Excellencies, dormant in human Nature', but in this very entry he is striving to *idealize* human feelings, to dematerialize them, as it were, otherwise they would be 'brutal', like the brutes (*CN*, I, 1637).[5]

The abrasive conflict between the imperious claims of his own more than usual organic sensibility and the idealizing pressures of his spiritual yearnings was to be long. Response to natural beauty, and mystical response at that, was not easily suppressed:

In looking at objects of Nature while I am thinking, as at yonder moon dim-glimmering thro' the dewy window-pane, I seem rather to be seeking, as it were *asking*, a symbolical language for something within me that already and forever exists, than observing anything new. Even when that latter is the case, yet still I have always an obscure feeling as if that new phaenomenon were the dim Awakening of a forgotten or hidden Truth of my inner Nature.(*CN*, II, 2546)

Yet another part of Coleridge could not accept meanings in nature which were not projections from within. In the years ahead the once lovely face of nature was to turn demonic. As late as *The Statesman's Manual* (1816) he could still extol 'the correspondencies and symbols of the spiritual world' to be found in nature, which is yet 'another book, likewise a revelation of God – the great book of his servant Nature'. But Coleridge subsequently set down next to this passage: 'At the time, I wrote this work, my views of *Nature* were very imperfect and confused' (*SM*, pp. 70, 71, n. 6). Of the supposed dependence of the soul on nature he declared that this

'confusion of God with the World and the accompanying Nature-worship
. . . is the Trait in Wordsworth's poetic Works that I most dislike, as
unhealthful, and denounce as contagious' (*CL*, v, p. 59). Julius Hare
reports Coleridge saying, 'No! Nature is not God; she is a devil in a strait
waistcoat' (*SM*, p. 71, n. 6).[6]

Pantheism became 'a handsome Mask that does not alter a single
feature of the ugly Face it hides' (*P Lects*, p. 433, n. 17). Once in his
hopeful youth, he had been 'All adoration of the God in Nature' (*Fears
in Solitude*, l. 182), a God who, in *Frost at Midnight*, 'from eternity doth
teach / Himself in all, and all things in himself' (ll. 61–2). Yet he would
come to scold Scotus Erigena for not having seen 'that his "Deus omnia
et omnia Deus" was incompatible with moral responsibility [for] Pantheism is but a painted Atheism'.[7]

Understanding the intensity and pervasiveness of Coleridge's convictions on this bedrock matter much clarifies his final views of human
nature. In 1818 he wrote of *The Friend*: 'The aim, the method throughout
was, in the first place, to awaken, to cultivate, and to mature the truly
human in human nature, in and through itself, or as independently as
possible of the notices derived from sense, and of the motives that had
references to the sensations' (*Friend*, i, p. 500).

Thus what is *truly human* is irrevocably divorced from the demands and
delights of the body, which is by now a bemired clog on the etherial
aspirations of the soul. In the later Coleridge the natural man is
characteristically 'degraded' (*CN*, iii, 3281), or 'depraved' (*P Lects*, p.
421). 'The age is so fully attached to the unnatural in taste, the preternatural in life, and the contra-natural in philosophy as to have left little
room for the super-natural', he complained inimitably in *Blackwood's* (xi
(Jan. 1822) p. 6), and in his notebooks he explained, 'My great aim and
object is to assert the *Superhuman* in order to diffuse more & more widely
the faith in the *Supernatural*.' In one of his last published works, *On the Con-
stitution of the Church and State*, he wrote that 'in all ages, individuals who
have directed their meditations and their studies to the nobler characters
of our nature, to the cultivation of those powers and instincts that constitute the man, at least separate him from the animal, and distinguish
the nobler from the animal part of his own being, will be led by the *supernatural* in themselves to the contemplation of a power which is likewise
super-*human* . . . ' (*C & S*, p. 44, and n. 2).[8]

In such a scheme, the teeming, protean, variegated world of nature,
which we know through our senses, is a temptation and delusion, a
painted whore, disguising satanic inner pollution. Thus far had Coleridge's long voyage on the mirage-shrouded seas of Idealism borne him
away from the brilliant sunlight of Wordsworth's

> language of the sense,
> The anchor of my purest thoughts, the nurse,
> The guide, the guardian of my heart, the soul
> Of all my moral being.   (*Tintern Abbey*, ll. 108–11)

The later Coleridge presents a poignant image of severely diminished emotional range and response. Suppressing the 'natural man' in himself, he willingly embraced the role of sedentary semi-invalid over the last eighteen years of his life. He left his wife when he was just thirty-four years old – never having been an ardent husband – and for the next twenty-eight years he was celibate, and struggled mightily to banish sexual images from his mind. He spent the long Highgate years more or less in the garb and stance of a priest, clad from head to toe in black, and declaiming against the evils of the age and the animal in us all. He was still a young man when he ceased to be a husband, father, brother, or lover to anyone. He did not ever see his daughter, Sara, between her tenth and twentieth years. He bade farewell forever to the 'dear gutter of Stowey' and the Quantocks when he was thirty-five, and never looked back on Grasmere, Keswick, or the Lake District after he was forty. He, once a worshipper of Nature, 'was well content to be a dweller in the "depths of the huge city" or its outskirts', in his astute grandson's words.[9] It is worth pondering that Coleridge's later writings were achieved in the teeth of these emotional constraints.

It is a mistake, of course, to paint an unrelievedly bleak picture. Counter impulses of feeling and belief were always present. But for Coleridge the philosopher, only the mind was involved in truly *human* life; all else flirted with the bestial.

At an early point in his long struggle with opium, and his frustrated love for Sara Hutchinson, which wracked him with guilt, Coleridge felt despairingly that

our *moral nature* is a power of itself; and not a mere modification of our common intellect / so that a man may have wit, prudence, sense &c &c, & yet be utterly destitute of a true *moral* sense. And when I observe the impotence of this moral sense, however highly possessed, unassisted by something still higher, and if I may so express myself, still more extra-natural, I own, it seems to me, as if the goodness of God had occasionally *added* it to our nature, as an intermediate or connecting Link between that nature and a state of Grace.   (*CL*, II, p. 1203)

The quest for grace, for 'something still higher . . . still more extra-natural', and the flight from the natural man, this was the great, anguished, and erratic odyssey of Coleridge's later life. These beliefs contribute to the conceptual obscurities of the critical and aesthetic writings of 1811–18. Many passages in the Shakespearean criticism are scarcely comprehensible without an awareness of Coleridge's need to project his deepest philosophical concerns upon Shakespeare's dramatic purposes. Thus he says that in *Hamlet*, Shakespeare 'meant to portray a person in whose view the external world, and all its incidents and objects, were comparatively dim and of no interest in themselves, and which began to interest him only when they were reflected in the mirror of his mind', and that in *The Tempest* 'all that belongs to Ariel is all that belongs to the delight the mind can receive from external appearances abstracted from any in-born or individual purpose'.[10] These remarks describe not Hamlet's mind, or Ariel's, but what Coleridge supposed was true of his own. 'The mind is affected by thoughts, rather than by things', he asserted in *Biographia Literaria*, 'and only then feels the requisite interest even of the most important events and accidents when by means of meditation they have passed into thoughts.' 'The man of genius lives most in the ideal world', he continued, and declared of himself, 'even before my fifteenth year, I had bewildered myself in metaphysics . . . History, and par-ticular facts, lost all interest in my mind' (*BLS*, I, pp. 20, 30, 39).

   'We are conscious of faculties far superior to the highest impressions of sense', we are told in 'The Principles of Genial Criticism', and 'that which is naturally agreeable and consonant in human nature . . . excludes the mere objects of taste, smell, and feeling' (*BLS*, II, pp. 234, 237). Statements which are in themselves baffling, or might be taken for merely rhetorical celebrations of the divine power of art, acquire much clearer and richer meanings against the developments we have been tracing. Thus, 'On Poetry or Art' hails poetry as 'purely human; for all its materials are from the mind, and all its products are for the mind. [Poetry] elevates the mind by making its feelings the object of its reflec-tion . . . . But please to observe that I have laid particular stress on the words "human mind," – meaning to exclude thereby all results com-mon to man and all other sentient creatures' (*BLS*, II, p. 254). This would seem to be a far cry from Milton's definition of poetry as 'simple, sensuous, and passionate', but very close to Kant's analysis of poetry as the greatest of the arts because 'it strengthens the mind by making it feel its faculty – free, spontaneous, and independent of natural determina-tion – of considering and judging nature as a phenomenon in accordance with aspects which it does not present in experience either for sense or understanding, and therefore of using it on behalf of, and as a sort of schema for, the supersensible'.[11]

   For Coleridge, truly human life 'begins in its detachment from Nature and is to end in union with God' (*SM*, p. 114 n. 3).[12] The parallel journey of the natural man's relations with his own body is traced in the final chilling sentence of 'On Poesy or Art': 'remark the seeming iden-tity of body and mind in infants, and thence the loveliness of the former;

the commencing separation in boyhood, and the struggle of equilibrium in youth: then onward the body is first simply indifferent; then demanding the translucency of the mind not to be worse than indifferent; and finally all that presents the body as body becoming almost of an excremental nature' (*BLS*, ii, p. 263).

The body had become at last, 'almost of an excremental nature'. It is part of the wonder and tragedy of this tormented genius that decades before, in the great stanzas that carried the accursed Mariner toward redemption, he had symbolized the cleansing of a corrupt soul in the blessing of once slimy water snakes, and had foreshadowed that sublime climax by turning the Mariner's fevered and pulsating eyeballs upon the corpses strewn about the rotting deck. The 'many men' he saw there were not loathsome, not excremental, but, startlingly, 'so beautiful'.

Coleridge was referring to his early rage for philosophy when he said in *Biographia Literaria*: 'Well were it for me, perhaps, had I never relapsed into the same mental disease: if I had continued to pluck the flower and reap the harvest from the cultivated surface, instead of delving in the unwholesome quicksilver mines of metaphysic depths' (*BLS*, i, p. 10). In view of his final, frozen recoil from the warm and vivid world of nature and the natural man, the same might more justly have been said on many of his somber post-Kantian meditations.

Notes

[1] On learning of his brother Francis's early death, Coleridge wrote to his brother George, 'Poor Francis! I have shed the tear of natural affection over him', a passage so strained and frigid that one can surmise that there was little natural affection there, as indeed there wasn't. Significantly, the twenty-two-year-old Coleridge went on to explain why in fact he felt little for his other brothers except indifference. 'Fraternal affection is the offspring of long Habit, and of Reflection' (*CL*, i, p. 53), he concluded, thereby asserting that fraternal affection is not natural, only customary. We see here 'natural' employed as a loose term, immediately followed by hard analysis wrung from his own bitter experience in the world.

[2] The whole passage is a variation on Franz Baader's 'unfortunately man can only stand above or beneath animals', quoted in Schelling's *Of Human Freedom*. See my *Coleridge, The Damaged Archangel* (1971), p. 133.

[3] *Coleridge on the Seventeenth Century*, ed. R. L. Brinkley (Durham, N.C., Duke University Press, 1929), p. 444.

[4] This conception, in various forms, is to be found everywhere in the aesthetic writings of Kant and Schiller, but without the emphasis on sensual experience as inherently beneath the dignity of man. 'The highest aim of art is to represent the supersensuous', wrote Schiller, and to represent 'the moral man independently of the laws of nature' ('On the Pathetic', in *Literary Criticism: Pope to Croce*, eds. G. W. Allen and H. H. Clark (New

York, 1941), p. 150). But such views in Schiller are balanced by his awareness of the 'nefarious influence exerted upon our knowledge and upon conduct by a preponderance of rationality . . . [and] of the damage caused when the functions of thought and will encroach upon those of intuition and feeling' (*On the Aesthetic Education of Man*, Letter 15).

5 The struggle of the secondary imagination to 'idealize' as well as to 'unify' has yet to be awarded its full significance.

6 This is oddly similar to what Henry Crabb Robinson tells us Blake said of the supposed 'atheism' in Wordsworth's poems: 'whosoever believes in Nature disbelieves in God. For Nature is the work of the Devil' (*Blake, Coleridge, Wordsworth, Lamb*, etc., ed. E. J. Morley (Manchester University Press, 1932), p. 23.

7 *P Lects*, p. 433, n. 7. Cf. 'For Pantheism – trick it up as you will – is but a painted Atheism' (*The Complete Works of Samuel Taylor Coleridge*, ed. W. G. T. Shedd (7 vols., New York, 1853), V, p. 417). 'I adore the living and personal God', he wrote in a letter at about this time, 'but who may not without fearful error be identified with the universe, or the universe be considered as an *attribute* of his Deity' (*CL*, IV, p. 894).

8 This emphasis on the supernatural in man seems far removed from the creative impulses behind *The Ancient Mariner* or *Christabel*; in an undated but late comment on Browne's *Religio Medici*, Coleridge wrote: 'he is the man of genius . . . who perceiving the riddle and mystery of all things even the commonest, needs no strange and out-of-the-way tales or images to stimulate him into wonder and a deep interest' (*Misc C*, p. 254).

9 *Letters of Samuel Taylor Coleridge*, ed. E. H. Coleridge (Boston, 1895), I, pp. 404–5, n.2. Coleridge's amazing capacity to absorb influences and models may extend even to his acutely sensitive response to nature during his great poetic period – a response one would ordinarily think of as the direct result of more than usual organic sensibility rather than something learned. 'In looking through the early poems', George Whalley has observed, 'I am struck by the general absence of vivid sensory images until the *annus mirabilis* and the conversation poems . . . . Very little of an exceptional sensibility breaks the opaque surface of a multifarious but received poetic manner until "This Lime-Tree Bower" ' ('Coleridge's Poetic Sensibility', in *Coleridge's Variety*, ed. John Beer (University of Pittsburgh Press, 1975), p. 3). In this respect Coleridge presents a startling contrast to Wordsworth and Keats, among many others one might name, poets whose characteristic sensual structure, like a gift for melody among composers, is present in their earliest compositions, however conventional the overall manner of their apprentice work.

10 *Coleridge on Shakespeare: The Text of the Lectures of 1811–12*, ed. R. A. Foakes (London, 1971), pp. 124, 111–12.

11 *Critique of Judgment*, trans. J. H. Bernard (2nd edn, rev. 1931), § 53 (Hafner Publishing Co., New York, 1966), p. 171.

12 In his late 'Death and the Grounds of Belief in a Future State', he was able to say, 'I feel myself not the slave of nature . . . *I* am praeternatural, i.e. supersensuous' (*CN*, III, 4060).

The imagination of Mrs Samuel Taylor Coleridge: unknown inspiration of an unknown tongue

MOLLY LEFEBURE

'If you ever have an owl dressed for dinner, you had better have it boiled, and smothered in onions, for it is not good roasted': Robert Southey in a letter of 14 September 1821, to his lifelong friend, Grosvenor Charles Bedford. Southey had been given an owl shot by his young neighbour Raisley Calvert (who explained that he had not known what kind of bird it was when he fired at it). As the Wordsworths were to be dining at Greta Hall, Southey decided that roast stuffed owl was a dish well suited to the author of *The Excursion* and so: 'I ordered it to be dressed and brought in, in the place of game that day at dinner. It was served up without the head, and a squat-looking fellow it was, about the size of a wood-pigeon, but broader in proportion to its length. The meat was more like bad mutton than anything else. Wordsworth was not valiant enough to taste it. Mrs W. did, and we agreed that there could be no pretext for making owls game and killing them as delicacies.'[1]

Southey's sense of humour was distinctly of the schoolboyish sort. He had a keen perception of the comical and the appearance of an owl on the Greta Hall dinner table when Wordsworth was the guest of honour must have struck him as altogether delightful, and even more delightful to see the Bard refuse the dish. This was the kind of thing that kept Southey laughing, and when Southey laughed all his household laughed with him; merriment is infectious. 'Sleeping, eating, drinking, talking & laughing in the dwelling house of Robert Southey Esqur Poet Laureat', to quote Mrs Samuel Taylor Coleridge, writing to Thomas Poole and describing the pleasures of family life with her brother-in-law at Greta Hall[2] and thereby conveying a happy impression of what was still a jolly menage even when the laughter concealed sore sorrows and increasing anxieties.

Southey was a lifelong devotee of *Tristram Shandy*, a book that may best be described, in the words of Quennell, as 'a study of the part that Chance plays in the evolution of the individual . . . and a tragicomedy of domestic disillusionment'.[3] Sterne saw the family as an organism apparently straightforward enough when viewed superficially; 'a simple machine' consisting of 'a few wheels', but in actuality strange, complex, fluctuating in mood and fortunes; the

79

wheels set in motion by so many different springs, and acted one upon the other from such a variety of strange principles and impulses, – that though it was a simple machine, it had all the honour and advantages of a complex one, – and a number of as odd movements within it, as ever were beheld in the inside of a Dutch silk-mill.

These observations applied to the family in general, and the Shandy Hall family in particular.

Southey detected a close resemblance between Greta Hall and Shandy Hall and furthermore he recognised in himself a Tristramish figure whose evolution as an individual had been strongly shaped by Chance in the guise of Samuel Taylor Coleridge, who had talked Southey into moving to Greta Hall in the first instance and there planted upon him an abandoned wife and three children, under circumstances which made it virtually morally impossible for the decent Southey ever to remove from Greta Hall elsewhere, or to rid himself of the encumbrance of an extra family to care for as his own. There was only one way in which to confront such an impossible situation and that was with laughter. Southey accordingly laughed and joked at the exhausting vicissitudes of his menage ('the Aunt Hill': the widowed Mrs Mary Lovell, another Fricker sister, being a third resident and penniless aunt): nonetheless we can perceive his merriment calcify as his predicament became less and less risible with the passage of time.

In order to support his many dependents Southey became a byword for his literary industry. From 1814 or thereabouts he, as a form of relaxation, began working on a book which he at first was tentatively calling 'Dr Dove' and ultimately was to publish as *The Doctor*; a tome of seven volumes, comprising collections of mottoes, anecdotes, fairy tales, nursery tales, social history, gossip, folklore and ballads, punning and play with words, attempts at serious etymology, and essays on every subject under the sun, ranging from the Greta Hall cats, and why Southey could not bear Sarah to be called Sally, to a famous example of Westmorland dialect, 'The terrible knitters o' Dent'. The book strikes today's reader as painfully discursive and all too often facetious; taken in small doses it makes an excellent bedside book and the more tedious passages guarantee an irresistible impulse to sleep. The length of the book was part of the joke of the thing (basically *The Doctor* was intended as an anonymous joke); the framework was loosely hung on the tale of Dr Daniel Dove (a doctor of divinity) and his horse Nobs, which tale might correctly be described as a shaggy horse story, for the humour lay 'in making it as long winded as possible' (we are not surprised to learn that in the first place it was Coleridge's story). The tale was never twice the same in its rendering, except as to names and leading features. Finally

Southey decided to turn it into a book with 'much of Tristram Shandy about it'[4] and much of Greta Hall embedded in it.

One chapter of *The Doctor* is hinged upon the old chorus, 'Hayley gayly gamborayly, higgledy piggledy, galloping draggle-tail dreary dun': Southey ruminates that though this is not in 'any known tongue' it may possibly be in an unknown tongue, and he continues,

There is a mystery in an unknown tongue; and they who speak it . . . may be in-spired for the nonce – though they may be as little conscious of their inspiration as they are of their meaning. There may be an unknown inspiration as well as an unknown tongue. If so what mighty revelations may lie unrevealed.[5]

In writing this chapter Southey undoubtedly had in mind Mrs Col-eridge's *Lingo Grande* (as her family called it) which she was creating and Greta Hall living with predominantly between 1807 and 1826: the 'language' being at its zenith in the last decade or so of this period. The origins of nursery rhymes and popular nonsense rhymes had not been researched in Southey's day; indeed Haliwell did not collect and print 'Mother Goose's Nursery Rhymes' until 1846. Southey amused himself with half playful, half serious speculation upon the origin of 'nonsensical' verse, accepting it as 'nonsense' per se; but, as Graves was to point out over a hundred years later 'sometimes what appears to be nonsense is no more than long out-of-date topical satire; sometimes the nonsense ele-ment has been added later, either because the original words were garbled or forgotten, or because their meaning had to be suppressed for political or moral reasons'. Furthermore, adds Graves, two or three hundred years of oral tradition in the nursery had played havoc with the 'nursery rhyme' texts before Haliwell collected and printed them. To continue to quote Graves upon this fascinating subject, 'Deliberately nonsensical rhymes for children first appeared in the eighteenth century, as a reac-tion against the over-sane verse of the over-sane Augustan Age, and even these were a . . . restrained sort of nonsense, based on puns and manifest self-contradiction' (for instance,

> The man of the wilderness asked of me:
> 'How many strawberries grow in the sea?'
> I answered him as I thought good:
> 'As many red herrings as grow in the wood').

It was not, says Graves, until Edward Lear and Lewis Carroll that 'nonsense of brilliant inconsequence studded with newly invented words came to be composed'.[6]

It may be urged that Lear and Carroll were in some degree anticipated by Mrs Samuel Taylor Coleridge. The traditional nonsense of punning, riddle-me-reeing and manifest self-contradiction was the sort of nonsense that appealed to Robert Southey and he kept Greta Hall merry with it. He played with words and punned and composed nonsense with huge gusto in this traditional vein; he was also a great man for practical jokes of the apple pie bed sort (and, as we have seen, roasted stuffed owl for Wordsworth). Southey's favourite sister-in-law, Mrs Coleridge, née Sarah Fricker, who had laughed with him and teased him ever since he had been a small boy, continued to partner him in his adult joking and quizzing and name inventing and 'funny things' in general: we find Southey writing to Hartley Coleridge, in June 1807 (when Mrs Coleridge was visiting the West Country with her children and their father) and observing (jokingly) that time makes everyone grow graver; 'This . . . has made me the serious man I am. I hope it will have the same effect upon you and your mother, and that when she returns, she will have left off that evil habit of quizzing me, and calling me names; it is not decorous in a woman of her years.'[7] But time did not sober Mrs Coleridge; she continued to quizz and call names and invent 'funny things', including a language of her own, and indeed became more, rather than less, exuberant with the passage of time, so that we find Southey in 1819 playfully threatening to quell her by importing 'an *aunt*-eater from Brazil'.[8]

It is clear that Southey was far from fully understanding Mrs Coleridge's vein of nonsense; particularly he failed to understand her 'language'. The fullest surviving account which we have of this language occurs in a letter from Southey to Grosvenor Bedford, dated 14 September 1821:

Dear Stumparumper,

Don't rub your eyes at that word, Bedford, as if you were slopy. The purport of this letter . . . is to give you some account (though but an imperfect one) of the language spoken in this house by Mrs Coleridge, and invented by her. I have carefully composed a vocabulary of it by the help of her daughter and mine, having my ivory tablets always ready when she is red-raggifying in full confabulumpatus. True it is that she has called us persecutorums, and great improprietors for performing this meritorious task, and has often told me not to be such a stuposity; threatening us sometimes that she will never say anything that ends in lumpatus again; and sometimes that she will play the very dunder; and sometimes bidding us get away with our toadymidjerings. And she asks me, how I can be such a Tomnoddycum (though my name, as she knows, is Robert), and calls me detesty, a maffrum, a goffrum, a chatterpye, a sillycum, and a great mawkinfort.

But when she speaks of you it is with a kinder meaning. You are not a vulgarum, not a great ovverum govverum. The appellations which she has in store for you are either words of direct endearment, or of that sort of objurgation which is the playfullest mood of kindness. Thus you are a stumparumper, because you are a shortycum; and you are a wattlykin, a tendrum, a detestabumpus, and a figurumpus. These are the words which come from her chapset when she speaks of you, and you need not be told what they signifump.

I dare say you have set up a whickerandus at this, and I hope you will not be dollatory in expressing the satisfaction which you derive from knowing you are thus decidedly in her good graces. Perhaps you may attempt an answer in the same strain, and show yourself none of the little blunderums who deserve to be bungated, but an apt pupolion, which if you do, you will deserve to be called as clever as De Diggle.

. . . It is much to be regretted that Mrs Coleridge's new language is not . . . investigated by some profound philologist. Coleridge, perhaps, by the application of Kant's philosophy, might analyze and discover the principles of its construction. I, though a diligent and faithful observer, must confess that I have but little insight into it. I can indeed partly guess why donkeys are in the language called jacks, and why peck is a nose; why some part of an elephant's trunk is a griper, but not why it is a snipe; why nog is a lump, bungay a bundle, and why trottlykins should stand for children's feet; but not why my feet and yours should be opprobriously termed hocksen and hormangorgs. So, too, when I hear needles called nowgurs, ladies laduls, whispering twistering, vinegar wiganar, and a mist fogogrum, or fogrogrum, I have some glimpse, though but a glimpse, of the principle upon which these mologisms are fabricated . . . But I should in vain seek to discover the *rationale* of other parts of this speech . . . And when I get at the meaning by asking an explanation, still no clue to the derivation is afforded. Thus, for instance, when it was said, 'Don't roakin there,' and I desired to know what was intended by this prohibition, the answer was 'Everybody says roakin;' and when I pressed for further information, I was informed that roaking was digging and grumping in a work-box. So, too, on the way from Mrs Calvert's one evening, I was desired to stop while she had gathered up her doddens, and that word was interpreted to mean a plaid, a pair of pattens, and an umbrella. If my foot happens to touch her chair, I am told that anything whidgetting the chair makes her miseraboble. If the children – the childeroapusses I should say – are bangrampating about the house, they are said to be rudderish and roughcumtatherick. Cuthbert's mouth is sometimes called a jabberumpeter, sometimes a towsalowset. When the word comfortabuttle is used, I suppose it may be designed to mean that there is comfort in a bottle. But by what imaginable process of language and association snoutarumpeter can be, as she declares it to be, a short way of calling mother, I am altogether unable to comprehend.

On one occasion, however, I was fortunate enough to see this extraordinary language in the mint, if I may so express myself, and in the very act of its coinage. Speaking of a labourer, she said, 'the thumper, the what-d'ye-callder – the undoer, – I can't hit upon it, – the cutter-up.' These were the very words, received and noted as they came from the die; and they meant a man who was chopping wood.

I must now bring this letter to a conclusion. The account indeed is very incomplete, but you may rely upon its fidelity; and though of necessity I have spelt the words according to their pronunciation, I hope that this has not occasioned any disvugurment, and that none of them in reading will stick in your thrapple. The subject cannot be so important to you as it is to me who live in a house where this language is spoken, and therefore have been obliged to pay attention to it. Yet it will not appear altogether incurious, connected as it is with the science of philology; and perhaps your regard for the inventor may give it a more than ordinary interest in your eyes . . .

P.S. I forgot to say that apple-dumple-dogs are apple dumplings, and that Dogroggarum is a word of reproach for a dog.[9]

(It is interesting to note that Southey made a subtle mispelling with 'snoutarumpeter'; Hartley, who in his letters to Derwent frequently refers to his mother by this name, spells it 'Snouterumpater', which suggests the *mater pater* theme and, one surmises, is an ironical comment on her part upon the equality of the sexes within the framework of the family: not an altogether farfetched suggestion inasmuch as there is firm evidence that Mrs Coleridge in her youth had been a keen disciple of Wollstonecraft and was a firm believer in sexual equality. The snout part of the name may possibly be connected with the fact that Mrs Coleridge had a somewhat more pronounced nose than had her husband. Indisputably, of course, after he had virtually abandoned his family Mrs Coleridge had assumed the chief role in the upbringing and guidance of her children.)

Further smatterings of the language are to be found here and there peppering the more intimate correspondence and lighthearted writings of Southey and that of the Coleridge progeny. Odd words, soubriquets and expressions survived Coleridge generations. We meet with wondrous words such as 'circumnambagious' and 'horse-mangandering'; sometimes in *The Doctor* Southey steals in 'a scurvy clogdogdo' or a 'side-ling toward an object crab-like' and though he may quote some strangely vague nursery rhyme source or merely use quotes and give no source at all we may well suspect that the true source is Snouterumpater.

The identifiable etymology of the lingo is immensely subtle, the sources far ranging and varied; old West Country speech, eighteenth-century drawing room refinements and witticisms, Cumbrian dialect, Cockney slang, echoes of Esteesian puns and conundrums, echoes from Hartley's ejuxrian fantasies, other echoes from the timeless currency of cottage firesides, from nursery rhymes and baby talk, schoolboy jokes and schoolroom howlers; fragmentary impressions of acquaintances and visitors over the years, pompous officials and dignitaries, excited radicals, enthusing Romantics.

Some of the words in her language were well established in everyday speech; the reason that they were evidently unknown to Southey (though known to Mrs Coleridge) was doubtless because she had the advantage of being a woman and a housewife, making daily contact with servants and shopkeepers, street vendors and mendicants; people from a stratum of society with which Southey, a man of letters chained to his desk, seldom had contact. The word 'roaking', which apparently so puzzled him, is the south western equivalent of the north country 'ratching' and means exactly what Mrs Coleridge said it did: 'digging and grumping'. As for 'doddens', that is a Cumbrian (viz. of Scandinavian origin = Norse, *dudra*, to quaver) variation on 'tots' or 'tottens', meaning rags, old clothes, worn and battered bits and pieces: a 'totter' in London street market parlance is a dealer in rags and old clothes (hence tottery and doddery, on your last legs, raggy and taggy and coming apart). 'Rudderish' Mrs Coleridge drew from 'rudding' or 'redding' (red smitting), the traditional practice of redding tups at rutting time, a season of wayward behaviour. 'Roughcumtatherick' is an ancient Cumbrian expression for one who has broken loose or is running wild, possibly deriving from a breaking away from the 'tedder styak' (the tether stake) for a grazing animal and, when traced far enough back into the mists of time like so many Cumbrian words ends up with the Old Norse: *tjóthr*, in this case.

These instances are merely given to indicate Mrs Coleridge's remarkable interest in words, the extent and catholicism of her vocabulary, the keen subtlety of her ear. Without these gifts, possessed in quite extraordinary degree, she could not have created a new 'language'. She revelled in human beings and their idiosyncracies of speech and behaviour. Though she relished drawing room society her vocabulary is proof of her enjoyment of the common world and common speech, so much more richly diversified in her day than in ours. We are left in no doubt of the acute perception which she brought to bear upon the world around her, providing source material for the mimicry with which she entertained her family and friends, and for her 'language'; more correctly experimental work in kaleidoscopic compression of verbal impressions and fancies; a dazzling expertise in the invention of portmanteau words and an exploitation of the subconscious pre-dating Lewis Carroll by a good half century and more.

Southey confessed to Bedford that he could discover no *rationale* of this language (expecting thereby to find the key to some system of derivation). To seek the rationale of a language, or code, which is largely a product of the subconscious can only be self defeating; but, of course, the subconscious was unrecognised in Southey's day (except by Coleridge who, as usual, was immeasurably ahead of contemporary thinking and in his notebooks probed and explored it, well aware of its existence if not having entirely decided how to define it). Southey, for his part, groped as in a glass darkly: 'There may be an unknown inspiration as well as an unknown tongue. If so what mighty revelations may lie unrevealed.'

These revelations have been made, or at least are in the process of being made, in the twentieth century, and for this reason we are able to understand much of Mrs Coleridge's language and to appreciate its significance. She had deep seated needs for inventing a private language, needs never analysed by her but only felt: release from the tensions of constant suppressed anxiety; the necessity to have something of her very own that could not be taken from her as everything else was taken; the need for privacy in a world which gossiped freely about her as the deserted wife of Samuel Taylor Coleridge. Fundamentally her language was a cypher affording her a species of cover (it is significant that one of the *aliases* which she bestowed upon herself was 'Mrs Codian'). Equally fundamentally it was her safety valve, permitting her, as it were, to let off steam. The language reveals that she was of an ironical turn of mind – a dangerous thing to be at the best of times. By using a private language Mrs Coleridge was able to give vent in safety to her irony; to pass comments on men and manners; to express herself without inhibition. By using a method of verbal shorthand she could reach to the private heart of things in a flash. For instance, to describe a man chopping wood as a 'thumper', an 'undoer' and a 'cutter-up' is to express, in a mere four words, a myriad of associated ideas and comments ranging from the sexual to the social. The result sounds, superficially, like nonsense; but it is really a garbling which makes possible a statement about the man and what he is doing and what he represents which could not be achieved by using a traditional speech method. Not that we should fall into Southey's error of supposing that she was working on this conscious level; her inspired garbling was a product of the imagination, she was swimming freely in that subconscious stream which, for lack of better definition we gropingly term inspiration.

It was both her good fortune and misfortune to live in the company of famous writers. Doubtless they stimulated her interest in words, but at the same time Mrs Coleridge became convinced that she herself was no good as a writer. She was, of course, chiefly evaluating her literary powers within the context of Dorothy Wordsworth's journals. We find Mrs Coleridge, in June 1823, writing to Poole,

I wish my dear friend, I could give you only a faint idea of a radiant sunset which we witnessed a few evenings ago! *Skiddaw* was converted to a mass of bright Amber and a vivid double rainbow was arching the other side of the vale, which was all over of a pale green light, such as you see through one of the compartments of a Claude-Lorrain Glass: Sara [her daughter] has given a very glowing description of this scene in some of her letters, but I am not 'good at these numbers' and shall only spoil the thing by meddling with it.[10]

Had she not been thus intimidated she might well have tried her hand at authorship; her letters reveal that she enjoyed writing and possessed a real gift for portraying everyday life, especially in its more comical aspects. People and incidents spring vividly from her pen. However instead of attempting literature she devoted her talents to the creation of a language of her own. A later age might well have encouraged her to commit this language to paper. But Mrs Coleridge was born before her time: her private language remained a private language, known only to the few, who wondered at it and laughed, seeing it simply as one of her 'funny things'.

Notes

1. *Life and Correspondence of Robert Southey*, ed. C. C. Southey (6 vols., 1849–50) V, pp. 98–9.
2. *Minnow Among Tritons: the letters of Mrs Samuel Taylor Coleridge to Thomas Poole*, ed. S. Potter (London, 1934), p. 105. Cited hereafter as *Minnow*.
3. Laurence Sterne, *The Life and Opinions of Tristram Shandy, Gentleman*, introduction by Peter Quennell (London, 1948), p. viii.
4. *New Letters of Robert Southey*, ed. K. Curry (2 vols., 1965) II, p. 130.
5. Robert Southey, *The Doctor*, ed. J. W. Warter (London, 1848), pp. 378–88.
6. Robert Graves, *The Crowning Privilege* (Penguin, 1959), p. 161.
7. Derwent Coleridge, *Memoir of the Life of Hartley Coleridge* (London, 1851), pp. xliii–xlvi.
8. *Selections from the Letters of Robert Southey*, ed. J. W. Warter (4 vols., 1856) III, p. 108.
9. *Ibid.*, III, pp. 270–3.
10. *Minnow*, p. 106.

'As much diversity as the heart that trembles': Coleridge's notes on the lakeland fells

WILLIAM RUDDICK

> You ask for the mystery
> Of my emotions
> To be revealed . . .
> But the bitter wind
> Or the mist that falls,
> The single raven
> Or the broken bough
> Are felt as much, and give
> As much diversity
> As the heart that trembles
> Or the voice that, longing
> Or in gladness, calls.

Peter Laver's poem 'Placing Sensitivities' neatly sidesteps a demand for self-revelation by asserting that the sights, sounds and bodily sensations experienced by anyone who lives in the Lake District are (or should be) as powerful and varied as any possible human contacts. The poem does not deny the vividness of personal feelings, but seems to externalise them into a natural vitality which absorbs them, while conversely also absorbing the poet's vivid perceptions of his surroundings into the poignantly suggested intensity of his heart's emotions.

Such a reciprocity of perceived and externalised inner sensations, of joys received from the beauty of the landscape and landscape features discovered to be objective correlatives for the poet's own emotions, can be sensed in the notebooks and occasional letters in which Coleridge records his discovery of the Lakeland landscape and (in particular) his solitary experiences of the infinitely varied terrain of the high fells. Coleridge's moods might vary: cries of joy and thankful ejaculations to nature could modulate into the gloomy thought that 'into a *discoverer* I have sunk from an *inventor*', for, as Kathleen Coburn remarks, one cannot but notice 'his association of observed natural phenomena with his own bodily and emotional states'; but on the whole the tone of his fell-walking prose between 1799 and 1802 is exultant. Discovering the fells offered Coleridge a whole new area of sense impressions and emotional stimuli, and though the prose works and poetry which he hoped to base upon his experiences were not to be written, the actual notebook prose in which he recorded his immediate sensations and impressions forms a body of topographical writing and personal recording of a wholly new and very remarkable kind.

The early tourists, who visited the Lake District with Fr. Thomas West's *Guide* or the tour journals of Pennant, Gilpin or Thomas Gray to tell them where to find the proper 'stations' and the correctly picturesque reactions to experience when looking at the views from them, did not walk about to any great extent. They travelled the usual tourist route from Keswick to Windermere in a carriage, were rowed round Derwentwater and Lake Windermere, and, if they felt brave enough to venture on the ascent of Skiddaw or (a little later) Helvellyn on foot rather than on the back of a pony, they were accompanied by a guide, who could point out the chief features of the landscape and revive the visitor's intrepidity with timely offers of a tot of brandy when they reached the heights. The walking tour as such only enters literature in the decade of Coleridge's first visit to the Lakes with the publication of Joseph Budworth's *A Fortnight's Ramble to the Lakes* in 1792. Budworth was a military man, active and hardy, and he made a succession of ascents which were not part of the regular tourist programme of the day. But he thought of mountains rather than fells, and even with the help of local guides he was clearly nervous on the steep slopes and kept well away from the scree. Like almost all the late eighteenth-century writers on the area he was a sightseer, not a resident. For deep knowledge and a close understanding of the Lakeland landscape we must wait till the Wordsworths and Coleridge are settled in the area. Late eighteenth-century tourists continued to swallow the tall stories about the terrible inaccessibility and awful hazards of the fells and high passes which Thomas Gray and other early visitors had half heard from the natives and half dreamed up for themselves, and they kept well away from the high ground.

Of course, as Molly Lefebure points out in *Cumberland Heritage*, the fells, mountains and high passes had always been traversed by the shepherds, miners and packhorse carriers of the region. But the tourists found the bare screes and fells frightening. The cult of the sublime and of Salvator Rosa made a few timid encounters with apparent danger (such as a ride along the road into the lower part of Borrowdale) quite popular. But high, empty, remote rockscapes were foreign to the aesthetic canons of the time, and the tourists felt no desire to experience them.

Coleridge first saw the Lake District in November 1799. In the previous two years he had doubtless heard a great deal about their native region from William and Dorothy Wordsworth and it was clearly a great joy to him that he was able to explore the area with William and (for part of the time) John Wordsworth as his guides. They gave him a comprehensive tour of the valleys and passes, lasting about three weeks. But in following their itinerary one must remember that the formation of Wordsworth's aesthetic sense had been powerfully affected by the publications of late eighteenth-century picturesque-topographical writers. He shared their pictorially orientated preference for a lowish viewpoint, from which the proportions of a landscape could be appreciated as if in a painting by Claude Lorrain or Richard Wilson. Although Wordsworth's response to landscape was enriched by time and travel, and although mountain experiences came to occupy a key significance in certain areas of his thinking (as witness the ascent of Snowdon passage in *Prelude*, 13) he remained basically faithful to the general tenets of the picturesque-topographical school, as his continued approval for West's *Guide* as late as the publication of his own *Guide to the Lakes* makes clear. So the three weeks' tour with Coleridge mostly kept clear of the higher ground.

In her chapter 'The First of the Fellwalkers' in *Cumberland Heritage*, Molly Lefebure maintains that 'Coleridge's notes for this introductory tour are rather subdued and his comments reveal him as deeply under the influence of Wordsworth.' My own reading of this section of the notebooks (*CN*, I, 494–563) rather suggests that on the early part of the tour, when Coleridge was new to the area and relying heavily on Wordsworth for information, the signs of Wordsworth's opinions are, inevitably, clear. But so too is the influence of picturesque-tourist literature, which Coleridge may have re-read in preparation for the trip. In a description of Hawes Water, written on Friday 1 November, early in the tour, Coleridge attempts to distinguish the various views from Wallow Crag by making a list of what are in effect 'stations' in the manner of West and describing the beautiful features of the landscape to be seen from each. Scattered references to Gilpin, West, Claude and Salvator Rosa are, indeed, to be found throughout Coleridge's Lakeland notes, but they soon represent nothing more than a kind of shorthand notation for suggesting particular kinds of effects. Coleridge's eye refuses to be tyrannised by the conventions of seeing which they stand for.

By the time the party reached Grasmere in the first week of November Coleridge had found his bearings. They embarked on an ascent of Helvellyn (the only high ascent of their tour) and Coleridge's brief notes written on the summit show what was to be his characteristic mode of recording the features of a high Lakeland view. The notes impart a sense of movement as he turns about; first due south, then clockwise round to the north east, and finally westwards, with a quick glance back again to the direction where he started. Viewing also involves a degree of movement along the high plateau to discover features that were hidden at first:

On the top of Helvellin
First the Lake of Grasmere like a sullen Tarn/ then the black ridge of mountain
– then as upborne among the other mountains the luminous Cunneston Lake
– & far away in the Distance & far to the Lake the glooming Shadow,
Wynandermere with its Island – Pass on – the Tairn – & view of the gloomy
Ulswater & mountains behind, one black, one blue, & the last one dun/
Greisdale Halse – Gowdrell Crag – Tarn Crag – that smoother Eminence on
the right is called Fairfield – (*CN*, I, 515)

At one stroke Coleridge breaks free from the conventions of picturesque-tourist descriptive writing. He makes no attempt to compose landscape features into a Claudian picture with a foreground, middle and far distances, or to create a Salvator Rosa-influenced mood piece of sublimity and horror. He breaks the rules by offering a moving panorama in which the spectator's head is free to move this way and that, and his body to turn about as he advances into a landscape. Coleridge draws on eighteenth-century descriptive terminology ('luminous' and 'glooming') but incorporates colours such as black and dun which formed no part of the word painter's conventional vocabulary.

The description of the view from Helvellyn conveys no great sense of Coleridge's emotions being involved with what he sees (the walk uphill had been a long one and the day was dull: the party seems to have been a little subdued), but from the early stages of the tour there are plentiful indications that his imagination was being stimulated beyond the customary bounds of topographical prose expression by the newly discovered landscapes of the Lakes. That 'despotism of the eye' which Coleridge was always to resist was even then in no danger of overwhelming his other senses or his creative fancy as he sought for meaningful analogies which might express the vital power of the scenery and its capacity to stimulate the poet's mind. On Wallow Crag Coleridge notes how one of the ridges is 'steep as a nose running behind the embracing Giant's arms' (the ridges on either side of it) as it runs down towards the lake (*CN*, I, 510). The lower part of Aira Force seems to spread 'into a muslin apron, & the whole water fall looks like a long-waisted Lady Giantess slipping down on her back . . . ' (*CN*, I, 549). From Place Fell Coleridge looks down on Ullswater to find

a large Slice of calm silver – above that a bright ruffledness, or atomic spor-
tiveness – motes in the sun? – Vortices of flies? (*CN*, I, 549)

Coleridge's eye moves onward, sharply responsive to the clear details of a sunlit landscape, to find yet more signs of vitality in brilliant light effects and the apparent energies suggested by the contours of the nearer hills:

How shall I express the Banks waters all fused silver, that House too its slates rainwet silver in the sun, & its shadows running down in the water like a column – the Woods on the right shadowy with Sunshine, and in front of me the sloping hollow of sunpatched Fields, sloping up into Hills so playful, the playful Hills so going away in snow-streaked Savage black mountains.   (*CN*, I, 549)

All around him Coleridge was sensing 'the one life within us and abroad', the 'informing and unitive energy that plays throughout nature'[1] which can surprise the eye into thinking 'Saddleback white and streaked' a cloud because of the lightness and texture of its colours at a distance and draw the poet's heart into a confession of his loss of self-awareness (akin in its simpler fashion to the Mariner's loss of the dead weight of self as he loses his identity in the spontaneous act of sympathy as he blesses the water snakes) when the seeming spirit and personality of a mountain take command of his imagination:

Ghost of a mountain – the forms seizing my Body as I passed & became realities – I, a Ghost, till I had reconquered my substance   (*CN*, I, 523)

The notebook entries of November 1799 show Coleridge advancing rapidly towards the full discovery of his characteristic manner of recording the forms and the imaginative impact of Lakeland scenery. One such entry, for instance, is a memorable attempt at capturing the varied aspects and energies revealed by travelling over a piece of high ground:

I climb up the woody Hill & here have gained the Crummock Water – but have lost the violet Crag. We pass thro' the wood, road ascending – now I am between the Woody Hill/ & a stone wall with trees growing over it & see nothing else – & now the whole violet Crag rises and fronts me – Then the waters near the upper end of Crummock . . .   (*CN*, I, 537)

William Gilpin had specialised in a staid and melodious prose describing the picturesque effects which modulate into one another as the spectator (usually in a boat, and therefore at lake level) advances steadily forwards into and through a landscape. But Coleridge's rapid notation of changing effects on rising ground, so precisely visual in regard to both distant features and close details as to seem an authentic record of the process of discovery actually being experienced, is without precedent in eighteenth-century tourist literature. Only Dorothy Wordsworth, among Coleridge's contemporaries, shares his gift for dynamic notation, but she shows nothing of his constant and highly characteristic desire to ascend in search of fresh revelations.[2]

In a letter to Tom Wedgwood of January 14 1803 Coleridge states his matured attitude to fell walking and his marked fondness for high ascents and viewpoints:

> In simple earnest, I never find myself alone within the embracement of rocks and hills, a traveller upon an Alpine road, but my spirit courses, drives and eddies, like a leaf in Autumn. A wild activity, of thoughts, imaginations, feelings and impulses of motion, rises up from within me . . . . The farther I ascend . . . the greater becomes in me the feeling of Life. (*CL*, II, p. 916)

The poetry of his Somerset years had already associated the joy of walking on high ground with the experience of finding a superior degree of spiritual and imaginative enlightenment. *This Lime-Tree Bower My Prison* offers a characteristic instance of this procedure.

Although the damp, misty weather of November 1799 might reduce the pleasure of mounting Helvellyn, it offered Coleridge stimulating glimpses of natural or (occasionally) man-made forms which seemed to cross the borderline between ideals and realities in a very exciting way. Lyulph's Tower

> rises emerging out of the mist, two-thirds wholly hidden, the turrets quite clear – & in a moment all is snatched away – Realities and Shadows (*CN*, I, 553)

A clear morning by Ullswater as the tour neared its close offered the amusing realisation that 'that round fat backside of a Hill' opposite formed, with its reflection in the water, '*one* absolutely undistinguishable form' of comically Platonic completeness (*CN*, I, 555). But most of all these magical discoveries of the one life and the relatedness of real objects with ideal concepts came to him when he was able to walk uphill.

The Wordsworths were strong walkers, but not fell walkers. The majority of the walks recorded in Dorothy's *Journals* were made on the then-empty roads, or on shepherds' paths such as the one up Easedale, relatively close to home. And walking was, for them, a shared experience which allowed them to respond together to the beauties of nature which Dorothy might afterwards record in her *Journal*. When Coleridge took his family to live at Greta Hall in July 1800 he was able to experience a new degree of self-immersion in the phenomena of the Lakeland landscape, but he soon discovered that he preferred a higher terrain than the Wordsworths did, and that he preferred to experience it alone. 'I *must* be alone', he wrote, 'if either my Imagination or Heart are to be enriched.' Yet he seems to have needed a degree of self-expression beyond that offered by purely internal self-communion quite frequently, and his notebooks became a steadily developing medium for expressing and recording his impressions while a walk, with all the emotional and aesthetic discoveries which attended it, was actually taking place.

Greta Hall offered Coleridge a magnificent panorama of lakes and mountains, and his initial burst of notebook and letter writing shows how exciting he found the chance to study a landscape in the endless diversity of light and colour effects which varying weather conditions and times of day brought into being. At this time he became fully engaged on what Kathleen Coburn rightly calls 'heroic attempts to find new words to describe these apperceptions, with results that sometimes suggest a much later development in the history of painting and poetry' (*CN*, I, p. xxxii). The comparisons with the work of certain of the French Impressionists which some critics have made are not overstrained: Monet painting his haystack at different times of day is engaged in an activity comparable to Coleridge noting down the aspects of his view from the upstairs study at Greta Hall at all manner of times and seasons. The domestic arrangements even gave him a readymade equivalent of a Claude glass, and he recorded the consequences of this with wry amusement:

My glass being opposite the window, I seldom shave without cutting myself. Some Mountain or Peak is rising out of the Mist, or some Slanting Column of misty sunlight is sailing across me – so that I offer up soap and blood daily, as an Eye-servant of the Goddess Nature.   (*CL*, I, p. 658)

As well as taking preliminary walks in order to master the topography of the area, Coleridge talked to local people. He soon realised (in Molly Lefebure's words) 'the ridiculous discrepancy between the exaggerated awe with which the picturesque tourists treated the fells and the confident manner in which the dalesfolk lived and worked in these reputedly hair-raising regions'.[3] He began, therefore, to plan more ambitious exploratory fell walks. At the same time he was finding the landscape round Keswick inspiring and was feeling his self-confidence as a poet and thinker revive. On the evening of Sunday 24 August he walked on Latrigg with his wife and child. He noted a remarkable cloud and light effect, characteristically discovered in the act of turning to go home:

As we turned round on our return, we see a moving pillar of clouds, flame & smoke, rising, bending, arching, and in swift motion – from what God's chimney doth it issue? – I scarcely ever saw in the sky such variety of shapes, & colors, & colors floating over colors. – Solemnly now lie the black masses on the blue firmament of – not quite night – for still at the foot of Bassenthwaite there is a smoky russet Light. – Tis 9 o'clock. –   (*CN*, I, 781)

Perhaps to Coleridge's Sabbath evening mind that pillar of clouds seemed like the one that led the Israelites across the desert to safety. He had found his Promised Land at Greta Hall: a child was about to be born to him, he was near the Wordsworths, and with returning inspiration he felt able to participate fully in the work of preparing a new edition of *Lyrical Ballads* and to imagine the possibility of completing *Christabel* as his major new contribution to the work. The notebook entries of August

1800 seem to record an experiment which he afterwards claimed to have made; by subjecting himself to the impact of powerful natural forces in the expectation that a comparable stimulation of his own creative imagination would ensue. At first, he claimed, the experiment had not answered:

> The wind from Skiddaw & Borrodale was often as loud as wind need be – & many a walk in the clouds on the mountains did I take; but all would not do.
>
> (*CL*, I, p. 643)

Eventually a chance over-indulgence in drinking released his mental powers, he claimed, 'and I proceeded successfully'. The notebook entries of this time, however, suggest that Coleridge was indulging in self-dramatisation after the event. The only reference to drinking is of a relaxed and jocular kind (*CN*, I, 791) and it comes in the midst of a succession of vivid, rapidly composed verbal sketches of the new landscape which he was mastering. By the time he had been at Greta Hall for five weeks, Coleridge had finished a sizeable draft of new material for *Christabel*, and he seems to have celebrated his success with a few days' strenuous exploration of the fells. The climax of this short holiday from composition came on Sunday 31 August, when he made the first recorded walk from Keswick to Grasmere along the tops (Calfhow Pike, Great Dod, Stybarrow Dod, Raise and Helvellyn).

In the course of this great walk Coleridge paused to make notes. The way in which his prose could now incorporate a rapid succession of exciting discoveries and powerful experiences while matching them with the exultant elasticity of his own mind and feelings is at once apparent:

> When I had wound round so as to come at the very head of the Gill I determined to wind up to the very top, tho' it led at least 3 furlong back toward Threlkeld – I went, my face still towards Wasdale, Ennerdale, Buttermere, &c till I reached the very top, then, & not till then turned my face, and beheld (O Joy for me!) Patterdale & Ulswater . . . (*CN*, I, 798)

As Kathleen Coburn notes, 'the use of the word "Joy" gives a very special sense of Coleridge's exuberance and creative mood'. He could match Nature's creativity by that of the manuscript poem in his pocket. He could choose when to see, and could control the timing of natural prospects and even natural surprises for himself. Nature even seemed willing to play a subservient role in the elation of the moment: 'the evening now lating', he thought of passing a stretch of high ground by, 'but Nature twitched me at the heart strings – I ascended it – thanks to her! Thanks to her – What a scene . . . ' (*CN*, I, 798, f37).

But on the summit of Helvellyn the strong chiaroscuro effects of the two great moonlit Edges recalled him again to a sense of the primal energies of the Creation, where Divine power seemed to have left the rocks in a state of frozen movement, as though their liquid state had but lately cooled into solid forms:

> travelling along the ridge I came to the other side of those precipices and down below me on my left – no – no! no words can convey any idea of this prodigious wildness . . . what a frightful bulgy precipice I stand on and to my right how the Crag which corresponds to the other, how it plunges down like a waterfall, reaches a level steepness, and again plunges!   (*CN*, i, 799, f40)

The elated poet had found a Salvator Rosa landscape of sublime terror to impress his mind, but he saw it from a totally un-Salvatorian viewpoint: he witnessed its terrors, like those of the imagined chasms in *Kubla Khan*, from above. And no ancestral voices rose from the depths to prophesy woes ahead. Coleridge scrambled down by Nethermost Pike and Seat Sandal. At eleven o'clock he reached Town End and gathered the Wordsworth household together for a recitation of the new part of *Christabel*.

The great range walk of 31 August 1800 formed a fitting climax to the 'honeymoon' period of Coleridge's initial happiness and creativity at Greta Hall. The prose account of the walk brings together and fuses in a style of remarkable economy, speed and specificity the deeper knowledge of the region which residence at Keswick had enabled Coleridge to amass so quickly. He and Dorothy Wordsworth are the first writers to preserve those sights and sounds of Lakeland which immediately recreate its physical reality for later generations. Each must have had gifts of observation and response which interested the other, but, as John Beer suggests, one can see Dorothy at times 'touched by his feelings for magical lights and mysterious energies actually manifesting themselves in nature'[4] while it is very difficult to see any very specific influence being exerted over Coleridge's prose by Dorothy in return. They shared, and perhaps helped each other to perfect, a gift for memorably fixing the actual: 'raspberry and milk coloured crags' . . . 'fine columns of misty sunshine sailing slowly over the crags' are characteristic examples from the entry describing Coleridge's ridge walk up Helvellyn. A few days earlier, on Saddleback, he had noticed 'no noise but that of the loose stones rolling away from the feet of the Sheep, that move slowly among these perilous ledges' (*CN*, i, 784).

But Coleridge's better-informed mind ranged, as Dorothy Wordsworth's could not do, from the infinitesimal to the vast in search of evidence for the working of natural energies towards form in ways which seemed akin to the operation of the human imagination, channelled and directed by the human will. Water, and forms analogous to those of water, particularly fascinated him. At the beginning of his great ridge walk to Helvellyn he noted how his own hills 'are the last surge of that enormous ocean formed by the mountains of Ennerdale, Butterdale, Wasdale & Borrodale' (*CN*, I, 798, f26). The analogy seemed strengthened a moment later when he caught a distant glimpse of the real sea. The 'forces' or waterfalls of the region always interested him, and nothing could be less like the explorations (or the prose) of the picturesque tourists than Coleridge's spatial explorations of the rocks, views, water courses and vegetation of the forces which he recorded from November 1799 onwards. Characteristic, but particularly delightful, is an account of Moss Force on Newlands Hause which the contemporary Cumbrian poet and topographical writer Norman Nicholson has more than once anthologised and selected for particular praise:[5]

The mad water rushed thro' its *sinuous* bed, or rather prison of Rock with such rapid curves . . . that in twilight one might have feelingly compared them to a vast crowd of huge white bears, rushing, one over the other, against the wind – their long white hair scattering abroad in the wind.

After this animated picture of hairy white bears playing leap frog in the dusk, Coleridge modulates into his more serious, speculative manner:

What a sight it is to look down on such a Cataract! The wheels, that circumvolve it, the leaping up and plunging forward of that infinity of Pearls and Glass Bulbs, the continual *change* of the *Matter*, the perpetual *Sameness* of the *Form* – it is an awful Image and Shadow of God and the World.

When engaging in strenuous fell walking in the hope of stimulating his creative powers so as to finish *Christabel*, Coleridge was acting upon a theory which attracted him for a time, that strong irritation of the nervous system through violent sense stimuli might awaken comparable energies in the central organic powers. Unfortunately irritations of a less philosophic sort were to assail him in October 1800 and for some time afterwards. First the new baby, Derwent, fell ill, then Wordsworth decided that *Christabel* was going to be out of tune with the new *Lyrical Ballads* collection as he envisaged it and persuaded Coleridge not to include it. This produced a bad crisis of confidence for Coleridge and he probably stepped up his intake of laudanum to steady himself, with the inevitable exacerbation of its side effects. Finally the damp lakeland winter worsened his tendency to rheumatism. Fell walking and the prose in which he described it could only be a summer pursuit for Coleridge, and in 1801 he was in such deep financial straits that when he eventually rose from his sick bed he had to prepare for a season of hack journalism in London. So little walking was done. He returned north in the spring of 1802, but his poor health, his despondency and the domestic turmoil which his friendship with the Wordsworths and his feelings for Sara Hutchinson only worsened boded ill for a recovery of vitality or better spirits. Yet recover he did.

The events which led up to the composition of Coleridge's *Dejection* have been much studied. But less attention has been given to the degree of recovery which he experienced in the summer which followed, and to the possibility that the record of his week's strenuous walking at the beginning of August 1802 constitutes a semi-private but definite affirmation of an alternative state of being to that chronicled within the poem.

Dejection is a poem in which the failure of the poet's 'genial spirits' is confessed in the context of a wild scene of disordered nature which acts as an externalisation and independent confirmation of the poet's anguished state of mind. The poem was originally addressed to Sara Hutchinson, and to her Coleridge makes his much discussed complaint that

> We receive but what we give,
> And in our life alone does Nature live.
> Ours is her wedding garment, ours her shroud.

But writing (perhaps also *completing*) the poem clearly served as a tonic to Coleridge. The letters show him delighting in this new proof of his own creativity: the poem is adapted, paraphrased, offered to a variety of correspondents. Domestic tensions at Greta Hall lessened for a while after a tremendous row late in May, and when the Wordsworths departed for Calais on 9 July, Coleridge was under less emotional pressure than he had been for a considerable time. Probably he took less opium as a result, which would speed his return to health. He planned a week's walking of the remoter fells with the help of Hutchinson's *History of the County of Cumberland* early in June. On Sunday 1 August he finally set off.

The tremendous week of fell walking (which included the first recorded ascent of Scafell by anyone other than a native of the region) is a testimony to the essential strength and recuperative energy of Coleridge's body and mind. He made notebook entries for all but the final (least arduous and already known) part of his tour, and in addition to this private record he also began a letter to Sara Hutchinson on the Wednesday. In this he transcribed considerable sections of the notebook account, with amplifications of detail and stretches of fresh narration in which he supplied incidents from memory which he had not had time to note down in the immediate circumstances (and excitement) of the walk.

Although neither notebook nor letter account is complete, it is possible to see in the latter a process akin to that which happened with *Dejection: A Letter* occurring once more (and, incidentally, at a time when *Dejection*'s transformation into a public document had not yet been completed by its publication in the *Morning Post*). Just as the private confessional poem to Sara Hutchinson was transformed in gradual stages into a general statement, so the private tour material in Coleridge's notebook could be written up for Sara, as a demonstration of recovered physical vitality and imaginative power. From the letter form to that of a picturesque tour book of a new and striking kind would not be too remote or difficult a transition, and the idea of a book on the Lakes had been in Coleridge's mind since the time of his first visit to the area with the Wordsworths. Together the notebook entries and their expansion in letter form bear witness to an astonishing recovery of resilience and a rebirth of self-confidence which is further suggested by other ideas for topographical writings which Coleridge noted down during the most arduous and exciting parts of his week's walking.

The notebook prose of Coleridge's Scafell tour with its almost simultaneous incorporation and amplification in the letters to Sara Hutchinson stands in a different relationship to public form and utterance from any of the other, essentially private notebook material relating to the Lakeland landscape and the fells. The letters occasionally indulge in a self-glorifying touch of the histrionic, as when the bald account of his difficult drop into Eskdale:

Good Heavens! what a climb! dropping from Precipices and at last should have been crag fast but for the chasm – (*CN*, I, 1218, f17)

is written up into a very sublime (rather Mrs Radcliffian) passage on the terrors of almost getting crag fast and eventually tottering to the bottom, shaking legs, heat bumps and all (*CL*, I, p. 451). But in the main they are precisely based on the notebook prose account. That account shows Coleridge not only able to 'receive . . . what we give' to Nature, but exultantly feeling that her wedding garment (of the richest tones and hues) has been thrown over him, and himself most comfortably attired and, indeed, lord of the feast. After months of depression and ill health he rejoiced in the exercise, the contacts with local people (with whom he always got on well), the bright weather, the contrasts between the beauty of the lower dales and the bare sublimity of the great high fells and the rich, strong colours everywhere.

The notebook entries of this week express Coleridge's elation. Observations flow from him in a torrent of exact, vivifying phrases (modern fell walkers have agreed on the precision of his scenic definitions and descriptions) and no one has ever caught better the contrast between the bareness of the great fells and the valley scenery below. Looking into Eskdale Coleridge notes

how then the Hill-ridge intermits and the vales become one/but never sure was lovelier human Dwellings than these nestled in Trees at the foot of the Fells, & in among the intervening Hills. (*CN*, I, 1222, f22)

His mind ranges everywhere, from the fact that on a steep slope up Scafell he sees himself

Ascend, stooping, & looking at my shadow, stooping down to my shadow, a little shorter than myself (*CN*, I, 1216)

to an amusing fancy for a future book:

The plan for one book the Genius of some place appearing in a Dream & up-braiding me for omitting *him*. (*CN*, I, 1214)

But running through everything is Coleridge's joy at the recovery of full physical and mental vigour. No fears assail him that he may lose his individual power of imagination under a mass of strong external sensations. To respond, to register and to record are now enough to satisfy his mind. Speculation and theorising are in abeyance as (to adopt Gerard Manley Hopkins's useful term) he catches the successive 'inscapes' of the high terrain. Briefly but exultantly he has become master of the great spaces he traverses and surveys.

Such an elation could hardly have lasted, and the complications of Coleridge's existence soon brought it to an end. In later tours, with Southey or (in Scotland now) with the Wordsworths, circumstances or his worsening psychological problems cause a noticeable muteness of tone in his prose notes. But in the notes made during Coleridge's two most active periods of fell walking, in the summers of 1800 and 1802, he fulfilled the promise of his first series of notes in November 1799. He developed a highly distinctive prose which moves further away from the aesthetic and formal procedures of picturesque-tourist writing than anyone else was to do until Ruskin and Hopkins began to make notes on the area much later in the nineteenth century. Coleridge brings into his prose the physical realities of the Lake District, as only Dorothy Wordsworth was capable of doing at that same time, and he writes of fell walking as no one had ever done before ('As I bounded down, noticed the moving stones under the soft moss, hurting my feet'). He appreciates the vitality and the connectedness of rocks, streams and growing things, and finds it possible not just to respond to them in the hope of stimulating his own creative powers, but ultimately (if briefly) to open himself to myriad revelations of the energies of nature as infinite correlatives to the energies of the human mind, without fear of being overwhelmed by nature's profuseness. Indeed through joy Coleridge becomes master of revealed energy, exulting in his ability to embrace it through the vigour of his own body and mind. The double irony lies in the fact that the great recoveries of the capacity for physical and mental adventure, and for joy, which followed the composition of the second part of *Christabel* and *Dejection* could not be sustained, and that the evidence of this transitory joy and the new manner of topographical prose writing which it generated should have lain hidden till our own time and the eventual publication of Coleridge's early notebooks.

Notes

1 John Beer, *Coleridge's Poetic Intelligence* (Cambridge, 1977), p. 127.
2 For an instance of Coleridge ascending in order to discover recorded by Dorothy herself, see *DWJ* under 23 April 1802.
3 Molly Lefebure, *Cumberland Heritage* (London, 1970), p. 134.
4 *Coleridge's Poetic Intelligence*, p. 272.
5 See Norman Nicholson, *The Lake District* (Harmondsworth, 1977), pp. 100–1 and comments in *The Lake Poets* (London, 1955), p. 129. Nicholson there concludes that 'if only Coleridge could have written like this more often there would have been no need for another guide to the Lakes'.

'Leaping and Lingering': Coleridge's lyrical ballads

STEPHEN PARRISH

I

One of the most colourful volumes of literary scholarship ever given to the world is a study of the working of Coleridge's imagination, 'an absorbing adventure along the ways which the imagination follows in dealing with its multifarious materials – an adventure like a passage through the mazes of a labyrinth, to come out at last upon a wide and open sky'. Now more than half a century old, *The Road to Xanadu* was composed in a style that has rather fallen out of fashion. Hardly any smart critics today write even like G. Wilson Knight, and post-structuralism has cultivated its own arcane splendours of language to overshadow the rococo magnificence of *Xanadu*'s mesmerizing rhetoric. Celebrated for a generation at Harvard with a Gilbertian tribute –

> My name is John Livingston Lowes;
> I'm a dealer in magical prose –

Lowes offered accounts of the poet's imagination of such spellbinding authority that we listen like a three-year's child while the critic has his will:

The 'deep well of unconscious cerebration' underlies your consciousness and mine, but in the case of genius its waters are possessed of a peculiar potency. Images and impressions converge and blend even in the sleepy drench of our forgetful pools. But the inscrutable energy of genius which we call creative owes its secret virtue at least in part to the enhanced and almost incredible facility with which in the wonder-working depths of the unconscious the fragments which sink incessantly below the surface fuse and assimilate and coalesce.[1]

This image of the well serves throughout the book to emblemize the mind of the poet, sometimes as 'a reservoir of memory', sometimes as the lodging place of denizens of the unconscious who stir about in its murky depths. I cannot refuse myself the gratification (as Wordsworth said when he took aim at *The Ancient Mariner*) of presenting one more fluent specimen (page 278) of Lowes's sparkling water-imagery:

the poem is not the confluence of unconsciously merging images, as a pool of water forms from the coalescence of scattered drops; nor is the poet a somnambulist in a subliminal world. Neither the conscious impressions nor their unconscious interpenetrations constitute the poem. They are inseparable from it, but it is an entity which they do not create. On the contrary, every impression, every new creature rising from the potent waters of the Well, is what it now is through its participation in a *whole*, foreseen as a whole in each integral part – a whole which is the working out of a controlling imaginative design. . . .

If metaphor is the key to understanding an abstraction like the conscious or subconscious mind, or the imagination, this metaphor of the well unlocks Lowes's understanding of Coleridge and remains available to us as an implement. We might be more tempted to make use of it if Lowes had used it with more control. It is a little startling to learn (on page 189) that when Coleridge seems to associate the iridescent colours of water snakes (in his poem) with the glistening colours of hoar-frost on snow in the sunlight (in his notebooks), 'the Spirit of the Well is once more dealing the cards for the shaping Spirit, with unerring art, to play'. This soggy underwater game has no place for players from a bewildering series of incompatible metaphors, both organic and mechanical, to which Lowes (understandably and forgiveably) has intermittent recourse. In his effort to portray what is in the end unportrayable, he speaks of Coleridge's mind as a loom with 'flying shuttles', as a stream with tributary rivulets, as a 'womb of creative energy', as the shaping spirit that moulds potter's clay, as a place where 'hooked atoms' work in tension, or where iron filings are drawn to a magnet, where 'tentacles of association' reach and cling, where a sort of 'alchemy' can blend and fuse and transmute.

It would be well to remind ourselves that these are Lowes's metaphors, not Coleridge's, and that they inevitably project Lowes's understandings of the working of his own imagination. The other great contemporary interpreter of Coleridge's mind, I. A. Richards (uncelebrated in song or ballad, I think, at least in his Harvard years), more prudent, more laconic, resorted sparingly to metaphor, and his knotted prose is, likewise no doubt, a reflection of his own complex, ingenious imagination.[2] Coleridge's imagination remains elusive and shadowy in *The Road to Xanadu*, lying perhaps just beyond the reach of metaphor, for another reason: Lowes never really believed that he was talking about the imagination as Coleridge discriminatingly defined it. His study of Coleridge, he confessed early on (page 95), convinced him 'that Fancy and Imagination are not two powers at all, but one. The valid distinction which exists between them lies, not in the materials with which they operate, but in the degree of intensity of the operant power itself.'

We had better turn away at this point from distracting visions of high-energy pumps, roiling the water in the well of memory, to seek for Coleridge's own metaphors of mind. A writer's metaphors of mind can, we have to suppose, betray unconscious as well as conscious notions. It is not

clear whether Freud ever recognized at the conscious level of his thinking that the two persistent images of mind that run through his writings
– the one of a landscape, with marshland and dry ground, the other of
a structure like a house – were both, by his own classification, female
symbols. Nor is it clear how serious Coleridge consciously intended to
be in his occasional evocations of the mind (containing the memory and
the faculties of Fancy and Imagination) in metaphor. Wordsworth offers
us abundant images of the mind, both the mind of man and the great
universal mind, throughout his poem on the growth of his own mind.
Coleridge could fashion summary definitions that still hold us transfixed:

The primary IMAGINATION I hold to be the living Power and prime Agent
of all human Perception, and as a repetition in the finite mind of the eternal act
of creation in the infinite I AM. . . .   (*BL*, I, p. 304)

And he could toy with metaphor, as in a chapter of 'Philosophical definitions' in the *Biographia* (II, p. 18):

GOOD SENSE is the BODY of poetic genius, FANCY its DRAPERY, MO-
TION its LIFE, and IMAGINATION the SOUL that is every where, and in
each; and forms all into one graceful and intelligent whole.

To finish off his catalogue of the 'Beauties' of Wordsworth's poetry in
the *Biographia* he drew on a rich nature description from one of his
favourite travel books:

in reading Bartram's Travels I could not help transcribing the following lines as
a sort of allegory, or connected simile and metaphor of Wordsworth's intellect
and genius. – 'The soil is a deep, rich, dark mould, on a deep stratum of tenacious
clay; and that on a foundation of rocks, which often break through both strata,
lifting their back above the surface. The trees which chiefly grow here are the
gigantic, black oak; magnolia magniflora; fraxinus excelsior; platane; and a few
stately tulip trees.'   (*BL*, II, p. 155)

In representing his own imagination Coleridge was less playful. As
Stephen Prickett has pointed out,[3] he deploys such symbols as the
spring, the cloud-covered mountain, and the Brocken-spectre, and even
seems to validate, in 'a long and bitterly self-analytical note' of 1805,
Lowes's master image, as he unhappily thinks back, while in Malta, to
'the beautiful Fountain or natural Well at Upper Stowey':

The images of the weeds which hung down from its sides, appeared as plants growing up, straight and upright, among the water weeds that really grew from the
bottom/ & so vivid was the Image, that for some moments & not until after I had
disturbed the waters, did I perceive that their roots were not neighbours, & they
side-by-side companions. So – even then I said – so are the happy man's
Thoughts and *Things* –

But perhaps the most explicit, and certainly the most poignant, image of his own imagination to be found in Coleridge's writing records his melancholy awareness that its shaping spirit has been suspended by affliction. Writing to Godwin in March, 1801 , to announce that as a result of Wordsworth's having 'descended' on him as from Heaven, 'the poet is dead in me', he explains:

> My imagination (or rather the Somewhat that had been imaginative) lies, like a cold Snuff on the circular rim of a Brass Candle-stick, without even a stink of Tallow to remind you that it was once cloathed & mitred with flame.
>
> (*CL*, II, p. 714)

Exactly three years had passed since the marvellous winter in which *The Ancient Mariner* had been composed – or forged, or fused, or coalesced – from what Lowes called 'the raw stuff of poetry', ladled up, we suppose, from the potent waters of the well. Whatever metaphor we favour – dried up, emptied, burnt out – we are faced with a startling discrepancy between Lowes's persuasive, rhapsodic account of the working of creative genius (in 1797 and 1798) and Coleridge's own sombre announcement of his imaginative extinction in 1801.

II

As we look back over these three years, it is hard to set aside suspicion that Wordsworth's descent upon Coleridge may actually date from the earliest days of their friendship. Wordsworth was the older, the more worldly, the stronger-minded, the dominant partner. 'I feel myself a *little man by his* side', Coleridge testified (*CL*, I, p. 325) with the enthusiasm of a convert. Wordsworth was nourished and fortified by just the sort of adulation that Coleridge lavished on his gifted friends (Humphry Davy was another such), and there is genuinely nostalgic warmth in the affectionate recall in the 1805 *Prelude* (XIII, 1. 407) of those happy days when the friends first 'Together wanton'd in wild Poesy'. What Wordsworth did for Coleridge is less clear. Critics have observed that images of nature can be found in Coleridge's verse only after 1797, but the superb blank-verse conversation poems, written in what W. J. Bate has called 'a late Augustan reflective mode', date from 1795, and Bate goes on to declare that by the end of the *annus mirabilis* Coleridge came to realize that 'he could do nothing with this particular kind of poetry that the "Giant Wordsworth," as he called him, could not do better'.[4]

This leaves the supernatural poetry, the genre that flared with such brilliance in a single year, then sputtered out in the extinction of the poet in Coleridge. Whatever its long-run effects, the intimacy with Wordsworth somehow brought into being two or three of the most original, and most distinguished, pieces of verse in what we now recognize as the Romantic revolution. Yet events of the *annus mirabilis* and after show that this verse rose not so much out of harmonious collaboration as out of deep and unresolved conflicts of critical opinion. It is, in fact, important to recognize a central irony in the English Romantic revolution in poetry: the partners in the revolution held, from the beginning, fundamentally differing notions of the genre under which their revolutionary poems, along with their manifestos, were gathered.

Wordsworth's notions of the ballad can be pieced together with some confidence from his specimens of the form and from his extended critical remarks. I have tried elsewhere to sum this notion up:[5] the ballad, for Wordsworth, was a version of pastoral, and a 'lyrical' ballad was lyrical in two respects – its passion ('all poetry is passion', Wordsworth declared) arose, as in any lyric, from the mind of the speaker or the dramatic narrator of a ballad tale, and it was heightened by the employment of 'lyrical' or rapid metre so as to convey this passion to readers unaccustomed to responding to the common language of men in common life.

Coleridge's theoretical notions of the ballad never got fully elaborated. When he spoke in *Biographia Literaria* (II, pp. 5–7) of 'the two cardinal points of poetry' that he and Wordsworth had talked about in 1797, he named one as 'the power of giving the interest of novelty by the modifying colours of imagination', and described his share in *Lyrical Ballads* in the eloquent language that gives special radiance to his best critical pronouncements:

it was agreed, that my endeavours should be directed to persons and characters supernatural, or at least romantic; yet so as to transfer from our inward nature a human interest and a semblance of truth sufficient to procure for these shadows of imagination that willing suspension of disbelief for the moment, which constitutes poetic faith.

But as he implied, the Preface of 1800 – 'half a child of my own Brain' he had once claimed (*CL*, II, p. 830) – spoke only of Wordsworth's kind of poetry. Since Coleridge never produced the essay he promised Byron in 1815 (*CL*, IV, p. 561), 'a Particular Preface to the Ancient Mariner and the Ballads, on the employment of the Supernatural in Poetry and the Laws which regulate it', we frequently have to piece together his principles by inference – by noting the unstated but implied positions that Wordsworth intermittently seems at pains to controvert. Coleridge's most extended analyses of Wordsworth's ballads (in late chapters of the *Biographia*) take the form of refutation, as do his lengthy remarks, in earlier chapters, on the subject of metre and diction with reference not to the ballad but to 'Poetry' or 'a Poem'. As for other central elements of Wordsworth's theory of the ballad, Coleridge pointed to '*the choice of his characters*' as the 'great point of controversy' between Wordsworth and his detractors, dismissed Wordsworth's dramatic technique as 'ventriloquism', and left us to suppose, without saying much, that he shared Johnsonian opinions of pastoral.

Yet, inexplicably, the partnership commenced in a shared enthusiasm for the ballad, a genre which certainly attracted the two poets for different reasons (Coleridge would have been excited by the music, the magic, the marvellous, and possibilities of allegory; Wordsworth by the common language, the dramatic frames, the closeness to simple life). Stimulated by their discovery of Bürger, whose ballads (in William Taylor's translation and in Scott's) appeared in 1796, and by their reading in Percy's *Reliques of Ancient English Poetry*, Wordsworth and Coleridge embarked in 1797 on a curious sort of collaboration. They appear to have followed a pattern that Coleridge had established in partnership with Southey and Robert Lovell. *Cain*, Coleridge later testified,[6] was to have been started by Wordsworth, and Coleridge was to add a second canto; the third canto was to be written by 'which ever had *done first*'. This pattern almost certainly accounts for the segments we have of *The Three Graves*: Wordsworth wrote the first two parts and handed them over to Coleridge, who added Parts III and IV; the last two parts remained unwritten.

The Three Graves, made up as it is of extended pieces of writing by both partners, ought to be more revealing of their differences than it has proven to be. A few comparative observations can be made. When he presented his portion of the poem in *The Friend* in 1809, Coleridge described it as a psychological study, a study of the working of the imagination. He had been drawn to the story, he explained, 'from finding in it a striking proof of the possible effect on the imagination, from an idea suddenly and violently impressed on it'; having been reading about witchcraft, he wanted to show 'the mode in which the mind is affected in these cases'. (*Friend*, II, p. 89). By this time Coleridge would have been acutely aware of Wordsworth's comparable claim for certain of his own ballads, as set down in the Preface of 1800 and elsewhere: they were psychological studies, studies of the way the imagination works, tracings of the fluxes and refluxes of the mind. But a central difference is evident at once: the imagination whose behaviour is studied in Coleridge's poem belongs to a person in the story; the imagination whose workings Wordsworth traced belongs, characteristically, to the narrator of the story. In his portion of *The Three Graves* Coleridge did preserve the fiction of a narrator, but his poem never approaches the dramatic monologue form in which

Wordsworth's most experimental ballads (like the parallel poem of *The Thorn*) were cast.

But the problem with using the separate portions of *The Three Graves* to discriminate the poets' respective practises is, simply, that Coleridge here tried to bend his practise to correspond to Wordsworth's. If we were to follow the track of John Livingston Lowes, we would endeavour to make something of an image or two that might be traced, say, to the Gutch notebook. Could

> The Sun-shine lies on the cottage-wall
> Ashining thro' the snow –

perhaps have flowered into the opening lines of *The Three Graves* (Part III)?

> The Grapes upon the Vicar's wall
> Were ripe as ripe could be;
> And yellow leaves in Sun and Wind
> Were falling from the tree.

But searching out possible transmutations of this order only evades the plain fact that this portion of *The Three Graves* is couched in a diction so plain, so simple, so Wordsworthian, as to seem, in Coleridge's voice, elaborately mannered, even a species of ventriloquism. How else could Coleridge have composed such a stanza as the following (from Part II) except by straining to force his language into the cadences of (Wordsworthian) common speech:

> He reach'd his home, and by his looks
>   They saw his inward strife:
> And they clung round him with their arms,
>   Both Ellen and his wife.

Or this stanza from Part IV:

> One evening he took up a book,
>   And nothing in it read;
> Then flung it down, and groaning cried,
>   Oh! Heaven! that I were dead.

With specimens like this at hand, we might irreverently wonder why Wordsworth should have had to turn, in the 1800 Preface, to Dr Johnson for an example of 'contemptible' matter:

> I put my hat upon my head
> And walk'd into the Strand . . . .

Coleridge's contempt for his own strained efforts to bend to his partner's notion of poetic diction grew over the years. When he reprinted his portion of *The Three Graves* in *Sibylline Leaves* (1817) he prefixed to it a most extraordinary disclaimer that touched on two central points in Wordsworth's manifesto of 1800, and signalled Coleridge's total dissent:

the language [of 'the following humble fragment'] was intended to be dramatic; that is, suited to the narrator; and the metre corresponds to the homeliness of the diction. It is therefore presented as the fragment, not of a Poem, but of a common Ballad-tale. Whether this is sufficient to justify the adoption of such a style, in any metrical composition not professedly ludicrous, the Author is in some doubt. At all events, it is not presented as Poetry, and it is in no way connected with the Author's judgement concerning Poetic diction.

No readers appear to have taken up this astonishingly open invitation to look upon the ballad as ludicrous, though the piece has not drawn much praise, either. Swinburne, to be sure, thought it magnificent, though his lyrical tribute reads almost like parody. Comparing Coleridge's common Ballad-tale to Wordsworth's dramatic (that is, 'lyrical') ballad, *The Thorn*, Swinburne proclaimed that

Coleridge, in his otherwise Wordsworthian poem of *The Three Graves*, has shown how a subject of homely horror, a tale of humble and simple wickedness, of simple and humble suffering, may be treated with poetic propriety and with tragic exactitude.[7]

Wordsworth, in his later years, had taken precisely the opposite view. Recognizing in Coleridge the sort of 'personal and domestic discontent' that made it difficult for him to portray suffering with sympathy, Wordsworth charged that Coleridge made *The Three Graves* 'too shocking and painful, and not sufficiently sweetened by any healing views'. He then went on, speaking to Barron Field after Coleridge's death, to utter a casual, trenchant, almost certainly wrong-headed remark that takes us back to the *annus mirabilis* and invites thoughtful examination: 'Not being able to dwell on or sanctify natural woes, he took to the supernatural, and hence his *Ancient Mariner* and *Christabel*.'[8]

III

As a matter of chronological fact, Coleridge took to the supernatural before his 'personal and domestic discontent' had risen to uncomfortable levels. He was attracted to Bürger's poems as early as 1796, and we can tell what he liked in Bürger from the Bürgeresque features he incorporated in *The Ancient Mariner*. These included not only the magical haunting air of miracle and terror that supernatural events evoke, as in the 'ghostlie crew' that whirled and danced in air, but what the *Monthly*

Magazine (in March 1796) called the 'hurrying vigour' of Bürger's 'impetuous diction', as in such lines as these:

> To and fro they are hurried about;
> And to and fro, and in and out
>   The stars dance on between.

John Beer has observed[9] that these features can be found in Scott's translation, as well as William Taylor's, and quotes two sufficiently suggestive stanzas:

> Tramp! tramp! along the land they rode;
>   Splash! splash! along the sea;
> The steed is wight, the spur is bright,
>   The flashing pebbles flee.

> The furious Barb snorts fire and foam;
>   And with a fearful bound
> Dissolves at once in empty air,
>   And leaves him on the ground.

Although Wordsworth paid Bürger the tribute of parody in *The Idiot Boy*, he hung back short of admiration, as an exchange of letters with Coleridge in 1799 reveals. Pronouncing Bürger to be a 'poet of the animal spirits', he complained stiffly that Bürger communicated 'no delicate or minute feelings', and more pointedly, that he failed to create character, other than his own. 'It seems to me, that in poems descriptive of human nature, however short they be, character is absolutely necessary . . . incidents are among the lowest allurements of poetry.'[10] Coleridge seems to have defended Bürger against these charges, ineffectually, and he had to report good-humouredly to Taylor that the argument broke up in 'metaphysical disquisitions on the nature of character', fortunately now lost.

But it is important to note that Wordsworth himself, by his own account, contributed two particularly striking supernatural incidents to *The Ancient Mariner* (besides suggesting the apparition of the skeleton ship with figures on it). These were the navigation of the mariner's vessel by his dead crew-mates, and the vengeance enacted for the albatross's death by tutelary spirits of the polar region (*WPW*, I, p. 361). It is not known when Wordsworth made these suggestions, but one fact of the poem's history may offer a clue. On 18 February 1798, Coleridge announced to Cottle that he had 'finished' his ballad in 340 lines (*CL*, I, p. 387). It was again (or still) 'finished' on 23 March, as Dorothy recorded in her journal. But by the time it went to the printer it had swollen out to 658 lines. It is teasing to speculate what sort of poem the earlier finished version was, though speculation might be fruitless were it not for Wordsworth's account of his contributions. As it stood in the 1798 volume the poem had seven parts as follows:

Part I	80 lines
Part II	58 lines
Part III	77 lines
Part IV	68 lines
Part V	131 lines
Part VI	132 lines
Part VII	112 lines

At the close of Part IV, 284 lines into the ballad, the Mariner feels a 'spring of love' gush from his heart, as he leans over the rail looking down into the shadow of the ship, and he blesses the water snakes 'unaware', with no more conscious premeditation than he had brought to the shooting of the albatross at the close of Part I. After this point the ballad seems to loop and wallow a bit, as though it were being stretched out, and it is not hard to imagine an original closing section of, perhaps, 56 lines (340 minus 284) which brought the mariner expeditiously home and completed his punishment, or his expiation. Could Wordsworth, we might wonder, having seen the first 'finished' version of 340 lines, have made his suggestions at this stage and prompted Coleridge to make insertions? The navigation of the vessel by the dead men falls in Part V of the 1798 text, and the vengeance exacted by tutelary spirits falls in Parts V and VI. (Readers may decide for themselves whether, if this speculation seem plausible, Wordsworth would have made *The Ancient Mariner* a better poem than he found it.)

Whatever the case, Wordsworth could hardly at any of these stages have disapproved openly of the supernatural, or attributed Coleridge's adoption of it to any sort of discontent. What is more likely is that he looked upon it as having nothing to do with the revolution in poetic taste he was committed to bringing about. The earliest manifesto of the revolution was not the 1800 Preface, but the 1798 *Advertisement*, and there Wordsworth had nothing to say about the supernatural, or indeed about two kinds of poetry: he speaks only of 'the language of conversation in the middle and lower classes of society' and the 'natural delineation of human passions, human characters, and human incidents'. These remarks made necessary some sort of apology for the odd, archaic language of *The Ancient Mariner*, and Wordsworth explained that the poem 'was professedly written in imitation of the style, as well as the spirit of the elder poets; but with a few exceptions, the Author believes that the language adopted in it has been equally intelligible for these last three centuries'.

For Wordsworth's indifference to the supernatural in 1798 there is another explanation: he had simply outgrown it. If we look back over what is now available of his juvenilia – his school-boy and Cambridge verse – we find much of it luridly Gothic, peopled with ghastly skeletal forms, spectres in 'clanking chains', the 'druid sons' of Superstition, moving or shrieking in a landscape of ruined castles and sable mountains 'array'd/ In gloomy blank impervious shade'.[11] Wordsworth is not likely to have been pleased to recognize, as he might well have done, echoes of this juvenile verse in *The Ancient Mariner*. Norman Fruman has pointed to one possible example.[12] Lines 330, 337–9 of the de Selincourt text of *The Vale of Esthwaite* –

> His bones look'd sable through his skin . . .
> But from his trembling shadow broke
> Faint murmuring – sad and hollow moans
> As if the wind sigh'd through his bones –

may perhaps glimmer through lines 181, 195–6 of *The Ancient Mariner*:

> His bones were black with many a crack . . .
> A gust of wind starte up behind
> And whistled thro' his bones.

It is tempting to generalize a little from these particulars, and to think of Coleridge's supernatural as equivalent to, perhaps a development from, Wordsworth's Gothic. The supernatural and the Gothic did not serve the same poetic function, but they could have arisen from the same psychological origins – a fascination with terror, with the marvellous, with a realm of sensibility beyond the real. The fact that Coleridge came to his realm with an explorer's fresh delight just as Wordsworth, wearied, turned away from it, may help to account for some of the differences that divided the partners in *Lyrical Ballads* almost from the start.

IV

Soon after his return from Germany in the spring of 1799 Wordsworth began to voice uneasiness about the possible 'injury' *The Ancient Mariner* had done to *Lyrical Ballads*. Fearful that 'the old words and the strangeness of it have deterred readers from going on', he proposed to his publisher to 'put in its place some little things which would be more likely to suit the common taste' (*EY*, p. 264). This uneasiness would have hung like a cloud over the conversations that accompanied renewed work on *Lyrical Ballads*. On 6 April 1800, Coleridge arrived in Grasmere, and upon his arrival Wordsworth made known his intention of putting together a second edition, as Coleridge reported to Southey on 10 April. When he left on 4 May Coleridge took some of the new poems with him to deliver to

Davy in Bristol (who was to read proofs), but steady partnership did not resume until the end of June, when Coleridge returned to the North to settle in with his family. About two weeks after their arrival, in mid-July, the first of the series of folio sheets copied out by Coleridge with some help from Dorothy (but little from William) went off to the printer, and dispatch of these sheets, containing new poems and revisions of old poems, ran on at intervals up into December.

During this period of shared labour and ongoing disputation Wordsworth composed the Preface, which like the *Advertisement* of 1798 concentrated on his own poems and developed his own theoretical position on the issues that divided him from Coleridge. The omission of any mention of the supernatural was what must have prompted Coleridge to project, rather wistfully a few months later, the writing of one or two essays of his own – on the 'Marvellous' in poetry, and on the 'Preternatural' (*CL*, II, pp. 707, 716). In between sessions of copying out Wordsworth's poems for the printer Coleridge undertook some spotty revisions of *The Ancient Mariner*, which was dislodged from the opening of Volume I and buried in the next-to-last position, just ahead of *Tintern Abbey*. There was not much he could do to meet Wordsworth's complaint, shortly to be spelled out, that the mariner had 'no distinct character', but he did remove some of the 'strangeness' that Wordsworth had worried about. A good deal of archaic language was modernized, and some of the most vivid stanzas in the poem were simply dropped. These look like reasonably good specimens of Wordsworthian Gothic, but with a clinical intensity that makes them seem rather like the naturalized supernatural:

> The moonlight bay was white all o'er,
>   Till rising from the same,
> Full many shapes, that shadows were,
>   Like as of torches came.
>
> A little distance from the prow
>   Those dark-red shadows were;
> But soon I saw that my own flesh
>   Was red as in a glare.
>
> I turn'd my head in fear and dread,
>   And by the holy rood,
> The bodies had advanc'd, and now
>   Before the mast they stood.
>
> They lifted up their stiff right arms,
>   They held them strait and tight;
> And each right-arm burnt like a torch,
>   A torch that's borne upright.
> Their stony eye-balls glitter'd on

In the red and smoky light.

I pray'd and turn'd my head away
Forth looking as before.
There was no breeze upon the bay,
No wave against the shore.

Whether Coleridge made these excisions and revisions at his partner's direction cannot be known, nor can we know (though we can guess) who decided on the reductive sub-title 'A Poet's Reverie'. (Lamb found the sub-title as comical as 'Bottom the Weaver's declaration that he is not a Lion, but only the scenical representation of a Lion'.)[13] But the revisions are less revealing of the critical dialogues going on in Grasmere and Keswick than the extraordinary note to the poem which Wordsworth composed and sent off on 2 October (after Coleridge had gone, briefly, to visit his family). It is hard to think of a comparable gesture – a contemptuous apology for the 'defects' in a poem which is supposedly being printed against the desire of its author! Even the tone and the manner of the note betray the strength of feeling that must have animated the two poets' dialogues:

I cannot refuse myself the gratification [it begins] of informing such Readers as may have been pleased with this Poem, or with any part of it, that they owe their pleasure in some sort to me; as the Author was himself very desirous that it should be suppressed. The wish had arisen from a consciousness of the defects of the Poem and from a knowledge that many persons had been much displeased with it.

As he went on to spell out the defects in the 'Poem of my friend', Wordsworth focussed, as he did in a paired note to *The Thorn*, on the central issues that discriminated his understanding of a lyrical ballad from his partner's: the issues of the choice of a speaking character, of dramatic propriety, and of poetic language.[14]

However stung he may have been, Coleridge deferred his response until 1817, when he was able in his turn to itemize some defects in Wordsworth's poetry. In 1800 and 1801 he spoke nothing but admiration, singling out in letters to friends *Michael*, *Ruth*, and *The Brothers* as the finest new poems in the collection. Only *Ruth* can be thought of as a ballad, and the centre of the controversy between the partners is once again revealed by Coleridge's puzzled complaint, two years later, to Southey about Wordsworth's alterations in *Ruth* for the edition of 1802 (which put into a speaker's mouth observations that were earlier heard in the poet's). These, together with some of Wordsworth's recent ballad poems, forced Coleridge at long last to recognize 'a radical Difference in our theoretical opinions respecting Poetry' (*CL*, II, p. 830).

Christabel raised other problems between the partners. The history of

Coleridge's struggle to finish it is too well known to need rehearsal. His failure doubtless sharpened Wordsworth's exasperation, for it obliged him first to cancel a portion of the Preface (which he later restored) then to compose a long poem to fill up the gap in the volume (to Coleridge's failure we owe *Michael*). The old theoretical issues appear to have arisen exactly as they had with *The Ancient Mariner*: covering his failure Coleridge explained gracefully to Davy in October that *Christabel* was 'so much admired by Wordsworth, that he thought it indelicate to print two Volumes with *his name* in which so much of another man's was included – & which was of more consequence – the poem was in direct opposition to the very purpose for which the *Lyrical Ballads* were published' (*CL*, I, p. 631). It is not hard to judge which of these conflicting explanations was the true one.

More important, however, than theoretical disagreements were the humiliation and the sense of defeat which Coleridge had to endure, and which, joined with his other multiple afflictions, brought him to an end as a poet. His letter to Godwin of 25 March 1801, in which appears the terrible image of his own imagination as a burnt-out candle, looked back over a period of nine months – April to December 1800 – and it is possible to think of these nine months as the critical turning-point in Coleridge's life. They cover his move to the north of England, the birth of his third child, his realization that his marriage was finally hopeless, prolonged illness, and his irrevocable commitment to life-long dependency on laudanum – a sufficient catalogue of 'personal and domestic distress'. Heightening the distress was his persistent veneration for 'the giant Wordsworth', whose industry and genius seemed more and more to mock Coleridge's numb incapacities. Pathetic tokens of these incapacities lie scattered through Coleridge's letters and notebooks, some agonizingly candid, some muted. Towards the end of the nine-month period of gathering despair (30 October 1800), Coleridge jotted down a little dramatic meditation which we can now perceive to be one of the saddest entries in the whole range of his marvellous notebooks: 'He knew not what to do – something, he felt, must be done – he rose, drew his writing-desk before him – sate down, took the pen – & found that he knew not what to do' (*CN*, I, 834).

V

While the main outlines of Coleridge's theoretical notion of the ballad emerge from the story of the controversies that stretched over the years of his partnership with Wordsworth, our final understanding of it has to rest upon our interpretation of the brilliant ballads he wrote. It should be clear to any reader of *The Ancient Mariner* that what principally separates Coleridge from Wordsworth is not his theory of diction, or metre, or the management of narrative, but the allegorical bent of his imagination. It was the sort of imagination that could transmute the mist and snow, the sun the moon and the stars, into symbol clusters, and could lift a 'common Faery Tale' (his own phrase for *Christabel*) to the level of myth (*BL*, II, p. 238). The working of such an imagination remains a mystery, obliging us to grope for metaphors to render it comprehensible, and for that reason we should in the end be grateful to John Livingston Lowes for providing us such opulent variety to choose from. As a gesture of gratitude, it seems appropriate to let Lowes have the final word (page 67):

Well, the subliminal ego doubtless deals the cards, as the throng of sleeping images, at this call or that, move toward the light. But the fall of the cards accepted, the shaping spirit of imagination conceives and masterfully carries out the strategy of the game. Grant all you will to the involuntary and automatic operations of the Well – its blendings and fusings, each into each, of animalcules, and rainbows, and luminous tracks across the sea, and all the other elements of chaos. There still remains the architectonic imagination, moving, *sua sponte*, among the scattered fragments, and discerning, latent in their confusion, the pattern of a whole. And the shadow of a sail in an old travel-book and the rude parallelism of a pair of sketches of porpoises and dolphins – themselves among the recollections tumbling over one another in the dark – may through an act of imaginative vision gather up the whole chaos into consciousness as a poised and symmetrical shape of light.

There is little need of further comment . . . .

NOTES

[1] I cite the revised edition of 1930, reprinted Boston: page 55.
[2] I refer to *Coleridge on Imagination* (New York 1950).
[3] *Coleridge and Wordsworth: The Poetry of Growth* (Cambridge 1970), pp. 84–85.
[4] *Coleridge* (New York and London, 1968), pp. 47–8.
[5] In *The Art of the Lyrical Ballads* (Cambridge, Mass., 1973).
[6] In his 'Prefatory Note' in the edition of 1828.
[7] *Miscellanies* (London 1886), p. 140.
[8] Field's 'Memoirs' were quoted by Ernest de Selincourt in *The Early Wordsworth* (n.p. The English Association 1936), p. 28n.
[9] *Coleridge the Visionary* (London, 1959), p. 147.
[10] Coleridge sums up and quotes Wordsworth's letters in writing to William Taylor (*CL*, I, pp. 564–6).
[11] Quotations are from *The Vale of Esthwaite*, the de Selincourt text in Volume I of *The Poetical Works of William Wordsworth*.
[12] *Coleridge, the Damaged Archangel* (New York 1971), p. 320.
[13] As he wrote to Wordsworth on January 30, 1801: *The Letters of Charles and Mary Lamb*, ed. Edwin Marrs (3 vols. 1975–) I 266.
[14] The two notes appeared at the back of Volume I of the 1800 *Lyrical Ballads*.

'Radical Difference': Wordsworth and Coleridge, 1802

LUCY NEWLYN

Coleridge's growing sense of distance from Wordsworth was accentuated, not caused, by his 'own peculiar lot' in 1802; and it did not always produce the envy and exclusion so clearly present in the *Letter to Sara Hutchinson*. The two men were in fact moving, intellectually and creatively, in opposite directions. Wordsworth at times seemed oblivious of change, and wrote as though the closeness of their earlier relationship still existed. But Coleridge became increasingly aware of ways in which they differed. In a series of justly famous letters, written during this year, one sees him not merely acknowledging divergence, but also (with a sort of doggedness) tracking down its causes. 'I rather suspect', he writes to Robert Southey, in July,

that some where or other there is a radical Difference in our theoretical opinions respecting Poetry – / this I shall endeavour to go to the Bottom of – and acting the arbitrator between the old School & the New School hope to lay down some plain, & perspicuous, tho' not superficial, Canons of Criticism respecting Poetry.
(*CL*, II, p. 830)

This is the germ of *Biographia Literaria*. 'Radical Difference' is something Coleridge believes to have grown from his increasing dissatisfaction with the 1800 *Preface*. Wordsworth's claim there, that the language of ordinary life is appropriate for poetry, seems questionable to him, though he cannot yet say why. Two weeks earlier, he had written to Sotheby:

In my opinion, Poetry justifies, as *Poetry* independent of any other Passion, some new combinations of Language, & *commands* the omission of many others allowable in other compositions. Now Wordsworth, me saltem judice, has in his system not sufficiently admitted the former, & in his practice has too frequently sinned against the latter.
(*CL*, II, p. 812)

This seems clear enough: poetry must be granted a degree of autonomy, and should in some cases have an obligation to be selective in what it takes from ordinary life. Wordsworth, by implication, is too wholesale in his use of everyday language, and follows too rigidly the theory of the 1800

117

Preface. In October, however, writing to Thomas Wedgwood, Coleridge seems less sure: 'in point of poetic Diction I am not so well s [atisf] ied that you do not require a certain *Aloofness* from [the la] nguage of real Life, which I think deadly to Poetry' (*CL*, II, p. 877). George Watson, misinterpreting the comment, writes that Coleridge 'has moved so far from the Preface that he feels poetic diction to "require a certain *aloofness* from [the la] nguage of real life," '.[1] In fact, he means precisely the reverse. The 'you' of 'you do not require' does not mean 'one'; it refers directly to Thomas Wedgwood, who has just criticised some of Coleridge's poems for their 'feeble expressions & unpolished Lines' (*CL*, II, p. 876). 'I sometimes suspect', he goes on to explain,

that my foul Copy would often appear to general Readers more polished, than my fair Copy – many of the feeble & colloquial Expressions have been industriously substituted for others, which struck me as artificial, & not standing the test – as being neither the language of passion nor distinct Conceptions.

(*CL*, II, p. 877)

Here, then, one sees Coleridge returning to the values of the 1800 *Preface*. He is expressing his own preference for a colloquial 'language of passion', as opposed to the 'polished' and 'artificial' diction admired by his readers. And he is doing so in terms that seem entirely to contradict his statement of three months before. It is important, first, that he makes these comments about his own poetic practice, and is not likely, therefore, to be bluffing; second, that he is seriously implying criticism of a man he would normally flatter.[2] One can hardly doubt that he is expressing a genuine opinion, yet the change of mind, within three months, seems perverse. An explanation for the discrepancy is needed.

Coleridge's statement to Sotheby in July, 'Poetry justifies, as *Poetry* independent of any other Passion, some new combinations of Language', does not deny the connection between poetry and passion; it requires that the language of real life should be refined to give poetry its intenseness. There is nothing inconsistent here with the thinking that lies behind the 1800 *Preface* – 'the Reader cannot be too often reminded that Poetry is passion: it is the history or science of feelings'[3] – and it is important that Coleridge remains faithful to this belief right through the period of his re-thinking, and on into *Biographia* itself.[4] Taking 'passion' as a central criterion, he first states carefully in Chapter Seventeen that 'the property of passion is not to *create*, but to set in increased activity' (*BLS*, II, p. 42), then makes a distinction between the poetic and undiscriminating use of ordinary language:

It is indeed very possible to adopt in a poem the unmeaning repetitions, habitual phrases, and other blank counters, which an unfurnished or confused understanding interposes at short intervals, in order to keep hold of his subject, which is still slipping from him, and to give him time for recollection. . . . But what assistance to the poet, or ornament to the poem, these can supply, I am at a loss to conjecture.

'Nothing', he continues, making clear his distinctions,

assuredly can differ either in origin or in mode more widely from the *apparent* tautologies of intense and turbulent feeling, in which the passion is of greater and of longer endurance than to be exhausted or satisfied by a single representation of the image or incident exciting it. (*BL*, II, p. 57)

Reading between the lines, one suspects that Coleridge sees in Wordsworth an inability to distinguish between these two kinds of language. It is not clear, however, whether he thinks of the lack of discrimination as a feature of Wordsworth's theory, or merely an occasional failure in his poetry. In the letter to Sotheby he puts forward both possibilities, but conducts his argument on a largely theoretical basis. In *Biographia* (where his main aim is to prove a disparity between the claims of the 1800 *Preface* and the poetry itself) he argues, again, in terms of the theory. But what, in both cases, is the real source of his unease?

To return to the letter Coleridge writes to Southey in July:

altho' Wordsworth's Preface is half a child of my own Brain / & so arose out of Conversations, so frequent, that with few exceptions we could scarcely either of us perhaps positively say, which first started any particular Thought . . . yet I am far from going all lengths with Wordsworth / He has written lately a number of Poems (32 in all) some of them of considerable Length (the longest 160 Lines) the greater number of these to my feelings very excellent Compositions / but here & there a daring Humbleness of Language & Versification, and a strict adherence to matter of fact, even to prolixity, that startled me / his alterations likewise in Ruth perplexed me / and I have thought & thought & thought again / & have not had my doubts solved by Wordsworth (*CL*, II, p. 830)

The criticisms seem to be levelled at individual poems, but it is not easy to say which. If one takes it that Coleridge has the language of real life in mind, only a small group out of the 32 lyrics is eligible. *The Leechgatherer* in its early form is presumably the poem estimated at '160 lines'; there is a scattering of 'lyrical ballads' like *The Sailor's Mother*, *Alice Fell*, *Beggars* (and possibly, *The Affliction of Margaret*); and Coleridge might also include such playful, garrulous poems as *The Tinker*, *To A Skylark* and *The Barberry Tree*. In each case, his criticism would have a good deal of justice. *The Leechgatherer*, before Wordsworth revises it, might easily be condemned for its 'strict adherence to matter of fact, even to prolixity' – indeed Sara Hutchinson's comment that it is 'tedious' amounts to the same thing.[5] Equally, the ballads of 1802 are a disappointment after their earlier counterparts. They slip into banality, and often seem too close to the events that inspired them. Of *Beggars*, for instance, Dorothy writes in her Journal for 13 March:

> After tea I read to William that account of the little Boys belonging to the tall woman and *an unlucky thing it was for he could not escape from those very words*, and so he could not write the poem. He left it unfinished and went tired to Bed.
>
> (*DWJ*, I, p. 123, my italics)

As for poems like *The Tinker* and *The Skylark*, there cannot be much doubt as to their 'daring Humbleness of Language & Versification':

> Right before the Farmer's door
> Down he sits his brows he knits:
> Then his hammer he rouzes
> Batter, batter, batter
> He begins to clatter
> And while the work is going on
> Right good ale he bouzes.   (*The Tinker*, ll. 9–15)

But even having acknowledged the appropriateness of Coleridge's remarks (and they are largely, it seems, value-judgements) one has not arrived at the centre of his critical position. Something in his reaction against Wordsworth's lyrics goes deeper than his specific objections might suggest, causing him first to make vague approving comments he cannot support ('the greater number of these to my feelings very excellent Compositions'), then to search for labels like 'daring Humbleness' or 'strict adherence to matter of fact' to explain his unease. The labels are not arbitrary, but they apply to so small a proportion of the lyrics that one senses deeper underlying reservations which Coleridge is not choosing to acknowledge.

Other letters, written during 1802, tell us a good deal more. The famous one to Sotheby, written on 10 September, contains a reaffirmation of values supposedly shared by Wordsworth in 1798:

> Nature has her proper interest; & he will know what it is, who believes & feels, that every Thing has a Life of it's own, & that we are all *one Life*. A Poet's *Heart* & *Intellect* should be *combined*, *intimately* combined & *unified*, with the great appearances in Nature – & not merely held in solution & loose mixture with them, in the shape of formal Similies. I do not mean to *exclude* these formal Similies – there are moods of mind, in which they are natural – pleasing moods of mind, & such as a Poet will often have, & sometimes express; but they are not his highest, & most appropriate moods.   (*CL*, II, p. 864)

The poet Coleridge has in mind is Bowles, whose 'perpetual trick of *moralizing* every thing' goes against his own most basic requirement: that 'every phrase, every metaphor, every personification, should have it's justifying cause in some *passion* either of the Poet's mind, or of the

Characters described by the poet' (*CL*, ɪɪ, p. 812). Judged by this criterion, Bowles is bound to fail. His poetry, at one time greatly admired and imitated by Coleridge, now seems to deny the values of the 'One Life'.

Coleridge would not have intended it to do so, but his critique of Bowles applies equally well to the Wordsworth of 1802. When he makes the concession – 'I do not mean to *exclude* these formal Similies – there are moods of mind, in which they are natural – pleasing moods of mind . . .' – he might very easily be thinking of *To A Butterfly*, or *To A Daisy*. It is interesting, in this connection, to notice that a number of Wordsworth's lyrics are grouped in 1807 under the heading 'Moods of my own Mind'. There is an acceptance of limitation in the slightness of the label, as though Wordsworth were himself conceding that 'they are not his highest, & most appropriate moods'. If one takes the analogy further, Coleridge's phrase 'merely held in solution & loose mixture' exactly describes the quality of Wordsworth's response in spring 1802:

> Oft do I sit by thee at ease,
> And weave a web of similies,
> Loose types of Things through all degrees,
>   Thoughts of thy raising;
> And many a fond and idle name
> I give to thee, for praise or blame,
> As is the humour of the game,
>   While I am gazing (*To A Daisy*, ll. 9–16)

Here, as in many of the 1802 lyrics, Wordsworth is writing about the workings of fancy, and is intrigued by the possibilities it opens up. Fancy is a sort of loose associationism. It does not bind thoughts and images tightly together, but allows them to proliferate, as though they had a will of their own: 'Loose types of Things through all degrees, / *Thoughts of thy raising*'. By implication, the process is rapid and aimless. It involves the thinker, not in a full engagement with the natural object, but in a sequence of namings and re-namings, which certainly do not seem to have their 'justifying cause in some passion . . . of the poet's mind'. Wordsworth is not making claims for fancy as more than a 'game'; in fact, he stresses its 'ease', 'fond'-ness, 'idle'-ness and 'humour'. Yet there is something magical in 'weav[ing] a web of similies' which gives the process a creative status. Later, in his *Preface* to *Poems*, 1815, Wordsworth writes, 'Fancy depends upon the rapidity and profusion with which she scatters her thoughts and images . . . or she prides herself upon the curious subtilty and the successful elaborations with which she can detect their lurking affinities' (*Prose Works*, ɪɪɪ, p. 36). This is by no means a limited claim: fancy is capable of 'insinuating herself into the heart of objects with creative activity' (*ibid*, p. 30). The language Wordsworth uses – 'curious subtilty', 'detect', 'lurking' and 'insinuating' – gives her an unpredictable, almost insidious, power. One recalls that in *Prelude*, Book Eight, the '*wilfulness* of fancy and conceit', intruding into human relationships, gives 'them new importance to the mind' (1805, VIII, 520–2). It is in this context that Wordsworth first defines the relation between fancy and passion:

> My present theme
> Is to retrace the way that led me on
> Through Nature to the love of human-kind;
> Nor could I with such object overlook
> The influence of this power which turned itself
> Instinctively to human passions . . .   (1805, VIII, 586–91)

Fancy may be capricious, but it is redeemed by its connections with human feelings. They allow it to find its way 'into the heart of objects' – to merge, in other words, with the creative imagination.

For the Coleridge of 1798, such merging had been a possibility. *Frost at Midnight* – in so far as poetry of this kind can offer definitions – had done so in Wordsworthian terms. Fancy (emblematised in the fluttering movement of the '*stranger*') had seemed at first to be a form of entrapment: evidence of the 'self-watching subtilising mind' (l. 27). But through a sequence of associations, activated and validated by emotion, it had led to the memory within a memory of church bells, which were 'most like articulate sounds of things to come' (l. 38). The 'most believing superstitious wish' of childhood (l. 29) – as opposed, by implication, to the introversion of the adult – was thus able to guide Coleridge from pure associationism into imagination. Fancy, in the process, had been exonerated. All quotations, here, refer to the text of *Frost at Midnight* published in the Quarto volume of 1798. When he came to revise the poem for publication in *Sibylline Leaves*, Coleridge made alterations that were in keeping with the disparagement of fancy that one sees in *Biographia*. Completely missing from the best known published text are lines in which he had carefully juxtaposed the seriousness and frivolity of fancy's workings, seeing creative potential alongside idleness:

> But still the living spirit in our frame,
> That loves not to behold a lifeless thing,
> Transfuses into all it's own delights
> Its own volition, sometimes with deep faith,
> And sometimes with fantastic playfulness . . .   (ll. 21–5)

In their place one finds the famous and much quoted lines about solipsism, in which, with a tone almost of contempt, Coleridge describes the fluttering '*stranger*'

> Whose puny flaps and freaks the idling Spirit
> By its own moods interprets, every where
> Echo or mirror seeking of itself,
> And makes a toy of Thought.   (ll. 20–3)

Damage is done, in the process of revision, to the logic of the poem: for how, if the workings of the fancy are so narcissistic, can release from the self be achieved? But in its own right, the alteration is fascinating, as a record of the major change that Coleridge's thinking has undergone.

All the evidence suggests that it is already an articulated change by 1802. The merging of fancy and imagination, possible for Wordsworth not only in the *Prelude* lines already quoted (which belong to October 1804), but right through into the *Preface* of 1815, is already by 1802 a closed option for Coleridge. *Biographia* – implicitly refuting the 1815 *Preface* – tells one very briefly what the division between these two faculties is, but the letter to Sotheby, written fifteen years earlier, gives us a clearer idea of why it should exist:

It must occur to every Reader that the Greeks in their religious poems address always the Numina Loci, the Genii, the Dryads, the Naiads, &c &c – All natural Objects were *dead* – mere hollow Statues – but there was a Godkin or Goddessling *included* in each – In the Hebrew Poetry you find nothing of this poor Stuff – as poor in genuine Imagination, as it is mean in Intellect – / At best, it is but Fancy, or the aggregating Faculty of the mind – not *Imagination*, or the *modifying*, and *co-adunating* Faculty. This the Hebrew Poets appear to me to have possessed beyond all others – & next to them the English. In the Hebrew Poets each Thing has a Life of it's own, & yet they are all one Life.   (*CL*, II, pp. 865–6)

The connection between this and Coleridge's criticism of Bowles must be apparent. Greek poetry deals with natural objects as though they were 'dead' – 'mere hollow Statues'. Any life they might seem to have is conferred on them, or 'included' in them, by an essentially limited faculty of the mind. This faculty interprets things not as parts or symbols of a whole, but as separate, fixed entities – each with its own diminutive property of conferred life. To put it in the terms applied to Bowles: imagination causes the '*Heart & Intellect*' to be '*combined, intimately* combined & *unified*, with the great appearances in Nature'; fancy holds the mind and natural objects 'in solution & loose mixture . . . in the shape of formal Similies' (*CL*, II, p. 864). Coleridge makes no allowance, as Wordsworth does, for the connection between fancy and human emotion. Godkins and Goddesslings do not have their 'justifying cause in some passion . . . of the Poet's mind', but are merely a decoration or afterthought. As he puts it, dismissively, in *Biographia*:

FANCY . . . has no other counters to play with, but fixities and definites. The Fancy is indeed no other than a mode of Memory emancipated from the order of time and space; and blended with, and modified by that empirical phenomenon of the will, which we express by the word CHOICE. But equally with the ordinary memory [it] must receive all its materials ready made from the law of association.   (*BL*, I, p. 305)

If Fancy really is no more than 'a mode of Memory emancipated from the order of time and space', it is both limited and dangerous – limited, because it can play only with 'fixities and definites' (the ready made materials of 'the law of association'); dangerous, because it has the capacity to run riot, destroying true poetry. In this respect it resembles the 'false diction' referred to by Wordsworth as 'the gaudiness and inane phraseology of many modern writers' in the *Advertisement* to *Lyrical Ballads*, 1798 (*Prose Works*, I, p. 116), and later defined more fully in the 1800 *Preface*:

Poets . . . think that they are conferring honour upon themselves and their art in proportion as they separate themselves from the sympathies of men, and indulge in *arbitrary and capricious habits of expression* in order to furnish food for fickle tastes and fickle appetites of their own creation.
                                                (*Prose Works*, I, p. 124; my italics)

There is no obvious connection between fancy and the language of ordinary life. But for Coleridge in 1802 they are felt to have an affinity. Just as fancy can be 'insinuating' in the *wrong* sense (like false diction, not like a 'creative activity'), so too can the 'daring Humbleness' of Wordsworth's language. To return, for a moment, to *Biographia*, and the end of Chapter Seventeen:

It is indeed very possible to adopt in a poem the unmeaning repetitions, habitual phrases, and other blank counters, which an unfurnished or confused understanding interposes at short intervals, in order to keep hold of his subject, which is still slipping from him, and to give him time for recollection; or in mere aid of vacancy, as in the scanty companies of a country stage the same player pops backwards and forwards, in order to prevent the appearance of empty spaces . . .

The phrase 'blank counters' and the stress on automatic movement – 'the same player pops backwards and forwards' – convey Coleridge's horror of anything that breaks down the poet's control of his own words, destroying the connection between language and emotion.[6] False diction, fancy, and 'daring Humbleness' have it in common that they are anarchic. They threaten the sanctity of poetic language, which should be (as Milton puts it) 'simple, sensuous, passionate'.

When Coleridge quotes this phrase, in his letter to Southey of July (*CL*,

II, p. 830), it is in the context of his dissatisfaction with Wordsworth. One feels that he turns to Milton in reaction against Wordsworth, because Milton allows him to think in his customary, symbolic, terms. Two months later, in the letter to Sotheby, he gives a long and detailed analysis of the famous passage in *Comus* about 'Haemony'. It is here that one sees him most carefully defining his own ideals:

all the puzzle [amongst Milton's commentators] is to find out what Plant Haemony is – which they discover to be the English Spleenwort – & decked out, as a mere play & licence of poetic Fancy, with all the strange properties suited to the purpose of the Drama – They thought little of Milton's platonizing Spirit – who wrote nothing without an interior meaning. 'Where more is meant, than meets the ear' is true of himself beyond all writers. He was so great a Man, that he seems to have considered fiction as profane, unless where it is consecrated by being emblematic of some Truth. . . . Do look at the passage – apply it as an Allegory of Christianity, or to speak more precisely of the Redemption of the Cross – every syllable is full of Light! (*CL*, II, pp. 866–7)

Coleridge preserves, here, an implicit distinction between the Bowlesian 'trick of *moralizing* everything', and the power Milton has to perceive and create through symbols. His interpretation of the passage from *Comus* seems far-fetched, and tells us little about Milton; but it does show how strongly Coleridge believes that poetry is 'consecrated by being emblematic of some Truth'. And it reveals, moreover, what sort of 'Truth' he has in mind:

Now what is Haemony? Αἷμα-οἶνος – Blood-wine. – And he took the wine & blessed it, & said – This is my Blood – / the great Symbol of the Death on the Cross. – There is a general Ridicule cast on all allegorizers of Poets – read Milton's prose works, & observe whether he was one of those who joined in this ridicule. (*CL*, II, p. 867)

Coleridge values symbolic vision, in this sacramental sense, more highly than any other mode of perception or creation.[7] Hebrew poetry comes nearest to embodying it, because 'In the Hebrew poets each Thing has a Life of its own, & yet they are all one Life.' Bowles and the Greek poets are farthest from it, because according to them 'All Natural objects [are] *dead.*' Neither words nor things point beyond themselves, or carry religious implications.

Coleridge is, in fact, with an extraordinary consistency, restating beliefs which go as far back as 1796. 'Is not Milton a *sublimer* poet than Homer or Virgil?' he had asked Thelwall, in a letter written in December of that year:

Are not his Personages more sublimely cloathed? And do you not know, that there is not perhaps *one* page in Milton's Paradise Lost, in which he has not borrowed his imagery from the *Scriptures*? I allow, and rejoice that *Christ* appealed only to the understanding & the affections; but I affirm that, after reading Isaiah, or St Paul's Epistle to the Hebrews, Homer & Virgil are disgustingly *tame* to me, & Milton himself barely tolerable.   (*CL*, I, p. 281)

Measured according to Coleridge's standards, which have remained the same in kind (if not in degree) since 1796, Wordsworth fails absolutely. By rights, he should be in the company of the 'Hebrew' poets: that, Coleridge feels, is the status he deserves for his earlier writing. But the lyrics of 1802 are limited, and lacking in symbolic potential. They reveal, by implication, a new poet: one who is content, like the bad commentators on Milton, that things should be 'decked out, as a mere play & license of poetic Fancy' (*CL*, II, p. 866) – one who has more affinities with Bowles, the discarded hero, than with the great precursors in a symbolic tradition.

This lowering of Wordsworth's status is confirmed for Coleridge by his neglect of *The Recluse*, which in its original conception had been designed to celebrate the 'One Life', and which he himself goes on thinking of in such terms.[8] Writing to Poole in October 1803, when he briefly assumes Wordsworth has gone back to working on it, Coleridge stresses the waste that is implied by the shorter lyrics: 'The habit . . . of writing such a multitude of small Poems was . . . hurtful to him. . . . I really consider it as a misfortune, that [he] ever deserted his former mountain Track to wander in Lanes & allies' (*CL*, II, p. 1013). In returning to *The Recluse*, Wordsworth is re-entering his 'natural Element'. He is confirming the values originally given him by Coleridge, in 1798, and writing a 'great work necessarily comprehending his attention & Feelings within the circle of great objects & elevated Conceptions' (*ibid.*) – a work, in other words, which has genuine affinities with Milton or 'Hebrew' poetry.[9]

Coleridge seems as a rule to have found it nearly impossible to analyse, or confront, the real source of his reservations about Wordsworth's writing. For an accurate, and in some ways moving, picture of his confusion at having to criticise the friend, 'to whom for the more substantial Third of a Life [he has] been habituated to look up', and for whom 'Love . . . begun and throve and knit it's joints in the perception of his Superiority', one has only to look at the letter written in May 1815, hesitantly explaining his reservations about *The Excursion* (*CL*, IV, pp. 571–3), but never once openly facing the depth of disappointment he feels. By comparison, the letter to Poole of 1803, quoted above, is unusually honest, since the emotional basis for the criticism it offers is tacitly acknowledged. It is a letter that should put Coleridge's exploratory criticisms of 1802 in perspective. Phrases like 'daring Humbleness of Language & Versification' or 'strict adherence to matter of fact, even to prolixity' (*CL*, II, p. 830) stand out as over-specific labels which are used to rationalize, even to explain away, the sense of disillusionment Coleridge is actually feeling. One could argue that this is simply a matter of articulation: that he is still wondering, in 1802, what is the cause of the unease, and that by 1803 he has things clearer in his own mind. It seems more likely, however, that 1802 is a time when he makes intuitive value-judgements, then blocks them on an intellectual level. This is partly because the reverence for his friend is a habit that sticks whatever else is changed; partly because he is surprised that Wordsworth, of all people, should be content to achieve so little.

Coleridge's thinking about fancy and imagination, cryptically summarised in *Biographia*, has a private history (part emotional, part intellectual) which I have tried in this essay to unfold. It goes back to the period in these writers' relationship when two separate things were happening: Wordsworth was composing his most overtly fanciful poetry, and Coleridge for the first time was downgrading fancy to the merely mechanical. A causal connection between the two cannot of course be absolutely proven, but Coleridge's disappointment and sense of betrayal, even when disguised, speak for themselves. As is so often the case with these two writers, the real causes of fundamental difference are not acknowledged. It is the disparity between, on the one hand, Coleridge's increasingly confirmed symbolic thinking, and, on the other, Wordsworth's entrenched literal-mindedness, that explains the growing divergence in 1802. Not, as Coleridge would have it, a disagreement about poetic diction. 'Radical Difference', then, is a more appropriate phrase than either poet perhaps realised: Coleridge's famous distinction between fancy and imagination rests on a profound, though unvoiced, criticism of his friend.

Notes

[1] *Biographia Literaria*, ed. George Watson (Everyman, 1975), p. xi.

[2] 'You are a perfect electrometer in these things' he confides to Wedgwood earlier in the same letter (*CL*, II, p. 877) – using a phrase he had once applied to Dorothy Wordsworth (*CL*, I, p. 331).

[3] See the Note to *The Thorn* in *Lyrical Ballads*, 1800.

[4] See particularly, *BL*, II, pp. 40–1. That Wordsworth too maintains the belief can be seen in his letter to Thelwall of January 1804, where he speaks of 'the passion of the subject', 'the passion of the metre', 'the Passion of the sense', and adds that he can scarcely 'admit any limits to the dislocation of the verse . . . that may not be justified by some passion or other' (*EY*, pp. 434–5).

[5] 'You speak of [the Leechgatherer's] speech as tedious', Wordsworth writes to Sara in June, outraged by her recent letter: 'everything is tedious when one does not read with the feelings of the Author – *The Thorn* is tedious

to hundreds; and so is the *Idiot Boy* to hundreds. It is in the character of the old man to tell his story in a manner which an *impatient* reader must necessarily feel as tedious' (*EY*, p. 367). The extreme defensiveness is typical of Wordsworth's state of mind in 1802, but the revisions made to *The Leechgatherer*, as a direct consequence of Sara's criticisms, show his absorption of her point of view.

6 Coleridge is not far, here, from Wordsworth's fear of anarchic language, described in the second of his *Essays on Epitaphs* as 'a counter-spirit, unremittingly and noiselessly at work to derange, to subvert, to lay waste, to vitiate, and to dissolve' (*Prose Works*, II, p. 85).

7 For comparable definitions of the sacramental, see *The Destiny of Nations*, ll. 18–20, *The Statesman's Manual* (*SM*, pp. 29–30), and *CN*, II, 2546. Robert Barth, S. J., in *The Symbolic Imagination, Coleridge and the Romantic Tradition* (Princeton, 1977), examines this aspect of Coleridge's thought in detail.

8 See the letter to Wordsworth of *c.* 10 September 1799, which clearly connects the idea of *The Recluse* with 'hopes of the amelioration of mankind' (*CL*, I, p. 527), and that of May 1815, in which the same idealistic claims are still preserved (*CL*, IV, pp. 574–15).

9 It was presumably Coleridge's admiration for 'Hebrew' poetry that made him write his *Hymn before Sunrise in the Vale of Chamouny* (September, 1802), which strains after religious sublimity in a sequence of sub-Miltonic exclamations.

Imagining Wordsworth: 1797 – 1807 – 1817

RICHARD GRAVIL

I

The symbiosis of Coleridge and Wordsworth is a well attested literary fact. One may debate the detail, and one may question some extrapolations of cause and effect, but no critic of the period can doubt that the verse of *Tintern Abbey*, for instance, and the feeling of *Frost at Midnight*, are the fruits of an exchange which was not merely intimate, but at its best generative of extensions of the human imagination. It is equally the case, however, though this is a view less often heard, that the long-term effect of the friendship was a weakening of each poet's confidence in his own identical voice. Wordsworth's 'descent upon Coleridge' is fairly well documented: there is evidence for supposing that Wordsworth's insensitivity to Coleridge's imagination was a primary cause of its extinction. Paradoxically, however, it has also been argued that Coleridge's imaginative efflorescence became dependent upon the proximity of his brother poet.[1]

That Wordsworth both fostered and stifled Coleridge's distinctive poetic voice is almost certainly true. But the idea that Coleridge was the weaker personality, which is in some sense assumed by all the current accounts of their relationship, seems to me to be open to radical question. Coleridge, after all, pursued his own course through life, and came to be regarded as the arbiter of Wordsworth's merit. Wordsworth not merely accepted Coleridge's status in that regard, to a degree which borders upon self-immolation, but devoted the major part of his lifetime to a labour ordained for him by Coleridge. He undertook to write, at Coleridge's behest, a long philosophical poem expressive of the younger poet's views to which he strove to subordinate his own. At the same time he subjected the more natural products of his own imagination to corrective revision in accordance with Coleridge's critical strictures.

With its critically retrogressive strictures on Wordsworth's theory and practice, *Biographia Literaria* is part of the history of a sustained rivalry, the most substantial single instalment of a running battle which goes back to 1798.[2] As Coleridge says in a letter of 1817, 'To the faults and defects of Wordsworth's poems I have been far more alive than his detractors, even from the first publication of the Lyrical Ballads, though for a long course of years my opinions were sacred to his own ear' (*CL*, IV, p. 780). Correspondence in 1801–3 with Godwin, Southey and Poole, including comment on the perversity of Fox and Lamb in preferring the poems Coleridge dislikes, makes clear the 'feelings of hostility' Coleridge already entertains towards those poems which he tosses and gores in 1817. That Wordsworth's reciprocal failure – and publicly owned failure – to respond to *The Ancient Mariner* fuels the long stand-off is not in doubt. Coleridge read in cold print in 1800 that:

The poem of my Friend has indeed great defects; first that the principal person has no distinct character . . . : secondly, that he does not act . . . thirdly that the events . . . do not produce each other; and lastly, that his imagery is somewhat too laboriously accumulated.

Against these perhaps characteristic defects, Wordsworth concedes some excellences too: *The Ancient Mariner* has 'many delicate touches of passion', 'beautiful images', 'unusual felicity of language' and versification both 'harmonious and artfully varied'.[3] It is barely surprising that as late as 1818 Coleridge still resented the Wordsworth household's 'cold praise and effective discouragement of every attempt of mine to roll onward in a distinct current of my own – who admitted that the Ancient Mariner and the Christabel . . . were not without merit, but were abundantly anxious to acquit their judgement of any blindness to the very numerous defects'. Nor, perhaps, is it surprising that in 1817 Coleridge chooses to balance Wordsworth's numerous defects against such oddly unimpressive excellences as 'an austere purity of language both grammatically and logically', 'a corresponding weight and sanity of the thoughts and sentiments', 'the sinewy strength and sanity of single lines and paragraphs', 'the perfect truth of nature in his images and descriptions' (an excellence somewhat nullified by his disparagement in the first paragraph of this chapter of 'faithful adherence to essential nature'), and 'a meditative pathos'. Until Coleridge comes to 'the gift of imagination in the highest and strictest sense of the word', compared with his less than graceful exertions of fancy, the list is faintly damning (*BL*, Chapter 22).

Wordsworth's censure of supernatural incident in poetry, in *Peter Bell*, and Coleridge's publication of 'The Three Graves' with its needling disclaimer that whatever Wordsworth might think, this kind of thing isn't poetry, are part of this history of almost marital sniping. So, I suspect is the sardonic postscript to the Duddon sonnets of 1820 in which one may hear a riposte to Coleridge's criticism (in a letter of 1815) of *The Excursion*. Conscious of the similarity in theme between his own 'Duddon' and Coleridge's unwritten 'Brook', Wordsworth admits to trespassing upon ground preoccupied, '*at least as far as intention went*, by Mr. Coleridge, who more than twenty years ago *used to speak of writing* a rural poem to be entitled "The Brook" '. After some further phrases admitting of a sardonic inflection, Wordsworth expresses the hope that his sonnets 'may remind Mr. Coleridge of his own more comprehensive design, *and induce him to fulfil it*'.[4] With one emphasis, 'more comprehensive design' must allude to the plans for 'The Brook', but with another it could well encompass Coleridge's comprehensive expectations of *The Excursion*.

The question, then, is not whether the friendship between Coleridge and Wordsworth masked a deep theoretical and imaginative rivalry, but what lay at the root of that continuing struggle. Why is *Biographia* so hostile to a large part of Wordsworth's poetry, and what broader ideal – present to Coleridge's mind in 1817, but perhaps from the outset of their friendship – licenses the severity of his critique?

There is some substance, one may feel, in Marilyn Butler's suggestion in *Romantics, Rebels and Reactionaries* (Oxford, 1981), that the *Biographia* should be seen in the context of ideological revisionism. In the chapter devoted to Coleridge's abhorrence of revolutionary principles, Chapter Ten of *Biographia*, Coleridge observes that Wordsworth's conversation at Nether Stowey 'extended to almost all subjects except physics and politics; with the latter he never troubled himself'. It would seem that, in the interests of commending Wordsworth to the propagandists of reaction, Coleridge is not content with assisting at the obsequies for Wordsworth's levelling muse: he extends to Wordsworth, in retrospect, his own 'withdrawal from the consideration of immediate causes', as he had put it in his letter to George Coleridge in April 1798. To depoliticise Wordsworth, after all, was a relatively minor imaginative exercise, for one who could say to Crabb Robinson, in December 1810, of no less a precursor than John Milton, that he was 'a most determined Aristocrat . . . and he would have been most decidedly hostile to the Jacobins of the present day' (*Misc C*, p. 388).

But Coleridge's imaginative revision of his friend began far earlier, and needs another hypothesis. The author of 'Constancy to an Ideal Object', it has been observed, is one who always aspired to liberate being from the accidents of temporal existence. 'Wordsworth' in this sense is a creation of Coleridge's need, an ideal Wordsworth liberated from the accidents of the existing Wordsworth's particular concerns. Coleridge did not rewrite 'Wordsworth' in 1817: he began to create the Wordsworth he revered as early as 1797 – from the earliest references to his friend as a Shakespeare without the 'inequalities' (June 1797), and an 'amiable giant' (March 1798). The ideal object to which Coleridge remained thus constant was the creation of a Wordsworth who is defined toward the close of *Biographia* – some two years after the publication of *The Excursion*, and a decade after Coleridge had heard *The Prelude*, as 'capable of producing . . . the FIRST GENUINE PHILOSOPHIC POEM'.

The process of transforming Wordsworth began early, but did not run smoothly. A 'semi-atheist' in 1796, Wordsworth has progressed by May 1798 to being one who 'loves and venerates Christianity', though Coleridge admits 'I wish he did more' (*CL*, I, pp. 216, 410). In May 1799 Coleridge is lamenting that the amiable giant 'has hurtfully segregated and isolated his being' (to Poole, *CL*, I, p. 491), which develops into an anxiety, by October 1803, 'lest a film should rise and thicken on his moral eye' (*CL*, II, p. 1013). Nevertheless, Coleridge can still, in January 1804, prophesy immortality to *The Recluse* as long as it is 'a faithful transcript of his own most august and innocent life, of his own habitual Feeling and Modes of seeing and hearing' (to Sharp, *CL*, II, p. 1024).

Corresponding entries in the Notebooks are still more illuminating than the letters. The Notebook equivalent of a well-known letter contains a strange metaphor of enshrinement:

I am sincerely glad that he has bidden farewell to all small poems – & is devoting himself to his great work – grandly imprisoning while it deifies his Attention & Feelings within the Sacred Circle and Temple Walls of great Objects & elevated conceptions.   (*CN*, I, 1546)

In the same month, October 1803, an entry on envy begins by analysing his reasons for feeling 'unkindly used' by Wordsworth.

A. thought himself unkindly used by B. – he had exerted himself for B. with what warmth! honouring, praising B. beyond himself, etc. etc. – B. selfish – feeling all Fire respecting every trifle of his own – quite backward to poor A. The up, askance, pig look, in the Boat, etc. Soon after this A. felt distinctly little ugly touchlets of Pain and little Shrinkings Back at the Heart, at the report that B. had written a new Poem/ an excellent one! & he saw the faults of B. and all that belonged to B. and detested himself dwelling upon them, etc.

At this point Coleridge makes a striking discovery.

And what was all this? – Evidently the instinct of all fine minds to *totalise* – to make a *perfectly congruous whole* of every character – & pain at the being obliged to admit incongruities . . .   (*CN*, I, 1606)

In an interesting aside, Coleridge compares his resentment of Wordsworth's incongruities with his resentment at Mr Pitt having been the author of the Irish Union, thereby subverting A's theory of 'Pitt's contemptibility'.

A later and painfully moving entry (October 1805) combines a comparison between Wordsworth and Empedocles, with a desire that Wordsworth might be perfected by an infusion of Coleridge's own spirit:

To W. in the progression of Spirit/ once Simonides, or Empedocles or both in one? O that my spirit purged by Death of its weaknesses, which are alas! my identity might flow into thine, and live and act in thee, and be Thou.

(*CN*, II, 2712)

Yet another entry laments how Wordsworth – immured within those elevated conceptions – ceases to include Coleridge in the old equality, and begins to pronounce, even to Coleridge, on 'points of morals, wisdom and the sacred muses' (*CN*, II, 2750).

Such entries reveal a stylites syndrome very clearly: Wordsworth, set upon his pillar by Coleridge, and kept there by Coleridge's entreaty, injures Coleridge's feelings by an increasing assumption of superiority. Wordsworth's persistence in modes of poetry which do not interest Coleridge is taken, in part, as a slight. More deeply, such dilatoriness contributes to an accumulation of disappointment and resentment.

Yet in the main, by 1799, Coleridge had found himself an amanuensis of unusual calibre. Wordsworth, captive and captivated, would spend the greater part of his creative life attempting to write a poem more dear to Coleridge than to himself . More than this, he meekly revises his other and more personal work in the light of Coleridge's unremitting criticism: and from early on, responds to the insidious pressure of generous praise for any verse which expresses Coleridgean conceptions in modes congenial to Coleridge. It is almost as though Wordsworth adopts Coleridge's view of himself – as an emergent bard undergoing necessary metamorphoses on the way to an end ordained by Coleridge.

Labouring dutifully at the philosophical poem, Wordsworth finds an ingenious excuse to produce something more congenial: he writes *The Prelude*, to which Coleridge accords generous praise in every respect except one: it is not (I will return for my reason for saying this) '*a Philosophical poem*'.

II

My suggestion that Coleridge denied to *The Prelude* the status of 'a Philosophical poem' conflicts with one's sense that he valued it above *The Excursion*, and saw in it philosophic themes philosophically handled. We have not only the late observation that it was 'superior on the whole to The Excursion' (a not unqualified commendation found in the *Table Talk*, 21 July 1832 [*Misc C*, p. 411]), but the fresher testimony of January 1807, in his poem *To William Wordsworth: composed on the night after his recitation of a poem on the growth of an individual mind.* Wordsworth's 'prophetic lay', he then recorded, was a pioneering investigation of human growth, of nature and nurture, of perception and of the creativity of perception.

> Of the foundations and the building up
> Of a Human Spirit thou hast dared to tell
> What may be told, to the understanding mind
> Revealable.   (ll. 5–8)[5]

Coleridge's response is couched in the vocabulary of friendly allusion. Wordsworth's poem, the later version suggests, has to do with 'Thoughts all too deep for words'; its author's powers are 'tides . . . and currents'; the poet's companionable stars and streams reappear in Coleridge's appreciation. He also appears to have grasped more clearly than most subsequent criticism what *The Prelude* is essentially about. By sub-titling his response (in its revised and considered version) ' . . . a poem on the growth of an individual mind' and by opening his praises by referring to its story as prophetic, not historic, Coleridge recognises that while he has been listening to a poetic Bildungsroman, and a crisis narrative (his apportioning of space recognises the proportions of Wordsworth's account of growth, crisis, and restoration), he has also been listening to an account of human possibilities which is intended to be normative, not idiosyncratic. He gives particular weight to the poem's closing theme:

> Then (last strain)
> Of Duty, chosen Laws controlling choice,
> Action and joy!

The Snowdon meditation is, of course, concerned precisely with this theme. Wordsworth's higher minds are gifted not with poetic speech, but with autonomy. In them Coleridge would recognise what he himself wrote of in his *Theory of Life*:

In Man the centripetal and individualising tendency of all Nature is itself concentrated and individualised – he is a revelation of Nature! . . . and he who stands the most upon himself, and stands the firmest, is the truest because the most individual, Man.

But 'the form of polarity, which has accompanied the law of individuation up its whole ascent' still pertains:

As the independence, so must be the service and the submission to the Supreme Will![6]

He might also have heard between Wordsworth's lines his own thoughts on those who are masters of Time, those whose lives express what, in the *Treatise on Method* he would call 'the initiative'. While the idle, in Coleridge's eyes, merely kill time, the higher mind 'may be justly said to call it into life and moral being . . . He organises the hours and gives them a soul', so that of him 'it is less truly affirmed that he lives in Time, than that Time lives in him'.[7]

Such, of necessity, would be the context of ideas in which Coleridge responded to Wordsworth's presentation of men

> Who are their own upholders, to themselves
> Encouragement, and energy and will . . .(*Prelude*, XII: ll. 261–2)

In *The Prelude* Wordsworth has shown how individuation depends upon action and joy; and how the project of an individual life is always open to reclamation or to loss. Coleridge's experience may not have made him comfortable with Wordsworth's belief that a life sustained by 'natural piety', by loyalty as it were to itself, may retain its trust in 'Emotions which best foresight need not fear / Most worthy then of trust when most intense' (*Prelude*, XIII: ll. 115–16). But insofar as the concept of 'duty' could be expressed by both poets in such terms as Wordsworth's 'obedience to paramount impulse not to be withstood' or to 'a moral law established by himself' (*Prose Works*, II, p. 24), Coleridge properly recognises in Wordsworth's concluding argument his own thinking. Both poets were engaged in the initiation of that stream of thought which was to be continued by Kierkegaard, Marcel and Jaspers, who also saw duty as preferable to the unrest of change, and the weight of chance desires, and – in Kierkegaard's formulation – found that duty and liberty are reconciled in love: for 'duty is as protean in its forms as is love itself, and it pronounces everything good when it is of love and denounces everything, however beautiful and specious it may be, if it is not of love'.[8]

A radical difference which this assimilation of Wordsworth and Coleridge obscures, however, is that Wordsworth's conclusion in *The Prelude* is lacking in any convincing use of a term equivalent to Coleridge's 'Supreme Will'. And this lack, not apparently felt by Coleridge in his poetic response to Wordsworth's reading, is nonetheless making itself subliminally effective in the shaping of Coleridge's lines.

In lines 61–75, Coleridge finds himself reflecting on his own life, and 'plucking the poisons of self-harm'. It is precisely because Wordsworth's celebration of naturally self-authenticating life is existentially stoic to the exclusion of any felt dependence upon a *higher* will, that Coleridge's feelings, in lines 61–112 follow in themselves the pattern of a crisis narrative. Coleridge has in fact paid scant regard to the emotional quality of Wordsworth's own crisis (the 'crisis' of *The Prelude* in Coleridge's reading is one in 'the general heart of human kind', line 36), since Coleridge always imagines Wordsworth to be one who watches 'calm and sure/ From the dread watch-tower of his absolute self' (ll. 39–40). The emotional crisis of *The Prelude*, then, is borrowed in 'To William Wordsworth' by its auditor, overcome by his

> Sense of past Youth, and Manhood come in vain,
> And Genius given, and Knowledge won in vain.   (ll. 69–70)

That the poem ends in prayer is easily misunderstood. It is not, surely, that Wordsworth casts a prayerful spell: rather it is prayer that enables Coleridge to rise. His poisonous sense of dependency upon the amiable giant can be cancelled only in a greater dependency, already prefigured in the litanic language which opens the final paragraph of the poem – 'O Friend! my comforter and guide! / Strong in thyself and powerful to give strength!'. Prayer is needed, not only because there is something troublous about sitting 'in silence . . . like a devout child' at the feet of a brother poet, but because Coleridge cannot otherwise bring to a calm resolution a poem which is threatening to revert to the condition of emotional storm which dominates the *Letter to Sara Hutchinson*. When Wordsworth's poem closes, the poet's bodily presence becomes a shade oppressive:

> And thy deep voice had ceased – yet thou thyself
> Wert still before my eyes, and round us both
> That happy vision of beloved faces . . .

Coleridge finds himself within the magic circle which has been for five summers and the length of nearly five long winters a token of the hollowness of Joy, the transientness of pleasure. As he found in the *Letter to Sara*:

> To visit those I love, as I love thee,
> Mary and William, and dear Dorothy,
> Is but a temptation to repine –
> The transientness is Poison in the Wine,
> Eats out the pith of Joy, makes all Joy hollow,
> All pleasure a dim Dream of pain to follow!

The *Letter to Sara*, however, is not the only poem in which we find an analogous recourse to prayer. We may read *To William Wordsworth* in one way if we think it is repressing the *Letter*. If we understand it as repressing *The Eolian Harp* – itself coiled at the heart of Dejection – we may see the gesture of prayer as containing a figure of renunciation. For prayer in *The Eolian Harp* has been used to deprecate an earlier witchery of sound, and earlier shapings of the unregenerate mind, speculations which spoke of the incomprehensible without the saving sense of Him

> Who with his saving mercies healed me,
> A sinful and most miserable man,
> Wilder'd and dark . . .

III

That it is a similar lack in *The Prelude* that disqualified it from the expected accolade, can be deduced from Coleridge's remarkable letter to Wordsworth expressing disappointment with *The Excursion*. Quoting lines 12–47 of *To William Wordsworth*, so that we cannot doubt his recall of *The Prelude* and its effect, Coleridge's letter of 30 May 1815 flatly proclaims '*This* I considered as "the EXCURSION" ': the second instalment of *The Recluse* he had anticipated

as commencing with you set down and settled in an abiding Home and that with the Description of that Home you were to begin a *Philosophical poem*, the result and fruits of a spirit so fram'd & so disciplin'd as had been told in the former. (*CL*, IV, p. 574)

This, unlike *The Prelude*, he had expected to exhibit 'the matter and arrangement of *Philosophy*':

I supposed you first to have meditated the faculties of man in the abstract . . . demonstrating that the Senses were living growths and developements of the Mind and Spirit in a much juster as well as higher sense, than the mind can be said to be formed by the Senses: . . .

(It is hard to say whether Coleridge felt that *The Prelude* had in any sense addressed itself to this question, as opposed to simply marshalling the data.)

The remainder of Coleridge's specification for the philosophical poem, it can hardly be said too emphatically, is not merely tangential to Wordsworth's proper concerns as a poet of the human mind, but wholly and radically incompatible with the argument of *The Prelude* and of the so-called 'Prospectus' to *The Recluse*. Wordsworth – and one must take the letter seriously and read it attentively if one is to grasp the fundamental intellectual dyspathy between two poets whose brilliant friendship had little to do with philosophical concurrence – was, in Coleridge's recollection,

to have affirmed a Fall in some sense, as a fact . . . the reality of which is attested by Experience & Conscience . . . and not disguising the sore evils under which the whole Creation groans, to point out however a manifest Scheme of Redemption from this Slavery . . . and to conclude by a grand didactic swell on the necessary identity of a true Philosophy with true Religion . . .

No service is done to either poet by supposing that Wordsworth, as opposed to 'Wordsworth', found the reality of a 'Fall' attested by conscience; or heard the whole Creation groaning for deliverance, or found manifest a scheme of redemption; or felt convinced of 'the necessary identity of true Philosophy with true Religion'.

That Wordsworth attempted to fulfil Coleridge's desire for upwards
of three decades is a sacrifice that can only have been motivated by a commanding veneration. He tried to conform, by repressing in himself what
Coleridge frowned on, to Coleridge's image of him: and in a miraculous
degree, he succeeded. *The Excursion* is the proper monument to Coleridge's revision of Wordsworth: a poem apologetic for its occasional
lapses into common speech, devoid of dramatised character or lapses into
the matter-of-fact, and preaching, in the language of the clerisy, the
necessity of a Platonised Anglicanism. It is not a more Coleridgean poem
in any positive sense: but it is a poem in which Wordsworth has carefully expunged all that he can identify in his former practice as having
displeased Coleridge. Coleridge, of course, wanted more than this. In
a memorable Notebook entry he sees the mental presence of Shakespeare,
Milton and Bruno as 'pure Action, defecated of all that is material &
passive' (*CN*, II, 2026): why should Wordsworth not achieve this ideali-
ty, not merely to posterity, but in existence? He is willing, as we have
seen, to contemplate his own death if that should contribute to the perfection of one poetic voice by a commingling of both (*CN*, II, 2712).

The Prelude, of course, is rightly preferred by Coleridge, as a superior
poem. Paradoxically, although he may not have recognised this, it is also
a more Coleridgean poem in the sense that Wordsworth succeeded in
some of its climactic passages in grafting on to a Wordsworthian stock
a Coleridgean bloom. Thomas McFarland observes, in his essay on their
symbiosis, that in Book V Coleridge's influence 'almost succeeded in
pulling Wordsworth out of orbit' but that Wordsworth's resistance takes
the form of writing a book about books in which 'he talks about almost
anything rather than books' (*Forms of Ruin*, pp. 85–6). Coleridge's success, however, is merely delayed.

Coleridge's imagination, it has not yet been sufficiently noticed,
habitually treats the data of perception in a symbolic or indeed an
eschatological manner to which Wordsworth's is ordinarily resistant. In
reading Wordsworth, as we see in his comments on the 'Salisbury Plain'
poetry in Chapter 4 of *Biographia*, Coleridge is liable to interpret a landscape inundated with a dramatised consciousness – in this case, that of
a mind haunted by guilt and sorrow – as revealing rather 'the tone, the
atmosphere, and with it the depth and height of the ideal world': few of
Wordsworth's characteristic effects are actually of this kind. (When Coleridge quotes, in Chapter 22 of *Biographia*, those Piel Castle lines which
describe the youthful poet as prone to add to what he sees 'the gleam, /
The light that never was on sea or land, / The consecration and the poet's
dream', it is immediately apparent that what Coleridge terms imaginative is in Wordsworth's mature judgement illusory.)

The 'spots of time' in *The Prelude* characteristically record experiences in which the natural or human world is perceived in a heightened and unfamiliar mode by a mind under the influence of physical or emotional disturbance. What is perceived, however, is not – in the boating, or birdsnesting, or poaching, or skating episodes, or the Paris spot, or on Salisbury Plain, or on Penrith Beacon – given the kind of doctrinal interpretation to which Wordsworth ascends in his two alpine spots, his hymn before nightfall in the Simplon Pass, and his hymn before a forgotten sunrise on Snowdon. In both instances, I believe, the candid reader must feel an unwonted layering in the rhetoric which is experienced as something distinctive, something unusually impressive, and yet disconcerting. The Simplon Pass experience becomes disturbingly impressive at the point where Wordsworth's rhetoric levitates from

> Black drizzling crags that spake by the wayside
> As if a voice were in them

to

> Characters of the great apocalypse
> The types and symbols of eternity

– which levitation is received by some readers, at least, as a fall from the authentic voice of experience.

The Snowdon meditation, too, moves from Wordsworthian experience to Coleridgean gloss, from what 'Nature thus/Thrusts forth upon the senses' to the bliss of 'higher minds' when encountering 'the consciousness/Of whom they are'. Despite the Norton note on the matter (*Norton 'Prelude'*, p. 464, note 4) the meaning is clear enough: in the kind of experience 'Snowdon' is about, higher minds become conscious of the yet Higher Mind whose creation they themselves are, or of Whom they are a part. My 'or', of course, recognises an ambivalence in Wordsworth's phrase, which in truth we should extend further to cover his later (1850) use of a lower case 'consciousness' and an upper case 'Whom': for Wordsworth is speaking of an innominate underpresence which it is open to Coleridge's higher mind – and there can be no doubt that the other higher mind so genially introduced in the closing book is Coleridge's – to experience as a person of the trinity, if he so desires. To Wordsworth it may remain, more congenially, a spirit in the woods, or an ever-during power subsisting at the heart of endless agitation. Capable, then, of Spinozist, or Berkeleyan, or Christian construction, Wordsworth's underpresence is ideally honed for Coleridge.

Ideally, in both senses, but still not in a way that could preclude a sense, on Coleridge's part, that Wordsworth had left something out. What Wordsworth cannot bring himself to do in his closing book – despite the

1850 recognition that we cannot all hold to our course 'unchecked, unerring, and untired,/In one perpetual progress smooth and bright', a recognition which would have done little to cheer Coleridge had it been offered in 1805 – is to move from a willingness to recognise the existence of some form of deity, to a personal conviction of sin. And that distinction was (as Thomas McFarland's *Coleridge and the Pantheist Tradition* has so comprehensively shown) at the heart of Coleridge's thinking.

When Wordsworth published *The Excursion* in 1814 he gave little sign of having resolved this ambivalence: indeed he advertised it in the 'Prospectus'. While this claimed in line 15 that his theme included 'melancholy Fear subdued by Faith', the implications of this capitalised 'Faith' are instantly nullified. For him, we learn in lines 33–4, Jehovah and all his angels are but another provisional myth by which people have figured to themselves the unfigurable – 'I pass them unalarmed'.

Wordsworth might agree with Schelling that it is of little consequence whether you call your sense of spirit Pantheism or something else – 'We gladly grant everyone his own manner of making intelligible to himself the age . . . The name does not matter; what counts is the substance'[9] – but to Coleridge, Wordsworth's failure to recognise what's in a name made the rest of his self-abnegating career seem just another of his (Coleridge's) failures. In the end, Wordsworth simply would not totalise. The great project succeeded in part: the poet of *The Excursion* is one who has deserted the 'Lanes and allies' of the affective life in which it pained Coleridge to see him wander, and abandoned his propensities for the dramatic mode and the matter-of-fact. Coleridge had in large, if negative, measure succeeded in realising his Idea of Wordsworth. For us, *The Prelude* and *The Excursion* are recognisable as the tremendous fragments of a fostered idea. But for Coleridge these were to be measured against the total idea: for one whose intention was – through *The Recluse*, or 'The Brook', or the 'Opus Maximus' – to pollinate the mind of the new age, the 'Wordsworth' project fell sadly short of the mark.

When Coleridge listened in January 1807 to the song of Wordsworth's self, he had recently written to Thomas Clarkson in terms which leave us in no doubt at all what his real judgement must have been of Wordsworth's misty allusions to the deity:

. . .But all the actions of the Deity are intensely real or substantial; therefore the action of Love, by which the Father contemplates the Son, and the Son the Father, is equally real with the Father and the Son – and neither of these three *can* be conceived *apart*, nor *confusedly* – so that the Idea of God involves that of a Tri-unity; and as that Unity or Indivisibility is the interest, and the Archetype, yea, the very substance and element of all other Unity and Union, so is that Distinction the most manifest and indestructible of all distinctions – and Being, Intellect, and Action, which in their absoluteness are the Father, the Word, and the Spirit will and must for ever be and remain the 'genera generalissima' of all Knowledge.

(Letter to Clarkson, 13 Oct. 1806, *CL*, II, pp. 1195–6)

In a sense the measure of Coleridge's imagination is that he could sincerely have felt that if Wordsworth were to produce 'a faithful transcript of his own most august and innocent life, of his own habitual feelings and modes and seeing and hearing' (*CL*, II, p. 1024) it would have ended up by inferring and revealing 'the proof of, and necessity for, the whole state of man and society being subject to, and illustrative of, a redemptive process in operation', or 'in substance, what I have been all my life doing in my system of philosophy' (*Table Talk*, 21 July 1832 [*Misc C*, pp. 410–11]). The measure of how masterful Coleridge's imagination could be is that Wordsworth's career took the course it did, in its long ascent towards baptism.

Notes

1   Major contributions to the study of this literary 'symbiosis' include Norman Fruman, *Coleridge: The Damaged Archangel* (New York, 1971), Stephen Parrish, *The Art of the 'Lyrical Ballads'* (Cambridge, Mass., 1973), chapter 3 of Mary Jacobus, *Tradition & Experiment in Wordsworth's Lyrical Ballads (1798)* (Oxford, 1976), John Beer, *Wordsworth in Time* (London, 1979), and of course Thomas McFarland's *Romanticism and the Forms of Ruin* (Princeton, 1981), particularly its first chapter on 'The Symbiosis of Coleridge and Wordsworth'. Lucy Newlyn's forthcoming study of 'echo and allusion' in their work will put the debate on a new level of particularity.

2   I have discussed the *Biographia*'s treatment of Wordsworth's poetry in some detail in 'Coleridge's Wordsworth', *TWC*, Spring 1984. The remainder of the first part of the present essay is closely based upon part of 'Coleridge's Wordsworth'. The deleterious effects upon Wordsworth's poetry are discussed (as they appear in 'Home at Grasmere' and *The Excursion*) in my 'Wordsworth's Last Retreat', *Charles Lamb Bulletin*, n.s. 43 (July 1983), pp. 54–67. In his essay on 'Coleridge's Interpretation of Wordsworth's Preface to *Lyrical Ballads*' (*PMLA*, 93, October 1978), Don H. Bialostosky deals very cogently with the confusions created by Coleridge, and sustained by those critics who assume that the theses attacked by Coleridge are in fact argued by Wordsworth.

3   Wordsworth's note appeared at the close of volume 1 of the 1800 edition.

4   *WPW*, III, pp. 503–4. Coleridge's remark on 'The Three Graves' is quoted in Stephen Parrish's essay above.

5   I am citing the standard text in *PW*. The ms. version of the poem given in that edition's Appendix 1 (L), and corrected in *Norton 'Prelude'*, pp. 542–5, is of course closer to the audition, and more personal, but like many early drafts it is also less clear. The later version, which is the one Coleridge quotes to Wordsworth in the 1815 letter, can be accepted as a more successful embodiment of what Coleridge thought. Lines 54–69 of the ms. version do not

appear in the revised poem. They elaborate on Coleridge's emotional response, and their ambivalence about how 'comfort from Thee' only 'scatter'd and whirl'd me' (ll. 56–9), and how 'thy Hopes of me . . . were troublous to me' (ll. 61–2) is consonant with the standard text.

6 *Hints Towards the Formation of a More Comprehensive Theory of Life*, ed. Seth B. Watson (London: John Churchill, 1848), p. 86.

7 *S. T. Coleridge's Treatise on Method as Published in the Encyclopaedia Metropolitana*, ed. Alice D. Snyder (London: Constable & Co, 1934), p. 13.

8 *Either-Or* (New York, 1959), vol. 2, p. 151.

9 F. W. J. von Schelling, *Of Human Freedom*, tr. James Gutmann (Chicago, 1936), p. 91.

The Otway connection

DAVID V. ERDMAN

When in his final version of *Dejection: an Ode* (in *Sibylline Leaves*, 1817) Coleridge wrote 'As Otway's self had framed the tender lay' (line 120) replacing the language of earlier versions ('Edmund's self' or 'William's self' or 'thou thyself', i.e. Sotheby!), he may have been making a substitution that 'disturbs every knowledgeable reader', as George Dekker believes (*Coleridge and the Literature of Sensibility*, p. 238). He may, on the other hand, have been inscribing a code reference to a precursor poem lying behind the whole symbiotic family of 'Intimations' and 'Dejection' odes by his dear friend Wordsworth and himself, the earliest surviving member being *The Mad Monk* of 1800.

In its immediate context, in Coleridge's verse letter to Sara dated 'April 4, 1802, Sunday Evening',[1] that portion of the 'lay' being recited by the wind as a 'Mad Lutanist' on a wind-harp is a tale of the moaning and screaming of a lost child, quite plausibly compared to Wordsworth's ballad of *Lucy Gray* – as it often is – although strictly Lucy Gray is never heard to moan or scream but is only said to sing 'a solitary song / That whistles in the wind'. Indeed Reeve Parker in *Coleridge's Meditative Art* (Ithaca, 1975, pp. 97–200) by associating the lost child with the 'groans and shudderings' of the preceding lines helps us recognize allusions to the female vagrant's tale in Wordsworth's *Adventures on Salisbury Plain* (and to Milton's fallen angels and routed pagan deities). As a retrospective identification of the complaining voice that 'moves' the complaining poet, however, it is true that, as Dekker says, 'Merely to mention Otway's name was to summon up a host of other ill-fated literary geniuses ranging from Spenser ['Edmund's self'] and Collins to Chatterton and Burns' (Dekker, p. 238). The failure of a poet's genial spirits was a common theme in the Augustan period, whose commentators 'recalled the neglect of Dryden and Milton and the still more ghastly – if apocryphal – end of Otway' (Dekker, p. 199).

For Coleridge, however, perhaps the point of his putting the name Otway into the 1817 version of 'Dejection', when he was himself a sadder but less desperate man,[2] was to dismiss in mockery the early identification of Wordsworth and himself with 'mighty Poets in their misery dead'

('Resolution and Independence'). What I wish to suggest also is that it was a way of commemorating, for himself and Wordsworth at least, the influence upon their dejection poems of *The Poet's Complaint of his Muse*, a seventeenth-century 'Ode' by Thomas Otway. I see the theme and shape of this ode lying behind *The Voice from the Side of Etna, or, The Mad Monk* published in *The Morning Post* of 13 October, 1800 – a poem which contains a stanza beginning 'There was a time' which has often been noticed as remarkably echoed in, and thus perhaps a source for, the first stanza of the 'Intimations' ode.

Since *The Mad Monk* belongs somehow to both Wordsworth and Coleridge and is itself a manifest and self-proclaimed parody – a parody as it were of the still unwritten 'Intimations' and 'Dejection' odes – there can even be a question as to whether these two odes existed in some form *before* the parody was written, or only later were written to fulfill its prophetic mockery.

There is mockery within mockery, indeed. What *The Mad Monk* declared *itself* to be, in a subtitle, was the parody of a gothic novel: 'AN ODE, in Mrs. RATCLIFF'S manner'. What it did not declare was its derivation from Otway's *Complaint*. In fact, when Julia Di Stephano Pappageorge investigated the novels of Ann Radcliffe, she discovered little discernible influence on the gothic recesses and insanity of *The Mad Monk*, but an impressively significant use of Radcliffe's *The Mysteries of Udolpho* in Coleridge's 'Dejection' ode. In brief, she discovered that the 'central thematic and atmospheric component of the poem, the poet's addressing the wind which "moans and rakes / Upon the strings" (ll. 6–7) of his "Aeolian lute" as a "Mad Lutanist" (l. 104), constitutes [a borrowing from and] an allusive reference to Ann Radcliffe's lute music' in the *Mysteries*, one of the novel's mysteries being the source of emotion-charged sounds 'made, we finally learn, by a mad nun loose in the forest'.[3]

This discovery, we may note, enables us to flesh out our understanding, hitherto only skeletal, of the process whereby Coleridge managed to replace the wind harp with 'the wind-as-harpist' and thus achieve the important shift from passivity to activity which George Dekker sees as the positive theme of *Dejection*.[4]

And if the subtitle to *The Mad Monk* of 1800 can lead us to an important source for the symbolic action of 'Dejection', perhaps the allusion to Otway in the latter poem may, even for the knowledgeable, point to the source of *The Mad Monk* as Otway and to its theme as a poet's *Complaint of His Muse*. Both Otway and the author of *The Mad Monk* are poets, each reporting on the madness of a brother poet. As we recognize the thematic and inter-personal similarities and contrasts involved, perhaps we may reasonably infer that the two monks of *The Mad Monk*, the mad one who complains that 'There was a time . . . ' and the sad one who reports the overheard complaint to readers of *The Morning Post*, are the same two poets who subsequently gave to the world an Ode intimating philosophic if not poetic 'Immortality' and an Ode distilling 'Joy' from 'Dejection'. These poets are, like Otways's mad poet, complaining of their muses' cruelty; yet they achieve through their complaints the tranquility of a philosophic and creative mind.[5] Reeve Parker's chapter on 'Dejection' documents how thoroughly and at times desperately Coleridge himself observed and believed in this result of 'meditative consciousness' (Parker, p. 181ff.). But let us now look at Thomas Otway and his poem.

*

Samuel Johnson, in his *Lives of the English Poets* (London, 1783), vol. I, p. 328, had this to say of Otway's poetry:

Of the poems . . . the longest is the *Poet's Complaint of his Muse*, part of which I do not understand; and in that which is less obscure I find little to commend. The Language is often gross, and the numbers are harsh. . . . His principal power was in moving the passions. . . . He appears to have been a zealous royalist: and had what was in those times the common reward of Loyalty; he lived and died neglected.

Coleridge and Wordsworth might have given stronger praise to the poet's 'power in moving the passions', but they would have regarded Otway's meteoric career, at court and in Grub Street, as a paradigm to avoid, whether or not one had to believe literally that his death at thirty-three had come from attempting to digest a charitable crust of bread on a long-empty stomach.

Otway's poem is – another disturbing truth – a loose and baggy monster of 21 stanzas totaling 704 lines; over 33 lines per stanza, though odic in pattern; while *The Mad Monk* is complete in 51 lines (8 stanzas); also, about a third of the way through, the *Complaint* shifts attention from the cruel Muse to her evil child, Libell – who need not concern us here.

In the relevant part of Otway's *Complaint* and in *The Mad Monk* the author interviews an insane friend (a poet or 'monk') who is in a suicidal frame of mind. Otway's suicidal friend is failing as a poet, and the Otway persona projects his own career anxieties upon him; in the Coleridge poem the reporter signs himself pseudonymously 'Cassiani, jun.', implying that the monk/poet interviewed on the 'side of Etna' (place of philosophical, suicidal associations) is his senior (recognizably Wordsworth) upon whom he projects his own career crisis.

Otway comes upon his friend, 'whose Muse was crazy grown', on a 'high Hill' (the high hill of Donne's Truth?), a place barren of anything but 'Heath, coarse Fern, and Furzes'. Coleridge locates his mad senior in vegetation that would suit the 'thoughts of more deep seclusion' of 'A Hermit or a Monk' such as the 'lofty cliffs' a few miles above Tintern Abbey had suggested to *his* theoretically reclusive friend.

The muse of Otway's friend has proved a very bawd, and has finally jilted him – a realization which overwhelms both poets. How had Otway's 'friend' (a fictional projection) got himself into this barren wilderness? He explains that he and his dear muse thought it might restore her sanity if they moved to the country, fleeing the 'nauseous Follies of the buzzing Town'. They had reached some place like Grasmere, where the Bard could 'lay him down' far from any path, but where the Earth was bare, and naked all as at her Birth (I quote in paraphrase) – a locale still responding to God's fiat to 'Let Grass and Herbs and every green thing grow' including 'fruitful Trees'.

The interviewed poet confesses, alas, that his rural effort to be a recluse has been a disaster. He had been blessed by his muse with 'Off-springs of the choicest kinds' and had been transported to a height whence he 'Look'd down and laugh'd at Fate'. Then all of a sudden, 'I round me look'd and found my self alone: My faithless Muse . . . was gone'. Plunged into dejection, he managed still to write, but produced only deformed baboons and apes as 'the hideous issue of my Brains'. Waking, he found that his ungrateful muse had robbed him of Time, Friends, Reputation, 'And left me helpless, friendless, very proud, and poor'. All the muses, he now knows, are prostitutes who serve the bawd Fortunne.

Otway is duly impressed – and goes on to explain that behind the whole ugly scam is a witch who corrupts states and is called (bless us!) 'The Good Old Cause'.

The interviewed poet sighs deep and cries, 'How far is Peace from Me?' It is nowhere in sight (we're only a third of the way through the poem) and future 'Joy' is farther away than ever.

Stanza 10 begins:

> A Time there was, (a sad one too)
> When all things wore the Face of Woe, . . .

This was enough to start Coleridge's Mad Monk who, when interviewed on the side of Etna, offered the same theme in reverse. To contrast good times and bad, Otway dwells on the bad, the Mad Monk on the good:

> There was a time when earth, and sea, and skies,
>   The bright green vale, and forest's dark recess,
> With all things , lay before mine eyes

> In steady loveliness:
> But now . . . .

And perhaps also to start Wordsworth on his 'Intimations' ode:

> There was a time when meadow, grove, and stream,
> The earth, and every common sight,
>> To me did seem
>> Apparelled in celestial light . . .
> It is not now as it hath been . . . .

(There may be echoes here of Otway's opening strophe about 'the Earth . . . naked all as at her Birth' *before* God had said 'Let . . . every green thing grow'.)

Or, also, the first lines of what became stanza VI of Coleridge's *Dejection*:

> There was a time when, though my path was rough
>> This joy within me dallied with distress,
> And all misfortunes were but as the stuff
>> Whence Fancy made me dreams of happiness:
> For hope grew round me . . .
> But now afflictions bow me down to earth: . . .
>> (ll. 233ff, *Letter to Sara*)

The thematic context, in each case, is the lament of a poet who has fallen upon the thorns of life from a state of 'loveliness'. But the 'Mad Monk' ode was published in October 1800. If the 'Intimations' and 'Dejection' odes are its offspring, did Wordsworth wait until 27 March 1802 to write his, on that 'divine' Sunday morning when, according to Dorothy Wordsworth's journal, 'At breakfast William wrote part of an ode'? Was he then just beginning the 'Intimations' – as the conventional assumption has been until recent questioning – or had he already written a first part, long ago? And on the next Sunday, 4 April, when 'William . . . repeated his verses' to the Coleridges (according to Dorothy), were these verses the 'Intimations' ode we know? And was the letter version of *Dejection* which Coleridge mailed to Sara Hutchinson, headed 'A Letter to—/April 4, 1802. – Sunday Evening' – was this his immediate response to Wordsworth's ode, and was it the first, the initial, version?

Mark Reed, in *Wordsworth: The Chronology of the Middle Years* (p. 156 & n) considers that Wordsworth had now been writing 'probably some part or all of stanzas I–IV', the rest in early 1804. George Dekker accepts these probabilities as to Wordsworth's Ode (in an extremely thorough investigation of the collaborative and literary and biographical context of the 'Dejection')[6] but he suggests the further probability that 'the essential components of *Dejection: an Ode* existed as actual stanzas of poetry *before* the verse letter to Sara Hutchinson was drafted' (p. 47).

Dekker's argument is that the verse letter dated 'April 4' is, 'in effect, an intermediate and in many ways deviant draft of *Dejection: An Ode*' (p. 54): a 'reshaping of lines already written – and written in a spirit nearer that of the correspondence of 1800–1801 and of the *textus receptus* of 1817' (p. 42). The verse letter, for instance, contains only two 'distinct echoes of the *Immortality Ode*' – lines 133–41, about dwelling 'in one happy Home' and crowning himself 'with a Coronal', and lines 294–5, both passages bearing 'all the marks of impromptu writing' (pp. 48–9). And I think it must be agreed that there is no evidence to prevent the supposition 'that the lines now comprising Stanzas I–II were composed well before 4 April 1802, as far back, perhaps as the the preceding spring or *even the summer of 1800!*' (p. 52: my italics) or earlier (see February echo noted below).

Dekker backs away from the longer interval, noting that the opening lines may well have been 'inspired . . . by Dorothy's description of the new moon which she and William saw on 5 March and which, very likely, Sara and Coleridge saw the same evening at Gallow Hill', but he remains radically sceptical about the patness of the April date, though 'it is as good a date as any for the poem which must have been put together about that time' (p. 52).[7]

A passage clearly belonging to an early form of the Ode is lines 211–15 in the verse letter, 121–5 in the published version. For Coleridge had echoed them in a letter to Thomas Poole of 1 February 1801:

O my dear dear Friend! that you were with me by the fireside of my Study here, that I might talk it over with you to the Tune of this Night Wind that pipes it's thin doleful climbing sinking Notes like a child that has lost it's way and is crying aloud, half in grief and half in the hope to be heard by it's Mother.

(*CL*, II, p. 669)

This, of course, is the passage that might have been composed by Otway or Edmund or William – or Sotheby! And it is a relevant coincidence that when Coleridge had been in what he presented as a suicidal mood in December 1796, he had written to Poole, after the collapse of Pantisocracy and of his *Watchman*, that to contemplate having to depend on Grub Street would be to have 'the evil Face of Frenzy' looking at him and to be haunted by 'the Ghosts of Otway [that name comes first!] and Chatterton' as well as by 'the phantasms' of his 'Wife broken-hearted, & a hunger-bitten Baby!' (*CL*, I, p. 275). (This helps us see why the starving poet Otway – or any other – might be responsible for the wind-music that tells of 'a little Child . . . Not far from home' who 'screams . . . to make it's Mother hear!')

When, five years later, Coleridge wrote his 'Letter to —' version of *Dejection* – leaving the blank in his title – he again associated Poole with this mother and child motif. He did address certain lines in this version to 'Sara' and 'dear Sara' and even 'dearest Sara', and he did, we assume, send it to Sara Hutchinson; yet he at first had not been certain to whom he might send it. Perhaps he had had in mind a round robin, on the theory expressed in the preface to his 1796 *Poems* and, as Reeve Parker notes, more illustratively in a notebook entry of 1803 'that has the excitement of fresh recognition' (supplied, I take it, by his having written 'Dejection' and published it):

One excellent use of communication of Sorrows to a Friend is this: that in relating what ails us we ourselves first know exactly what the real Grief is – & see it for itself, in its own form & limits. Unspoken Grief is a misty medley, of which the real affliction only plays the first fiddle – blows the horn, to a scattered mob of obscure feelings.   (*CN*, I, 1599)

At any rate, a month after the date of the verse letter of 1802, on 'May 7, Friday', writing a cheerful letter to 'My dear Poole', Coleridge, having inserted transcriptions of '2 pleasing little poems of Wordsworth's' (the second of which concludes with the line, 'And love & thought & Joy!') adds this revealing and self-critical remark:

I ought to say for my own sake that on the 4th of April last I wrote you a letter in verse [the 'Dejection' of course]; but I thought it dull & doleful – & did not send it –

God bless you, dear Friend! & S.T.C.—
(*CL*, II, 801)

We must note Coleridge's inclusion of self in the blessing. Possibly, with only a month's time, the fresh recognition had not had time to work; perhaps the draft which Coleridge almost sent to Poole in April lacked the lines of Joy and rejoicing at the end of the Sara version; perhaps they were there but with a gloomy echo like 'Otway's Self' instead of 'William's Self' in line 210.[8]

However that may be, instead of shaping a climax of rejoicing for a version to send to Poole with this May letter, Coleridge found it easier to copy out for Poole Wordsworth's cheerful lines *To a Butterfly* and *The Sparrow's Nest*. Both, interestingly enough, celebrate Wordsworth's blessedness in having a 'Sister' who has served as his muse ever since he was a 'Boy': 'She gave me eyes, she gave me ears, / And humble Cares & delicate Fears . . . ' (*WPW*, I, p. 227).

The fact that the names Otway and Wordsworth can function as interchangeable stand-ins for the 'Mad Lutanist' of expressive grief points clearly to Wordsworth as that 'other' poet whom Coleridge cryptically recognizes in such disguises as that of the insane friend of Otway and the insane Monk on the side of Mt Etna. As a Wordsworth-watcher in 1800, what Coleridge imagines might drive his senior insane must be the killing-off of 'Lucy' if Lucy can be understood as the muse who gave him eyes and ears, i.e. his Sister as shield of his soul. The point *The Mad Monk* makes is, if we bear Otway in mind, that to murder the maiden muse is to bring on insanity and the end of genial spirits. Perhaps one thing Coleridge is saying in that poem is that William's great flaw is his failure to appreciate either Dorothy or S.T.C. But to get the discussion on firm ground, we need to examine the human context of interpersonal (and interpoetical) relations as they developed in 1800 and threatened, by 1802, to make 'all Joy hollow' for Coleridge and suspend his 'shaping Spirit of Imagination' (April letter, lines 161, 242). If we recognize the newspaper 'Monk' poem of October 1800 as Coleridge's parody of Wordsworth's domestic and poetic acts and thoughts during the spring and summer preceding, in spirit a sequel to his *Monthly Review* parodies of other poets and himself, in 1797, as 'Nehemiah Higginbottom', we are able to recognize some of the ingredients in the developing personal symbiosis of our two personae in this season as they began the life that earned them the cognomen 'Lake Poets'.[9]

In April 1800 Coleridge made his first visit to Dove Cottage and learned that Wordsworth had decided to publish 'a second Volume of Lyrical Ballads, & Pastorals', and was already turning out poems for it. By early May Coleridge was back in Bristol, with some of these to show to Poole and Davy, and (apparently) with the first part of *Christabel*, which Davy praised highly. To bring the poets closer together, Dorothy Wordsworth was on the look-out for housing, and by the end of July the Coleridges moved into Greta Hall, in Keswick – where they resided for the next twelve years.

The *Lyrical Ballads* project was still, by unwritten contract so to speak, a joint undertaking, but William's relegation of S.T.C. to share the chore work with Dorothy must from the start have produced in Coleridge the uneasy emotions that surfaced in *The Mad Monk*. William was willing to write most of the poems, and was dashing them off in merry haste to clear his mind for the serious work they all felt to be the important thing on his agenda, the great *Recluse*. Coleridge was willing, he himself felt, to do most of the negotiating with the publisher. 'Indeed', observes Wordsworth's biographer, Mary Moorman, 'Coleridge could not have worked harder for the *Lyrical Ballads* if they had been his own "great work" instead of a small work by his friend. The manuscripts of the poems and letters about their publication . . . show how much of the labour of correspondence and preparation he undertook'.[10] How could Coleridge, in his secret rivalrous self, not take comfort from the very smallness of what the 'greater man' was occupied with – a comfort that enabled him to strike a magnanimous pose? Wordsworth's name was to go on the volume, a publication to be justified by sales, not immortality, and at the end of the year Coleridge would profess to be 'especially pleased that I can now exert myself loudly and everywhere in their favour without suspicion of vanity or self-interest' (*CL*, I, p. 654). This to the publisher, Thomas Longman. A few days later, writing to Francis Wrangham (who had reviewed the first *Lyrical Ballads* in the *British Critic* as if all were by Coleridge) he was true to his word and, making clear that the new volume was all by Wordsworth, insisted: 'He is a great, a true Poet – I am only a kind of a Meta-physician' (*CL*, I, p. 658). At the same time he was careful to distance himself from Wordsworth in Wrangham's mind: it was Wordsworth who owed Wrangham this letter, but Coleridge had to write it for him, since Wordsworth was a vile procrastinator: and Wrangham was not to think of them as intimates: 'Wordsworth & I have never resided together – he lives at Grasmere. . . . His address is . . . . As to our literary occupations they are still more distant than our residences' (*CL*, I, p. 658).

This guarded ebullience occurred in December, but in the spring it had been understood that Coleridge was also contributing to the new volume. Some time in June, when he was in Bristol showing some of Wordsworth's contributions (and reading *The Brothers*) to Humphry Davy and Thomas Poole, he had the first part of *Christabel* to show them; Davy heard or read it and was full of praise.[11] Yet something made Coleridge put off showing it to the Wordsworths for many weeks – either his wish to complete it first, or his anxiety lest William disapprove of it as heartily as he had of *The Ancient Mariner*. (*Christabel*, too, might spoil the sales.) Dorothy records that on 31 August 'Coleridge read us a part of *Christabel*. Talked much about [not the poem but] the mountains, etc. etc.' (*DWJ*, I, p. 58).

Finally, on 4 October, Coleridge having sat up 'all the night before, writing essays for the newspaper', arrived at Dove Cottage drenched with rain, with a 'second part of *Christabel*' to read. The Wordsworths (or Dorothy at least) were 'exceedingly delighted' (*DWJ*, I, p. 64). And the next morning 'Coleridge read *Christabel* a second time; we had increasing pleasure. A delicious morning' (*DWJ*, I, p. 64). Though he had been 'intending to go', Coleridge stayed on two days. During that time, alas, the delightful work of *his* muse was held at arm's length and then effectively slain.

Dorothy and William were working on 'an addition to the Preface'; after tea the second day they 'read *The Pedlar*' (William's emphatically Wordsworthian self-assertion). And then, in Dorothy's laconic words, they 'Determined not to print *Christabel* with the L.B.' (*DWJ*, I, p. 64). There was talk, perhaps only meant to be talk, of publishing a separate volume with *Christabel* and *The Pedlar* (i.e. *The Ruined Cottage*), but nothing came of that.

Coleridge even accepted this with open cheer (as Mary Moorman deduces, the decision was 'unanimous'). Or, in a kind of parody of good cheer, he went overboard in explaining the decision to Davy (on October 9; *CL*, I, p. 631). Now the problem was not that the poem was unfinished but that it was getting too long: 'The Christabel was running up to 1300 lines' – that would be almost double the number that survive, but he is less likely to have thrown half of the poem away than to have been working up his statement to a high degree of falsity – and that the poem was 'admired by Wordsworth' but *not* by its author! 'I would rather have written [Wordsworth's] Ruth, and Nature's Lady ['Three years she grew . . . '] than a million such poems' as *Christabel* (see *CL*, I, p. 632 for even more of this self-abasing mockery).

Indeed, Coleridge carried it off so well that, for instance, on Wednesday morning, the 22nd, they 'were very merry' at Dove Cottage, according to Dorothy, although William (trying to write *Michael* and having a hard time lifting up its stones) 'composed without much success at the sheepfold' – and Coleridge came in to dinner having 'done nothing'. After supper, 'Wm. read *Ruth*, etc. . . . Coleridge *Christabel*' (*DWJ*, I, pp. 68–9).

Another part of the collaboration, more directly involving the one who declared himself 'only a kind of a Meta-physician' (see above – I think he split the word to make a pun: he could be the physician of Wordsworth in this respect), was the 'addition to the Preface' which William and Dorothy were 'employed all the morning in writing' on that Sunday when Coleridge 'read *Christabel* a second time' (*DWJ*, I, p. 64). This is not the place to give more than a quick look into the collaborative agonies and conflicting accounts of that Preface, but only to note that while the Wordsworths were busy on it they did not involve Coleridge, and that when Coleridge was telling Davy that *Christabel* was expendable and that it was a 'delightful' thing that Wordsworth's ballads *had* been written, he went on to talk about the work he had most 'at my heart', defining it as an 'Essay on the Elements of Poetry . . . in reality . . . a *disguised* System of Morals & Politics', yet indicated no connection with the *Lyrical Ballads*. Years later Wordsworth would maintain that *he* had written the Preface, but 'solely to gratify Coleridge', and that he could remember the very spot, 'a deserted quarry in the vale of Grasmere' (a setting as barren as the pathless spot where the poet Otway interviewed his friend the 'wandring Bard'), where Coleridge 'pressed the thing upon me' and Wordsworth agreed 'out of sheer good nature' (Moorman, p. 492).

Now let us look at the particular poems by Wordsworth that were pressed upon Coleridge during the weeks before publication of *The Mad Monk* and what message the great poet may have seemed to be sending to his Meta-physician. In the first week of August 1800, Dorothy and Coleridge were at work copying for the printer enough of Wordsworth's new poems to complete a fourth sheet of copy for the *Lyrical Ballads*. Dorothy copied out *Strange Fits of Passion*. Coleridge copied *She Dwelt among the Untrodden Ways*, and *A Slumber Did My Spirit Seal*, writing directions for the printer. A few days later *'Tis Said That Some Have Died for Love* was copied by Dorothy, with notes by Wordsworth and Coleridge (Reed, II, p. 78). These seem the poems that could have inspired the lamentations of *The Mad Monk*, for they all have to do with the fear – then the reality and the 'difference to me' – of the death of the poet's beloved 'Lucy'.

What the author of *The Mad Monk* claims to be overhearing is the Complaint of a poet who has murdered his muse and gone insane. The long debated question, ever since George McLean Harper and Emile Legouis published the record of Wordsworth's secret affair with Annette Vallon, has ranged from the proposition that 'Lucy' was Annette, to conjectures that she was Dorothy ('murdered' to stop their incest – not really a likely proposition; or to prevent their love from becoming incestuous – rather more probable) or some still undiscovered woman. Coleridge made one suggestion – in a mocking *Epigram* in the *Morning Post* of 11 October 1802, the week after the Wordsworth wedding – to the effect that, though 'strict and holy' in his own eyes, Wordsworth was still associating with a prostitute named Annette. Reading back from that ironic charge (*Spots in the Sun* was its title) we may suppose that the insanity of the overheard 'Monk' of 1800 was derived from the thought that he was killing off his beloved Annette – slowly, by distance? Or by some current decision?

What I think likely is that in 1800 when Coleridge was reading the 'Lucy' poems with Dorothy, he assumed that William was secretly saying to himself and Dorothy (as in early versions of *Nutting*) that they must avoid in England the ostracism their intimacy had provoked in Germany; that, in effect, the Dove Cottage family should include a proper wife for William – as they all finally agreed (in the good Christian part of their hearts).

In 1802, while Coleridge was still pitying himself for his entrapment in a domestic establishment that prevented him from doing more than hold hands with Sara Hutchinson, we find that it was Wordsworth who wanted to enlarge *his* trap. Indeed he sought both from his Muse and his Meta-physician advice – and approval of an arrangement whereby *he* could cut himself loose from (to use Coleridge's language to Poole, quoted above) the 'phantasms' of a wife and daughter out of wedlock, Annette and Caroline, now within visiting distance because of the Peace of Amiens, and thus be able to propose marriage to Mary Hutchinson (a phantom, but a 'phantom of delight', who would prove to be 'a Woman too!') and thus also be able (this was the beauty part) to keep the muse his Sister within a respectable family – which could also include (why not?) S.H. and S.T.C.

It was precisely to talk this over with Coleridge that Wordsworth kept him up all night on 3 April 1802, impelling his weak-willed friend to exercise his 'own tenderness of Heart' and 'disinterested Enthusiasm for others, and eager Spirit of Self-sacrifice' (which Coleridge possessed, he later felt, because of his 'being & having ever been, an unfortunate unhappy Man'). One of the Griefs expressed in the *Dejection* lines addressed to Sara Hutchinson the next day is Sara's precarious status in the proposed household.

I am quoting what Coleridge claimed were his unexpressed thoughts on the occasion, in a belated notebook entry made on midnight, 12 May 1808, pouring out his repressed feelings – having that day, for the first time (he told himself) allowed himself to utter his 'Complaints . . . relatively to [Wordsworth's] conduct towards me, and that of [erased: perhaps naming Mrs Coleridge & Mary & Dorothy]'. He has been cruelly treated 'by almost every one' *because* of his eager sacrifice of self. 'O God! if it had been foretold me, when in my bed I – then ill – continued talking with [Wordsworth] the whole night till the Dawn of the Day, urging him to conclude on marrying [Mary Hutchinson]' (*CN*, III, 3304).

A comparable self-despising can be found in the curse he put on himself in 1821 (for falsehoods he had circulated that led to the duel in which John Scott was shot): 'If I had the craft of the Draftsman, I would paint . . . myself as a Dutch Mercury . . . the God of . . . prudential Interest . . . of Thieves, Tradesmen, Diplomatists, Pimps, Heralds, and Go-betweens – the soothing, pacifying God'.[12]

Kathleen Coburn in her note on the 1808 entry, after observing that Coleridge's multiple agony included his resentment at Wordsworth's separating himself from one woman to marry another with 'the sort of freedom for which Coleridge longed but which his conscience did not permit him', adds that 'A better consequence of the night's talk was *Dejection: An Ode*, written the next day.' Nor must we accept Coleridge's cruel self-contempt as the deepest truth about his ambivalent sentiments about his greatest Friend. In self-contemning moments he could express bitterness about his friend as well. The 'Dejection' triumphs, not only over his own dejection but over his envy, and, in the version published on Wordsworth's wedding day and the anniversary of his own, constitutes, as Reeve Parker suggests, 'an epithalamic gesture' of tremendous sincerity.

Parker can keep us from overcrediting the finality of Coleridgean expressions of resentment, by calling our attention to another *Morning Post* poem, published three weeks earlier and constituting the prelude to this epithalamion: the 'Hymn Before Sun-rise, in the Vale of Chamouni', which he reads 'as an allegorical celebration of Wordsworth's emergent being as poet and husband' expressing 'Coleridge's perhaps envious but certainly yearning blessing of the marriage as the event to . . . domesticate and humanize, in effect to realize, the sublime austerity of his Friend' (p. 160). As Parker reads the evidence in his letters and in Dorothy's journals – a sampling of which I have presented above – what Coleridge saw as he watched Wordsworth productively at home in Grasmere was 'that Wordsworth was emerging, like Mont Blanc, from the dark night of doubts and personal anxieties that had, at least to Coleridge's mind, beset him, and that he was entering on a career of radiant and productive creativity, secure in the undersong of domestic affections Coleridge likened to the "still hive at quiet midnight humming" ' (Parker, p. 158).

Fortunately, before he sent *Dejection* to the *Morning Post*, Coleridge had cleared up some of the ambiguities of the verse-letter – for instance the two passages that distinctly echo the 'Immortality' ode but ambiguously express the 'Spirit of Self-sacrifice' into which he was entering for the great occasion. The first, as Dekker (p. 49) observes, does not make clear 'whether he is wishing the Wordsworths and Hutchinsons all dead and in Heaven or all living together in one house in Grasmere':

> When thou, & with thee those, whom thou lov's best,
> Shall dwell together in one happy Home,
> One House, the dear *abiding* Home of All,
> I too will crown me with a Coronal –
> Nor shall this Heart in idle Wishes roam
>   Morbidly soft! (ll. 113–18)[13]

One message conveyed by the 'Intimations' ode which Coleridge was struggling to accept in silence – or ambiguity – was that since Wordsworth was winning the palms that would certify his attainment of 'the philosophic mind', without any help from colleagues other than the brooks and hills, the writing of his philosophic epic, *The Recluse*, might not require help from Coleridge. (Actually, we know that Wordsworth panicked when his friend decided to leave England without supplying his schema.) From the occasionally bitter Coleridgean point of view, the title itself can be read as announcing that the poet was given, even in childhood, intimations of his poetic immortality. And in a curious way, Wordsworth's great 'Poem to Coleridge' (posthumously entitled *The Prelude*) would also, in its closing tribute to Coleridge as loving and understanding friend, imply both an appreciation of his generous and mediating service – and reticence about his philosophic mind or genial spirits. I refer to the conclusion of the 1805 version; the 1850 version, in a passage revised after Coleridge's death, drops all this and gives credit primarily to Coleridge's religious faith.[14]

*

Manifestly the complicated and fluctuating intimacy of these two poets involved shifting proportions of admiration and mistrust. There was something in Wordsworth which he himself spoke of as a belief that he had 'a talent for command'. He had studied military history and tactics in his boyhood; he could grieve for Buonaparte (over what reverses he does not specify) until that unhappy warrior seized the imperial crown.[15] His definition of the 'Character of the Happy Warrior', composed about the time he was completing the 'Intimations' ode, contains a large element of self-definition – for instance, 'a natural instinct to discern / What knowledge can perform', a soul 'alive to tenderness' and 'homefelt pleasures' yet even as a commander in 'the heat of conflict' able to hold firm to the decisions which he had 'In calmness made' (ll. 8–9, 26, 35, 53–4, 60). When he firmly excluded *Christabel* from the *Lyrical Ballads* while praising it, he was exercising that talent.

Evidently there was something in *The Ancient Mariner* and *Christabel*, not to mention *Kubla Khan*, that he responded to as a commander confronting demon power. It was what Coleridge called 'pure imagination', i.e. imagination uncontrolled by will.[16] Wordsworth himself had a great empathy with power *under control*: the 'force' (pun) of a waterfall that was held in stationary control (like emotion recollected in the mind of a poet who has thought deeply, too deeply for tears). Such powers were to Wordsworth legible as characters of 'the great Apocalypse', all 'like workings of one mind'. But the great poems of Coleridge, fragmenting implosions and explosions not firmly held in check, were rather too much either for their author or his 'Father Confessor'.

On the other hand, there was something in Coleridge that made him portray the shooting of albatrosses yet wish to be commanded by a powerful institution or a 'commanding genius'. In intermittent 'pants' he embraced and resented powerful control. By setting a strong force in motion – in a poem or in his relations with others – and then not controlling it, he could remain free of competition and judgment (anyone's final decision must await the completion of the Opus) and thus forcefully defiant, cryptically. As Reeve Parker observes, 'The stimulating friendship with Wordsworth cost Coleridge dearly, for he invested Wordsworth with a power destructive of his own self-assurance' (p. 218). Coleridge was not simply imagining things when he poured forth into a diary or blurted in an intimate letter, grievances against his commanding friend. And

Wordsworth was not being paranoid in sensing a powerful hostility in these poems, with their vertiginous enticements and open endings.

To conclude this discussion I should like to draw upon a recent collection by Warren Stevenson (in 1983) of essays he published in various journals in 1962, 1973, and 1976 – sadly overlooked by bibliographers (those of the Romantic Movement at least) – which he now titles *Nimbus of Glory: A Study of Coleridge's Three Great Poems* (Salzburg, 1983).[17]

Behind *Kubla Khan* and the Tartars of *Purchas his Pilgrimage*, with their ancestral voices prophesying war, Stevenson notes a 'subtle claim on the sympathetic attention of Coleridge' in their possession of qualities which Wordsworth had and Coleridge lacked, 'those qualities of warlike bravery and decisiveness in which Coleridge seems to have regarded himself as being deficient, and for which he retained a certain childlike admiration. One thinks of his undergraduate escapade of running away to join the dragoons. Compare the following note: "Every thing, that has been known or deemed fit to win woman's love, I have an impulse to make myself – even tho' I should otherwise look down upon it – I cannot endure not to be strong in arms, a dazzling Soldier . . . " ' (*CN*, III, 3158, f. 42, Stevenson p. 44). The unhappy warrior, dejected when he thinks of the Grasmere commander girdled by Dorothy and Mary and Sara, buries his grief in writing a Second Part (not to be finished) of *Christabel*.

Stevenson's reading of the heroine's relationship to Geraldine as 'a subconscious symbolical representation of Coleridge's relationship to Wordsworth' (pp. 12ff.) is impressive in its details:

> Christabel is Coleridge the poet – the true poet, the author of *The Ancient Mariner* and *Kubla Khan*: Sir Leoline, her father, is STC – Coleridge's self-deprecating way of referring to himself as the mere social being, versifier, family-man, and friend. Sir Leoline is 'weak in health' and 'seldom sleepeth well'; his wife is dead, and life has become a kind of living death for him. 'Each matin bell, the Baron saith, / Knells us back to a world of death.' STC was unhappily married and made similar laments. . . . Geraldine, the malignant demon whom Christabel unwittingly succors, is a transmogrification of Wordsworth – rather, of the worst element in Wordsworth's nature. . . .
>
> Christabel's inability to tell the truth is itself the curse. . . . [Her] silence . . . prophetically symbolizes the congealing of Coleridge's poetic impulse; and her sense of sin and confusion is part of her spiritual death, which is conceived of as a vicarious atonement for the sin of Geraldine.

Stevenson finds an important iconographic explanation of Geraldine's mysterious 'bosom and half her side' as 'lean and old and foul of hue' in a passage in Collins's *Ode on the Poetical Character* which Coleridge pointed to as having greatly inspired him. Collins describes a magic band or girdle, woven on the day of creation of the world, which is the emblem of poetic genius – the very thing at issue here. In Spenser it is the magic girdle of Venus, which bursts when put on by an unchaste woman. The same symbol of poetic power is the druid circle – which Coleridge in *Kubla Khan* calls for as his proof of inspiration – and which Wordsworth had used, as Stevenson notes, in *The Vale of Esthwaite* to hint at his own bardic initiation:

> The spectre made a solemn stand,
> Slow round my head thrice wav'd his hand.

Stevenson's summary, an intriguing exercise of fancy, is worth full quotation:

Geraldine's deformity is thus vitally linked to the total symbolic structure of the poem, which deals *on one level* with the psychic conflict and poetic rivalry of Wordsworth and Coleridge. When she unbinds her cincture and inner vest, Geraldine is at once revealed as 'poetically unchaste', a false aspirant to the title of divinely inspired poet, and she symbolizes that part of Wordsworth antithetical to his own and Coleridge's creative imagination. Her foul and deformed side, the mark of her shame and seal of her sorrow, symbolizes both Coleridge's intuitive apprehension of Wordsworth's 'hidden vice', and his deep unconscious feeling that Wordsworth has arrogated to himself the title of divinely inspired poet, while denying it to Coleridge, the true aspirant.

And there is much more, the Wordsworthian aspect of the Ancient Mariner; Wordsworth as Peter Bell the Potter, who 'struck – and struck again', echoic contrary of the youth in his 'elfin pinnace' who also 'struck and struck again' when a threatening peak 'as if with voluntary power instinct / Upreared its head'. And the two bards in *Kubla Khan*. But Stevenson's full account of this component of Coleridge's three great symbolic poems must be read for the Coleridge-watcher interested in Coleridge's watching of Wordsworth to see quite how fully this line of investigation seems to me consistent with and more all-embracing than my own attempt to 'read' the poets' Odes as Complaints of their muses – in Otway's sense – and of that evil child of poetical unchastity, the monster named Libell.

Notes

[1] In July 1977 a variant draft of this Letter turned up (see G. Dekker, *Coleridge and the Literature of Sensibility* (New York, 1978), p. 249), but I cite the one long known and cited. Within the lines it addresses 'Sara', but the heading leaves a blank for the name. The newly discovered version, in the hand of Mary Hutchinson, is actually addressed to Sara, I gather from Dekker – though he was allowed to see it at Sotheby's but not quote and may only mean to report that Sara is addressed within the poem, as in the familiar version. He saw several differences in wording but reports that 'it is substantially the same poem as the verse letter'.

² Compare Wordsworth's putting the name Oswald into the 1841 version of *The Borderers*.

³ 'Coleridge's "Mad Lutanist": A Romantic Response to Ann Radcliffe', *BRH*, 82 (1979), pp. 222–35.

⁴ Dekker, p. 113, quoting John O. Hayden, 'Coleridge's "Dejection: An Ode" ', *English Studies* (April 1971), pp. 1–5.

⁵ This cannot be said of the parody, of course, the 'agony' of whose protagonist escalates from seeing the trickling stream as the blood of the Rosa he 'struck' (and struck again?) to a wish to 'be for ever dead!' – to the 'deep dismay' of the listener, who withdraws to his 'goat-herd's tent' remarking that there is 'no moon!'!

   N.B.: For the evidence of Coleridge's authorship of *The Mad Monk*, which is now generally accepted (as it was before we debated the question), see 'Who Wrote *The Mad Monk*? A Debate', Stephen M. Parrish and David V. Erdman. *Bulletin of the New York Public Library*, 64 (1960), 209–37 below. Stephen Parrish argued that there was so much Wordsworthian diction in the poem that Coleridge could not have written it; I argued that his using it served the purpose of parody. Parrish in reprinting his essay (Parrish, *The Art of the Lyrical Ballads* (Harvard, 1973), pp. 189–213) concedes that 'such evidence can be ambivalent' and cites a compromise suggestion by Robert Woof, to the effect that Coleridge 'wrote the poem in parodic imitation' not of Wordsworth but 'of the kind of writing that Wordsworth and Coleridge attacked' in the 1800 Preface (209 and n). Parrish's own conclusion is that 'it is impossible to imagine that *The Mad Monk* can be all Coleridge's and not at all Wordsworth's'. A nice point alongside my own, that it is a document of their symbiosis. And that it was a *private* parody goes with Parrish's further point that 'no reader could have been expected to know what it was a parody of, the pertinent poems of Wordsworth's being unpublished' (211 and 212).

⁶ *Coleridge and the Literature of Sensibility*, passim.

⁷ There could, of course, have been an earlier draft with different opening lines.

⁸ Dekker (p. 239) does assemble a parallel between the two odes – and Wordsworth's *Resolution and Independence* understood as 'Wordsworth's "answer" to Coleridge' – to which he then adds the slightly upbeat finale of Otway's drama of triple suicide, *The Orphan*. The argument is that 'So long as feeling can be kept alive, something can be made of pain and misfortune.' Hence a tale of groans and pain followed by 'A tale of less affright, / And tempered with delight', can be loosely attributed to Otway. (Or, I should think, to any of the hundreds of tragedies that in some way purge the fright.)

   Growing more knowledgeable, however, I begin to see the embarrassing potential of a plot which places twin brothers [say, William and Samuel] in rivalry for their sister's love, one attempting and one achieving incest; all three self-destroyed. The 'Mad Monk' managed only one 'murdered' maiden!

⁹ For an extensive and penetrating discussion of the literary and psychological aspects of the Coleridge–Wordsworth interaction, we are all deeply indebted to the chapters in Thomas McFarland's *Romanticism and the Forms of Ruin: Wordsworth, Coleridge and Modalities of Fragmentation* (Princeton,

1981). Giving equal attention to 'Coleridge's Anxiety' and to the anxiety of Wordsworth, McFarland updates an earlier article which opened the topic, 'The Symbiosis of Coleridge and Wordsworth', and demonstrates the tidal pull of the thoughts and acts of each upon the other.

10 Mary Moorman, *William Wordsworth: A Biography; the Early Years, 1770–1803* (Oxford, 1957), p. 488.

11 See M. Reed, *Wordsworth: The Chronology of the Middle Years* (Cambridge, Mass., 1957), p. 65.

12 *CL*, V. p. 190. See my discussion of this in 'Coleridge and the ''Review Business'' ', *TWC*, 6, i (Winter 1975), pp. 3–50.

13 See Dekker, pp. 48–9, 294–5.

14 See XIII 246–68; XIV 275–301.

15 See A. G. Grosart, ed., *The Prose Works of William Wordsworth* (3 vols., 1876), III, p. 451, on Wordsworth's military interests. Wordsworth's sonnet of May 1801, *I grieved for Bonaparte*, was probably prompted by Napoleon's stifling the republics of Switzerland on his way to empire.

16 For a clarification of Coleridge's remarks to Mrs Barbauld on *The Ancient Mariner*, see P. Magnuson, *Coleridge's Nightmare Poetry* (Charlottesville, 1974), p. 81.

17 Warren Stevenson's original articles were: (1) '*Christabel*: a Reinterpretation', *Alphabet*, 4 (June 1962); (2) '*Kubla Khan* as Symbol', *Texas Studies in Literature and Language*, 14, iv (Winter, 1973); (3) '*The Rime of The Ancient Mariner* as Epic Symbol', *Dalhousie Review*, 56, iii (Autumn, 1976).

Imagining Robespierre

NICHOLAS ROE

> O friend, few happier moments have been mine
> Through my whole life than that when first I heard
> That this foul tribe of Moloch was o'erthrown,
> And their chief regent levelled with the dust.
>
> (*The Prelude*, x, ll. 466–9)[1]

So Wordsworth tells Coleridge of his feelings when he heard of the death of Robespierre in summer 1794, while crossing the Leven Sands. 'Great was my glee of spirit, great my joy', he recalls. Coleridge's reaction to the news was different. He immediately collaborated with Southey on a tragedy, *The Fall of Robespierre*, and he continued to explore Robespierre's character and motives in his political lectures of 1795. Coleridge's interest in Robespierre was shared by the leading reformist John Thelwall, and both agreed that the British prime minister Pitt lacked Robespierre's political skill. Coleridge went further, though, and used Robespierre as a foil in his developing idea of the imagination. When he wrote about Robespierre's death in *The Prelude* Wordsworth knew that Coleridge had not shared his feelings at the time, and that his friend's complex response to Robespierre was ultimately of the greatest importance to himself. Why then did Wordsworth insist so emphatically upon his exultant feelings,

> 'Come now, ye golden times',
> Said I, forth-breaking on those open sands
> A hymn of triumph,   (x, ll. 541–3)

– recalling Robespierre's death as a moment of personal vindication?

The 'golden times' never came. France did not recover the revolutionary idealism of former years, and no longer provided a model for political and social change in Britain. Despite his 'hymn of triumph' and renewed confidence in the future, the execution of Robespierre was the beginning of the end of Wordsworth's revolutionary commitment. In the following months Wordsworth's thinking was much influenced by *Political Justice*, until the inefficiency of Godwinian rationalism as a means to social progress became increasingly apparent. This was the time,

161

perhaps early in 1796, when Wordsworth 'Yielded up moral questions in despair'.

In *The Prelude* Wordsworth claims that

> then it was
> That thou, most precious friend, about this time
> First known to me, didst lend a living help
> To regulate my soul. (x, ll. 904–7)

Coleridge and Wordsworth first met in September 1795, but they had no marked mutual influence until two years later. Nevertheless, Wordsworth deliberately presents Coleridge as a redeeming figure in Book Ten, a 'living help' in the aftermath of personal crisis, the successor to his schoolmaster and poetic mentor William Taylor whose grave Wordsworth had visited on the very day he had heard of Robespierre's execution back in August 1794. When Wordsworth reminded Coleridge of that day, he did so in the knowledge that the fundamental differences in their response to his downfall, and in their personal experiences over the next three years, provided the immediate context for their early meetings and mutual commitment to poetry in June 1797. Those differences are the subject of this essay.

1: Treason and Terror

Many years after the French Revolution, William Godwin looked back to the time when he had 'blazed as a sun in the firmament of reputation' as the author of *Political Justice*. For Godwin, 1794 was memorable not for the Terror in France nor for the execution of Robespierre, but for an event in London,

the trial of twelve persons under one indictment upon a charge of high-treason ... – it was an attempt to take away the lives of men by a constructive treason, & out of many facts no one of which was capital, to compose a capital crime – the name of the man in whose mind the scheme of this trial was engendered was Pitt – [2]

In May 1794 the leaders of the London Corresponding Society and Society for Constitutional Information had been arrested and imprisoned in the Tower and Newgate jail. *Habeas Corpus* was suspended on 23 May, and the prisoners were held over the summer until formally charged with treason on 2 October. Thomas Hardy, Horne Tooke, and John Thelwall were then brought to trial – and acquitted – during the next two months. Godwin had contributed to the acquittals by attacking the trumped-up treason charge in his pamphlet *Cursory Strictures*, which first appeared in the *Morning Chronicle* on 21 October and was certainly read by Coleridge and Wordsworth then or very shortly afterwards.

In Book Ten of *The Prelude* Wordsworth also recalls the treason trials which remained as vivid a memory for him as they had for Godwin. His condemnation of the government is unequivocal –

> Our shepherds (this say merely) at that time
> Thirsted to make the guardian crook of law
> A tool of murder
> (X, ll. 645–7)

– and it recalls his nightmare dreams of the massacres at Paris earlier in Book Ten,

> Such ghastly visions . . . of despair,
> And tyranny, and implements of death . . .   (X, ll. 374–5)

The similarity between Pitt's 'tool of murder' and French 'implements of death' was deliberate. Unlike Godwin, Wordsworth did not believe that the scheme of the treason trials had been 'engendered' in Pitt's mind. Pitt had no capacity for originality. He was an imitator, and a foolish one at that,

> Though with such awful proof before [his] eyes
> That he who would sow death, reaps death, or worse,
> And can reap nothing better, childlike longed
> To imitate – not wise enough to avoid.
> (X, ll. 648–51)

The 'awful proof' Wordsworth had in mind was of course the Terror in France, which culminated in Robespierre's death on 28 July 1794. In spite of this example Pitt's government persisted in 'composing a capital crime', as Godwin put it, and charging the reformists with high treason. If found guilty, they would presumably have been executed. In *The Prelude*, Wordsworth draws a direct analogy between the 'unjust tribunals' of Paris and those in London. His comparison also extends further, for Wordsworth implies that Pitt's schemes had pushed Britain to the threshold of violence that would bring about his own downfall. In sowing death through his childlike imitation of Robespierre, he too would reap nothing but death.

Wordsworth's recollection of the treason trials in Book Ten was written during autumn 1804, exactly ten years after the event. The date is important, for his portrayal of Pitt as Robespierre's imitator has a curious link with work on the last seven stanzas of *Intimations* in the spring of the same year. In stanza seven of *Intimations* Wordsworth had described the four-year-old child's restless urge to imitate, adopting one role after another,

> But it will not be long
> Ere this be thrown aside

> And with new joy and pride
> The little actor cons another part
> Filling from time to time his humourous stage
> With all the persons down to palsied age
> That Life brings with her in her Equipage
> As if his whole vocation
> Were endless imitation   (ll. 99–107)[3]

The child's joy in fitting his tongue to a succession of adult roles is sadly ironic. The 'earnest pains' of his imitation only serve to hasten the loss of his own 'heaven-born freedom' as a child. He blindly provokes the 'inevitable yoke' of years that lead to the prison-house of adult life. In Book Ten of *The Prelude*, however, the 'little actor' is William Pitt, and his wilful 'conning the part' of Robespierre is a matter for condemnation. The child in *Intimations* impatiently throws aside one role to adopt another, innocently unaware that he is at strife with himself. Pitt, on the other hand, had only one vocation: to imitate the man whose execution should have stood as a warning example,

> Though with such awful proof . . . childlike longed
> To imitate – not wise enough to avoid.

The portrait of Pitt as a perverse child is peculiar to Wordsworth in 1804.[4] But Wordsworth was not alone in regarding the treason trials ten years earlier as an imitation of Robespierre's Terror in France. Besides recalling the stanza from *Intimations*, the passage in Book Ten of *The Prelude* may also have been influenced by Wordworth's reading of Coleridge's *Conciones ad Populum*, and by John Thelwall's political journal *The Tribune*. Coleridge and Thelwall both agreed that Pitt was an imitator of Robespierre. Furthermore, their attitudes to Robespierre himself also coincided.

Thelwall was acquitted of high treason on 5 December 1794 and that night he celebrated his freedom over dinner with his wife, William Godwin and Thomas Holcroft.[5] Two months later he resumed his political lectures at Beaufort Buildings in the Strand. To guard against the misrepresentation of spies and informers, the lectures were transcribed verbatim and then published in *The Tribune*. On 23 May 1795 *The Tribune* contained Thelwall's third lecture on 'The Prospective Principle of Virtue', which was based upon his reading of Godwin's *Political Justice*. Wordsworth was in London at this time and given his friendship with Godwin, and his democratic politics, he may well have been in the audience at Beaufort Buildings when Thelwall made a sustained 'comparison between the character of Robespierre and the immaculate minister of this country'.[6] Thelwall argued that the arrests in 1794, the suspension of *Habeas Corpus*, the charges and the trials were a policy of terrorism copied from the French, and designed to remove all opposition to the Government. 'I will ask you', he said,

what might have been the situation of this country, if the late prosecutions had succeeded? . . . who knows, when you once begin a system of massacre, and especially *legal* massacre, for opinion, where you can stop? I do not believe that *Robespierre* meditated, in the first instance, those scenes of carnage into which he at last was plunged . . . I have strong suspicions in my mind, that, if they had touched the life of an individual who stood at the bar of the Old Bailey, the gaols of London (and we all know we have abundance) would have been as crammed as ever the prisons of Paris were, even in the very dog-days of the tyranny of Robespierre.[7]

Thelwall was self-dramatising and given to exaggeration, but since his life depended on the outcome of 'the late prosecutions' his suspicions were understandable, nor were they peculiar to him alone. The government had been frustrated by the acquittals at the Old Bailey, and this offered a further opportunity to attack Pitt as an unsuccessful imitator of Robespierre. In his lecture, Thelwall developed the characters of Robespierre and Pitt, but to the disadvantage of

that Minister who, without the energy of Robespierre, has all his dictatorial ambition; who, without the provocations which Robespierre and his faction experienced, has endeavoured, vainly endeavoured, to carry into execution the same system of massacre for opinion, of sanguinary persecution for proclaiming truth, of making argument High Treason, and destroying every individual who dared to expose his conduct, or oppose his ambitious views.[8]

Thelwall damns Pitt for endeavouring to execute a 'system of massacre for opinion', and – ironically enough – for failing to succeed in his ambitions. At the same time, he almost acquits Robespierre, who had introduced his system of terror after 'provocations'. The provocation he had in mind was the European coalition against France, which he believed had encouraged the leaders of the republic to adopt extreme and violent policies. In *The Prelude* Wordsworth makes a similar point,

> And thus beset with foes on every side,
> The goaded land waxed mad　　　　　　　(x, ll. 311–12)

– and at the end of his lecture 'On the Present War' in *Conciones* Coleridge takes the argument full circle by identifying Pitt, not Robespierre, as ultimately responsible for the Terror in France:

It was a truth easily discovered, a truth on which our Minister has proceeded, that valour and victory would not be the determiners of this War. *They* would prove finally successful whose resources enabled them to hold out the longest. The commerce of France was annihilated. . . . Immense armies were to be supported. . . . Alas! Freedom weeps! The Guillotine became the Financier-General. – That dreadful pilot, Robespierre, perceived that it would at once furnish wind to the

sails and free the vessel from those who were inclined to mutiny. – Who, my
Brethren! was the cause of this guilt, if not HE, who supplied the occasion and
the motive?   (*Lects 1795*, p. 74)

Coleridge's judgement of contemporary events was remarkably acute.
Britain had joined the war against France in February 1793. The following month, French armies under General Dumouriez were defeated at
Neerwinden in Holland, and also in Belgium. The simultaneous
rebellion in the Vendée put the republic at risk from within. Coleridge's
analysis of the financial ruin caused by maintaining large armies at a time
when war sapped commerce and trade was correct. Throughout 1793 in-
flation and the shortage of goods meant that prices rose steeply, adding
in turn to unrest in Paris and elsewhere in the country. In response, the
National Convention sought to consolidate the powers of central government. Representatives were sent to the armies and into the provinces to
bolster revolutionary enthusiasm, recruit soldiers, and root out counter-
revolutionaries. The Revolutionary Tribunal was set up at Paris, and on
6 April the Committee of Public Safety was established to direct executive
government and policy. As Coleridge indicated, the machinery through
which the Terror was implemented was set up in spring 1793 as a
response to threats from inside and outside the republic. He had genuine
grounds for his claim that by maintaining a war of attrition against
France, Pitt had in fact supplied the 'occasion and the motive' for the
Terror.

In 1795, Coleridge and Thelwall agreed that Robespierre had been
'provoked' into the Terror. At the same time, their need to condemn the
repressive policies of the British government led both to compare Pitt un-
favourably with Robespierre. Like their analyses of the immediate causes
of the violence in France, their insights into Robespierre's character and
motives are also strikingly similar.

Robespierre was executed on 28 July 1794 and his death was first
reported in the London *Times* on 16 August.[9] Six days later Southey
wrote to his friend Horace Bedford telling him that, with Coleridge, he
had written 'a tragedy upon [Robespierre's] death in the space of two
days!' This 'tragedy' was, of course, *The Fall of Robespierre*, and Southey
continued his letter to Bedford by giving his 'opinion of this great man',
who he believed had been

sacrificed to the despair of fools and cowards. Coleridge says 'he was a man whose
great bad actions cast a dis [astrous] lustre over his name.' He is now inclined
to think with me that the [actions?] of a man so situated must not be judged by
common laws, that Robespierre was the benefactor of mankind and that
we should lament his death as the greatest misfortune Europe could have
sustained . . .[10]

Coleridge's response was more complex than Southey suggests, and he never actually hailed Robespierre as the 'benefactor of mankind'. But Southey's letter does anticipate Coleridge's dedication to the play where he says that he has 'endeavoured to detail . . . the fall of a man, whose great bad actions have cast a disastrous lustre on his name' (*PW*, II, p. 495). In the opening speech of the play, Robespierre is described as

> Sudden in action, fertile in resource,
> And rising awful 'mid impending ruins;
> In splendour gloomy, as the midnight meteor,
> That fearless thwarts the elemental war (*PW*, II, p. 496)

– and just visible through the gloom is Milton's 'dread commander' in *Paradise Lost*,

> above the rest
> In shape and gesture proudly eminent
> Stood like a tower; his form had yet not lost
> All her original brightness, nor appeared
> Less than archangel ruined, and the excess
> Of glory obscured . . . (I, ll. 589–94)[11]

Robespierre's awful stature recalls Satan's towering presence, his 'disastrous lustre' the obscured glory of the fallen archangel. Rather than seeing Robespierre as 'the benefactor of mankind' as Southey had done, Coleridge presents him as heroic rebel, undaunted by the ruin brought upon himself. Like Satan he retains traces of his 'original brightness' in his resourcefulness and swiftness to action.

Despite the obvious debt to Milton, however, *The Fall of Robespierre* does reveal Coleridge's own interest in Robespierre's character and motives subsequently explored with greater insight in his political lectures. There is also evidence that the similarity between Thelwall's and Coleridge's ideas of Robespierre in 1795 may have been influenced by Thelwall's reading of the play. In late September 1794 five hundred copies of *The Fall of Robespierre* were published at Cambridge by Benjamin Flower. At least 125 copies were sent to London, one hundred to Kearsley the bookseller and twenty-five to George Dyer (*CL*, I, p. 117). Dyer was a friend of Thelwall's and may have sent a copy to him in the Tower. This would explain what appear to be echoes of *The Fall of Robespierre* in Thelwall's 1795 lecture 'On the Prospective Principle of Virtue':

Robespierre had a soul capacious, an imagination various, a judgement commanding, penetrating, severe. Fertile of resources, he foresaw, created, and turned to his advantage all the events that could possibly tend to the accomplishment of his designs. The mind of Pitt is barren and inflated, his projects are crude, and his views short sighted.[12]

Thelwall's lecture develops Coleridge's idea of Robespierre as 'Sudden in action, fertile in resource', into a Machiavellian hero who turns all to his advantage. Thelwall's purpose was to present Pitt in an unfavourable light and he did so by stressing Robespierre's resourceful energy and the quality of his mind. Where Robespierre was vital and creative, Pitt's mind was 'barren and inflated', lifeless and flatulent. Where Robespierre could foresee and manipulate events to his advantage, Pitt was myopic and his politics inept. 'Having viewed these facts', Thelwall concluded, 'it is impossible to doubt which of these characters we must prefer.'

This lecture was delivered and published in London during May 1795, some eight months after the publication of *The Fall of Robespierre* and almost a year after the death of Robespierre himself. Three months before, in February 1795, Coleridge had delivered 'three political Lectures' at Bristol. One of these was his *Moral and Political Lecture*, published during February and subsequently expanded to form the 'Introductory Address' to *Conciones* which was published the following November. Coleridge's additions in the 'Introductory Address' included a history of the different factions that had held power in France. His portrait of Robespierre is close to Thelwall's, but it differs significantly in Coleridge's emphasis on the contradictions of Robespierre's character,

Robespierre . . . possessed a glowing ardor that still remembered the *end*, and a cool ferocity that never either overlooked, or scrupled, the *means*. What that *end* was, is not known: that it was a wicked one, has by no means been proved. I rather think, that the distant prospect, to which he was travelling, appeared to him grand and beautiful; but that he fixed his eye on it with such intense eagerness as to neglect the foulness of the road. (*Lects 1795*, p. 35)

So the Machiavellian politician turns visionary, and Coleridge implies that Robespierre might have redeemed himself had his 'grand and beautiful' prospect ever been realised. It is probable that this idea of Robespierre was influenced by Coleridge's reading of his speeches to the National Convention from which he had already drawn material for *The Fall of Robespierre*. In his major speech on political morality, delivered 5 February 1794, Robespierre defended the original ideals of the French Revolution but countenanced violence as a means of ensuring the rights of man. 'What is the objective toward which we are reaching?' Robespierre asked, and then declared the object of the Revolution to be

The peaceful enjoyment of liberty and equality; the reign of that eternal justice whose laws are engraved not on marble or stone but in the hearts of all men, even in the heart of the slave who has forgotten them or of the tyrant who disowns them.[13]

In reaffirming the principles of 1789 Robespierre also defined the 'distant prospect' to which Coleridge refers in his 'Introductory Address'. But within minutes of advocating the 'peaceful enjoyment of liberty and equality' Robespierre claimed that only by 'sealing our work with our blood, we may witness at least the dawn of universal happiness – this is our ambition, this is our aim'.[14] He then described the 'goadings' and 'provocations' the republic had endured from its enemies:

Externally all the despots surround you; internally all the friends of tyranny conspire; they will conspire until crime is deprived of all hope. It is necessary to annihilate both the internal and external enemies of the republic or perish with its fall. Now, in this situation your first political maxim should be that one guides the people by reason, and the enemies of the people by terror. . . . Terror is only justice that is prompt, severe, and inflexible; it is thus an emanation of virtue . . .[15]

Robespierre's speech confirms Coleridge's insight into his contradictory motives, 'His cool ferocity that persuaded murder, / Even whilst it spake of mercy!' (*PW*, II, p. 516). The abstract foundations of Robespierre's political maxim – 'reason', 'justice', 'virtue' – also correspond to those of *Political Justice*,

> the philosophy
> That promised to abstract the hopes of man
> Out of his feelings,   (x, ll. 806–8)

– and for Coleridge this abstraction was the fundamental flaw in Godwin's system. By invoking 'reason' and 'justice' to justify terror, therefore, Robespierre also appears as an ancestor of Rivers, the Godwinian rationalist and murderer in Wordsworth's *Borderers*. In *The Prelude*, Wordsworth further identified Robespierre's politics with Godwin's philosophy by using the terror as an extended metaphor for his Godwinian speculations and the despair which preceded his composition of *The Borderers* in autumn 1796.

Robespierre's 'great bad actions' did not merely challenge Coleridge's and Wordsworth's allegiance to France. Although the Terror ceased with his death, his shadow endured and remained a disturbing presence for long afterwards. Both Coleridge and Wordsworth discovered in Robespierre a distorted reflection of their own political and philosophical positions. For Coleridge, the realisation had a formative influence on his idea of the 'elect', and also upon his thinking about the working of the individual mind within the universe of the 'One Life' – the 'living help' he was to bring to Wordsworth when they met at Racedown in June 1797.

2: The poet who might have been

During 1794 and 1795: increasingly repressive domestic policies coupled with food shortage and the burden of the war with France appeared to make revolution in Britain a possibility. At the same time, France no longer offered a model for peaceful change elsewhere, as it had done before 1792. As Coleridge put it, 'The Example of France is indeed a "Warning to Britain" ' (*Lects 1795*, p. 6). The same realisation underlies Wordsworth's concern in his letter to William Mathews of 8 June 1794, where he says that he 'recoils'

from the bare idea of a revolution; yet, if our conduct with reference both to foreign and domestic policy continues as it has been for the last two years how is that dreadful event to be averted?   (*EY*, p. 124)

Wordsworth answered his own question by proposing a scheme of political education to be conducted through the pages of *The Philanthropist*. His principal aim was to avoid a repetition of the violence witnessed in France. 'I deplore the miserable situation of the French', he told Mathews,

and think we can only be guarded from the same scourge by the undaunted efforts of good men in propagating with unremitting activity those doctrines which long and severe meditation has taught them are essential to the welfare of mankind.   (*EY*, pp. 124–5)

In June 1794 the doctrines Wordsworth had in mind were the 'rules of political justice' to which he refers elsewhere in the same letter. *The Philanthropist* would propagate Godwin's principles of passive enquiry and his belief in the perfectibility of mankind, thereby fostering peaceful change in Britain. His reliance on the efforts of 'good men' like Mathews and himself recalls his question in *A Night on Salisbury Plain*,

> whence but from the labours of the sage
> Can poor benighted mortals gain the meed
> Of happiness and virtue, how assuage
> But by his gentle words their self-consuming rage? (ll. 510–13)[16]

In 1794 the French Revolution was consuming itself in blood and Wordsworth took the guiding task of the sage upon himself, the 'gentle words' of Godwin as his text. *The Philanthropist* would bring *Political Justice* to the 'benighted mortals' of Britain, and direct their potentially destructive rage to a worthier end.

'I know that the multitude walk in darkness', Wordsworth told Mathews on 8 June, 'I would put into each man's hand a lantern to guide him'. His prophetic claim is relevant to the state of Britain in 1794, and also significant in his subsequent development as a poet. He is echoing Isaiah, 9, 2,

The people that walked in darkness have seen a great light: they that dwell in the land of the shadow of death, upon them hath the light shined.

As a prophet of the Godwinian enlightenment, Wordsworth's *Philanthropist* was the 'lantern' that would guide the benighted people of Britain ('the land of the shadow of death') to future reformation. The plan for *The Philanthropist* is in fact a first utterance of Wordsworth's prophetic wish. It is heard again early in 1800 in the 'Prospectus' to *The Recluse*, and subsequently in the closing lines of *The Prelude* where the imagination replaces Godwinian rationalism as the means of future redemption.

In June 1794 the 'rules of political justice' offered Wordsworth certainty and guidance at a time when all seemed tending to 'depravation'. But Godwin's 'rules' drew only contempt from Coleridge. Like Wordsworth, in 1795 Coleridge also took the burden of the sage upon himself. For Coleridge, though, the only 'gentle words' that might prevent violence were those of religion:

In that barbarous tumult of inimical Interests, which the present state of Society exhibits, *Religion* appears to offer the only means universally *efficient*. The perfectness of future Men is indeed a benevolent tenet, and may operate on a few Visionaries, whose studious habits supply them with employment, and seclude them from temptation. But a distant prospect, which we are never to reach, will seldom quicken our footsteps, however lovely it may appear . . . . (*Lects 1795*, pp. 43–4)

The *efficiency* of religion lay in the certainty of 'an infinitely great revolution hereafter', simultaneously the establishment of a just society and the promised millennium. This, he believed, might serve as a means of popular restraint – 'Rest awhile / Children of wretchedness!' – and an alternative to the bogus prospect of perfection offered by rival visionaries. The 'studious' visionaries Coleridge had in mind were Godwin and his disciples, the 'dim-eyed Sons of Blasphemy' among whom Wordsworth numbered himself during 1795. Coleridge was right in thinking that *Political Justice* was popular among the intellectual leaders of the reform movement at this time. Prominent members of the Corresponding Society such as John Thelwall, John Binns, Francis Place, and Coleridge's Cambridge hero William Frend were all influenced by Godwin's thinking. Thelwall consistently used *Political Justice* in his lectures to advocate peaceful reform, but Coleridge thought that it might have the opposite effect. He detested Godwin's atheism, and believed that the philosophy of *Political Justice* might lead to a moral and political breakdown and ultimately to violence similar to that of France during the terror.[17] But where Coleridge could reject Godwin's position unequivocally, Robespierre was a more problematic figure.

In their various lectures during 1795 Coleridge and Thelwall both presented Robespierre as a man of vision, although their purposes in doing so were different. Thelwall claimed Robespierre had a 'capacious' soul, a 'varied' imagination, and that Pitt was in every way his inferior. Coleridge would have agreed, but he found the paradoxes of Robespierre's character and mind even more fascinating. Where Thelwall was content to describe, Coleridge was concerned to analyse. Thelwall's Robespierre was of political significance only, but Coleridge's Robespierre had a direct bearing upon his thinking about the imagination.

Coleridge's earliest definition of imagination comes at the beginning of his *Lecture on the Slave Trade*, which he delivered 'by particular desire' on 16 June 1795. 'To develope the powers of the Creator,' Coleridge says,

is our proper employment – and to imitate Creativeness by combination our most exalted and self-satisfying Delight. But we are progressive and must not rest content with present Blessings. Our Almighty Parent hath therefore given to us Imagination that stimulates to the attainment of *real* excellence by the contemplation of splendid Possibilities that still revivifies the dying motive within us, and fixing our eye on the glittering Summits that rise one above the other in Alpine endlessness still urges us up the ascent of Being, amusing the ruggedness of the road with the beauty and grandeur of the ever-widening Prospect. Such and so noble are the ends for which this restless faculty was given us – but horrible has been its misapplication.   (*Lects 1795*, pp. 235–6)

This is one of Coleridge's most important statements about the imagination, and it foreshadows the definitions of primary and secondary imagination in *Biographia*. The seminal significance of this passage, however, lies in its immediate implications for Coleridge rather than in anticipating his position twenty years later. By redeploying the dying revolutionary motive to progress in the 'restless faculty' of the imagination, Coleridge found his own solution to the dilemma confronting a whole generation caused by the complete failure of the French Revolution. The *Lecture on the Slave Trade* offers a momentary insight into the more extended process of development in Coleridge's thinking about the 'One Life' between 1795 and 1797. It was this gradual translation of 'splendid Possibilities' from revolutionary politics to the individual mind that was to sustain Coleridge through years when Wordsworth – who had made a parallel reinvestment of hope in Godwin's philosophy – suffered a crisis of despair. Coleridge's power to bring Wordsworth a 'living help / To regulate [his] soul' depended upon his having made this transition, the nature of which he had recognised as early as June 1795. Its revivifying influence flows through Wordsworth's poetry of spring 1798, in his revised conclusion for *The Ruined Cottage*, in his study of the narrator of that poem in *The Pedlar*, and in the lyrical poems written at this time and subsequently published in *Lyrical Ballads*. It is not an exaggeration to claim that the emergent idea of imagination in the *Lecture on the Slave Trade* represents a turning point in the development of English Romanticism, upon which the subsequent literary careers of Coleridge and Wordsworth depended. That idea of imagination, in turn, was conditioned by Coleridge's insight into its 'horrible misapplication' by Robespierre during the Terror.

Robespierre's misapplication of imagination was caused by his lack of *patience*. 'Permit me', Coleridge asked Thelwall on 17 December 1796, 'as a definition of this word to quote one sentence from my first Address',

'Accustomed to regard all the affairs of Man, as a Process, they never hurry & they never pause.' In his not possessing *this* virtue, all the horrible excesses of Robespierre did, I believe, originate. (*CL*, I, p. 164)

Coleridge's definition of patience comes from his discussion of the 'thinking and disinterested Patriots', with whom he identified himself, in his 'Introductory Address'. These patriots were the reformists Joseph Gerrald, Thomas Muir, Thomas Fysshe Palmer and Maurice Margarot, all of whom had been tried for sedition during 1793–4 and transported to Botany Bay. Like Robespierre they were distinguished for their visionary power, but also for the restraint which he had not possessed:

Theirs is not that twilight of political knowledge which gives us just light enough to place one foot before the other; as they advance the scene still opens upon them, and they press right onward with a vast and various landscape of existence around them. Calmness and energy mark all their actions. (*Lects 1795*, p. 40)

The thinking and disinterested patriots are, in fact, the prototypes of Coleridge's Elect in *Religious Musings*,

> Who in this fleshly World, . . .
> Their strong eye darting thro' the deeds of Men
> Adore with stedfast unpresuming gaze
> Him, Nature's Essence, Mind, and Energy!
> And gazing, trembling, patiently ascend
> Treading beneath their feet all visible things
> As steps, that upward to their Father's Throne
> Lead gradual – else nor glorified nor lov'd. (ll. 57, 58–64)

Robespierre, in comparison, was too presumptuous. He might have belonged among the Elect but for the impatience which betrayed his own vision and usurped God's providence, that 'strong controlling love / Alike from all educing perfect good'. This alone could have reconciled

Robespierre's 'means' to the 'distant prospect' he had in view, and avoided the excesses of the terror. As it was, Robespierre remained unregenerate. He was a patriot *manqué*, a distorted reflection of Coleridge's own image. He appears as a grotesque parody of the 'disinterested Patriots' and the Elect, divided against himself and his country,

> – to prevent tyranny he became a Tyrant – and having realized the evils which he suspected, a wild and dreadful Tyrant . . . – he despotized in all the pomp of Patriotism, and masqueraded on the bloody stage of Revolution, a Caligula with the cap of Liberty on his head.   (*Lects 1795*, p. 35)

Coleridge drew this passage in the 'Introductory Address' to *Conciones* from the first act of *The Fall of Robespierre*. In the 'Address' the theatrical metaphor works to highlight the contradictory fragments of Robespierre's political personality, a tyrant ruling in the name of liberty. Coleridge even coined a new word – 'despotize', meaning to act the part of a despot – to define the split in Robespierre's psyche which he believed had been caused by his impatience, equivalent for Coleridge to a lack of faith.[18] Not surprisingly, he found an identical dislocation in atheist Godwin's *Political Justice*, 'a book which builds without a foundation, [and] proposes an end without establishing the means'.[19] Robespierre's politics and Godwin's philosophy lacked a foundation in the 'universally efficient' powers of God, and were inevitably self-defeating. Robespierre rushed headlong to attain his 'distant prospect', and the spectacle horrified and fascinated Coleridge. At the other extreme was Godwin, the 'studious Visionary' who denied the existence of God and passively awaited the triumph of truth through the exercise of human reason. Coleridge contemptuously dismissed Godwin's vision of future perfection as an ideal state 'which we are never to reach'. His deeper fear, however, was that Godwin's ideas might be used by less patient individuals to justify extreme, and possibly violent, means of social and political change. It was this possibility that fed his concern about the popularity of *Political Justice* 'among the professed Friends of civil Freedom' (*Lects 1795*, p. 164). These doubts about the moral effects of *Political Justice* never became a reality. But they did have an imaginative fruition, in Wordsworth's *Borderers* and later in *The Prelude*.

In Book Ten of *The Prelude* Wordsworth recalls the 'miserable dreams' that he experienced during the Terror:

> Such ghastly visions had I of despair,
> And tyranny, and implements of death,
> And long orations which in dreams I pleaded
> Before unjust tribunals, with a voice
> Labouring, [and] a brain confounded . . .   (X, ll. 374–8)

His night-visions of despair and confusion before those 'unjust tribunals'
subsequently reappear in Wordsworth's account of his Godwinian
speculations about society and human nature. He says that he dragged
'all passions, notions, shapes of faith / Like culprits to the bar' (x, ll.
889–90). Here, though, Wordsworth is both prosecutor and defendant
and is divided against himself over the 'bar' of Godwinian rationalism,
endlessly prevented from reaching a verdict,

> thus confounded more and more,
> Misguiding and misguided   (x, ll. 887–8)

– in exactly the way that Coleridge believed Robespierre had been con-
founded by the means he had adopted to save France. With the republic
threatened from outside and within the country, he had been pushed into
terrorism to protect the gains of the Revolution,

> And thus beset with foes on every side,
> The goaded land waxed mad . . .   (x, ll. 311–12)

A little later in Book Ten, Wordsworth once again uses identical
language to describe his thinking under the influence of *Political Justice*.
'My mind was both let loose', he recalls, 'Let loose and goaded',

> I took the knife in hand,
> And, stopping not at parts less sensitive,
> Endeavoured with my best of skill to probe
> The living body of society
> Even to the heart.   (x, ll. 862–3, 872–6)

The guillotine has become a surgeon's knife, and the surgeon is Wordsworth himself performing an operation of vivisection upon 'the living
body of society', as Robespierre had sought to purge the internal enemies
of France and 'seal our work with our blood'. Through a series of
deliberate and striking verbal parallels, the madness of the 'goaded land'
is internalised as the disturbance of Wordsworth's mind,

> now believing,
> Now disbelieving, endlessly perplexed
> With impulse, motive, right and wrong   (x, ll. 892–4)

– until he 'Yielded up moral questions in despair', bringing ruin upon
himself as Robespierre had done. However, Wordsworth's extinction as
a Godwinian being carries an intimation of future restoration in its echo
of Matthew, xxvii, 50,

Jesus, when he had cried again with a loud voice, yielded up the ghost

– but the resurrection was shortly to follow. For Wordsworth in *The
Prelude*, despair gives way to Dorothy's healing presence, Coleridge's

friendship and under their influence his own reincarnation as a poet.

Book Ten of *The Prelude* imaginatively associates Robespierre's politics with Godwin's philosophy, Wordsworth's confused Godwinian self with the author of the Terror. Wordsworth wrote this section of *The Prelude* in 1804, when the shortcomings of Godwin's philosophy had long been obvious to him. Nevertheless, it apparently insists that this realisation originally contributed to his moral despair and, moreover, that the very nature of that despair in some way fostered his receptivity to Coleridge's ideas when they met in 1797.

Like Coleridge in *The Fall of Robespierre*, Wordsworth's allusions to *Paradise Lost* in Book Ten of *The Prelude* identify Robespierre as Satan, the serpent that marred the early peaceful years of the Revolution with violence. But his effort to damn Robespierre momentarily relaxes at one point where he admits that even during the 'rage and dog-day heat' of the Terror he had found

> Something to glory in, as just and fit,
> And in the order of sublimest laws.
> And even if that were not, amid the awe
> Of unintelligible chastisement
> I felt a kind of sympathy with power – . . .   (x, ll. 412–16)

Wordsworth never gloried in the executions at Paris, but the implications of this passage are almost as disturbing. His 'kind of sympathy' with Robespierre's absolute power ironically resembles his 'ready welcome' for *Political Justice* in 1794, as a means to guard against the scourge of violence in Britain. In *The Prelude* his memory of Godwin's philosophy is of an 'unimpeachable' power

> To look through all the frailties of the world,
> And, with a resolute mastery shaking off
> The accidents of nature, time, and place,
> That make up the weak being of the past,
> Build social freedom on its only basis:
> The freedom of the individual mind,
> Which, to the blind restraint of general laws
> Superior, magisterially adopts
> One guide – the light of circumstances, flashed
> Upon an independent intellect.   (x, ll. 820–9)

The 'resolute mastery' and magisterial guidance recall Wordsworth's letter to Mathews of 8 June 1794, where he had based his hopes for social freedom upon Godwin's ideas. Four months before Wordsworth wrote that letter, in his speech on political morality, Robespierre had made an equally sweeping claim for 'virtue and equality', which he identified as the 'soul of the republic'. Robespierre too had shaken off the frailties of feeling and other 'accidents' of human nature, and presented republican virtue as

> a compass to direct you through the tempest of the passions and the whirlwind of the intrigues that surround you. You have the touchstone with which you can test all your laws, all the propositions that are laid before you. [20]

Moments later, Robespierre used that 'touchstone' to justify his ruthless equation of terrorism with justice. In *The Prelude*, Wordsworth presents Godwin's philosophy as a similar touchstone, 'to the blind restraint of general laws / Superior'. But where Robespierre openly advocated the use of violence, Wordsworth hints darkly at the similar end to which Godwin might have guided him. He does so by defining Godwinian rationalism

> – the light of circumstances, flashed
> Upon an independent intellect

– in words taken from the mouth of a man who would persuade murder. As is well known, these lines originally appeared in *The Borderers*, where Rivers congratulates Mortimer for killing the old man Herbert:

> You have obeyed the only law that wisdom
> Can ever recognise: the immediate law
> Flashed from the light of circumstances
> Upon an independent intellect.
> Henceforth new prospects ought to open on you,
> Your faculties should grow with the occasion. (III-v-ll. 30–5)[21]

It has less frequently been pointed out that the 'new prospects' and growing faculties contingent upon Rivers' 'immediate law' ironically correspond to the 'ever-widening Prospect' and 'restless faculty' in Coleridge's *Lecture on the Slave Trade*. The anti-Godwinian thrust of Wordsworth's irony lies in the conditional 'ought to open', 'should grow', and in the immediate context of the play where the only prospect discovered is death. In the character of Rivers Wordsworth has, in fact, realised Coleridge's long-standing fears about the similarities between Godwinian abstraction and Robespierre's visionary politics.

Coleridge published his *Lecture on the Slave Trade* in the fourth issue of *The Watchman*, 25 March 1796. He omitted much of the definition of imagination in the lecture as originally delivered on 15 June 1795, and unless Wordsworth read the manuscript in Bristol the following September it seems unlikely that he was familiar with it when he wrote *The Borderers*. He did, however, receive a copy of *Conciones* sent by James Losh on 20 March 1797, but this was probably after completion of a first draft of the play (*EY*, p. 186). Nevertheless, Wordsworth must have known Coleridge's criticisms of Godwin at least since their meeting in September 1795, when they would certainly have differed over the merits of *Political Justice*. Two years later, Rivers' speech offers striking evidence of the extent to which their ideas later coincided when they met again at Racedown in June 1797, and of Wordsworth's receptivity to Coleridge's influence.

The shadowy figure presiding over that meeting was not Godwin – whose influence had been exorcised – but Robespierre, in whose life and death Coleridge and Wordsworth recognised the man they could have been. And that realisation ultimately led each of them to discover his own true identity as poet, the man Robespierre might have been but never was.

Notes

[1] All references to *The Prelude* will be to the 1805 text in *Norton 'Prelude'*.

[2] William Godwin, ms. autobiographical fragment in the Abinger-Shelley collection at the Bodleian Library, Oxford. The ms. is undated, but the paper is watermarked 'Fellows 1807'. I am grateful to Lord Abinger for permission to quote from Godwin's papers.

[3] Quoted from the text in Jared Curtis, *Wordsworth's Experiments with Tradition. The Lyric Poems of 1802* (Ithaca and London, 1971), p. 167.

[4] For a discussion of the relation of *Intimations* to *To H.C.* see Lucy Newlyn, 'The Little Actor and his Mock Apparel', *TWC* (Winter 1983), pp. 30–9.

[5] William Godwin, *Diary*. Abinger-Shelley collection, Bodleian Library.

[6] John Thelwall, *The Tribune* (3 vols., London, 1795–6), I, p. 254. Cited in future as *Tribune*.

[7] *Tribune*, I, p. 258.

[8] *Tribune*, I, p. 254.

[9] *The French Revolution. Extracts from The Times 1789–1794*, ed. N. Ascherson (London, 1975), pp. 114–15.

[10] *New Letters of Robert Southey*, ed. K. Curry (2 vols., New York and London, 1965), I, pp. 72–3.

[11] John Milton, *Paradise Lost*, eds. J. Carey and A. Fowler (London, 1968).

[12] *Tribune*, I, p. 259.

[13] *The Documentary History of Western Civilisation. The French Revolution*, tr. and ed. P. Beik (London, 1971), p. 278. Cited in future as Beik.

[14] Beik, p. 279.

[15] Beik, p. 283.

[16] *The Salisbury Plain Poems of William Wordsworth*, ed. S. Gill (Hassocks, Sussex, 1975), p. 37.

[17] For Coleridge's doubts about the moral effects of *Political Justice*, see the *Third Lecture on Revealed Religion, Lects 1795*, pp. 164–5.

[18] See my note, 'Robespierre's Despotism and a Word Coined by Coleridge', *N & Q* (August, 1981), pp. 309–10.

[19] *Third Lecture on Revealed Religion, Lects 1795*, p. 164.

[20] Beik, p. 281.

[21] William Wordsworth, *The Borderers*, ed. Osborn (Ithaca and London, 1982), p. 210. The text quoted is from the ms. published by Osborn as 'The Early Version (1797–99)'.

Coleridge's *Dejection*: imagination, joy, and the power of love

J. ROBERT BARTH, S.J.

Poetic origins are often obscure, as witness the genesis of Shakespeare's sonnets or the history of Keats' two Hyperions. Among such mysteries, the relationship between Coleridge's verse 'Letter to Sara Hutchinson' (written on 4 April 1802, but first published only in 1937) and his *Dejection: an Ode* (published in the *Morning Post*, 4 October 1802, Wordsworth's wedding-day) has been a matter of considerable discussion and debate.[1] Although it is evident that the one is a drastic revision of the other, it remains unclear what were Coleridge's poetic purposes in making the revision, and what was in his mind in publishing it on the wedding-day of his friend Wordsworth, which was also the seventh anniversary of his own unfortunate marriage to Sara Fricker.

A cogent case has been made that 'Dejection' has its origin as much in Coleridge's relationship with Wordsworth as in his frustrated love for Sara Hutchinson. The first four stanzas of Wordsworth's 'Immortality Ode', in which Wordsworth laments his loss of the 'visionary gleam', were written just days before Coleridge composed his verse-letter to Sara, and it was two years before Wordsworth was able to complete it. Written as they are on what appears to be a similar theme, it is difficult not to see the two poems as 'in some sense in a dialogue with each other'.[2] The sense of 'dialogue' is deepened when one realizes that Wordsworth's own stanzas echo clearly a poem of Coleridge written two years earlier – *The Mad Monk* (1800), which begins:

> There was a time when earth, and sea, and skies,
>   The bright green vale, and forest's dark recess,
> With all things, lay before mine eyes
>   In steady loveliness:
> But now . . .   (ll. 9–13)

Wordsworth's answer to his sense of loss, written two years later, was a re-affirmation of the strength still to be found in the world of nature: 'Yet in my heart of hearts I feel your might' (l. 193).[3] Coleridge's answer to his loss, it has been said, was rather to turn inward, despairing of nature as a healing power: 'O Lady! we receive but what we give' (l. 47). If this is so, the two friends had certainly parted company poetically and philosophically long before their friendship was ruptured in 1810.

Perhaps even more tantalizing is the question of the relationship between the two major versions of Coleridge's poem, the verse-letter and the *textus receptus*. As to the poetic superiority of one over the other, each version has its proponents. As Reeve Parker writes, the *Letter to Sara* 'has been called an incomparably greater poem . . . chiefly on grounds of its being a less disguised personal lament over marital unhappiness, ill-health, and weakened poetic power'. There are others, however, 'who prefer the final, shorter ode form for its greater lyric dignity and who find the sprawling earlier text embarrassing in its self-pity'.[4]

John Beer, for example, seems to give the nod to the earlier version: 'Both poems have their peculiar value. *Dejection* stands to its predecessor rather as an engraving may stand in relation to an original painting. Its points are made more sharply and stringently: but in order to hear the full throb of Coleridge's unhappiness the greater length of the earlier version is needed.'[5] Humphry House, too, although he admits that 'a case cannot be made for the full coherence of the original version', argues for its overall superiority, stressing especially what he sees as its greater artistic unity; he argues, in effect, that *Dejection* betrays the essential unity of the original.[6] George Watson, on the other hand, insists that 'there can be no doubt of the superiority of the final version, where the original 340 lines have been reduced to a tight-packed 139. . . . On the whole, . . . the reduction of the ode to its familiar form is a continuous triumph of critical acumen'.[7] In the last analysis, it comes down no doubt to a matter of poetic taste, a conflict (as Reeve Parker characterizes it) 'between those who like confessional sincerity in art and those whose inclination is for the orderliness of form'.[8]

We are faced, however, with the two major versions of the poem; and one question that seems continually to be urged in the recent history of Coleridge criticism is Coleridge's purpose in changing the form of the poem so drastically. Some critics have suggested that Coleridge found it necessary, for personal reasons, to hide (or suppress) the real origins of his feelings; others, that he realized his real theme was the loss of his 'shaping spirit of Imagination', and so pruned and reshaped the poem to highlight that loss; and still others, that, having experienced such deep grief, he used *Dejection* to explore the process of grief with which the experience began. Each of these approaches has something to recommend it, nor should they be thought of as necessarily exclusive of one another.

The first of these views – that Coleridge found it necessary to suppress the real origins of his feelings – may be represented by Beverly Fields' interesting psycho-analytic study, *Reality's Dark Dream.* [9] Her case can be fairly enough summed up in these words from her Conclusion:

> The shifts in organization appear to have been made partly for reasons of coherence but also partly in order to suppress as far as possible the real reasons for his depression. It was undoubtedly far easier for him to assign the cause of the depression to metaphysical speculation than it would have been to let the poem stand as a revelation of the sadomasochistic fantasies that paralyzed his feeling and his behavior.   (p. 166)

Other, less psycho-analytic readers, like Max Schulz and Charles Bouslog, also see Coleridge's desire to camouflage his real feelings as the reason for his revision of the poem. [10]

The second reading – that Coleridge realized his real theme was the loss of his 'shaping spirit of Imagination' – is persuasively argued by Paul Magnuson in *Coleridge's Nightmare Poetry.* [11] Magnuson finds, in effect, not two versions of the same poem but two quite distinct poems. The *Letter* focuses on 'the pain he has caused Asra' (p. 108), while *Dejection* focuses on himself – his own pain, his own loss.

> The Letter is nearer the spirit of the earlier Conversation Poems in that there is an imagined exchange of sympathy, but in 'Dejection,' he faces a far more fundamental problem. If he himself has lost joy, and if he is the victim of strong feelings, then his blessing could well turn into a curse upon himself and Asra.
>   (p. 109)

The only shared experience between them is that of grief (p. 111). He has lost, perhaps forever, his old sense of the One Life. As Magnuson puts it, 'We project a meaning upon nature, and whatever we receive from nature is only a reflection of our minds' (p. 114), but since the poet has lost joy and his 'shaping spirit of Imagination' (l. 86), for him the world is now without meaning. There is still hope for 'the Lady', since her soul is still alive – and so for her things can still live – 'their life the eddying of her living soul!' (l. 136) – but for him there is no life in the world because there is no life within him: 'O Lady! we receive but what we give.'

The third view – that Coleridge, having experienced such deep grief, used *Dejection* to explore the process of grief itself – is articulated by Reeve Parker in his splendid book *Coleridge's Meditative Art.* [12] The ode was, in effect, a gesture 'offered to reassure the Grasmere circle that he was capable of transcending the impulses toward despair and unseemliness that were so much responsible for the original letter' (p. 181). The original letter is merely an expression of grief, while the more shapely, more carefully crafted ode is an exploration of the state of grief in which the poet finds himself. This exploration is, in effect and even perhaps in intention, a kind of therapy. As Coleridge had argued in the Preface to his *Poems* of 1796, from the intellectual labor of poetic composition 'a pleasure results which is gradually associated and mingles as a corrective with the painful subject of the description'.[13] Thus there is, in Parker's phrase, 'a salutary egotism in poetic composition' (p. 181).

Parker thus finds *Dejection* a much more positive poetic experience than do many other critics. He believes, in fact, that modern readers of the poem often read into it their own preoccupations:

In emphasizing the elements of personal distress discernible in and through the poem and in seeing it as a lament over suspended poetic imagination, readers . . . have presumed a greater continuity than actually exists between the concerns of a poet like Coleridge, at the turn of the nineteenth century, and the characteristic preoccupation of many twentieth-century writers with alienation, self-doubt, and distrust of the artful imagination.   (p. 181)

There is an entry from 1803 in one of Coleridge's notebooks which Parker believes sheds light on Coleridge's 'heuristic' motives in *Dejection*: 'One excellent use of communication of Sorrows to a Friend is this: that in relating what ails us we ourselves first know exactly what the real Grief is – & see it for itself, in its own form & limits' (*CN*, I, 1599).[14] With the help of the controlling metaphor of the poem, the storm, the poet is able to dramatize his situation – and in doing so, is able to 'generalize' his grief, to (in a phrase of Coleridge) 'abstract the thoughts and images from their original cause' and to reflect on them 'with less and less reference to the individual suffering that had been their first subject'.[15] When the poet returns, late in the poem, to an awareness of the wind that still rages, he is able to achieve, in Parker's phrase, an 'absolute distancing of wind and poet' (p. 200). He is not under the control of the wind, but rather can hear in it different voices, as he soon reveals – hearing first the voices of violence and war, then a new voice, 'A tale of less affright / And tempered with delight' (ll. 118–19). He can now hear in the wind the voice of Wordsworth's Lucy Gray, and it is a voice of life in the face of the lonesome wind.

For Parker, then, the 'sounds less deep and loud' at the end of stanza VII are 'correlative to a mind that, having gone through the process of deliberately exploring the melancholy grief with which the poem opens, is winning its way to a substantial calm' (pp. 206–7). Having achieved this calm, the poet is then able 'to "send his soul abroad" in the blessing that constitutes the final stanza' (p. 207).

Without in any way denying the cogency of Parker's approach, with which I find myself generally in considerable agreement, I would like to go on to suggest that there is a motif implicit in 'Dejection' which is quite compatible with the exploration of the process of grief – a motif which has been given little or no attention.

Let me begin with the *Letter to Sara*. No one would deny, I suspect,
that the *Letter*, whatever else it is about – loss or grief or despair – is also
about love. It may be love lost or grieved over or despaired of, but any
careful reading makes it clear how preoccupied the original poem is with
love. And this love ranges through the whole spectrum of possibilities.
The most obvious – and indeed central – love is what we may call his
'romantic' love for Sara Hutchinson. She is his 'best belov'd! who lovest
me the best' (l. 120); she is 'My Comforter! A Heart within my Heart!'
(l. 250); she is the 'Sister & Friend of my devoutest Choice!' (l. 324). She
is beyond question the central figure of the *Letter* addressed to her. At the
same time, however, the context in which she is placed must be taken account of: she is constantly seen as part of a whole domestic scene, as in
'that happy night / When Mary, thou & I together were, / The low decaying fire our only Light' (ll. 99–101), or when he speaks despairingly of
visiting 'those, I love, as I love thee, / Mary, & William, & dear Dorothy'
(ll. 157–8). It is not only Sara, but the loving circle of which she is part,
that is the object of his love and longing. This is not to say that there is
no romantic or sexual component in his longing for Sara; there clearly
is. It is to suggest, however, that there is more than one kind of love at
issue, not only in the poem but even in his relationship with Sara.

With this peacefully remembered scene of domestic tranquillity, Coleridge contrasts his own home: 'My own peculiar Lot, my house-hold
Life / It is, & will remain, Indifference or Strife' (ll. 163–4). It is, perhaps
even more movingly, 'my coarse domestic life' (l. 258). There is joy, to
be sure, in the love of his children: 'My Little Children are a Joy, a Love,
/ A good Gift from above/' (ll. 272–3). But his grief (perhaps over the
failure of his own domestic life) lessens the joy of even this great love:
'This clinging Grief too, in it's turn, awakes / That Love, and Father's
Joy; but O! it makes / The Love the greater, & the Joy far less' (ll. 287–9).

There is love of Nature in the poem, too, for he goes on to apostrophize
its beauty:

> These Mountains too, these Vales, these Woods, these Lakes,
> Scenes full of Beauty & of Loftiness
> Where all my Life I fondly hop'd to live –
> I were sunk low indeed, did they *no* solace give.   (ll. 290–3)

But even they have failed him, for – and here the Wordsworthian
parallel will be evident – 'They are not to me now the Things, which
once they were' (l. 295).

Thus there is in the *Letter to Sara* a whole range of human loves: romantic and sexual love, love of family, love of children, love of friends, love
of nature.[16] All are either lessened or lost or in some way frustrated. One

may well say that the *Letter* is about loss, but I suggest that even more fundamental to it is the question of what it is that is lost: love of every kind. The most basic dichotomy of the *Letter* is between Coleridge and Sara – the one who has lost love and the one who is still surrounded by it, as the last stanza continues to insist:

> Sister & Friend of my devoutest Choice!
> Thou being innocent & full of love,
> And nested with the Darlings of thy Love . . .   (ll. 324–6)

Whatever else it is, the *Letter to Sara* is a poem about love and its loss.

Against this background, it is perhaps startling to discover that while the word 'love' (or its cognates – loved, lover, and beloved) appears twenty-one times in the *Letter*, its only cognate in *Dejection* is, ironically, 'loveless' in line 52. Does this mean that a motif that was so prominent in the earlier version has been completely written out of the later one? I would like to suggest that what was explicit throughout the *Letter* has simply gone underground, becoming an implicit principle of action in *Dejection*. I would like to argue, in fact, that the word 'loveless' – 'The poor loveless ever-anxious crowd' – is a key to the poem.

My argument turns around the interpretation one gives to the much-quoted line, 'O Lady! we receive but what we give'. This line is most commonly taken to refer to the poet's relationship with nature: that he is arguing, in effect, against Wordsworth's belief in the healing power of nature. Nature has no power to affect our lives; our response to nature is determined by our own feelings, by the projection of our selves. And if our feelings, or our inner selves, have lost their sense of life, then there is nothing but the blankness of despair.

This may indeed be the initial meaning of the line, but it does not, I think, remain its sole meaning. This understanding of the relationship of nature and self does last, to be sure, through the two stanzas that follow – stanza V, which extols joy, 'this strong music in the soul', and stanza VI, which laments the passing of that joy. Stanza VII, however, marks a decisive turn away from this view:

> Hence, viper-thoughts, that coil around my mind,
>   Reality's dark dream!
> I turn from you, and listen to the wind,
>   Which long has raved unnoticed.   (ll. 94–7)

Putting aside the almost solipsistic view of himself and nature, he finally allows himself really to listen to the wind, to allow *its* power to work in him. At the beginning of the poem, he had projected his own feelings onto the wind – and so could hear only his own depression. This is precisely what had led to his reflection: 'We receive but what we give'. Later, after rejecting this self-centred and self-pitying attitude ('Hence, viper-thoughts!'), he is able to let nature touch him, and he finds that it is heal-ing. Perhaps Wordsworth is right after all.[17]

Therefore stanza IV was a self-pitying, wrongheaded view, which the poet now finds strength to reject; and the vehicle for this discovery is the wind. His perception of the wind had begun as superstition (the folk-beliefs concerning the weather) and self-projection; but through the pro-cess of the poem he has come to see it as a natural force from which he can learn: it has its cycles, from wild to gentle, as he does himself.[18] And as the wind gentles down – singing 'a tale of less affright, / And tempered with delight' – so does his own soul. He was right in stanza IV:

> And from the soul itself must there be sent
> A sweet and potent voice, of its own birth,
> Of all sweet sounds the life and element!   (ll. 56–8)

And this voice is the voice that issues forth from him at the end of the poem, offering blessing to one he loves. It is perhaps no accident that in stanza IV this voice is contrasted with 'the poor loveless ever-anxious crowd' – because we come to see that it is the voice of love, of one who has learned that only if he is open to receive will he be able to give. Had he not opened himself to the voice of nature – first wild but ultimately healing – he would never have found his own voice. But he did find it, and in the closing lines of blessing it is indeed 'a sweet and potent voice', newly potent because it now speaks not out of self-pity but out of loving concern for another.

The pattern of this poem is, in fact, no different from that of a number of others of Coleridge's poems. It is the same pattern found in *This Lime-Tree Bower My Prison*, in which the poet overcomes his dejection by enter-ing into the feelings of Charles Lamb as he enjoys the country sunset:

> and sometimes
> 'Tis well to be bereft of promis'd good,
> That we may lift the soul, and contemplate
> With lively joy the joys we cannot share.   (ll. 64–7)

What is this but an act of love: a giving of oneself to another? And so with the Ancient Mariner, who is able to move out of his isolation by an act of imaginative sympathy with the watersnakes:

> A spring of love gushed from my heart,
> And I blessed them unaware.   (ll. 284–5)

Whatever name one may give to such an act, it is a movement of love: a going-forth out of the self to encounter the being of another. In the last analysis, Coleridge is not content to remain one of the 'loveless ever-anxious crowd'; he does not remain mired in 'dejection'. Through the ministry of nature, he is able to love. *Dejection* remains, therefore, in its transformation from the *Letter to Sara*, a love poem; but it becomes a love poem in a broader and deeper sense – now not merely the lament of a frustrated lover, but an ode to the power of love itself, which can bring him out of dejection into calm, out of selfishness and self-pity into generous-hearted blessing.

But if *Dejection* is about love, it is also about imagination and joy – for the three are inextricably bound together – and about the power of art. That *Dejection* is concerned with imagination is perhaps the best known truth about the poem: the poet is dejected at least in part because he has lost his 'shaping spirit of Imagination'. He has allowed the understanding – the analytic faculty, the power of mind that deals with parts and with merely sense impressions – to take away his power to shape his experience of the world into a meaningful whole: 'by abstruse research to steal / From my own nature all the natural man' (ll. 89–90).

What is it, though, that has brought him to this sad pass? Surely it is the loss of joy, the very joy that he wishes for the 'virtuous Lady'. Joy is

> the spirit and the power,
> Which wedding Nature to us gives in dower
> A new Earth and new Heaven.   (ll. 67–9)[19]

It is joy that can enable one to bring together man and nature, heaven and earth, sense experience and spiritual reality, and it is at the same time joy that celebrates the union of all these things. The 'natural man' could feel joy, for he was in harmony with nature and could not only perceive but feel the unity of all creation. His faculties all in harmony, he could appreciate the 'wholeness' of experience and rejoice in it, for wholeness and joy are functions of one another. Hence the joyful exclamation of 'The Eolian Harp': 'O! the one Life within us and abroad' (l. 26). However, having 'by abstruse research' narrowed down his vision of the world, the poet can now see only parts of the great world. And with the loss of wholeness, joy is lost.

For joy is not only a feeling but a power of perception; it affords both creative vision and emotional exaltation. Joy or 'delight' is, in fact, a prerequisite not only for harmonious living but for the writing of poetry. As Coleridge had written of the Abyssinian maid:

> Could I revive within me
> Her symphony and song,
> To such a deep delight 'twould win me,
> That with music loud and long,
> I would build that dome in air . . .   (*Kubla Khan*, ll. 42–6)

This is, I suggest, precisely the role of *Lucy Gray*, the tale 'tempered with delight'. The poet has revived within himself, or the wind has raised within him, or better yet, the poet and the wind in fruitful concert have revived a song – not the song of the Abyssinian maid but the song sung by the little girl. As Irene H. Chayes says, 'the poet of "Dejection" begins in his reverie to re-compose another man's poem and for the moment becomes a poet again'.[20] His imagination has come to life again.

But we are concerned for the moment with the role of joy. How can a tale that tells of the suffering of a frightened child – her moans and grief and fear – be a cause of 'delight' for the poet, or indeed for anyone? The answer has to do with the nature of aesthetic experience. The wind is, after all, a 'Poet, e'en to frenzy bold' (l. 109). Through the agency of the wind and the power of the poet's poet-friend, the actual experience of grief (both Coleridge's grief and the grief of the lost child) is transformed into a tale, an artistic form, which distance the listener from the actual experience, giving it shape and meaning. The terrifying experience is sublimated to another level of reality, a mythic level, which is both meaningful and sustaining. For myth universalizes our experiences, showing them to be part of the larger experience of mankind; and by binding us to each other through our common humanity, especially through our common experience of suffering, myth allows us to draw strength from each other. It is thus we learn that mankind survives, even in the face of diminishment and loss. Therefore the experience the poet could not bear becomes through art (the 'tale' which the wind tells) not only bearable but even hopeful.

This is not to say, of course, that in the 'tale' the grief is taken away. It still retains, for the reader as well as for the poet, a strong sense of the terror of the child irretrievably lost. It is, however, 'tempered' by art, so that the grief is bearable and life can go on. And if the tale of the wind has made the child's grief bearable to the hearer, so the poet's tale of his own grief (his poem, *Dejection*) may serve the same function, giving him enough 'distance' from his grief that he can bear it – and that life can go on.

Rachel Trickett has remarked that the secret of morality in Wordsworth is that love must precede understanding.[21] Her comment recalls Shelley's famous dictum in the *Defence of Poetry* that 'the great secret of morals is love, or a going out of our own nature and an identification of ourselves with the beautiful which exists in thought, action, or person, not our own'.[22] What Trickett, like Shelley, has in mind of course is not merely morality but poetry, as a distillation and articulation of the highest human values. And if this is true of Wordsworth, it is no less true of Coleridge; without love there can be no poetry. Without love, no joy; without joy, no working of that shaping power, imagination.

But since the three – love, joy and imagination – work so closely in concert, any one of them can help to rouse the others. In *Dejection*, the momentary return of imagination and imaginative delight – in the poet's recollection of *Lucy Gray* – can stir in him a return of love, moving him to the loving gesture of blessing which closes the poem, and can hold out at least the hope of a more personal joy for him, as he prays the gift of joy for one he loves.

One question yet remains: what did Coleridge mean by publishing *Dejection* on Wordsworth's wedding-day and his own anniversary? I would like to suggest that he intended the poem as a kind of ironic epithalamion, for himself rather than for his friend. For Coleridge's tribute to the power of love is bound up, however subtly, with the nuptial imagery of the first half of the poem. The nuptial portrayed is, of course, the marriage between nature and man, and it is joy which presides over the solemnity:

> Joy, Lady! is the spirit and the power,
> Which wedding Nature to us gives in dower
> A new Earth and new Heaven.   (ll. 67–9)

But this wedding involves, paradoxically, both life and death:

> And in our life alone does Nature live:
> Ours is her wedding garment, ours her shroud.   (ll. 48–9)

And yet, if our union with nature implies death, it does so in a sense analogous to sexual union as 'a little death' – a death which can bring about new life, in this case indeed 'a new Earth and new Heaven'. So too the 'phantom light' (l. 11) – the ghost of the old moon held in the arms of the new – implies death, while the new moon affirms life. The old moon must die if the new moon is to be born. (One might even suggest that the 'silver thread' with which the phantom light is 'rimmed and circled' might point ahead to the 'wedding garment'.) Thus the phases of the moon, which are of course cycles of nature, are caught up in the nuptial imagery, which itself, as Robert Siegel has suggested, 'reflects the theme of imaginative wholeness'.[23]

However, in striking contrast to the ideal marriage described in stanza v, in which Joy,

> wedding Nature to us gives in dower
> A new Earth and new Heaven,

there is the poet's own wedding with nature (stanza VII), which brings forth nct 'a new Earth and new Heaven' but a terrifying storm. The storm is not to last forever, though, for the poet hears at length another voice of nature:

> A tale of less affright,
> And tempered with delight.

And if the poet's stormy wedding with nature – which is indeed more like a divorce than a marriage – may be seen as metaphor for Coleridge's ill-fated marriage to Sara Fricker, then the incomplete but longed-for union with the kinder face of nature ('tempered with delight') may be taken as a metaphor for his impossible yet somehow sustaining union with Sara Hutchinson.

Coleridge's marriage to Sara Fricker is over, no doubt, leaving behind only a 'phantom light' like that of the old moon, and marriage to Sara Hutchinson is only a longing. But if the song the poet hears in the wind is indeed *Lucy Gray*, then there is at least a sustaining dream at the end. Lucy Gray is dead, to be sure, but she is still alive as a dream, a mythic reality, as Lucy 'sings a solitary song / That whistles in the wind'. So too the poet's love for 'the other Sara' is alive for him, at least as a comforting dream.

But this love is not merely a dream; like the song sung by Lucy Gray, it has something of the healing power of myth. As Coleridge's spiritual divorce from his wife is reflected in his divorce from nature, from 'the one Life within us and abroad', the 'sympathy between his soul and Sara Hutchinson's looks forward to a new wedding of his soul to nature'.[24] And he too, I might add, like Lucy Gray, sings his 'solitary song' – this poem – that 'whistles in the wind', affirming life even in the midst of death.

This is indeed the power of love: to bless, to heal, even – and even in the face of dejection – to bring the hope of joy. And the power of love is, as we have seen, for Coleridge as for Wordsworth, deeply bound up with imaginative power. Wordsworth wrote, at the end of *The Prelude*:

> This spiritual Love acts not nor can exist
> Without Imagination.
>> (*Norton 'Prelude'*, XIV, ll. 188–9, 1850 text)

Coleridge would stress, I think, the corollary: that imagination cannot exist without love. He could write this poem only because the love he thought he had lost was not wholly dead in him, because – whether or not his love was returned – he was still, or perhaps again, capable of giving love. Perhaps indeed his gift of love was all the greater because it was at last unconditional love, given not for his sake but for the sake of the beloved, given whether or not it was returned. In that generous-hearted gift of self lay his hope.

Notes

[1] The text of the *Letter to Sara Hutchinson* used throughout will be that of *CL*, II, pp. 790–98; it may also be found in S. T. Coleridge, *Poems*, ed. John Beer (London: Everyman's Library 1974), pp. 272–80. The text of *Dejection: an Ode* is that of *PW*, I, pp. 362–8; this edition will also be used for all other references to Coleridge's poetry.

[2] George Watson, *Coleridge the Poet* (London, Routledge and Kegan Paul, 1966), p. 78. See also Fred Manning Smith, 'The Relation of Coleridge's *Ode on Dejection* to Wordsworth's *Ode on Intimations of Immortality*', *PMLA*, 50 (1935), pp. 224–34.

[3] The text of Wordsworth used throughout will be *Poetical Works*, ed. Thomas Hutchinson, rev. Ernest De Selincourt (London, Oxford University Press, 1936).

[4] Reeve Parker, *Coleridge's Meditative Art* (Ithaca, Cornell University Press, 1975), p. 180.

[5] *Poems*, ed. Beer, p. 257.

[6] *Coleridge: The Clark Lectures 1951–52* (London, Rupert Hart-Davis, 1953), p. 137; see also pp. 133–7.

[7] *Coleridge the Poet*, pp. 74–5.

[8] *Coleridge's Meditative Art*, p. 180. A different focus of this distinction is given by Max F. Schulz in his bibliographical essay, 'Coleridge', in *The English Romantic Poets, A Review of Research and Criticism*, ed. Frank Jordan (third edn; New York, MLA, 1972): 'It is probably safe to say that those interested in Coleridge the man and in the biographical facts behind the composition of the poem will prefer the "Verse Letter," while those concerned with literary questions of theme and form will be drawn to "Dejection" ' (p. 203).

[9] Beverly Fields, *Reality's Dark Dream: Dejection in Coleridge* (Kent, Ohio, Kent State University Press, 1967), pp. 101–64.

[10] See Max Schulz, *The Poetic Voices of Coleridge* (Detroit, Wayne State University Press, 1964), p. 140; and Charles Bouslog, *Modern Language Quarterly*, 24 (1963), pp. 42–52.

[11] Paul Magnuson, *Coleridge's Nightmare Poetry* (Charlottesville, University Press of Virginia, 1974), pp. 107–25.

[12] *Coleridge's Meditative Art*, pp. 180–209.

[13] *PW*, II, p. 1136; quoted by Parker, pp. 181–2.

[14] Quoted in Parker, p. 182.

[15] *The Complete Works of Samuel Taylor Coleridge*, ed. W. G. T. Shedd (New York: Harper and Brothers, 1856), IV, p. 435; and see Parker, p. 193.

[16] This spectrum of loves in the *Letter to Sara* may account, in some measure, for the different addressees of its various versions: the very personal 'Sara' of the original; 'William', 'Wordsworth', and 'dearest poet' (in the version Coleridge sent to William Sotheby in a letter of 19 July 1802; *CL*, II, pp. 813–19), emphasizing his close personal relationship with his poet-friend; 'Edmund' (in the version published in the *Morning Post* on 4 October 1802; see *PW*, I, pp. 362–8, notes), again celebrating friendship, though distanced by the use of another name; and 'Lady' (in the *textus receptus* published in *Sibylline Leaves* in 1816), returning to the romantic love of the original verse letter, but again distanced by the use of the generic and more formal mode

of address. Coleridge's complex thought and feeling give validity to each of these in turn.

17 An opposite view of the wind metaphor is taken by Panthea Reid Broughton in her subtle and perceptive essay 'The Modifying Metaphor in "Dejection: An Ode" ': 'Coleridge was really very skeptical . . . of the Wordsworthian faith in the active universe' (*TWC*, IV (1973), p. 242). Although she later sees Coleridge able to use the closing image of the 'eddy' as a fruitful metaphor, in Broughton's view Coleridge begins by 'dispelling the familiar Romantic metaphor of the Aeolian harp. . . . Outward forms, though they may rescue Wordsworth, fail Coleridge; he awaits their intervention to no avail. And thus the central Romantic metaphor debilitates because it encourages him to wait passively for a shift in the weather before he can change his tune' (p. 243). I suggest rather that the poet's waiting has changed from passive to active ('I turn from you') as he opens himself at last to the natural influence of the wind which he had shut out. For a view similar to Broughton's see Marshall Suther, *The Dark Night of Samuel Taylor Coleridge* (New York, Columbia University Press, 1960), pp. 124–8.

Unlike Broughton, M. H. Abrams, in 'The Correspondent Breeze: A Romantic Metaphor', sees the wind as truly an agent for change in the poet's mind: 'By the agency of the wind storm it describes, the poem turns out to contradict its own premises: the poet's spirit awakens to violent life even as he laments his inner death' (*English Romantic Poets: Modern Essays in Criticism*, ed. M. H. Abrams (2nd edn; London, Oxford University Press, 1975), p. 39). R. H. Fogle, too, in 'The Dejection of Coleridge's Ode', assumes 'that Coleridge as a metaphysical realist and a Romantic poet of nature is expressing his experience through the interaction of his thoughts and emotions with natural symbolism and imagery' (*ELH*, XVII (1950), p. 73).

18 In 'Structure and Style in the Greater Romantic Lyric', M. H. Abrams writes: 'On Coleridge's philosophical premises, in this poem nature is made thought and thought nature, both by their sustained interaction and by their seamless metaphoric continuity' (*Romanticism and Consciousness: Essays in Criticism*, ed. Harold Bloom (New York, Norton, 1970), p. 223).

19 Attention has been called to the echo here of Revelation 21:1 ('And I saw a new heaven and a new earth'), but I have not seen reference to the possibly even deeper roots of this passage in Isaiah 65:17ff., where the role of joy is made explicit: 'For, behold, I create new heavens and a new earth: and the former shall not be remembered, nor come into mind. But be ye glad and rejoice for ever in that which I create: for behold, I create Jerusalem a rejoicing, and her people a joy. And I will rejoice in Jerusalem, and joy in my people: and the voice of weeping shall be no more heard in her, nor the voice of crying.' With the notes struck not only of joy but of creativity, together with the fact that in Revelation Jerusalem becomes the Bride, it is difficult not to hear echoes of both passages in Coleridge's lines.

20 Irene H. Chayes, 'Rhetoric as Drama: An Approach to the Romantic Ode', *PMLA*, 79 (1964), p. 70.

21 'Wordsworth's Moral Imagination', lecture delivered by Rachel Trickett at the Wordsworth Summer Conference, Grasmere, 3 August 1983.

22 Percy Bysshe Shelley, 'A Defence of Poetry', *Shelley's Prose*, ed. David Lee Clark (Albuquerque, University of New Mexico Press, 1954), pp. 282–3.

23 Robert Siegel, 'The Serpent and the Dove: The Problem of Evil in Col-

eridge's Poetry' (Ph.D. diss., Harvard University, 1968), p. 236. I am more generally grateful to Siegel, too, for his illuminating discussion of the wedding theme, which has considerably influenced my own reading of the poem.

[24] Siegel, p. 238.

Imagining naming shaping: stanza VI of
Dejection: an Ode

PETER LARKIN

I

But now afflictions bow me down to earth:
Nor care I that they rob me of my mirth,
But oh! each visitation
Suspends what nature gave me at my birth,
My shaping spirit of Imagination

John Spencer Hill finds compelling reasons for believing that July –
September 1802 'were crucial months in the shaping of the theory of the
Imagination' for Coleridge, a period which is straddled by the *Letter to
Sara Hutchinson* in April and the Ode's publication in October.[1] The
material of stanza VI remains fairly constant between the two versions,
though subject to some transposition within the overall scheme of the
poem, and only condensed to one stanza in the later text. Both versions
reflect Coleridge's concern with the nature of imagination he was in process of exploring beyond the borders of his Ode, though the concern is
as much in evidence, if rather more problematically, within the poem
itself. The question of how the different modes of Coleridge's writing
(poetic or theoretical) relate to each other is closely bound up with their
author's sense of personal vocation, or with how an authorial voice
distributes itself between overtly critical, poetic or philosophic texts.
From the perspective of the *Dejection* Ode, Coleridge appears taken up
with the problem of which 'voice' might best name imagination. Which
voice names most essentially, and is this the same as the voice which best
authorizes a description of names? What relation exists between the
voices of critic, poet or philosopher, and is one voice rather than another
responsible for supervising that relation? Or is the very possibility of relation itself only discernible at the level of opposition, or where one voice
infiltrates another? How, then, does the word 'Imagination' speak in the
Ode? Its resonance (and here pathos) as poetic diction would seem to depend in no small part on its equal involvement within the language of Coleridgean theory.

Coleridge characterized the poetic diction of the moderns in the

Biographia as 'an amphibious something made up, half of image, and half of abstract meaning' (*BLS*, I, p. 15). 'Imagination' in the Ode may have its own need to remain amphibious, for a name that is as much at home outside a poetic text as inside may distract, bearing as it does a trace of theoretic ambition and coolness, from the purely subjective trammels of dejection, even while identifying the cost of dejection. What of the Ode's dejection? We may need to turn to Coleridge the philosopher in any case to gain dejection's full import, or acquire some objectification of dejection's irreducible object. For the philosophic critic of the *Biographia* 'the spirit is not originally an object' (*BLS*, I, p. 185). A dejected spirit, such as we meet with in the Ode, however, seems reduced to some contrary origin where it is constantly found by an 'object' which insists on being identified with it. The spirit appears thrown back on an unwanted objecthood from which it can no longer recognize itself as a power of the subject. If Coleridge's idealist (and itself undejected) formulation hints at the grounds of a contrary dejection in which the object, not the spirit, is original, the Ode itself had long anticipated him; there dejection is both acknowledged and partly relieved by recourse to naming a poetic Power (imagination), whose loss, though disabling, is nevertheless somewhat mitigated by a sense that 'Imagination' is a term of growing theoretic sophistication that is equally a Coleridgean achievement. It is as if Coleridge is fully aware that in a time of loss he is addressing himself by a far better name (imagination in every sense a work of his own shaping) than he had seemed to do in times of more pressing plenitude. Such an imagination-as-theory could well become, one might suppose, evangelical, and in featuring in a poem as an integral part of that poem's diction, is there to seek out imaginative loss in order to proclaim the good news of the imagination's own self-understanding. Ultimately, though, the Ode does not employ the term 'Imagination' simply as an analytical key to the poetic field, and so as a surrogate of poetry, but in order to be open to the theoretical resources which might neighbour that field, and upon which it might to some extent lean. Coleridge's universal I of I-magination does not dispute the priority of poetic dejection, but it does complicate the workings of dejection. If there seems no such thing as an *interpretative* dejection for Coleridge (however un-innocent interpretation might be), the interpretative presence underlying 'Imagination' is a trace poetry may trope on, not simply as the power of imagination-lost, but as a name (however variously compounded) speculating or spiriting other dimensions through which to view that loss. Such a trope would seem to shape imagination's name as the Ode names it.

Stanza VI seems as much involved with fancy as imagination. Fancy (more frequently named in Coleridge's verse hitherto) may be, however, as fancy, not much other than a care-free form of imagination, a proto-form of the thought of poetic power, though one which still has earlier access to the life of poetry. Fancy, though, may deal in transformations of the mind that cannot be fully underwritten by a thoughtful poet. In the Ode, a joy which dallies with distress seems too easily squandered, unserious under stress:

> There was a time when, though my path was rough,
>> This joy within me dallied with distress,
> And all misfortunes were but as the stuff
>> Whence Fancy made me dreams of happiness . . .   (ll. 76–9)

Visions of unhappiness so trifled with may lead to dejection's long dalliance unless they can become involved in a conceptualizing purity fancy alone cannot supply. Tilottama Rajan sees the visionary power evoked by fancy here as partaking of something always borrowed, a process in which that which is 'not my own, seemed mine' (l. 81), and she concludes that, for Coleridge, emptiness of self may always have been more primary.[2] In stanza VI we find Coleridge immersed in trying to figure the transition from one 'primary' that seems to rob his power of strength to another mode of making prior, one which in bearing a trace of transcendental reflection may evade an unacceptable object which recognizes too much of itself in the self. To imagination, there may be no primary that has *always* been more primary; and if not, the resulting pluralization will occur at the very point where 'Imagination' blends its own originary, vocational poetic status with the revisionist priority of interpretative terminology. However, any transition from fancy to imagination in this stanza is not itself the fruit of a philosophic distinction, but a slide of figuration. Though we know that by September 1802 Coleridge was writing to a friend contrasting 'the *modifying* and *co-adunating* Faculty' of imagination with the 'aggregating Faculty' of fancy, the names of the two poetic powers in stanza VI are, as names, blocking the way to interpretation as anything more than a detour between them (*CL*, II, pp. 865–6). If interpretation (as the trace of another mode of writing) is present at all, it represents for Coleridge a device for pluralizing the primary whereby an empty self (that seems to underly fancy) is on its way to having its name changed, and with it a whole set of ontological assumptions. Desynonymization itself remains more purely a product (and liability) of imagination: imagination's collusion with conceptuality images itself as a leading edge cutting across fancy, isolating fancy as a questionable mode of vision with no powers of revision, so that imagination may retain to itself the full scope of strategic difference embedded within visionary understanding, an essential part of its amphibious survival kit.

So, while fancy in this stanza appears fused with the past, imagination seems of the present but suspended, or, as Paul Fry says, a suspense 'lingering in play'.[3] The presentments made by imagination seem more properly translated into the terms of fancy while it remains a matter of dealing in immediate or local images, whether of self or nature. Imagination itself seems less than imaginable until it grows more abstruse.

Beyond this ghostly suspension of imaginative activity, and its displacement towards the discredited reminiscences of fancy, lies a more radical substitutional shaping into the Spirit of Imagination. It is a substitution likely to involve a shuttling between poetic and theoretic domains (though the shuttling is part of the suspension). Theory does not blend with poetry without some liability, however. The rigour of theory may mutate into a poetic substance no less problematic than dejection itself. Poetry may have no way of distinguishing rigour from those 'fixities and definites' which (rigorously) define a sliding towards fancy rather than imagination (BLS, I, p. 202). Coleridge was fond of warning that metaphysical systems become popular 'not for their truth, but in proportion as they attribute to causes a susceptibility of being *seen*' (BLS, I, p. 74). If imagination cannot wholly sublimate its origins in the seen, imagination-as-theory is even more implicated in giving sight to an object of the mind. We have already noted in stanza VI some divergence between a fancy implicated in nostalgia and an imagination which presides over a statement of definitively surrendered power. Owen Barfield writes on Coleridge the theorist: 'it would appear to be . . . memory-cum-fancy that gives rise to "fixities and definites" '; imagination itself, Barfield later remarks, 'is precisely an advance of the mind towards knowing itself in the object'.[4] The memory of power seems something of an embarrassment to 'Imagination' in stanza VI: power remembered seems more like fanciful memory than the wholly imaginative. Barfield directs our attention to two further points: imagination (as understood by Coleridgean theory) must dissolve and dissipate the *same* fixities and definites which fancy can only rearrange; fancy evidently takes a hand in producing fixities as such.[5] In the *Dejection* Ode, however, the dissolving power of imagination is largely suspended (is confined to colluding with its suspension), and the process of recalling imagination becomes contaminated by fancy's more privileged role in rememoration. An imagination suspended increasingly swerves towards its more theoretic pole, but the language of theory may not be sufficiently distinguishable in poetry from the language of fancy, the latter already heavily implicated in situating imaginative failure. The sense of loss may arise no less from Coleridge's intuition in the Ode that only fancy can play the terms of 'Imagination' (as a conspiring form of poetic diction) back into the life of his poetry. To a philosophic eye, works of the imagination may always in practice stray to the fanciful, since the root-term 'imagination' is always secondary to the differentiations it provokes. As Jean Pierre Mileur insists, poetic imagination is as secondary to the 'natural' perception of the primary imagination as fancy is to imagination itself.[6] From the *Biographia* again we learn that imaginative dimness may lead to an excessive reliance on the senses, bringing superstition and fanaticism in its train (*BLS*, I, p. 19). 'Imagination' in stanza VI, if truly naming its own poetic dimming, would seem to show excessive reliance on fancy on the one hand and theory on the other.

If both fancy and imagination in stanza VI are by no means the prudent products of desynonymization, despite the traces of theory which underlie the stanza, words like 'nature' and 'natural' seem much more easily to move away from identity. Stanza IV affirms that 'in our life alone does Nature live' (l. 48); but this seems not the life of the 'natural man' of stanza VI who has appropriated nature's name to himself, but has no sure life of his own since his 'nature' is all that can be subtracted from the poet's beleaguered self. In dejected self-differentiation alone does a residue of a 'natural man' henceforth live. He is that aspect of the self which can be identified with nature's gift at birth. The 'shaping spirit of Imagination' seems more receiver than giver, or, in the language of dejection, more object than subject. What nature holds in its gift the spirit of imagination? Presumably it is an original self prior to the 'Nature' of stanza IV. Only thence can 'Nature' receive, assimilating to itself all that is natural in the 'natural man', though the power of the original self is, as a birth-gift, linked to a birth that is itself a purely natural or extrinsic event. Yet the time of birth does not seem coeval with fancy's 'dreams of happiness', but to be a birth-time linked to a spirit which shapes imagination's self-understanding, but at the cost of being precisely that 'time' which is no longer fully available as a poetic presence, but remains suspended over the stanza as a detachable power of reflection or shadowy trope. That suspended 'what' given by nature at birth is not simply, for Coleridge, to be identified with imagination, but is what imagination shapes, a shaping that may have equal business with suspension. Too natural a birth produces, as in 'The Nightingale', a natural babe rather than the babe as original self, one which lisps not shapes, mars by imitation rather than articulates origin. That such contingency appears benign in 'The Nightingale' suggests that natural birth does not coincide with imagination until, under the weight of dejection, natural birth becomes the fixing place, a fanciful fixity, of original power lost. Nature, as Coleridge was to write towards the end of his life, 'mocks the mind with it's own metaphors' (*CL*, V, p. 497). A Nature that lives only within our life is a weak projection, too lax an appropriation of Nature's image by a power which has its own designs on the image. The 'more original union' between all the elements of the Coleridgean universe needs recourse to a trace of self derived from an extra-poetic language if it is to escape a damaging inversion of subjective idealism under the pressure of dejection. For Coleridge, the self's relation to Nature might be described as one involving a 'tensional continuity' in which the asymmetry of domains is reimagined as harmonizable when held under positive stress. Dejection then emerges as a tragic loss of the capacity to apply pressure to the relation, but not the loss of the principle of continuity itself (a principle which can still be applied by interpretation) unless dejection fall into the horror of its condition as negative universalizer. Against this, Coleridge summons in stanza VI an invocation to imaginative loss haunted by a trace of imagination-as-theory which is itself able to invade the horizon at which dejection could become universalizable as theory; in so doing, it is paradoxically assured that dejection remains implicated at the level of trope as is 'Imagination' itself. In neither field of theory-into-trope or trope-into-theory can a victory over dejection be assured, but the chiasmic shuttling of domains acts out a suspension that is itself the only truly native trope in a poem of otherwise uncertain figurative power. Coleridge, that is to say, steals enough dejection from the dejected man to continue the claim of one able to write imagination's name, a name at once aggressively 'proper', a literalization of itself fiercely self-referring, but of weakening sense unless it substitute for itself a role in theory.

Imagination troping on itself as virtual theory is thorough enough to contaminate its own (poetically dark) figuring of the cost of analytical powers. Fry believes Coleridge's tracing of a discourse unfolding its inspirational sources in this poem is itself an 'abstruse research'.[7] The abstruse, it seems, is the abstract muse, or an abstract ruse, an intensely active desynonymizer of self and nature, an infection of the whole which traces the global modifications of imagination itself. If 'abstruse research' was Coleridge's 'sole resource', his afflictions, unlike the earlier dallying distress, allow of no fanciful substitutions. Abstruseness does not thereby emerge to a new level of literalness, however; abtruse research arrests the play of fancy, but can only suspend imagination as a figure *of* the arrested, and becomes drawn into the complicities of that arrest. 'Imagination' is thus led to the margins of a dejected poem as a term for power-suspended on the one hand, but on the other, induces a new invasion of figurable theory. This figuration, deeply collusive, links imagination-lost to the deathly effect of abstract theorizing, a process already begun, though, in the abstract formulation of a 'shaping spirit'.

The figure-of-theory, not surprisingly, is at odds with its own letter which within its own domain would sublimate trope as concept. 'Shape', Kenneth Burke remarks, 'is characteristically a troublous word in Coleridgese'.[8] Coleridge in 1818 contrasts shape as against form as being 'super-induced', 'the Death or the imprisonment of the Thing' (*CN*, III, 4397), and Burke points out similarly threatening connotations in 'Religious Musings' and 'The Ancient Mariner' which show that the prevailing tonality of 'shape' was already at work in the 1790s. Within the *Dejection* Ode, the gerund 'shaping' suggests a more positive figuring and figurative power, but it is one which as essentially binds itself to the noun of 'Imagination', and through it, to the abstruser superinducements of theory. It is here that there can be a surplus of recognitions, or an apparent substitution of loss for loss, one that seeks to outplay the deathly habit of dejection in favour of a lost imagination which knows a theory plays its loss, that theory is here all too needful a 'shape'. Theory may not know, nevertheless, how it is that 'Imagination' names.

II

If it were possible to become a stronger interpreter in the course of writing a poem, what poetic resource could signal this? If 'Imagination' appears more like an essentially repressed interpretative term in 'Dejection', there may be some chance of repression and figuration coinciding. Within a dejected poem, though, repression is likely to be underpower and patchy, 'Imagination' floating free enough to claim some kinship with its homonymic role as a seminal Coleridgean principle, though one muted by manifestation within a threatened poetry. But what self is poetry? What degree of supplementation can it tolerate before becoming an *e*jected form? If 'Imagination' is caught up within a symbolic adumbration of theory, we again approach a dark calculus of parts and wholes under the general 'infection' of dejection. Is too overt a calling upon imagination, too apocalyptic a sounding out of loss, itself part of the pathology of dejection? Once introduce imagination, and the resulting collusion of everything with everything else may become unsavoury, at least until blocked by the name of 'Imagination' itself, which not only stalls any stable figural-repressive economy by too overt or 'weak' a mention of itself, but may go on to compromise any effective transposition of reference from one type of text to another. The name grows common to less and less, though seemingly remorselessly expan-

sive in potential meaning. Thomas McFarland, in a discerning essay on
Coleridge's theory of the secondary imagination, sees imagination as being for Coleridge less an '*a priori* theory of poetry than . . . a means of connecting poetic, philosophic, and theological interests'. 'Imagination', he
continues, 'is therefore primarily a connective developed because of Coleridge's commitment to systematic philosophizing. It would not appear
to be rewarding, accordingly, to try to make very much critically of its
presence in particular poems.'[9] It may never be over-rewarding to trace
a theory's practice within the fabric of an individual poem, especially as
the 'theory' may be a trace of all that holds itself over against the poetic
act. The Dejection Ode, perhaps luckily therefore, is not at all times a very
rewarding poem, and it compromises theory by naming it as 'Imagination'. Such a name signals its otherness from poetry, as well as being the
poem's failed genius. Naming as such may hold out the chance of failing from within a fairly precise locus, however, one that will make possible the figure of suspension. If imagination (-as-theory) is, as McFarland
proposes, a Coleridgean connective, a bridge between system and origin,
it is one which becomes deeply inclusive of any source-text, whether
poetic or philosophic, in a way which differentiates the reference of imagination rather than facilitating a greater fluency of inter-textual relation. The potential crossing between poetry and theory is as much a
double-crossing, in that the need for a connective is here (from the
perspective of a weak poem like 'Dejection') *too* symmetrical, and reveals
a common need for mutual support that rapidly descends into a struggle over imagination's name, a struggle that blocks the bridge from either
end. For imagination, whether as the force of poetry or the transcendental
adequacy of theory, seems no longer a common term. The struggle is to
appropriate it as a proper name.

Coleridge would seem to have glimpsed in 'Dejection' the possibility
of collusion between an imagination-lost in poetry and an imagination-
found in theory; this would certainly have been to have reversed the flow
of imagery from a poetic recognition of the locus of nature's life towards
a more elaborate subsumption of nature within the classification of a
'poetic' faculty – the force of the classification making the poetry itself
derivative. Imagination is not left to shuttle undecidably between poetry
and theory, however, for Coleridge's poem is still bent, from within a dying fall though it may be, on reconstituting the poetic word. Though imagination as poetic vision is a weak figure in the poem, and drifts towards
its extra-poetic supplement, imagination-suspended is much stronger
and far less tolerant of any invasion from the margins of theory. Suspension, to be sure, figures the substitution of a weaker field of writing (dejected poetry) for a stronger one (innovatory theory), but the figure itself

subsumes poetry's fallenness to theory by casting theory as the foundation of itself, a 'founded' figure which induces the much more potent trope of willing suspension. Imagination-suspended does not itself mediate but takes mediation as its vehicle so as to trail supportive theories of mediation. Coleridge, in a notebook entry dating from 1805, was to liken a man's imagination 'fitfully awaking & sleeping' to the 'odd metaphors & no metaphors of modern poetry' (*CN*, II, 2723). This rehearses the pattern of his own fitful alternation between poetry and theory, neither of which has a sufficiency of original power (either may sleep or awake in the other). Within such a suspension 'Imagination' is named, as at once the term for all metaphor, but itself suspended within poetry as a distinctive 'no metaphor' summoned by loss, but equally (by virtue of suspension) blocking any direct path to the priority of theory. Only within the trope of suspension can imagination become a 'no metaphor'. The figure engages with the image of its own literalness (an image that is equally a conceptualized ground) as the suspending within suspension, as the otherwise unimageable feature of its own power of trope; a power which also ultimately entraps theory (were not 'theory' supplemented by this present essay) by emptying imagination's reference. Imagination becomes within *Dejection* a privileged disfiguration made possible by the (troped) suspension of figuration, but is no new equivalent of the literal. And that is to complicate (unfatally) the matter of dejection's power over the poet. A 'shaping spirit of Imagination' would be surplus to the structural needs of any poem in terms of a poet's reviewing of his equipment (at best, as in Wordsworth's 'Imagination!' apostrophe in *The Prelude*, VI, likely to lead to an arrest) were not such a top-heavy intervention treatable from within suspension. Suspension allows some play whereby the poetic figures exhausted by dejection can echo as wise theories outside the standard proprieties of the poem. Coleridge at this point appears a distracted poet – the inconsistencies of his Ode have been the targets of criticism more than once – but his image-play leads straight out of the poem to a 'bridge' with theory rather than forming any poetic logic of its own. The trope maintains this suspension-bridge across which much will set out but nothing arrive. The figure figures the interpretative relevance of its own play, indifferently finding and losing itself within suspension. For there is no meta-figure as such, one that might manipulate both poetry and theory; there are only the multiple domains of the one figure. Nor can any secure level of meta-theory adequately conceptualize the suspending of imagination, for Coleridge is still strong enough to want to contaminate the theory of imagination as such.

'Such *he* is: so he writes', writes Coleridge of Wordsworth's mild, philosophic pathos in the *Biographia*, but a philosophic self set more rigorously upon defining imagination surely writes *before* he is (*BLS*, II, p. 123). The priority of knowing over being is a figure which powerfully haunts 'Dejection', both as poison and cure, before being displaced by the more potent figure of suspension itself. It is suspension which interminably shuttles between figure and concept, which is to say it successfully subdues the trope of shuttling to its own purposes, for suspension remains a more universal horizon than either figure or concept which it entrammels. What such a willing suspension of poetic/theoretic disbelief wills is poetic diction. In 'Dejection' a poet can believe his own theory *as* theory rather than poetic myth and so comes to suspend himself as poet. Suspension clings to theory *as* theory as the ground of its trope, for theory believes tropes have power. The poet sees himself as secondary to a stronger interpreter (the philosopher) who is himself secondary to a yet stronger poet (Wordsworth). Poetic weakness is thus related to poetic strength via the intervening of theory, and the impulse to mediatory relation is not imagination but its suspension, which establishes a lineage rather than a sphere of radiance. For a poet to suspend his imagination may not result in his substituting his own weakness for another's strength, but a subtle pathway has been set up whereby Coleridgean and Wordsworthian imagination both detour through the theory of imagination (a theory equally resistant to both poets); that theory, however, is more successfully troped on from within *Dejection* than anywhere else. Imagination, as Coleridge can still know it, freezes dejection in stanza VI rather than subdues it, but this may allow time for other offerings to other names during the later stages of the poem. Here, imagination has hardened neither to retrospective symbol nor to extrinsic formula, but, in suspension, engages dejection over a common abyss. Dejection grows contingent in the void, less than all-inclusive, while imagination grows recondite. And whose name shall be the less common?

III

Our names, and but our names can meet   *An Exile*

In a well-known passage in the *Biographia*, Coleridge introduces imagination as an intermediate faculty between active and passive ways of thinking; the whole gravitational process of alternating attention can be likened to a man 'trying to recollect a name' (*BLS*, I, p. 85). Coleridge's own swings between poetry and theory (each potentially active or passive in relation to the other) is a continuous attempt to recollect the name of agination', or recollect that it is a name. *Aids to Reflection* will identify the name of a thing with the condition of its real existence, linking '*nomen* with *numen*'.[10] Robert Demaria writes that '*Proper* names are nothing less than the type of words for Coleridge, and as the *substance* (in Lockean terms) of reality, they must be identified with the type of whatever is, or life.'[11] In *Dejection* we witness a struggle between two types, or between type and antitype: the strife of dejection and imagination, each of which has claims to recognize Coleridge by a name more haunting than his own, each capable of suppressing it or substituting for it. Geoffrey Hartman identifies such compulsive but devious naming as the work of a 'spectral name' which interposes itself between a given or baptismal name as more truly 'proper', though it is usually kept secret because 'sacred to the individual, or numinous (nomen numen)'.[12] Imagination, which is involved in characterizing the mode of relation between general and particular, implicates itself in the semantico-grammatical distinction between common and proper names. Hartman, employing a classic account of proper names as 'pure signifiers that have only a referent . . . but no concept or signified' pushes onward his name – pleading to suggest that '(p)erhaps the second-order discourse we call ''metalanguage'' . . . aspires to the same magic, that of pure signification'.[13] Is Coleridgean imagination in the Ode a spectral name, then, able to ward off dejection, a warding that secretively awards itself proper status? If so, its ward is a place of wounding within suspension itself. As suspended, the name of 'Imagination' can, as we have seen, no longer signify imagination-as-vision without recourse to a trace of theory. That trace comes to be regathered within the general trope of suspension, a trope which 'Imagination' must surely name overall rather than denoting only the 'what' of suspension. A proper name cannot itself trope, its 'sense' being too weak to allow of more forceful displacements; rather, it becomes the I-magic of suspended sense, one whose referent, the namer, grounds within his naming a trope upon a suspended name. Is he dejected in doing so? In dejection he has abandoned a baptismal name in favour of a spectral one which must suspend itself if it is to have any reference. Coleridge, that is to say, reduces to a 'transdiscursive author' in order to open a space for the tremors of imagination otherwise less than fully native to either poetry or theory;[14] as the name of its own (dispersed) author, imagination itself becomes a tenuous mountain-birth whither interpretation never clomb, marooned at a height unrealized by poet also unless sufficiently potently suspended by it. To question the function of imagination in Coleridge's poem is to be on the verge of naming it properly. While in Germany in May 1799, Coleridge had proposed in a letter to Josiah Wedgwood to write up his ideas in the form of a biographical study of

Lessing, or 'under a better name, than my own ever will be' (*CL*, I, p. 519). In the 'Dejection' Ode of 1802 we read a biography of dejection which yet resists dejection's claim to title it fully: imagination-suspended is a better name for Coleridge than his own dejection ever can be, and as spectral-proper is a name that has not itself been rejected in love.

The oblique invocation to imagination in *Dejection*, with its complex pathway between weak and strong poetry, itself borrows the Wordsworthian form of 'Imagination! thou shouldst be living at this hour'. Jonathan Culler notes that 'an apostrophe seems to make a deflection of the message'.[16] In the same way that a proper name might be said to 'deflect' its own descriptive powers, the naming of imagination in the Ode allows, through its name, a virtual apostrophe to become actual. Coleridge, however, while wanting to come into imagination's presence and reprove its suspension, would seem to have repressed the apostrophe by diverting his voice through the said of interpretation. Theory is not to be troped on without a residue which resists pure figuration, but nor can it, by the same token, impose a common meaning upon the name 'Imagination'. 'Invocation', according to Culler, 'is a figure of vocation';[16] it is also, we sense, a figure of a vocable. As for vocation, Fry sees Coleridge here as 'disjected, cast out of his vocation in having misconceived it'. The poet 'scatters any conceivable poetic form into so many *disjecta membra poetae*'.[17] This is a casting out still able, though, to name its loss at a point identified by dejection with a name that overshadows any dejected locality as such; imagination's proper name reckons with the spectral presence of a conceiver, a poet-theorist, whose Ode, though perhaps onomatoclastic in its fragmented and uncompletable name as an ode *to* imagination, emerges as a name-maker of imagination.[18] Who, though, is left to pronounce the name? Poetry and theory may instruct the name, but perhaps only dejection comes to pronounce it, to evince its utterability. In that sense, Coleridge's Ode remains an ode *of* dejection.

Reason cannot, Coleridge notes in *The Statesman's Manual*, 'in strict language be called a faculty, much less a personal property, of any human mind'. It is to be appropriated no more than one can 'make an inclosure in the cope of Heaven' (*LS*, p. 70). It is imagination, however, rather than reason, which recognizes what is heaven-like in the 'cope' of heaven, but the space of such a recognition is not the provision of reason which can acknowledge no locality within itself. Imaginative recognition thus falls back to a lesser sphere where its 'inclosures' gain no purchase on a universe of meaning it alone has irreversibly but groundlessly envisioned. If reason, from the pure solvency of its own self-adequation, cannot class itself as a faculty, much less as a personal property, imagination must contract from the common term of the cope it recognizes to the inclosure of its own name, a name whose ground is (as reason) a suspension, but as a recognition of the shapes of reason a 'suspended' ground, a site still within heaven's cope.

The name of imagination entails another, equally scrambled, personal appellation more often met as 'Asra' in Coleridge's verse, though in *Dejection* he prefers the greater suspension of 'Lady', a common and descriptive name that clearly has a proper reference. This Lady may be a spirit whose shape is still in place. Does 'Imagination' name Coleridge as homage-maker as much as image-breaker within this afflicted poem? The tracing of a weaker self by means of another name (Asra) already has its equivalent in poetry's unequal self-companioning in theory. Both theory and the Lady are recognitions of the other which inherits the suspended heart of the poem, and gradually equips its recovery of a heart-language. It is an equipping which enables the imagination to know that the other is itself 'not far from home' (stanza VII, l. 123) though in a way the other itself cannot be imagined to know. Such knowing is known *for* the other by an imagination which simultaneously echoes orientation and nearby disorientation from within its own labyrinthine channels through poetry and theory, either of which may entail loss or gain. Imagination supervenes the relation, but as a power suspended modifies only so far as a naming. The Lady alone can offer to the poet's self what the self recognizes is there to be given through imagination, but since she has no certain life beyond the imagination's (name's) naming of her, the suspension remains, though one not far from the home recognized. Coleridge still does have a name by which to call on Asra, one not debarred from acceptance as is his own.

George Whalley suggests we view Coleridge as describing imagination in his poem to Sara, not as a faculty, but as a state or condition of the person inseparable from the quality of perception.[19] In his *Philosophical Lectures* Coleridge was to go on to record that '[a] man of genius finds a reflex to himself, were it only in the mystery of being' (*P Lects*, p. 179). The reflex-type, the genus of genius, *can* only rebound on mystery, where the naming of a mediatory power becomes the mediation of its name, the hearer and caller of other names, a name proper in its difference from any description, but improperly assignable or spectral as the difference of reflex itself. A poem's difference from imaginative power is one of dependence, while that of theory is one of independence, but both fully articulate their modes of difference. Neither names imagination as its own priority without wounding itself, though in the case of a poem, its difference from the power it would assume may be especially realized through its defeasibility at the hands of interpretation. But

such an asymmetry of relation returns the suspension of imagination to
a poetic fold, its flaw, its ward.

Notes

1 Samuel Taylor Coleridge, *Imagination in Coleridge*, ed. John Spencer Hill,
(London, Macmillan, 1978), p. 8.
2 *The Dark Interpreter: the Discourse of Romanticism* (Ithaca, Cornell University
Press, 1980), p. 232.
3 *The Poet's Calling in the English Ode* (New Haven, Yale University Press,
1980), p. 11. Cited hereafter as Fry.
4 *What Coleridge Thought* (London, Oxford University Press, 1972), pp. 88–9.
Cited hereafter as Barfield.
5 Barfield, p. 86.
6 *Vision and Revision: Coleridge's Art of Immanence* (Berkeley, University of
California Press, 1982), p. 8.
7 Fry, p. 173.
8 'Kubla Khan', in *Language as Symbolic Action: Essays on Life, Literature, and
Method* (Berkeley, University of California Press, 1966), p. 212.
9 'The Origin and Singnificance of Coleridge's Theory of Secondary Imagination', in *New Perspectives on Coleridge and Wordsworth*, ed. Geoffrey H.
Hartman (New York, Columbia University Press, 1972), p. 202.
10 *Aids to Reflection and the Confessions of an Inquiring Spirit* (London, George Bell,
1884), p. 153.
11 'Coleridgean Names', *Journal of English and Germanic Philology*, 77 (1978),
p. 35.
12 *Saving the Text: Literature, Derrida, Philosophy* (Baltimore, Johns Hopkins
University Press, 1981), p. 125. Cited hereafter as Hartman.
13 Hartman, pp. 126–7.
14 The term 'transdiscursive' is applied by Michel Foucault to an author considered to have initiated a new discourse, rather than simply to have written a particular book. Coleridge is clearly the author of 'imagination' in this
extended sense. Interestingly enough, Foucault considers the question of
the free, meaning-endowing subject as essentially a 'suspended' one. See
'What is an Author?', in *Language, Counter-Memory, Practice; Selected Essays
and Interviews*, ed. Donald F. Bouchard, trans. Donald F. Bouchard and
Sherry Simon (Oxford, Blackwell, 1977), pp. 131–7.
15 'Apostrophe', *Diacritics*, 7 (1977), p. 59. Cited hereafter as Culler.
16 Culler, p. 63.
17 Fry, p. 182.
18 Cf. 'Literature is at once onomatopoeic (name-making) and onomatoclastic (name-breaking)' (Hartman, p. 128).
19 Quoted in *Imagination in Coleridge*, p. 26.

Mythopoesis: the unity of *Christabel*

ANTHONY JOHN HARDING

'Christabel', as Walter H. Evert wrote in 1977, has 'eluded critical consensus', and despite a steady flow of commentary continues to baffle interpretation.[1] The poem evidently owes something to the Gothic romance, and many critics, including Evert himself, have pointed out the affinities between the figure of Christabel and the Gothic heroine – young, dutiful, innocent and terribly vulnerable. These affinities can be overemphasized, however, and on their own they do not provide a sufficient basis for the understanding of the poem. Its remoteness from novelistic narrative is apparent in many of its most important episodes, not the least of which is the frightening metamorphosis of Christabel in Part II of the poem into a stumbling, hissing double of Geraldine. No-one expects a Gothic tale to obey canons of literary realism, but something is happening here that refuses to be confined even within the rather extravagant parameters of credibility that apply to the Gothic prose tales Coleridge could have known. Both events and characters are polysemous in the way we usually expect myth to be polysemous. Some of the conflicting critical accounts of the poem which now puzzle us by their inconsistency may turn out to be harmonious after all, if we take slightly higher ground and examine the poem's mythopoeic elements.

In particular I would argue that it is a mistake to see Christabel as a character in a versified novel, a 'heroine', and therefore in any sense to be 'on her side', whether we welcome or abhor the intrusion of Geraldine into her mother-blessed world. For all the 'gothicism' of her surroundings, the title 'heroine' is as wrong for Christabel as it would be for Wordsworth's Lucy. As Jean-Pierre Mileur observes: 'The attempt to create a narrative romance out of the situation at the poem's center is thwarted by the inaccessibility of a causal center or source of motive.'[2] Attempts at reading the poem as a tale of sexual initiation, or the transition from 'innocence' to 'experience' in some related sense, simply do not explain enough, because they provide no adequate explanation of the particular form Christabel's transformation takes.

The approach I wish to explore, then, is that of treating *Christabel* as an instance not of novelistic narrative, nor yet of parable or allegory, but of Romantic mythopoesis. That is, I wish to draw the poem closer to Blake's *Visions of the Daughters of Albion* and Shelley's *Prometheus Unbound*, and proportionately to distance it from Lewis's *The Monk* and Radcliffe's *The Mysteries of Udolpho*, applying to Coleridge's poem something like Shelley's dictum that a poem (as distinct from a 'story') is 'the creation of actions according to the unchangeable forms of human nature, as existing in the mind of the creator, which is itself the image of all other minds'.[3]

The first problem we encounter in treating *Christabel* as mythopoesis is obviously that of the poem's unity or disunity: both the relatedness or unrelatedness of the poem's two parts, and the completeness or incompleteness of the diptych, if we envisage it as a diptych. Assuming that Coleridge's own remarks (as reported by James Gillman and Derwent Coleridge) establish the poet's unfulfilled plans for the poem, we have dutifully searched for proleptic evidence that the completed poem would have been a parable showing how 'the virtuous of this world save the wicked', or how 'the holy and innocent do often suffer for the faults of those they love', and we sometimes read back into the Geraldine of Part I the characteristics of the shape-shifter demanded by the improbable series of events which Gillman gives us as a summary of the projected Parts III and IV.[4]

H. W. Piper's 'The Disunity of *Christabel* and the Fall of Nature' is more respectful of the poem as it stands now, but Piper has to sacrifice narrative cohesion by treating Part II as a failure, an abortive attempt to resume in 1799 and 1800 the interests and themes of 1797. To Piper, Geraldine's ambiguity in Part I reflects Coleridge's incipient unhappiness with the view of nature canonized in *Lyrical Ballads*: that the natural order is benevolent even when it appears for the moment evil. In support of this interpretation he cites *Kubla Khan* and *The Ancient Mariner* as two nearly contemporary poems in which 'the setting plays a vital part in the working out of the poem', though he appears to feel that the 'setting' of *Christabel* Part I is much more ambiguous than the settings of the other two poems. Both the setting and Geraldine's duplicitous character 'call into question the moral purposes of the natural order'.[5]

It is misleading, however, to speak of the 'settings' of *Kubla Khan* or *The Ancient Mariner* as if they had the same independence from the poet's consciousness, the same kind of 'outness', as the pastoral farms of *Tintern Abbey* or the hazel-trees of *Nutting*. Even in his conversation poems Coleridge is far more concerned with nature internalized, or nature as God's symbolic language (*Frost at Midnight*), than with nature as 'independent' entity. Kathleen Coburn's remark about *The Ancient Mariner* is pertinent: 'For Coleridge, nothing is more strange, more mysterious than the mind itself, especially the frightened, or troubled, or guilty mind' – and Coleridge himself, on his voyage to Malta in April and May 1804 (during which he had several unpleasant dreams), saw that poetry may be (in Alethea Hayter's phrase) a 'rationalized dream'.[6] Geraldine is surely an embodiment of mental, not of 'outward forms'. It is instructive that Piper has some difficulty in transferring his argument about Geraldine-as-nature to the second part of the poem. His solution – which is to treat the second part simply as less skilful than the first, indicating that Coleridge had lost sight of the fruitful ambiguities of Part I – imposes a further unnecessary penalty on the search for thematic and narrative unity in the poem.

Yet the unfinished state of the poem, and its division into two parts, are not the only features it has which stand in the way of a consistent parabolic interpretation. Unlike, say, Spenser, who keeps the momentum of events going by constantly reminding us (not least through the steady onward-pacing rhythm of his nine-line stanza) that each scene is but part of a larger unfolding pattern, Coleridge allows and encourages us to 'freeze' the action, by having the narrator break into his own narrative:

> A sight to dream of, not to tell!   (l. 253)

> Can this be she,
> The lady, who knelt at the old oak tree?   (ll. 296–7)

> Why is thy cheek so wan and wild,
> Sir Leoline?   (ll. 621–2)

These interruptions almost too strenuously underline the fact that the hold which the poem exerts on a reader derives in large part not from the sense of narrative expectation ('how will she get out of this one?') but from the intrinsic power of a central, heartstopping image. Even in some prose romances, such images fail to be neutralized by subsequent rescues or escapes, and therefore interrupt the narrative rhythm of the tale. Readers of Lewis's *The Monk*, for instance, surely remember the image of Agnes imprisoned in the vault and clasping to her breast the decaying body of her child, long after they have forgotten how she came to be there or how she was rescued. So in Part I of *Christabel* the image of Geraldine, with corpse-like bosom and side, holding Christabel 'As a mother with her child' (l. 301), is frozen for us by the narrator. It too parodies storgè or mother-love, as well as erotic love, and anticipates the world of *The Pains of Sleep* in its psychosexual ambiguity:[7]

> Desire with loathing strangely mixed
> On wild or hateful objects fixed.

> Fantastic passions! maddening brawl!
> And shame and terror over all!
> Deeds to be hid which were not hid,
> Which all confused I could not know
> Whether I suffered, or I did . . .   (*PW*, I, p. 390)

The impact of such images can only partly be explained through the kinds of interpretation usually offered – that they are emblems of life-in-death, or a horrible parody of mother-love, here given connotations of necrophilia. Through such commentary, we try to express our sense that such images momentarily violate some of the most radical structures of human knowledge, primarily the distinction that we make between living and dead, and between birth-event and death-event. The middle ground between such opposites, as Jane A. Nelson points out (citing Edmund Leach), is the focus of taboo. Mythical thought works from the awareness of such opposition towards a resolution, which is to be achieved by the introduction of a third, anomalous category: the *revenant*, the incarnate god, the virgin mother. As Nelson shows, the narrativity of *Christabel* is closer to non-literary myth than to literary narrative proper – which is not necessarily to say that it is artless. The poem poses a problem in poetic and mythopoeic logic, '*the re-union of what in this world is divided*'; and the sense of division and opposition which pervades the poem is embodied chiefly in 'familial and sexual' relationships – Leoline and Christabel, Geraldine and Christabel, Leoline and Geraldine.[8] It was a problem that haunted Coleridge for many years, if not to the end of his life. One of the Malta notebooks contains the entry 'Mem. To examine whether Dreams of Terror & obscure Forms, ugly or not, be commonly preceded by Forms of Awe & Admiration with distant Love' (*CN*, II, 1998).

It is notable, however, that in Coleridge's *poetry* the perception of division or opposition very often shows itself in the form of a threat not to the stability of outward things, nor even to psychic stability as such, but to *the very possibility of poetic utterance itself*. The *Ode to the Departing Year*, written at the close of 1796, which 'prophesies, in anguish of spirit, the downfall of this country', ends:

> I unpartaking of the evil thing,
>   With daily prayer and daily toil
>   Soliciting for food my scanty soil,
> Have wail'd my country with a loud Lament.
> Now I recentre my immortal mind
>   In the deep Sabbath of meek self-content;
>   Cleans'd from the vaporous passions that bedim
> God's Image, sister of the Seraphim.   (*PW*, I, p. 168)

The phrase 'I unpartaking of the evil thing' should not be read as the poet's claim to moral superiority. It is spoken in the character of national prophet, and is a recognition of the fact that in order to utter prophetic words at all the poet must be blessed with unity of being. Biblical thought constantly images evil as 'double-mindedness' (Psalms 12:2, 51:6, 119:113), while the forked tongue or sharp-edged (cutting, splitting) tongue is the dominant metaphor for false or deceitful utterance (Psalms 52:2, 57:4, 140:3). Similarly, the inability to speak one's thought because of disunity in the inward being is a theme common to several poems of Coleridge that abjure the prophetic stance. In the 1796 sonnet *When they did greet me father*, for instance, the poet's attempt at prayer is frustrated by 'Th'unquiet silence of confused thought/ And shapeless feelings' (*PW*, I, 153), where the apparent self-contradiction of 'unquiet silence' focuses the speaker's dilemma, inner turmoil preventing the prayerful response demanded by the occasion. A different kind of inner disharmony prevents the Ancient Mariner from voicing the prayer he knows he should speak: as he longs for death, for self-annihilation, he cannot at the same time affirm his being (or the being of Being) through prayer. In *The Pains of Sleep*, too, the first thing in the poet's mind is the possibility of utterance itself, and the intimate connections between poetic utterance, love, and prayer. The attempt to pray, like the initiation into love, presupposes and requires wholeness in the self.

When the prayer-state is successfully achieved in Coleridge's poetry, there is usually a corresponding emphasis on unity of being, as at the conclusion of the 1807 poem *To William Wordsworth*, written after Coleridge heard Wordsworth read *The Prelude* (then known, of course, simply as 'the poem to Coleridge') at Coleorton:

> Scarce conscious, and yet conscious of its close
> I sate, my being blended in one thought
> (Thought was it? or aspiration? or resolve?)
> Absorbed, yet hanging still upon the sound –
> And when I rose, I found myself in prayer.
>
> (*PW*, I, p. 408)

Silent prayer, presumably, just as Christabel's prayer on behalf of her lover (l. 36) is silent, indicating perfect community between the person praying and the one prayed to – no need for the intervention of speech.[9] The language of familial and sexual relationship which Coleridge adopts in *Christabel* should not blind us to the fact that the primary 'division and opposition' the poem is concerned with is not in 'the world', nor even in sexual or familial 'identity', but in the profoundest reaches of the praying self: an experience corresponding to Wordsworth's sense of treachery and desertion in the place /'The holiest that I knew of . . .'.[10] In *Christabel*, as in *The Pains of Sleep*, the victim is also the doer of evil ('Sure I have sinn'd', l. 381), while the agent, Geraldine, the 'worker of these harms', looks more like a victim, 'still and mild' (ll. 298, 300). Still more to the point, in Part II the moment that dominates the narrative, the moment for which everything else seems only a preparation, is the moment when Christabel's power of speech is paralysed:

> Christabel in dizzy trance
> Stumbling on the unsteady ground
> Shuddered aloud, with a hissing sound.   (ll. 589–91)

Here the narrative comes to a final halt, save for the 'Conclusion to Part II' which is really a second way of describing the same condition, the same discovery of treachery and desertion within the self. The loving father, compelled to utter his 'love's excess' by sheer pressure of emotion, finds that his words slip, slide, and perish, betraying an unsuspected rage and pain alongside the love. If the father's words, as suggested here, are 'wild', like a monster that, once set free, exhibits destructive powers his maker never intended him to have, then the bitterness they express is nevertheless *there*, part of their content, whether 'unmeant' or not. From this perspective the 'Conclusion to Part II' appears to be a commentary not on a moral truth, at least in the first instance, but on a truth about speech, and about its frightening disconnectedness from willed thought and meaning. The fathers Leoline and Coleridge are their own victims in the sense that each is 'responsible for' the utterance, even though the bitterness it expresses was unwilled, or unmeant (just as Coleridge feared at times that he might have been in some obscure way 'responsible for' the loathsome images summoned up in his dreams):[11]

> pleasures flow in so thick and fast
> Upon his heart, that he at last
> Must needs express his love's excess
> With words of unmeant bitterness.
> Perhaps 'tis pretty to force together
> Thoughts so all unlike each other;
> To mutter and mock a broken charm,
> To dally with wrong that does no harm.
> Perhaps 'tis tender too and pretty
> At each wild word to feel within
> A sweet recoil of love and pity.   (ll. 662–72)

In this wildly associative, dreamlike, and amoral moment, parallel not only to Leoline's rage but also to Christabel's dizzy trance, human relationship is turned to 'sorrow and shame', love to 'rage and pain', and prayer to 'a broken charm'. Coleridge has perhaps recognized in this image the horror of his own state – the paralysis of poetic and prayerful utterance.

Hazlitt – if it was Hazlitt who wrote the review of the 'Christabel' volume in the *Examiner* for 2 June 1816 – was quite right to say of Coleridge that 'he comes to no conclusion'.[12] There is no 'conclusion' because the real subject of *Christabel* shows affinity not so much with traditional narrative poetry as with Blakean mythopoesis. Like *Visions of the Daughters of Albion*, Coleridge's poem depicts a strangeness in human existence; and instead of moving forward to an easy resolution, it ends with the dominant image of a human soul in its temporally divided and speechless state, as if recognizing that a miraculous hair's-breadth escape would be at best a weak palliative. Each part of *Christabel* focuses on a distinct moment of horror arising from some profound division and havoc in the self: the first part on the displacement of Christabel's mother's spirit by the sinister Geraldine, the second part on the desperate situation of Christabel struggling to speak her peril but unable to do so, 'O'ermastered by the mighty spell' (l. 620). Both moments exist outside the normal moral cause-and-effect paradigms of the dayworld: both are 'dark sayings' unfolding the 'disquietness of heart' that emerges unsummoned from a prayerful moment of 'Deep inward stillness & a bowed Soul' (*CN*, I, 259).

These biblical phrases (they are from Psalm 49:4, Psalm 43:5 and Psalm 44:25) come from an entry in the Gutch memorandum book, possibly a list of references to be used in a projected Essay on Prayer. The phrases group themselves around an experience similar to the ones adumbrated in *CN*, I, 257, an outline of the prayer experience. In *Christabel* and *The Pains of Sleep*, however, the preparation for prayer and the gradual composing of the mind to a state of calm contemplation are followed by the terrible irruption of loathsome phantoms, the sense of evils done and suffered, which contaminates the still mind of the worshipper and taints the prayers he is struggling to utter. With her mother's spirit near, or at least not banished, Christabel prays in 'gentle vows' (l. 285), pious tears just beginning in her eyes – 'both blue eyes more bright than clear,/ Each about to have a tear' (ll. 290–1), another image of motherhood. After her mother's spirit is banished and replaced by Geraldine the desire to pray remains ('praying always', she 'prays in sleep', l. 322), but there is a change – 'tears she sheds – / Large tears that leave the lashes bright', ll. 315–16 – and she moves now 'unquietly' (l. 323). In Christabel's troubled sleep we confront the third stage of prayer as Coleridge described it: 'Repentance & Regret – self-inquietude' (*CN*, I, 257).

Some psychoanalytical criticism of Coleridge has perhaps tended to obscure an important aspect of the 'absent mother' motif in *Christabel*: that for Coleridge the idea of mother-love is closely associated with prayer and the ability to pray. Coleridge's memories of childhood prayer, as Kathleen M. Schwartz points out, always involved his mother – never his father – and the outline of the Essay on Prayer associates prayer closely with mother-love (*CN*, I, 263, and compare *CN*, I, 750).[13] Sir Leoline's kind of piety seems by contrast distinctly patriarchal – or Urizenic: 'Each matin bell, the Baron saith, /Knells us back to a world of death' (ll. 332–3).

Part I of *Christabel*, then, speaks of a Christabel-element in the human spirit which is openhearted, generous, naturally prayerful and loving. In the language of the Gutch memorandum book (based on Psalm 22:3), the Christabel-in-us 'inhabit[s] God's praises' (*CN*, I, 259). She is orphaned, however, by the departure of a certain kind of spirituality that is associated with womanhood and motherhood. This deprivation leaves her vulnerable to the irruption of the tyrannous Geraldine. In mythopoeic terms it is entirely credible that the 'unchangeable form', Christabel, should accept as well-intentioned and even pitiable the Geraldine-element, which presents itself as an emissary of higher powers (ll. 227–8), or as descended from 'a noble line' (l. 79).

That-which-is-Geraldine is, however, specious, deceitful, potent and capable of imposing its will on Christabel, as is shown by its deformed shape underneath the 'silken robe' (l. 250). 'Geraldine' may here be glossed not merely as nature (Piper's view) but the natural man, existence-in-the-flesh, Blake's Rahab. She belongs to a long and dishonourable tradition of succubae and temptresses, including most notably Spenser's Duessa, in whom the double aspect of the flesh – beautiful to view, but subject to corruption and exercising a tyrannical power over the soul – is imaged (compare *The Faerie Queene*, I, viii, l. 47). The result of this psychomachy is the transformation of unaffected piety, and the holy sleep of a calm soul (*CN*, I, 191), to a state of 'self-inquietude'. Geraldine's oldest ancestors are Eve and the serpent; she is woman as patriarchal religion sees her: duplicitous, seductive, a snare and a delusion, identified with the flesh, an embodiment of 'lower powers':

Now this is the present unhappy state of Man; our *lower* powers are gotten uppermost . . . . The *Woman* in us still prosecutes a deceipt like *that* begun in the Garden; and we are wedded to an *Eve*, as fatal as the Mother of our Miseries.[14]

The worst consequences are saved for the second part of the poem, however, as Christabel finds herself unable to enlist the help of her father, whose piety is of the morbid, death-obsessed kind, in contrast to the fresh-air-and-wildflower piety of Christabel's mother. Instead Sir Leoline seems strangely attracted to Geraldine's specious grandeur, as a pharisaical piety is often pruriently attracted to what it affects to despise. Worse still, Christabel is shown 'passively' imitating the serpentine look of 'dull and treacherous hate' thrown in her direction by Geraldine (ll. 605–6), and in the midst of her trance unable to make any sound other than a serpent's hiss. As in the nightworld of *The Pains of Sleep* it is the evildoer who has all along enjoyed the appearance of virtue, while the victim is shown guilty of complicity in her own downfall. Interpretations that view Christabel's downfall as purely or primarily sexual in nature surely narrow the significance of most of Part I of the poem. Christabel fails to read the warning signs – Geraldine's refusal to pray, the tongue of light in the dying fire (ll. 142, 159) – with the result that Christabel, the embodiment of spiritual wholeness, quickly permits herself to accept Geraldine, the embodiment of carnality, existence-in-the-flesh, as what she appears to be, a lady of 'noble line'. Sure Christabel has sinned, and as she sinned in Geraldine's person she is punished by being turned into Geraldine. This is the justice of the imagination, the same justice that is properly meted out to Milton's Satan:

> a greater power
> Now rul'd him, punisht in the shape he sinnd,
> According to his doom: he would have spoke,
> But hiss for hiss returnd with forked tongue
> To forked tongue, for now were all transformd
> Alike . . .[15]

The forked tongue is no more than a recognition, a rendering into physical terms, of the fact that Satan and the rebel angels have deceived themselves as well as their victims Eve and Adam. Christabel too – callous though this may sound – has deceived herself. She is at least partly subject now to the tyranny of Geraldine, and of those Geraldine serves, the ambivalent powers of 'the upper sky' (l. 227). The spell is 'lord of [her] utterance' (l. 268) to such an extent that she cannot explain the danger to her father but can only blurt out a desperate entreaty that he send the deceiver away (ll. 616–17).

A close connection is assumed here between speech, especially prayerful utterance, and wholeness. Christabel appeals to Sir Leoline by her mother's soul (l. 616), a reminder that prayer grows from the unity of being suggested in the image of mother and child, rather than from the relationship of father to child; compare the narrator's reiterated prayer 'Jesu, Maria, shield her well!' (ll. 54, 582). There is even a hope that the undeceived and single-natured poet Bracy may be able to banish the evil 'With music strong and saintly song' (l. 561). As far as this narrative is concerned, however, that-which-is-Christabel is deeply compromised by its contact with that-which-is-Geraldine, and the consequences are fatal to poetry itself: to be forced into silence, robbed of the power of utterance, is equivalent to the complete loss of 'poetic space', the power of projecting from the self an answering and reciprocally self-confirming otherness, the power to affirm Being as the ground of self.

Paul H. Fry has argued that Wordsworth and Coleridge rejected the older identification of 'poetic space', or the system of relationships that gives meaning to poetry, with the order of genres. In the new Romantic poetic, Fry suggests, 'poetic space is what we half perceive and half create on the basis of an ad hoc symbiosis of mind with nature'. The function of symbolism within this poetic is 'the making-present of some universal power that is universally absent until by magic the *nomen* grows numinous . . . . Were it not antinomian, defiant of determinism by externally given origins, this faith would attach itself to the office of prayer.'[16] If *Christabel* is essentially, as I have proposed, a poem about poetic utterance, depicting a state in which the inward stillness necessary for such utterance, as it is for prayer, is destroyed by disquietness of heart and self-deception, then Coleridge seems to have rejected any 'ad hoc symbiosis of mind with nature' almost before it even produced any results, suspecting, with Blake, that nature and the natural man are not only ambiguous but tyrannous, deceitful usurpers claiming descent from the 'noble line' of Being itself. The substitution of the fleshly Geraldine for the absent mother-spirit is a horrible actualization of the way in which that-which-is-Christabel, in its orphaned loneliness, makes the natural man its adoptive parent: and in Part II of the poem the stultifying of prayerful utterance is the inevitable consequence. If Christabel had been able to speak to Geraldine, she might have said something like this:

> Thou, mother of my mortal part,
> With cruelty didst mould my heart,
> And with false self-deceiving tears,
> Didst bind my nostrils, eyes and ears,
>
> Didst close my tongue in senseless clay
> And me to mortal life betray.[17]

For the prophetic poet, poetic speech must assert itself in absolute freedom from the mortal part, the 'evil thing', and to allow the lower powers of mortal life to close around the mind is to resign oneself to tongue-tied silence.

Notes

This essay is based on a paper presented at the 1983 Wordsworth Summer Conference in Grasmere, England. I am grateful to the organizers of the Conference, especially Richard Wordsworth and Jonathan Wordsworth, for the opportunity to present and discuss the paper, and to my fellow participants for their many constructive suggestions.

1 Walter H. Evert, 'Coadjutors of Oppression: A Romantic and Modern Theory of Evil', in *Romantic and Modern: Revaluations of Literary Tradition*, ed. George Bornstein (Pittsburgh, University of Pittsburgh Press, 1977), p. 37. For the texts of Coleridge's poems I use *PW*. References to *Christabel* (*PW*, I, pp. 213–36) are by line number.

2 Jean-Pierre Mileur, *Vision and Revision: Coleridge's Art of Immanence* (Berkeley, University of California Press, 1982), p. 63.

3 'A Defence of Poetry', in *Shelley's Poetry and Prose*, ed. Donald Reiman and Sharon Powers (New York, W. W. Norton, 1977), p. 485.

4 These reports can conveniently be consulted in Humphry House, *Coleridge: The Clark Lectures 1951–52* (London, Rupert Hart-Davis, 1953, rpt 1969), pp. 126–8.

5 H. W. Piper, 'The Disunity of *Christabel* and the Fall of Nature', *EC*, 28 (1978), p. 217. Robert Schwartz also emphasizes the 'disunity' of the poem: 'the narrative, while promising the unity of a continuous and discernible meaning, rarely does more than . . . inform us of a second level of experience' – that is, the supernatural one ('Speaking the Unspeakable: The Meaning of Form in *Christabel*', *University of South Florida Language Quarterly*, 19, Nos. 1–2 (1980), p. 34). Edward Dramin points to numerous instances of parody in the gothicism of the poem, but stops short of saying that parody is its unifying feature (' "Amid the Jagged Shadows": Christabel and the Gothic Tradition', *TWC*, 13 (1982), pp. 221–8).

6 Kathleen Coburn, 'Coleridge and Wordsworth and "the Supernatural" ', *University of Toronto Quarterly*, 25 (1956), p. 125; Alethea Hayter, *A Voyage In Vain* (London, Faber and Faber, 1973), p. 50.

7 For 'storgè' see my *Coleridge and the Idea of Love*, p. 162.

8 Jane A. Nelson, 'Entelechy and Structure in "Christabel" ', *SIR*, 19 (1980), pp. 385–7. See also Jonas Spatz, 'The Mystery of Eros: Sexual Initiation in Coleridge's *Christabel*', *PMLA*, 90 (1975), p. 113.

9 Kathleen M. Schwartz, in 'Prayer in the Poetry of S.T.C.', Diss., Princeton University, 1975, p. 26, argues that Coleridge was more at home with contemplative prayer, 'the fusion of the self with the divine', than with petitionary prayer.

10 *Oxford 'Prelude'*, X, 380–1. 1805 text.

11 See David S. Miall, 'The Meaning of Dreams: Coleridge's Ambivalence', *SIR*, 21 (1982), p. 69.

12 *Coleridge: The Critical Heritage*, ed. J. R. de J. Jackson (London, Routledge and Kegan Paul, 1970), p. 205.

13 Kathleen Schwartz, 'Prayer in the Poetry of S.T.C.', p. 23.

14 Joseph Glanvill, 'Against Confidence in Philosophy and Matters of Speculation', 1676, quoted in Donald Greene, 'Latitudinarianism and Sensibility: The Genealogy of the "Man of Feeling" Reconsidered', *M Phil*, 75 (1977), pp. 169–70.

15 John Milton, *Paradise Lost*, ed. B. A. Wright (London, Dent, 1962), p. 343 (Book X, ll. 515–20).

16 Paul H. Fry, *The Poet's Calling in the English Ode* (New Haven, Yale University Press, 1980), pp. 134–5.

17 William Blake, 'To Tirzah', *Poems*, ed. W. H. Stevenson and David V. Erdman (London, Longman, 1971), p. 591.

Kubla Khan

In Xanadu did KUBLA KHAN
A stately pleasure-dome decree:
Where ALPH, the sacred river, ran
Through caverns measureless to man
   Down to a sunless sea.
So twice five miles of fertile ground
With walls and towers were girdled round:
And here were gardens bright with sinuous rills,
Where blossom'd many an incense-bearing tree;
And here were forests ancient as the hills,
And folding sunny spots of greenery.

But oh! that deep romantic chasm which slanted
Down the green hill athwart a cedarn cover!
A savage place! as holy and enchanted
As e'er beneath a waning moon was haunted
By woman wailing for her demon-lover!
And from this chasm, with ceaseless turmoil seething,
As if this earth in fast thick pants were breathing,
A mighty fountain momently was forced:
Amid whose swift half-intermitted Burst
Huge fragments vaulted like rebounding hail,
Or chaffy grain beneath the thresher's flail:
And mid these dancing rocks at once and ever
It flung up momently the sacred river.
Five miles meandering with a mazy motion
Through wood and dale the sacred river ran,
Then reached the caverns measureless to man,
And sank in tumult to a lifeless ocean:
And 'mid this tumult Kubla heard from far
Ancestral voices prophesying war!

   The shadow of the dome of pleasure
   Floated midway on the waves;
   Where was heard the mingled measure
   From the fountain and the caves.
It was a miracle of rare device,
A sunny pleasure-dome with caves of ice!

   A damsel with a dulcimer
   In a vision once I saw:
   It was an Abyssinian maid
   And on her dulcimer she played,
   Singing of Mount Abora.
   Could I revive within me
   Her symphony and song,
   To such a deep delight 'twould win me,
That with music loud and long,
I would build that dome in air,
That sunny dome! those caves of ice!
And all who heard should see them there,
And all should cry, Beware! Beware!
His flashing eyes, his floating hair!
Weave a circle round him thrice,
And close your eyes with holy dread:
For he on honey-dew hath fed,
And drank the milk of Paradise.

1816 version

The Crewe Manuscript of *Kubla Khan*

In Xannadù did Cubla Khan
A stately Pleasure-Dome decree;
Where Alph, the sacred River, ran
Thro' Caverns measureless to Man
Down to a sunless Sea.
So twice six miles of fertile ground
With Walls and Towers were compass'd round:
And here were Gardens bright with sinuous Rills
Where blossom'd many an incense-bearing Tree,
And here were Forests ancient as the'Hills
Enfolding sunny Spots of Greenery.

But o! that deep romantic Chasm, that slanted
Down a green Hill athwart a cedarn Cover,
A savage Place, as holy and inchanted
As e'er beneath a waning Moon was haunted
By Woman wailing for her Daemon Lover:
From forth this Chasm with hideous Turmoil seething,
As if this Earth in fast thick Pants were breathing,
A mighty Fountain momently was forc'd,
Amid whose swift half-intermitted Burst
Huge Fragments vaulted like rebounding Hail,
Or chaffy Grain beneath the Thresher's Flail:
And mid these dancing Rocks at once and ever
It flung up momently the sacred River.
Five miles meandring with a mazy Motion
Thro' Wood and Dale the sacred River ran,
Then reach'd the Caverns measureless to Man
And sank in Tumult to a lifeless Ocean;
And mid this Tumult Cubla heard from far
Ancestral Voices prophesying War.

The Shadow of the Dome of Pleasure
Floated midway on the Wave
Where was heard the mingled Measure
From the Fountain and the Cave.
It was a miracle of rare Device,
A sunny Pleasure-Dome with Caves of Ice!

A Damsel with a Dulcimer
In a Vision once I saw:
It was an Abyssinian Maid,
And on her Dulcimer she play'd
Singing of Mount Amara.
Could I revive within me
Her Symphony and Song,
To such a deep Delight 'twould win me,
That with Music loud and long
I would build that Dome in Air,
That sunny Dome! those Caves of Ice!
And all, who heard, should see them there,
And all should cry, Beware! Beware!
His flashing Eyes! his floating Hair!
Weave a circle round him thrice,
And close your Eyes in holy Dread:
For He on Honey-dew hath fed
And drank the Milk of Paradise.

This fragment with a good deal more, not recoverable, composed, in a sort of Reverie brought on by two grains of Opium, taken to check a dysentery, at a Farm House between Porlock and Linton, a quarter of a mile from Culbone Church, in the fall of the year, 1797. S. T. COLERIDGE.

The languages of *Kubla Khan*

JOHN BEER

A close reading of *Kubla Khan* makes one aware of an irresolution in the imagery which stands in marked contrast to the homogeneity of the verse. Throughout the poem there runs a strong incantatory strain, within which we become aware of an ingenious poetic language. The feminine rhymes in the second, third and fourth stanzas bring in a lightness and variation which is regularly superseded by a powerful and strong iambic movement. The effect of inevitability becomes stronger each time, until the final lines of the last stanza, which have the quality of a charm.

There is, however, a contrast of effect between the rhythmic movement of the verse, impressive in the subtlety of its patterning, and the visual imagery of the poem, which is not only hard to fix into a landscape pattern but is constantly contracting and expanding in the mind, moving between pictures of an objectively visible scene and suggestions of vast unseizable subterranean spaces and forces.

As a result, the reception of the poem will vary according to the degree of submission to its more 'enchanting' aspects. One can allow one's mind to be taken over by its rhythm, while contemplating the shifting landscapes described and suggested as one might in a dream. As soon as the conscious mind takes over, on the other hand, questions will begin to pose themselves. It will then become obvious that the poem also has the arbitrariness and reductive economy of much dream work. The fact that a Greek river is flowing through a Tartar landscape, with an Abyssinian maid somewhere in the background, may not be particularly troubling, for the mind can deal easily with such superpositions; but the 'sunny pleasure-dome with caves of ice' may seem all too convenient and rounded a package for the amount of symbolic freight that it seems by then to be carrying. We know from Coleridge's notebooks that he had been attracted by the account of an image of ice in an Indian cave which waxed and waned in accord with the waxing and waning of the moon – a marvellous piece of symbolism for correspondences of process between nature and the human mind; but since this idea is not presented in the text of the poem itself it cannot be explored except by subsequent association. Equally, we may suspect that the genius of the last stanza is, like other such figures, standing on a mountain top, and that somewhere in that landscape there is a self-renewing spring of inspiration to counter the disordered fountain of stanza two – but again these are elements to be inferred by the reader from clues such as the honey-dew, not to be found directly presented in the text. At such points, therefore, we glimpse that this poem is inviting a different reading from those to which modern criticism usually points us – a reading which will treat the language of the poem as a threshold which we cross to enter into a imaginative world corresponding to Coleridge's own at the time when he wrote the poem. That world is constructed partly in alignment with mythological symbolisms which Coleridge himself had been exploring; but it is also in intimate relationship with the landscapes of the writers who meant most to him when he was thinking in visionary terms. To explore the poem to its depths, therefore, is to become aware of various poetical languages: some largely symbolic, arising from the mythological constructions of previous civilizations, some verbal, echoing relevant passages in writers whom Coleridge valued. As the poet's work is done, all play together in a structure which is larger than that of the presented text.

The language of myth and symbol

The text of the Crewe manuscript[1] (reprinted above, p. 219) is the closest we have to that of *Kubla Khan* as it was originally written down. For the purpose of the present discussion I shall assume that that original writing took place during a walking tour to the Valley of Rocks in the late autumn of 1797, and that when he composed it Coleridge was in a state of less than complete consciousness. I have elsewhere[2] presented the case for making such assumptions and attempted a reconstruction of the conversations that might have taken place between Wordsworth and Coleridge as they left Porlock and passed through the woods beyond (specifically mentioned by Dorothy Wordsworth in a letter on that occasion), emerging from time to time to see splendid views across the Bristol Channel to the mountains of Wales. Issues of life and death might well have preoccupied them as they observed and discussed the country around them and perhaps began evolving ideas for the landscape of seasonless death in *The Wanderings of Cain*. The rocks lying scattered in the Valley of Stones, equally, might have directed their minds to the destructive power of the earth, resisting all attempts to recreate an earthly paradise. And so (to continue the reconstruction) when Coleridge was taken ill on the return journey and retired to a lonely farmhouse, the scene was set for a meditation on the nature of earthly powers, whether in the world outside or within the individual.

One other point may be noted. If the retirement was to Ash Farm, the place that fits Coleridge's description best, it was an area of unusual magnificence, from which the enclosed valley which surrounds Culbone stretches down to the sea.[3] It is even possible that Coleridge knew something of the history of the place: how Ash Farm, along with the vale as a whole, had been repossessed in the middle of the eighteenth century by its owner, who had proceeded to cultivate it. Earlier it had been for many years a place of banishment, for lepers and others, and then in-habited by discharged servants from India, who moved about it burn-ing charcoal for the rising metal industries of the country. English charcoal-burners were still at work there in the late 1790s.[4] To this day it is an unusually peaceful and even magical place – even though it dif-fers in equally obvious ways from the language of Coleridge's poem.

But whatever the effect of the actual visible landscape on Coleridge's mind as he came to compose his poem, there can be no doubt that other landscapes were already there, imprinted during his reading of mythology and travel and associated with his more esoteric specula-tions. Indeed if Coleridge's retirement to the lonely farmhouse took place during the return from the November visit to the Valley of Rocks, at a time when the two poets were actively planning *The Wander-ings of Cain*, it would also be natural to suppose (in view of the philological habits of mythologists at that time)[5] that Coleridge's sight of the words 'In Xamdu did Cublai Can build a stately Palace'[6] evoked an immediate connection between Can and Cain. And in that case a number of connections in the poem become more readily explicable. For Cain is a natural emblem of the daemon in humanity turned to destruction. As the son of Adam in whom the Fall is realized, he knows that all men must now die; although he has never experienced Paradise he has learned what it was like and knows that he cannot regain it. The desperation of his plight is displayed both in the murder of his brother and in subsequent attempts to recreate lost paradise. In eighteenth-century lore, it was commonly supposed that the widespread cults of sun-worship and enclosures sacred to the sun had been initiated by Cain and his descendants in their attempts to recreate the Eden that had been lost. Later, in the persons of Tubal-cain and his descendants, the enterprise became centred in the working of metals, with all the ambiguity implied by an activity that could involve the making either of weapons or of agricultural implements – or for that matter of musical instruments.[7] As the activity of creation goes on, sometimes manic in its intensity, the ultimate aim is always to recreate and repossess a former state of wholeness – a state which, though lost, is still sensed in the subconscious.

With the central myth of Cain and his ambiguous activities, two further mythological strains can be connected. The first is the myth of Isis and Osiris, in which the idea of the lost glory is further elaborated into the loss of Osiris and the usurpation of the sun by the destructive Typhon, while Isis undertakes incessant wanderings in the hope of recreating her lover. If Osiris were ever to be recreated by Isis Typhon would be vanquished and disappear, but since she cannot discover his virile member, her work must always be defeated, her unsuccessful quest being imaged in the waxing and waning of the moon. So the world remains trapped between the workings of a destructive sun and a deprived moon which reaches the form of plenitude only to lose it again. Were Osiris to be revived, on the other hand, the world would be dominated by a sun that united heat and light creatively, as imaged in the figuration of sun-gods such as Apollo, deity of healing and music.

The dialectic implicit in the Osiris and Isis myth (for it is the heat of Typhon and the light of Isis that would be blended in the restored Osiris) becomes focussed on the male–female relationship in the myth of Alpheus and Arethusa. There was an enclosure sacred to the sun by the river Alpheus in Greece, but the main myth connected with Alpheus himself was of his search for the nymph Arethusa: when he rediscovered her they rose up blended in the Arethusa fountain in Sicily.[8]

Once the running together of these myths and others is seen to provide the main structure of meaning in the poem, it becomes possible to understand how a Tartar paradise can associate so readily with a Greek sacred river. The paradisal imagery in the remainder of the first stanza may also be seen as precisely apt – for most of the elements mentioned, the sacred river, the enclosure, the incense-bearing trees and the sunny spots – are traditionally associated with sun-worship.[9] In the second stanza, by contrast, all that is ambivalent in such traditions comes to the fore: the fountain is destructive, the woman is separated from the daemon-lover who still attracts her, nature is distorted and humanity doomed to war. A miraculous reconciling of the various elements – fire and ice, earth and water, sunny dome and cave of ice, river of life and sea of death, is imaged in the music created by the echo of the fountain in the cave – but imaged only. It is not until the final stanza that the possibility of a true reconciliation is glimpsed in the figure of the restored sun-god who reconciles everything into harmony. The Abyssinian maid can be identified as a priestess of Isis, Abyssinia being the abode of secret wisdom as well as the site of the Nile springs. The poet creating his dome in air reminds us of Apollo, building with his music a temple that all could see.[10] But although the scene closes with the genius having tasted paradisal elements of honey-dew and milk (suggesting the original paradisal spring of which all earthly fountains are pale copies), there is still a wistfulness in 'Could I revive within me . . . ': the scene figures an aspiration, not an accomplished fact. In one sense the poem ends triumphantly, for the images of honey-dew and milk consummate the various streams of mythological imagery involved, including the food of the Old Testament Messiah who will redeem man from Cain's condition as well as that of many pagan gods.[11] There is also however insubstantiality in a vision that seems to last only so long as the musician is there to make it and convince his audience. The concluding sense is of harmony, not of loss, but that harmonization is shot through with fragility.

I have written at greater length about this elsewhere, bringing together more evidence for the establishing of such mythological links, and for Coleridge's knowledge of the traditions involved. I have also argued that the various ideas are further held together by the imagery and lore of genius, that favourite eighteenth-century theme, so that when we think of sun and moon or of spring and river, we are really looking at aspects of the daemonic, where constructive and destructive factors are working together in creation or falling apart in destructiveness and loss. With the aid of such interlinking themes, I have argued, Coleridge was able to bring together some of the issues that he had been contemplating in his more esoteric investigations, presenting back to himself a satisfying image of his own aspirations. Such lore as I have come across since I first wrote on the subject has helped to support and further delineate this pattern. A possible strand which I had overlooked was pointed out by Richard Gerber, who drew attention to the resemblance between Cybele (Kubele) in Greek mythology and Cubla (Kubla).[12] The sight of Cubla's first name, he suggests, might well have aroused this run of imagery, also, in Coleridge's mind. Cybele is earth-goddess, but an earth-goddess associated rather with destruction than with growing; the cults of priests devoted to her drove themselves into frenzies; her common depiction was with a crown of walls and towers, suggesting military defence. If the disorders of the second stanza are seen as evidences of her powers manically and destructively in action, her presence not only gives another dimension to the 'walls and towers' that Kubla decrees but adds to the suggestion of sun-worship the need to propitiate fearful elements in earthly nature. The combination of Cybele and Cain in the name of Cubla Can would thus initiate the cross-currents of self-assertion and vengeance in the poem still more vigorously.

In all these ways the poem emerges as a structure of images and symbols by which a complex interpretation of human experience – and especially of the daemonic element in that experience – is being suggested. Yet this perception does not give us the whole poem. To some degree the images clothe themselves naturally in Coleridge's words, yet we are some way from seeing why particular patterns of language and metre and particular choices of words should have emerged. The discussion so far assumes that Coleridge's mythological interests did not begin when he sat down to write his poem but had long been a feature of his thinking. When, after all, he had claimed to his brother at the age of eighteen, 'I may justly plume myself that I first have drawn the nymph Mathesis from the visionary caves of abstracted idea, and caused her to unite with Harmony. The first-born of this Union I now present to you . . .', he was already exploring imagery which reappears in the last stanza of *Kubla Khan* (*CL*, I, p. 7). This was not the only language he had learned to speak, however: he had also been devouring and assimilating the work of previous poets and writers who worked in similar ways. Their language can be seen behind his, evidencing a series of poetic relationships, some intimately detailed, others strong but general, which call for further examination.

To carry it out will involve the pursuit of literary echoes, in a manner that has been much used in connection with *Kubla Khan*. There is a well-known tradition for such studies, established by John Livingston Lowes, whereby one finds a previous use of a striking word (which is then printed in italics)[*] and presents it in connection with the corresponding line in *Kubla Khan*, where the word is also italicized.[13] (In Lowes's case, however, one finds that many of the usages he cites could be duplicated several times from other travel-books, so that cases he notes often prove simply to be striking instances of a more general imagery.)

I have discussed elsewhere some of the problems raised by this kind of work, pointing out the hazards of trying to establish with precision rules for pursuing influences from one work to another, but also proposing as a simple rule of thumb that coincidence is less likely to be at work if one can trace a phrase rather than a single word, or if a number of echoes from a previous writer rather than a single one, seem to be at work.[14] Accordingly, I concentrate here on authors who are known to have impressed Coleridge deeply in youth, and look for clusters of usage rather than single, isolated words. It is a further element among my assumptions that where such words recur what is likely to be at work is not just a simple distinguishable 'echo' but a whole context, informing particular words with recollection of the larger matrix of meaning in which they originally appeared. There is always a danger that such arguments will become circular, obviously, but readers who care to check my method by look-

---

[*] I shall do this myself and to avoid confusion silently suppress italics in the original texts.

ing up important words in writers not mentioned will find it harder than they may expect to establish rival patterns of previous usage. Shakespeare, for instance, uses many of the words to be found in the poem, yet I have traced in his work no pattern or cluster of usages that is particularly significant for *Kubla Khan*.

The language of genius and sensuousness

Insofar as the symbolism of *Kubla Khan* can be seen to bring together various strands of mythology and traditions of interpretation from the past, its interest is inevitably limited for a modern reader, who has ceased to assign supreme authority to the Bible as a historical record. In such terms it may look at best like the poetry of an inspired comparative mythology, written by a happier Mr Casaubon. But there is more to the matter than that. Just as Blake at this time was trying to forge a new mythology for his age to replace what he thought of as an outworn and discredited Christianity, Coleridge valued the myths of antiquity less for themselves than for what they suggested about the further possibilities of human creativity. They were to be read as embodying perennial traditions of human inspiration, of genius.

As such, these ideas had already had a long history in Coleridge's mind. They can be associated for example with his general interest in romance as a whole – an interest which had begun as a child with his early absorption in the *Arabian Nights*, and continued apparently throughout the reading of his childhood and youth, taking in first the popular fiction of the time such as *Tartarian Tales* and then, in adolescence, imaginative philosophers such as the Neoplatonists and visionary mystics such as Jacob Boehme.[15]

When we turn to Coleridge's earlier poems we find many examples of words and images that look forward to his most visionary poem, but we also notice a particularly significant cluster around the year 1793. This had been a year both of pleasure and disaster for Coleridge. The trial of William Frend in the Senate House had been an exciting event in Cambridge, followed by a Long Vacation in the West Country where he had enjoyed some lively company. It was then, probably, that he helped prepare for the Society of Gentlemen in Exeter the paper (described in *Biographia Literaria*)[16] in the course of which he compared Erasmus Darwin's *Botanic Garden* to the Russian palace of ice, 'glittering, cold and transitory', and 'assigned sundry reasons, chiefly drawn from a comparison of passages in the Latin poets with the original Greek, from which they were borrowed, for the preference of Collins's odes to those of Gray'.

His attitude to Erasmus Darwin was not one of complete dismissal of course: for years afterwards his poems would be touched by images that he had come across in the *Botanic Garden*, while *Zoönomia* would help stimulate his thinking about the nature of life.[17] Rather, Coleridge was seeking to extend Darwin's achievement, to find a way of writing about scientific matters in verse which would reconcile them with other themes: theology, politics, the human mind. Evidences of this quest can be found both in his reading and in his early poetry. At times, however, it was the quality of the aspiration itself, as celebrated by his more rhapsodic poetic predecessors, that possessed him. Already in 1748 there had appeared Thomson's *Castle of Indolence*, in which the bard roused those who would listen with the strings of his harp, 'The which with skilful touch he deftly strung, / Till tinkling in clear *symphony* they rung . . . '. With the aid of the muses he had then sung to the ten thousands thronging mute around him a song which included the invocation,

> 'Come to the beaming God your hearts unfold!
> Draw from its *fountain* life! 'Tis thence alone
> We can excel. Up from unfeeling mould
> To seraphs burning round the Almighty's throne,
> Life rising still on life in higher tone
> Perfection forms, and with perfection bliss . . .'   (II, xlviii)

This sublimated sun-worship was matched by the elevation given to the divine intelligence by Mark Akenside, whose *Pleasures of Imagination* had appeared in its first version a year or two before. In both versions appeared the lines,

> From Heav'n my strains begin: from Heaven descends
> The flame of genius to the human breast,
> And love, and beauty, and poetic joy,
> And inspiration.   (I, 55–8)

– to be followed by a long account of the ways in which the human mind could pursue the heavenly intelligence into all its intricate paths of creation. Nature had a particularly central part to play: to quote the first version,

> Nature's kindling breath
> Must fire the chosen genius; Nature's hand
> Must point the path, and imp his eagle-wings,
> Exulting o'er the painful steep, to soar
> High as the summit; there to breathe at large
> Æthereal air, with bards and sages old . . .   (I, 37–42)[18]

In the first version, the aged sage Harmodius teaches the poet about the secrets of the universe, recalling a visionary experience in which the 'Genius of human kind' appeared before him in heavenly radiance. After the first pleasurable landscape there was a change of scene:

> A solitary prospect, wide and wild,
> Rushed on my senses. 'Twas a horrid pile
> Of hills with many a shaggy forest mixed,
> With many a sable cliff and glittering stream.

The long description which follows contains few verbal parallels with the second stanza of *Kubla Khan*, yet there is a distinct resemblance of emblematic form, particularly in the movement from rough energetic water to calm stream:

> Down the steep windings of the channeled rock
> Remurmuring, rushed the congregated floods
> With hoarser inundation; till at last
> They reached a glassy plain, which from the skirts
> Of that high desert spread her verdant lap,
> And drank the gushing moisture, where confined
> In one smooth current, o'er the lilied vale
> Clearer than glass it flowed.

In this vale, protected by the cliffs above, the sage also saw another sight:

> On the river's brink
> I spied a fair pavilion, which diffused
> Its floating umbrage 'mid the silver shade
> Of osiers.

As he looks at this scene, the sage sees a shaft of sunlight and learns that the pavilion, with its shadow on the waters, is 'the primeval seat / Of man', designed as a place where human youth can grow up nurtured by the goddess of wisdom – who is accompanied in turn by another goddess, the fair Euphrosyne. When the goddess of wisdom discovers that the young man is in fact attracted only to her companion she complains to the father-god, who replaces Euphrosyne with an avenging demon; the young man almost despairs. At this point, however, his goddess intervenes: he feels her inspiration 'Vehement, and swift / As lightning fires the aromatic shade / In Æthiopian fields', and with her help is roused to do combat; at once Euphrosyne appears again, promising never to leave him:

> She ended; and the whole romantic scene
> Immediate vanished; rocks, and woods, and rills,
> The mantling tent, and each mysterious form . . .

The sage awakes to be instructed by the moral of what he has seen: happiness will always accompany virtue – but only so long as virtue is followed for herself alone.[19]

The landscape, it must be repeated, bears little relation in strict ver-

bal terms to that described in *Kubla Khan*: occasional 'rills' and 'rocks'
feature in many other such passages. But in its general form, its pitting
of savage scene against paradisal plain, its rough waters and calm waters
and its general moral that pleasure, if pursued directly for itself, will give
rise to an avenging demon, whereas the following of virtue will be accompanied by true inspiration, it bears a strong resemblance to the structure
of Coleridge's poem.

Coleridge knew Akenside well by 1796, voicing admiration then for
his combination of 'head and fancy'; his own philosophical poetry bears
the touch of his influence at many points. He also imitated him in a poem
dated tentatively in 1794, and it seems likely that he already knew him
by 1793. In that year, however, his chief poetic heroes seem to have been
the two figures mentioned in the *Biographia*: Gray and Collins.

Collins, certainly, was figuring strongly in his consciousness then: after
he had met Miss Fanny Nesbitt while travelling in a coach, he had addressed several poems in his style to her. One of them, *On presenting a Moss
Rose to Miss F. Nesbitt*, was actually written on the back flyleaves of a copy
of Collins's *Poetical Works*.[20] His devotion that summer is further
demonstrated by the poetic texture of his 'Songs of the Pixies'. The lines
which begin the fifth section, for instance,

> When Evening's dusky car
> Crown'd with her dewy star
> Steals o'er the fading sky in shadowy flight . . .

condense various lines in Collins's 'Ode to Evening', such as

> The Pensive Pleasures sweet
> Prepare thy shadowy Car

and

> Thy Dewy fingers draw
> The gradual dusky Veil . . .

The 'fading sky' echoes Gray's *Elegy*, 'Now fades the glimmering landscape . . .' and Gray is actually quoted in the line, 'A youthful Bard
"unknown to fame" '.

Both Gray and Collins seem to be echoed in *Kubla Khan*. As John Ower
has pointed out,[21] Gray's *Progress and Poesy*, which begins with an invocation to the 'Aeolian lyre', continues with a description of poetry imaged
as a river:

> From Helicon's harmonious springs
> A thousand *rills* their *mazy* progress take:
> The laughing flowers, that round them blow,

> Drink life and fragrance as they flow.
> Now, the rich stream of *music* winds along
> Deep, majestic, smooth, and strong,
> Thro' verdant vales, and Ceres's golden reign:
> Now rowling down the steep amain,
> Headlong, impetuous, see it pour:
> The *rocks*, and nodding groves rebellow to the roar.

Elsewhere in Gray's poem there is also a reference to fields 'where *Maeander*'s amber waves / In lingering Lab'rinths creep'. The landscape is not so close as in Akenside's poem, however, nor are the verbal reminiscences overwhelmingly convincing, since they could easily be matched elsewhere in the poetry of the period. The two most impressive elements are the fine management of the poetical movement and the use of such a landscape to describe not simply genius, but poetic genius. Coleridge was no doubt aware of Dr Johnson's harsh criticism of these lines in his *Lives of the Poets* (1781), but whatever common sense might say he was also likely to be touched by the seductive charms of their rhetoric. The attractiveness of Collins is displayed in a letter of 1796 to John Thelwall:

Now Collins' Ode on the poetical character – that part of it, I should say, beginning with – 'The Band (as faery Legends say) Was wove on that creating Day,' has inspired & whirled *me* along with greater agitations of enthusiasm than any the most *impassioned* Scene in Schiller or Shakspere ... Yet I consider the latter poetry as more valuable, because it gives *more general* pleasure – & I judge of all things by their Utility. – I feel strongly, and I think strongly; but I seldom feel without thinking, or think without feeling.   (*CL*, I, p. 279)

The poet who could write that had evidently been very powerfully drawn by Collins and in fact the lines he mentions have a close relevance to the ending of *Kubla Khan*. Published in 1747, they take to a further stage the imagery of genius projected by Akenside. Poetry is seen as having been born when the Creator, having made the world, retired with Fancy:

> Seraphic Wires were heard to sound,
> Now sublimest Triumph swelling,
> Now on Love and Mercy dwelling;
> And she, from out the veiling cloud,
> Breath'd her magic Notes aloud.
> And Thou, Thou rich-hair'd Youth of Morn,
> And all thy subject Life was born![22]

This image of a goddess inspiring with her song is followed by a concluding section, in which Milton is portrayed as the poet to have fulfilled the ideal of poetic genius, in a career never to be repeated by anyone else. By a neat stroke he is projected into a paradisal scene like that which he himself created – an Eden which lies high on a rocky cliff, guarded by 'holy *Genii*'. I have quoted the lines elsewhere [23] and there is no point in trying to condense them, since it is not particular verbal resemblances that are in question here but the movement as a whole. Collins's verse, like Coleridge's, takes on the inevitability of an incantatory chant which undermines the sense of what is being said: a repetition of the miracle by which the inspired poet, hearing his 'native strains' from Heaven, reproduced them for his hearers is being pronounced impossible, but the ecstatic movement of the poem does not altogether confirm the pessimism of the statement.

The figure of the inspiring female and the inspired poet in his elevated paradise are clearly of significance for the final stanza of Coleridge's poem – the movement of which is still less ready to affirm the impossibility of regaining it. It is in another poem of Collins's, however, that we find the closest resemblances to Coleridge's poem. John Livingston Lowes long ago noted the significance of the singing of Melancholy as described in 'The Passions':

> And dashing soft from *Rocks* around
> Bubbling Runnels join'd the Sound;
> *Thro'* Glades and Glooms the *mingled Measure* stole,
> Or o'er some *haunted* Stream with fond Delay,
> *Round* an *holy* Calm diffusing,
> Love of Peace, and lonely Musing,
> In hollow Murmurs died away.[24]

While the 'mingled Measure' gives Coleridge a key phrase for his third stanza, the movement of the lines as a whole contributes to the close of the second. Influences can be traced still further, in fact, since behind Collins's 'Thro' Glades and Glooms the mingled Measure stole' one may discern the shape of Dryden's '*Through* all the *compass* of the notes it *ran*'). Coleridge's 'Thro' Wood and Dale the sacred river ran' sounds even closer to Dryden than to Collins, but whereas Dryden then moves to a powerful succeeding line: 'The diapason closing full in Man', Coleridge, like Collins, allows the movement to pass to an indeterminate close, the 'died away' of Collins being matched by his own 'sunk in tumult to a lifeless ocean'. (We may also note in passing, as another possible echo of Dryden, the line that ends a section in Wordsworth's 'School Exercise' (1784–5): 'Through all my fame the pleasing accents ran.')[25]

The subversive attractions of Collins were the effects of a sensuousness not altogether afraid of itself. Collins's delight in the oriental, similarly, found an echo in Coleridge's love of Eastern tales. Many resemblances can be traced between these exotic stories and details in Coleridge's poem – indeed, given its subject-matter, it would be surprising if they could not – the most striking occurring in the writings of an author who (though Coleridge may not have known it) was imitating Eastern tales rather than translating them. It was James Ridley's *Tales of the Genii* (the very title of which would appeal to that genius-haunted age) that seem to have engaged his imagination most fully. Ridley's book contained a convincing analogue for Kubla's dome of pleasure: the Genius of Riches produces for the delight of the merchant Abudah a dome which shines so brightly that he can hardly look in its direction – a dome of gold with pillars of precious stones, with intermediate spaces of crystal, so that the inside of the dome can be seen from every direction.

In such tales, however, the proposal of pleasure is usually ominous. When Hassan Assar, Caliph of Baghdad, found himself in a delightful wooded landscape and met a beautiful houri, they leapt to embrace one another, but as they did so were divided by a 'dismal *chasm*'. And while they stood on either side, 'viewing the horrid fissure and the dark abyss', 'wild notes of strange uncouth warlike music were heard from the bottom of the pit'. The moral of the event is the same as in Akenside's natural paradise: the caliph is told that it has happened because he had allowed himself to be over-influenced by 'the outward appearance of things'. Abudah, similarly, had been taken through a beautiful landscape, with woods of spices and perfumes breathing sweetness over the cool stream as the boast followed 'the *meanders* of the current'; but when he tried to open a chest in the centre of the temple the scene turned to darkness and destruction: the ruins of the temple falling in '*huge fragments*' while those who survived ran to and fro in despair, tearing each other to pieces.[26]

However attractive the siren voices of pleasure, whether in Collins's cadences or in the attractions of Eastern romance, their appearance signalled danger. The pursuit of pleasure was likely to be followed by an unhappy turn of fate. And even if Coleridge escaped the tentacles of this idea for a time during the summer of 1793, with its agreeable flirtations and poetic effusions, they re-enfolded themselves all too firmly around him just after. When he returned to Cambridge he was already beset by debts; there are also suggestions of amorous adventures with women of the town. All would be redeemed, he trusted, when he again won the medal for Greek verse which he had already gained the year before. 'Astronomy' being the set subject he made it the occasion for an effusion on genius, portraying Newton as a scientific discoverer with all the trappings of inspired genius, gazing into the spring of creative energy and inebriated by the 'holy ecstasy' that seized him.[27] The conclusion expressed his aspiration to join Newton in the celestial ranks of genius.

Unfortunately, however, he was not awarded the prize, and with the failure his financial embarrassments became overwhelming, so that he ran away to London. There still remained in the tradition of romance that further turn of fortune by which the victim might after all find himself transformed suddenly into a position of power. When the merchant Abudah had been overtaken by the catastrophe described earlier, he had passed into the 'dungeon of lust' from which he was able to rise only with great difficulty; yet when he finally managed to complete the long cavernous ascent he suddenly found himself on top of a mountain, acclaimed as their sultan by the voices of ten thousand.[28] Coleridge, likewise, was evidently hoping for a magical event which would transform his fortunes into prosperity. With the little money he had left he bought a ticket in the lottery, but the stroke of luck he hoped for eluded him. In despair, he volunteered for the army, where he stayed until rescued by his brothers.[29]

The disaster of late 1793 had been a chastening experience, and Coleridge was never to be carried away so fully again. Henceforward it would be his stated preference to combine feeling with thought and to choose the useful in preference to the attractive. Yet the very existence of *Kubla Khan* is a witness to the hold over his imagination which the poetry of genius and the arts of Eastern romance still retained. Among other things, this is a poem about sensual pleasure – including erotic pleasure: the delights of vision, sounds and scents in the first stanza convey suggestions such as those which are overtly expressed in the Song of Solomon, where the bride describes herself as a wall, her breasts like towers, and promises to be a spice-laden garden to her lover.[30] The second stanza likewise suggests the disorders of lust (the working of grievous sexual energies, emblematized in the rough chasm and violent fountain, is made manifest in the woman wailing for her daemon-lover). The figure of genius in the last stanza, similarly, is recognizably an inspired lover, resembling the lover who in the Song of Songs comes into his garden to gather myrrh and spice, to eat honeycomb with honey and to drink wine with milk. It seems likely, as Lowes suggested, that when Coleridge read of Kubla's paradise garden in Purchas's *Pilgrimage*, he was reminded of the false paradise of Alcadine, described just before the parallel passage in Purchas's *Pilgrimes*, with its pipes that ran with 'Wine, *milke, Honey*, and cleere Water' and 'goodly *Damosels* skilfull in *Songs* and Instruments of *Musicke* and Dancing'.[31] With such images in the background it is hardly surprising that Coleridge should write of his mountain of inspiration first as 'Mount Amora', changing it to Milton's Amara only when the censor of his consciousness had had time to intervene. The pleasures of sensuousness, which had been tantalizing him before the disaster of 1793, had by no means lost their hold on his unconscious mind.

However, the effluxions of an unchecked libido are not sufficient to account for the poem's language, either. Other echoes inhabit the garden.

The language of collaboration

Coleridge had not been alone in finding 1793 a momentous year. While he had been enjoying the doomed pleasures of that summer and autumn Wordsworth had been enjoying different pains and pleasures, to be recalled in *Tintern Abbey*. During that summer, at a time when his sensuous response to nature was acute ('The sounding cataract haunted me like a passion') he had been beset by gloomy thoughts as he saw British ships preparing for war off the Isle of Wight. Passing across Salisbury Plain, with its Druidic remains, he had been haunted by a Hardy-like sense that the patterns of human creativity and violence must always repeat themselves, so that hopes raised by the French Revolution were bound to be illusory. He had comforted himself a little by recollection of the Druids' more benevolent activities, but it was not until he passed into the Wye Valley and saw a different kind of scenery, one which seemed to impress itself irresistibly on the human consciousness, that he had felt more reassured. Perhaps, after all, there was a hidden force in nature that was working for humanity's amelioration.[32]

In the autumn of 1797, the convergence between Wordsworth and Coleridge reached its closest point. For the first and only time they actually planned to write poetry together: *The Wanderings of Cain* and (when that idea failed) *The Ancient Mariner* (*PW*, I, p. 287). The ensuing year was marked by shared observations, enthusiastic discussions and interlinking speculations, in the course of which Wordsworth's powers became steadily more manifest. Although Coleridge's intelligence was essential to the inspiration of Wordsworth at this time, he constantly assigned to his friend the dominating place. 'The giant Wordsworth!' is a typical phrase (*CL*, I, p. 391).

If we accept that *Kubla Khan* is a poem about genius it becomes natural to ask whether Wordsworth's genius, affirmed so enthusiastically by Coleridge, was not also a presence in the poem. And here it is relevant to recall the distinction which appears in some of Coleridge's later works between two different forms of genius: 'commanding' genius and 'absolute' genius (*BL*, I, pp. 31–3). The man of commanding genius was one whose genius was directed primarily outwards: he might be the man of power who would direct the making of a great harbour, or an aqueduct that brought water to the desert, or lay out a great palace, temple or landscape garden. Such men were however at the mercy of circumstance – to quote Wordsworth, they

> obeyed the only law that sense
> Submits to recognize; the immediate law,

> From the clear light of circumstances, flashed
> Upon an independent Intellect.[33]

In less propitious times, therefore, they would emerge as the agents of destruction, becoming the warmakers, the mighty hunters of mankind. Men of absolute genius, by contrast, can 'rest content between thought and reality, as it were in an intermundium of which their own living spirit supplies the *substance*, and their imagination the ever-varying *form*' (*BL*, I, p. 32). Applying this formula back to *Kubla Khan*, it will be evident that it expresses well the distinction between the kind of genius displayed by Kubla Khan in the first two stanzas and that of the inspired genius in the last. It can also be seen as relevant to Wordsworth himself: a man of considerable powers who had considered joining the Girondist cause in France and so been in danger of devoting those powers to the cause of violent warfare (– and who, for that matter, had left there a woman enslaved by love for him). At the time when Coleridge came to know him well, on the other hand, he was devoting himself more and more to works of what might better be called 'absolute' genius – works in which he drew on his own inward powers in the hope of exhibiting to other human beings the nature of their own potential creativity. So it is hardly fanciful to read in the development of the poem an account of Wordsworth's own progress. We need turn only to Coleridge's reported description of Wordsworth in the following spring, when he was talking to Hazlitt about his 'matter-of-factness':

His genius was not a spirit that descended to him through the air; it sprung out of the ground like a flower, or unfolded itself from a green spray, on which the gold-finch sang. He said, however (if I remember right), that this objection must be confined to his descriptive pieces, that his philosophic poetry had a grand and comprehensive spirit in it, so that his soul seemed to inhabit the universe like a palace, and to discover truth by intuition, rather than by deduction.

('My First Acquaintance with Poets', *H Works*, XVII, p. 17)

We might equally recall his description of Wordsworth in a notebook some years later in October 1803:

I am sincerely glad, that he has bidden farewell to all small Poems – & is devoting himself to his great work – grandly imprisoning while it deifies his Attention & Feelings within the sacred Circle & Temple Walls of great Objects & elevated Conceptions . . .   (*CN*, I, 1546)

Just as Coleridge at this time had turned away from immediate politics to study the 'causes of causes' so Wordsworth was looking into the principles underlying all human behaviour. He was drawn to look for an absolute truth which would, when found, be compulsively clear to all. But while he cherished the dream of writing what Coleridge hoped would be 'the *first* and only true philosophical poem in existence' (*CL*, IV, p. 574), a poem which would present and help to solve the riddles of human existence, he was also subject to self-doubt and the fear that his sense of inspiration might be illusory – so that when he began *The Prelude* the 'Was it for this . . .?' theme (his own version of 'Could I revive within me . . .') was at first dominant.[34]

Coleridge's admiration for Wordsworth's strength was not new: it went back to his discovery of *Descriptive Sketches* in 1793, when he had been seized by the power of passages such as the description of the storm. Reading them, he wrote later, he was struck by a vigour which recalled the vegetable processes in which 'gorgeous blossoms' rise out of a 'hard and thorny shell':

The language was not only peculiar and strong, but at times knotty and contorted, as by its own impatient strength.   (*BL*, I, p. 77)

There is a sense, then, in which *Kubla Khan*, with its pictures of commanding genius in the first two stanzas and of absolute genius in the last, is a poem about the actualities, the vulnerabilities and the potentialities which Coleridge perceived in Wordsworth's powers. In addition, the language of the poem is often very close to that of the early writing of both poets. There is a particularly close relationship to Wordsworth's *Descriptive Sketches*, for example. As usual we need to be on our guard, since a young poet is likely to be working from the favourite diction of his contemporaries; even so, however, it would be hard to find an eighteenth-century poem which ran so closely to the vocabulary of *Kubla Khan*. The very opening:

> Where there, below, a *spot* of *holy ground* . . .

contains three key words in Coleridge's poem; the convergences continue – at least in the imagery – when the poet goes on to say that if such a spot could be found it would be in a language where, among other things, 'murmuring rivers join the song of ev'n', and where

> Silence, on her wing of night, o'erbroods
> Unfathom'd dells and undiscover'd woods;
> Where rocks and groves the power of water shakes
> In cataracts, or sleeps in quiet lakes.   (ll. 9–12)

Any reader who cares to trace the parallels between individual words and phrases in *Kubla Khan* and in the writings of the two poets will be struck by the very large number of such convergences. There are points, however, where one or other poet seems to be in the ascendant. In the case of the second stanza, for instance, Wordsworth's usages provide an even closer parallel than Coleridge's. Consider his '*deep chasms* troubled by roaring streams' (*Borderers*, 1.1805), '*Slant* watery lights' (*Evening*

Walk, l. 92), light streaming '*athwart* the night' (*Guilt and Sorrow*, l. 144), 'the full circle of the *enchanted* steeps' (*Evening Walk*, l. 350), 'While opposite, the *waning moon* hangs still' (*Descriptive Sketches*, l. 219). It is the constant appearance of these words in contexts of landscape, and of a landscape made numinous by a juxtaposition of beauty with fear, which makes for this constant sense of connection. It is only at the 'daemon-lover' that the relevance of Coleridge's early poetry (e.g. 'She that worked whoredom with the Daemon Power' (Religious Musings, l. 332)) becomes decidedly more significant.

The inference which might be drawn from this is that Wordsworth's idea of genius stood in the tradition which associates it with feelings of fear and wonder aroused in a numinous landscape, and that Coleridge was aware of the fact, so that when that theme entered *Kubla Khan* it was Wordsworth's poetic language that came most readily to his mind. This effect emerges still more strikingly when we look for points of what might be 'intensive' influence – points where there is a cluster of such words. Wordsworth's 'Were there, below, a *spot* of *holy ground*' has already been mentioned.

For an equally intense influence from Coleridge's own verse we should need to turn to his recent *Osorio*, which includes a line describing the 'innumerable company' who 'in broad circle',

> *Girdle* this *round earth* in a dizzy *motion*   (*PW*, II, p. 551)

'Girdle' was probably not in the original manuscript of *Kubla Khan*, as we have seen, but even so we can still find three direct verbal parallels – including the use of 'this . . . earth' and the striking resemblances between 'dizzy motion' and 'mazy motion'. If we then look for those words in the poem which had been previously used by Coleridge, but not by Wordsworth, we find words such as 'incense', 'milk', 'mazy' and 'honeydew' – words, that is, of sensuous pleasure and suggestion. And here, we may legitimately suspect, we are looking at the language of genius that comes more naturally to Coleridge himself from his own past.

To say this is to raise a wider issue. Human beings set to remember objects or sentences are much more likely to remember those which they have already *expressed* in some form.[35] In particular, they remember their own previous *constructions*. We should expect, similarly, that in a poem such as *Kubla Khan* where, as we have seen, the passive side of the artist's mind seems to have been unusually prominent, that which he had done before would provide a most ready means of expression. Whereas he would be likely to recall Wordsworth's lines in terms of their *significance*, in other words, he would at the same time be treading more widely in his own memory, sometimes producing tangential effects from past poems whether or not there was a bond of significance as well ('dizzy motion' – 'mazy motion' is a good example of such a connection: strong in repetition of movement and sound, lighter in terms of actual significance). We should also expect that where parallels of diction and significance concurred there might be a very intensive effect. A good example can be found in his *Monody on the Death of Chatterton*, where Chatterton's inspiration is described in the lines:

> *See*, as *floating* high *in air*
> Glitter the *sunny Visions* fair,
> His *eyes dance* rapture, and his bosom glows!   (*PW*, I, p. 127)

No less than seven of the strong words in these lines are found in *Kubla Khan*, and the congruity of theme goes without saying. If Wordsworth is the master of the numinous wild landscape, Coleridge's voice comes into its own with descriptions of ecstatic poetic inspiration.

Such are the general patterns that seem to emerge from an inspection of earlier usages by Wordsworth and Coleridge that are echoed in the poem. It is also profitable to turn to the various words which had not previously been used by either poet. This list, which is not long, would include such words as *pleasure-dome* (as opposed to *pleasure* and *dome* separately), *measureless* (as opposed to *measure*), *sinuous*, *greenery*, *at once and ever*, *ancestral* and *revive*. First, obviously, we look for evidence of Coleridge's innovatory skills – and we are not disappointed, since the *Oxford English Dictionary* gives no use of 'greenery' before *Kubla Khan*; the idea of reviving *within oneself* looks more sophisticated than the usages recorded there, also (though here we may be on less sure ground). The most unusual word to a modern eye, 'momently', is not in fact a new coinage, but both Coleridge and Wordsworth enjoyed using it afterwards, as we shall see.

The passage which is brought most into prominence when we look for words not previously used by either poet is the one that follows immediately after 'momently was forced':

> *Amid whose swift* half-intermitted *burst*
> *Huge fragments* vaulted *like* rebounding hail,
> *Or* chaffy grain *beneath the* thresher's flail . . .

The words previously unused by Coleridge (represented here of course by *lack* of italics) make up a large and distinctive knot within the poem as a whole; and the list (apart from 'flail', which is used rather memorably in 'the *measured* echo of the distant *flail*' in *Descriptive Sketches* l. 770) is shared with Wordsworth. The other striking feature of these lines is their descriptive skill. It is as if when Coleridge moves into representation of energy he manages also to break free of poetic practice, his own and others'. We cannot forget, of course, that the image of threshing is biblical: Isaiah (40:15) had spoken of the Lord as threshing the mountains and making the hills as chaff, and his imagery had been presented as an example of the biblical sublime by Lowth, whom Coleridge read in 1796.[36] Yet there is also a freshness here, a vivid realization of the images being drawn into service. When Coleridge copies phrases of biblical rhetoric into his notebooks (perhaps as fuel for projected rhetoric) they sometimes look perfervid and overblown; here the phrases have been fully assimilated into verse with a life of its own.

This is the nearest we come to a passage of direct originality in the poem. Elsewhere, as we have seen, Coleridge's originality is to be found working indirectly by way of previous poetic languages – not only Wordsworth's but those of eighteenth-century poets such as Gray and Collins. If we now move still further back, to a poet who stands behind these poets, we may begin to understand more precisely the kinds of pressure from the past that are being exerted on certain particular words and phrases, reminding us of other and older languages.

The language of loss

We have already suggested that the wistfulness towards Milton expressed by poets such as Gray and Collins might prompt a response less despairing than their own. They might mourn the impossibility of ever matching Milton's achievement, yet the very ecstasy of the language in which they did so could prompt a different response: that very language was perhaps waiting to be developed by a new Milton, if one should arise. And was it after all impossible to imagine a poet of equivalent strength? 'What if you should meet in the letters of any then living man, expressions concerning the young Milton . . . the same as mine of Wordsworth', wrote Coleridge to Poole in 1800, 'would it not convey to you a most delicious sensation?' (*CL*, I, p. 584). Meanwhile he was cherishing his own dreams of writing an epic poem (*CL*, I, pp. 320–1).

Yet if one tried to array Milton too readily in the singing robes of genius and sensuousness the paradox threatened to come full circle, since he himself, despite his insistence ('On Education', para. 17) that true poetry was 'simple, sensuous and passionate', had imposed severe limits on sensuous indulgence. Unless he went the full course with Blake and decided that Milton himself had erred in his view of pleasure, the young man who hoped to rival him must take on himself the same burden of moral

knowledge, the same belief that in every sensuous paradise there must
lurk a deadly serpent.[37]

Coleridge always accepted that knowledge, seeing his own life
as a constant series of movements between pleasure proposed and guilt
supervening. The paradigm is clear enough in *The Eolian Harp*, where,
as soon as he has set forth a speculative philosophy which might reconcile sensuous experience with the divine he rebukes himself (through
the imagined intervention of Sarah) for such 'unhallowed thoughts'
(so, incidentally, invoking the figure of the Lady in *Comus* when
she unlocks her lips in 'this unhallowed air' (l. 757)). When he and
Sarah enjoyed their married bliss in their Clevedon cottage later
on it was with an under knowledge of admonition, a sense first signalled
in his poem *Reflections on having left a Place of Retirement* by the passing Bristol
'son of Commerce' who was made to 'muse / With wiser feelings', declaring that it was 'a Bléssèd Place' (*PW*, I, p. 106). The ironic reference is
of course to Satan in *Paradise Lost*, Book Nine passing through Eden like
one 'long in populous city pent' before the Fall and looking with muffled
envy, 'stupidly good', at the happiness he sees there. For Coleridge,
however, the moral points differently, towards himself and Sarah. They
will be forced to take on Adam's fate and, in the interests of social responsibility, leave their paradise. The admonitory Miltonic note sounds for
them, also.

In *Kubla Khan*, likewise, every phrase with an echo of *Paradise Lost* is
shot through with plangency of foreknowledge. The very line with which
the poem opens recalls Adam, seeing

the destind walls
Of *Cambalu*, seat of Cathaian *Can* . . .   (IX, ll. 387–8)

– a foresight clouded with the double irony of Adam's knowledge that
this will be a post-lapsarian paradise, doomed to decay, and the reader's
that, as with the others to be catalogued, that decay has by now been
realized.

So with other words in the poem that recall *Paradise Lost*. Likenesses
are accompanied by telling differences. If the sacred river recalls the river
that flowed through Eden, the actual description of it, progressing
through caverns to a sunless sea, is in contrast with Milton's description
in Book Four of his river before the Fall, when it divided, part returning
to well up again in a spring near the Tree of Life. As Coleridge writes of
'sinuous rills', similarly, we are likely to be reminded that Milton's river-
fountain went on to water the garden 'with many a rill'; the word
'sinuous', which had not appeared before in Coleridge's poetry or Wordsworth's, was elsewhere used by Milton to describe the worms and

serpent-like creatures which for all their attractive colouring were to become pests after the Fall (IV, l. 481).

The undertone of admonition emerges more strongly in the second stanza. The word 'savage' occurs during Satan's entry into Paradise: 'Now to the ascent of that steep savage hill/ Satan had journeyed on' (IV, ll. 172–3). The 'cedarn cover', similarly, recalls his return just before the Fall:

> Nearer he drew, and many a walk traversed
> Of stateliest covert, cedar, pine, or palm . . .   (IX, ll. 434–5)

– the word 'cover' looking forward simultaneously to Adam's cry after the Fall: 'cover me ye pines, / Ye cedars, with innumerable boughs, / Hide me, where I may never see me more' (IX, ll. 1088–90). The woman wailing for her daemon-lover suggests Eve after the Fall – particularly if we recall the rabbinical tradition, known no doubt to both Milton and Coleridge, that the tempting of Eve took the form of actual sexual temptation by Satan [38] (there might also be a distant echo from the temptation of Samson in Milton's drama, by Delilah, who describes herself '*Wailing* thy absence in my widowed bed').[39]

The remainder of the stanza moves into a pattern which recalls the shape of *Paradise Lost* as a whole. The violent fountain is redolent of the vast destruction during the War in Heaven and the natural disorders after the Fall. When the river that flows from it moves with a mazy motion we recall not merely Gray's *Progress of Poetry* but Milton's river, which 'flowed with mazy error' – the strange foreboding note is sounded once again within a description of Paradise.[40] The ancestral voices prophesying war recall some of the grim visions of the future presented to Adam in the final books of *Paradise Lost*, while the syntactical form of the line recalls the faces that threatened from the walls of Eden as Adam and Eve departed: 'fierce faces threatening war' (XI, l. 641).

It is in the last stanza that the presence of *Paradise Lost* is most crucial, for there it intrudes with its admonitory implications on the most ecstatic statements in the poem, importing ambiguity. The most intensive echo comes, as has often been noticed, from the passage where Milton describes the later paradises which were to recall Eden, notably the one

> . . . where Abassin kings their issue guard
> Mount *Amara*, though this by some supposed
> True *Paradise*, under the Ethiop line
> By Nilus head . . .   (IV, ll. 280–3)

It is peculiarly appropriate that Coleridge's paradise should, by implication, be situated by the source of another sacred river, the Nile, in view both of the sun/moon, Isis and Osiris imagery in the poem and of the lore surrounding the troglodytes of Abyssinia (including their supposed invention of the dulcimer, a form of lyre).[41] Immediately before that description in Milton's poem there is another which is also appropriate:

> that Nyseian isle
> Girt with the river Triton, where old Cham
> Whom Gentiles Ammon call and Lybian Jove,
> Hid Amalthea and her florid son
> Young Bacchus from his stepdame Rhea's eye . . . (IV, ll. 275–9)

It is not simply that the infant Bacchus, as a young divinity, was nurtured on milk and honey, but that Rhea (as Richard Gerber points out) is an alternative name for Cybele, so that the threat from the destructive earth-mother moves in the background of Milton's narrative also.[42] Throughout Milton's description, moreover, we are reminded that these are all false paradises: they may image Eden, but none can actually replace it. The 'symphony and song' may remind us of the 'dulcet symphonies and voices sweet' in Book One of *Paradise Lost*; if so, we are simultaneously reminded that the 'fabric huge . . . Built like a temple' which was raised to their sound was none other than Pandaemonium, the meeting-place of the devils (I, ll. 710–57). And even when we see the words 'deep delight' we may recall that the nearest parallel in *Paradise Lost* is also admonitory:

> But if the sense of touch whereby mankind
> Is propagated seems such dear *delight*
> Beyond all other, think the same vouchsafed
> To cattle and each beast . . .   (VIII, ll. 579–82)

At this point a reinforcing echo is provided by that other master of the false paradise, Spenser. When Atin arrives at Acrasia's Bower of Bliss to rouse Cymochles, he finds him surrounded by 'a flock of *Damzelles*', charming him with sensuous pleasures, including 'sweet wordes, dropping like *honny dew*'. He is shocked to see him 'Thus in still waves of *deep delight* to wade' (II, v, 32.4–35.2). These warning echoes from *Paradise Lost* and *The Faerie Queene* link with the fact that the dome is built 'in air' – not, apparently, on the solid earth.

Although the language of *Paradise Lost* is one of the clearest presences in the poem it speaks with no simple voice: it offers sounds and sights of paradise but in the act reminds, always, that Eden is not to be permanently or totally regained. That alternation between attraction and admonition, each redoubling on the other, contributes strongly to the note of plangency in Coleridge's poem.

The language of *Paradise Lost* is not the only voice of Milton in the poem, as we shall see later, but the echoes from it, including the trisyllabic

Xanadu for 'Xamdu' (probably prompted unconsciously by the sound of Milton's 'Cambalu') and the Amara of the last stanza, are so strong that we do well to attend to them – and to the note that they portend. They point to the deepest division with Coleridge's own psyche and so to the hindrances he experienced as a poet when his moral consciousness was actively in play.

The language of mediation

Whenever the language of *Paradise Lost* emerges recognizably in *Kubla Khan* it introduces a tension between the aesthetic and the moral which reinforces the tension between the first two stanzas.

No-one after Milton quite succeeded in recreating that tension on a large scale: it perhaps required the impetus and momentum of an enthusiasm for the baroque if it were to be sustained for so long. Coleridge might have seemed unusually well qualified to revive the strain by his alternations between sensuous delight and deep guilt; but in fact the very extremity of their operation disabled him. The naturally welling language of his poetic imagination would regularly be turned to impotence or restraint as some act of extravagance was followed by moral reproach, whether from the external world or from his own conscience.

In such a situation the poetry of William Cowper had an important and subtle role to play. To 'the head of fancy of Akenside' and 'the heart and fancy of Bowles' in his catalogue of critical appreciation Coleridge added 'the "divine chit-chat" of Cowper', his terms acknowledging the sharpness of the tension that needed to be resolved (*CL*, I, p. 279).[43] Cowper had succeeded in the difficult task of reconciling the religious with the warmly sociable and finding a single diction that would contain them.

In the 1790s Cowper's ability to walk such tightropes had proved valuable in another context. For young radicals he was a figure of markedly liberal views who had yet contrived to remain acceptable across the whole range of contemporary society – his secret having been to propitiate the household gods of his age by blending his warm sensibility with a firmly moral uprightness. The resulting diction provided a secure form of discourse in times of difficulty. For Coleridge, who knew the alternate states of sensuous acceptance and gnawing guilt, and who had sometimes been plunged into depths of despair not unlike those which Cowper knew, the offered mode of mediation was of unusual value, for it marked the limits within which sensuousness could be indulged by the virtuous without danger.

During 1797–8 Cowper's mediation was to be particularly valuable to Coleridge as he wrought the art of his 'conversation poems' to its finest pitch. His presence in the greatest of them, *Frost at Midnight*, where his writing becomes a scaffolding from which Coleridge can build a more delicate diction of his own, has been noticed by more than one critic.[44] The relation of Cowper's poetry to *Kubla Khan* is of a different kind: providing a safety net for Coleridge in his aspirations to the sublime. That attempt to bring together poetry and philosophy, pursued seriously on a limited scale by Akenside, more light-heartedly by Darwin, found a strong yet sober advocate in Cowper, whose imagery was not altogether removed from that in Coleridge's closing lines. 'Philosophy', he wrote,

> baptiz'd
> In the pure fountain of eternal love
> Has eyes indeed . . .
> . . . Piety has found
> Friends in the friends of science, and true prayer
> Has flow'd from lips wet with Castalian dews.
> Such was thy wisdom, Newton, Childlike sage!
> . . . Such too thine,
> Milton, whose genius had angelic wings,
> And fed on manna!   (*The Task*, III, ll. 243–5; 249–52; 254–6)

(The last phrase was to be used by Hazlitt in later years to describe Coleridge, as he remembered him in 1798, at the height of his inspiration.)[45]

In *Charity* Cowper describes how the philosopher, studying astronomy, 'Drinks wisdom at the milky stream of light' (l. 319). Such lines provide secure underpinning for the more sensuous and ecstatic picture of genius in *Kubla Khan*. Elsewhere Coleridge's poem echoes large sections, rather than individual lines of Cowper's work, the reminiscences being usually not of words but of more general ideas. A good example is the account of the Sicilian earthquake in Book Two of *The Task*, a passage which may well have come to the minds of Wordsworth and Coleridge when they visited the Valley of Rocks and considered the kind of force that could have brought about such a scene. 'Alas for Sicily!' Cowper begins, 'rude *fragments* now / Lie scatter'd where the shapely column stood.' The scene is then explored as one which has displayed the power of God and of God's wrath, sounds of pastoral pleasure having given way to the noise of his punitive workings, desolation replacing what was formerly a paradisal scene:

> How does the earth receive him? – With what signs
> Of gratulation and delight, her king?
> Pours she not all her choicest gifts abroad,
> Her sweetest flow'rs, her aromatic gums,

> Disclosing paradise where'er he treads?
> She quakes at his approach. Her hollow womb,
> Conceiving thunders, through a thousand deeps
> And fiery *caverns* roars beneath his foot.

In the whole long passage of nearly sixty lines (II, ll. 75–132), there are some exact verbal links with *Kubla Khan*: '*fragments*', '*paradise*', '*caverns*', '*rocks*', 'Immense the *tumult*'; but they are few and scattered. It is the transition from sensuous paradise to destructive upheaval, exhibiting the two sides of God's activity, which is closest to Coleridge's poem. This sense of threat to an ordered plan is a recurring theme in Cowper. At one point he pictures 'th'omnipotent magician' Capability Brown raising a 'palace' for his patron, changing everything in the landscape – woods, hills and valleys:

> And streams, as if created for his use,
> Pursue the track of his directing wand,
> *Sinuous* or straight, now rapid and now slow,
> Now murmuring soft, now roaring in cascades –
> Ev'n as he bids!   (III, ll, 778–82)

Unfortunately, however, the expense of such building bankrupts the owner, and so he never enjoys what he has created. Similarly with another magical work of construction: the Russian palace of ice, the 'brittle prodigy' built by the Empress Anna at St Petersburg, to which the young Coleridge compared Erasmus Darwin's poetry:

> 'Twas transient in its nature, as in show
> 'Twas durable: as worthless, as it seem'd
> Intrinsically precious; to the foot
> Treacherous and false; it smil'd, and it was cold.   (V, ll. 173–6)

This is yet another vivid variation on the theme (which dogged Cowper even more than others in his age) that any paradisal enterprise is likely to involve a complementary element of threat, deceit or fragility.

But while Cowper's ideas contribute firmly to the transition between the first and second stanzas of *Kubla Khan*, his verbal influence is more often mediating and reconciling. The larger diction of Coleridge's lines, with their mingling of elegance and artistry, owed something to the neatly turned cadences of Cowper's discourse; we may note further that 'spot' is a favourite word of his ('Think on the fruitful and well-watered *spot*' (*Expostulation*, l. 418)) and that some of the less common words and phrases, such as '*sinuous*' (in relation to a stream), '*meandering*', '*this earth*', '*decree*', and '*tumult*' all occur at least twice in his work.[46]

Interestingly, however, the influence of Cowper seems to appear most directly when Coleridge revises his poem for publication many years later. When he substitutes for 'hideous tumult' 'ceaseless tumult', he is not only softening the diction of the line but substituting for a word more common in Milton than in Cowper a word which might well recall Cowper's line 'By ceaseless action all that is subsists' (*The Task*, I, l. 367) – a line likely to have appealed to Coleridge's interest in the role of energy and the nature of Being, and following closely on a description of a thresher with his flail, sending the chaff flying (I, ll. 355–9). Similarly, when Coleridge changes 'With walls and towers were compass'd round' to 'were girdled round', the increase in elegance is reminiscent of Cowper's 'The blooming groves that girdled her around' – used again (in *Heroism*, l. 6) of Etna and Sicily.

Cowper's language affected Coleridge's creating consciousness in various ways. His description of the Sicilian earthquake, where a sense of the earth's ambiguous power was overlaid by that of God's vengeance, added weight to the note of admonition that had run through Milton's descriptions of Paradise; his use of sensuous imagery for inspired knowledge gave backing to Coleridge's more unrestrained enthusiasm. Such influences, however, belonged properly to the speculative activity that had preceded the making of *Kubla Khan*. The role of Cowper's diction, as recalled in the making of the poem itself, tended to be a restrained and restraining one, helping to mould the sensuous elegances of the diction and particularly evident when Coleridge came to cast a revisionary eye over what had been created in a more passive state of mind. As opposed to the 'threshold' language which is the poem's most distinctive feature, this was a language of the circumference, fostering yet limiting at the same time. Its role, though muted, was still, given Coleridge's precarious purchase on the idea of genius, a valuable one.

The language of magical transformation

Although Cowper's language helped provide defensive cover for the advance from Milton's admonitory sublime to a sublime that would encompass larger areas of sensuous experience, its full value as a mediating agency emerged only when Coleridge was writing his meditative verse. There, in what are often known as the 'conversation poems', Cowper's delight in the power of human sensibility to respond to delicate phenomena in nature was extended into a full-scale exploration of the relationship between mind and nature, based on intimate sensuous observation. When Cowper praised inspired knowledge, by contrast, the moral reservations concerning human limitation which underlay his imagery of threatened paradise necessarily cast their shadow across that larger aim also. By the 1790s, moreover, the growth of specialized knowledges was making the creation of an all-embracing scientific theory still more difficult, reinforcing the sense that any projected totality of knowledge might prove to be no more than a doomed construction.

The precariousness of the framework for such a unified view as provided by philosophies such as those of Locke and Newton had been further demonstrated in Coleridge's time when the attempt of the French *philosophes* to build a new order on the basis of nature interpreted by reason had turned to destruction, defeated by flaws in human nature itself. There was, nevertheless, an older tradition of unified knowledge which had not been altogether discredited by recent events. During the Renaissance the Pythagorean philosophy, which linked the order of nature to that of music, had been an inspiration to poets and thinkers alike. This philosophy, unlike that which had been recently fashionable, did not rely upon an optimistic view of general human nature; on the contrary, it assumed that a harmonized knowledge would be reached only by a few, and under special conditions.

By the 1790s the revival of interest in various forms of Platonism meant that a young man such as Coleridge would be particularly alert to the potency of that tradition, which had been at its height in the late sixteenth century and still active in the early seventeenth, attracting, among others, the young Milton. And so it is apposite to recognize that despite the many echoes of *Paradise Lost* in *Kubla Khan*, the presence of Milton himself there is not limited to that of his greatest poem. When the echoes are from a word which has strong roots in Milton's early career, in fact, the connotations are often different, belonging rather to the magical world of art. The word 'haunt', for example, always a word with good overtones in Milton's writing, is used memorably in *L'Allegro*:

> Such sights as youthful poets dream
> On summer eves by haunted stream.   (ll. 129–30)

When we read that the shadow of the dome of pleasure 'floated midway on the wave', similarly, we might, if we were thinking only of *Paradise Lost*, recall Satan, 'With head uplift above the *wave*' while his other parts 'lay *floating* many a rood'; but such echoes fade as soon as we reach back into the early poetry and remember the time of peace that greets the birth of Christ, 'While Birds of calm sit brooding on the charmed *wave*', or Sabrina, sitting 'under the glassy cool translucent *wave*'.[47]

An echo of this kind, where the use of 'wave' completed a held moment of formalized enchantment, recalls, in turn, other poets who stand behind the early Milton. We have already noted two apparent echoes from Spenser, and it is a little surprising that his possible presence in *Kubla Khan* has been so little attended to in view of the overt 'Elizabethanism' of the sentence about Xanadu which Coleridge records as having been his starting-point:

... wherein are fertile Meddowes, pleasant springs, delightful Streames, and all sorts of beasts and game, and in the middest thereof a sumptuous house of pleasure ...

The word 'stately', which Purchas then used to describe Kubla's palace, is a favourite word of Spenser's, as we discover early in *The Faerie Queene*:

> A *stately* Pallace built of squared bricke,
> Which cunningly was without mortar laid,
> Whose *walls* were high, but nothing strong nor thick,
> And golden foile all over them displaid,
> That purest skye with brightnesse they dismaid
> High lifted up were many loftie *towres* ...   (I, iv, 4)

An enchanting sight, one might think, but as Spenser's epigraph has already revealed, this is the House of Pride – a place therefore of foreboding, not of permanent pleasure. Yet such buildings remain, like the Bower of Bliss, images of true beauty: we need think only of Spenser's lines to Sir Walter Raleigh, 'In whose high thoughts Pleasure hath built her bowre' – the last phrase of which he uses elsewhere to describe both true love and the good life.[48]

There are a number of words which, though figuring in sources examined so far, stand out in Spenser with particular clarity. In the 'Visions of Bellay', for example, we find the lines:

> ... Which, like incense of precious Cedar tree
> With balmie odours fill'd th'ayre farre and nie   (XI, ll. 3–4)

– a collocation which suggests that the incense-bearing trees and the cedarn covers were one and the same in Coleridge's imagination. 'Beware' is a particularly Spenserian word, as are 'savage' and 'haunt'. To Spenser, too, we turn for several uses of the phrase '*compassed round*' – for example,

> That turrets frame most admirable was
> Like highest heaven *compassed around.*[49]

(This is a good example of a Spenserean brightness darkened by a Miltonic overtone, for Milton's two uses of the phrase are 'With terrors and with clamours compassed round' and 'In darkness, and with dangers compassed round' (of Satan and himself respectively).)[50] As Richard Gerber points out, Spenser's most significant use for our purposes comes in the description of the mural crown of the Thames in *The Faerie Queene*:

> In which were many *towres* and castels set

> That it *encompast round* as with a golden fret.
> Like as the mother of the Gods, they say, . . .
> Old Cybele, arayd with pompous pryde . . .   (IV, xi, ll. 27–8)

Here the walls and towers by the river turn into the crown of Cybele's pride, forging another possible link in the imagery of ambiguous earth-powers. It should also be noted, however, that whereas the links with *Paradise Lost* can often be established within the implications of particular phrases or place-names, Spenser's presence is often more diffusive in effect. Consider, for example, the line

> So *did* the Gods by heavenly *doome decree* . . .
> (*The Ruines of Rome*, VI, l. 11)

The fascination of this echo is that if accepted it imports into the second line the implication that when Kubla Khan was decreeing his pleasure-dome he was also decreeing his pleasure-doom. Yet it is working through associations primarily of sound rather than of sense. And as one investigates such possible echoes from Spenser one is often unusually aware of a whole poetic context that is there giving life to the word or words. Coleridge himself wrote of *The Faerie Queene*,

It is in the domains neither of history or geography; it is ignorant of all artificial boundary, all material obstacles; it is truly in land of Faery, that is, of mental space. The poet has placed you in a dream, a charmed sleep, and you neither wish nor have the power, to inquire where you are, or how you got there. (*Misc C*, p. 36)

A similar atmosphere of enchantment (working also through the general dreamwork of the poem) seems to cling to many of the words in *Kubla Khan* which have Spenserian parallels; it comes particularly to the fore in Coleridge's third stanza, where the 'miracle' that is described reconciles heat and cold, a relationship the paradoxical nature of which had fascinated the Elizabethans. Shakespeare was fond of it: ' . . . hot ice and wondrous strange snow. /How shall we find the concord of this discord?'; 'To bathe in fiery floods or to reside /In thrilling region of thick-ribbed ice'; 'O, who can hold a fire in his hand /By thinking on the frosty Caucasus? . . . Or wallow naked in December snow/ By thinking on fantastic summer's heat?'; 'There may as well be amity and life/ 'Tween snow and fire, as treason and my love'.[51] Between these opposites human sensation sometimes recognizes strange points of concord: when Coleridge drew up a list of illustrations for his favourite saying 'Extremes meet', the first was a quotation from *Paradise Lost*: 'The parching Air / Burns frore, and Cold performs the Effect of Fire.'[52] This, however, was torturing, a foretaste of the state where the damned are constantly hurried back and forth to burn in 'beds of raging fire' and 'starve in ice' by turns (II, ll. 598–603). Coleridge's own search was for points of positive correspondence between such extremes, allowing them to be reconciled into a more beneficient unity. 'Socinianism moonlight – Methodism a Stove / O for some sun to unite heat & light' (*CN*, I, 1233). It is an equivalent miracle that is envisaged in the third stanza of *Kubla Khan*.

There is also an erotic strain here, of course: since the most common correlatives of fire and ice in Elizabethan times were lust and chastity. Here, too, if Coleridge looked for the point of reconciliation and harmony between apparent opposites, he would be taken further into the heart of Renaissance poetry. The phrase 'of rare device' leads on to *The Faerie Queene*, which contains lines such as 'So fashioned a Porch with rare device' (of the Bower of Bliss), 'A work of rare device and wondrous wit' or 'could be fram'd by workmans rare device'.[53] Yet here again the most relevant parallel turns out to be one which has the phrase in a less exact form:

> That fire, which all things melts, should harden yse;
> And yse, which is congeal'd with senselesse cold,
> Should kindle fyre by wonderfull devyse!
> Such is the powre of love in gentle mind,
> That it can alter all the course of kynd.   (*Amoretti*, xxx)

Love, for the Elizabethans, was the key which could work such miracles of transformation, and so it remained for Coleridge. His ideal of a love which could reconcile the extremes of heat and ice into a temperate sensuousness had already been well figured in poems such as Milton's early *Arcades*, where the nymphs and swains approaching the Countess, 'Sitting like a goddess bright,/ In the centre of her light', comment:

> Might she the wise Latona be
> Or the towered Cybele,
> Mother of a hundred gods;
> Juno dare not give her odds . . .   (ll. 20–3)

The Apollonian and the Dionysiac emerge here figured respectively as Latona (mother of Apollo and Diana), or Cybele, multi-breasted earth-mother: they are seen as reconciled in Milton's Countess just as they are to be in Coleridge's 'Abyssinian maid'. In Milton's poem the 'Genius of the Wood' goes on to address the swains themselves:

> Of famous Arcady ye are, and sprung
> Of that renowned flood, so often sung,
> Divine Alpheus, who by secret sluice,
> Stole under seas to meet his Arethuse . . .   (ll. 28–31)

Creative dialectic is again in play, this time between Alpheus and Arethusa, and continues as the Genius describes his own beneficent work in nature, fostering and protecting growing things everywhere while at night he can relax and attend to the 'celestial sirens' harmony':

Such *sweet* compulsion doth in *music* lie
To lull the daughters of Necessity,
And keep unsteady Nature to her law,
And the low *world* in *measured motion* draw
After the heavenly tune, which none can hear
Of human mould with gross unpurged ear . . .   (ll. 68–73)

We are close here to the inner music that Coleridge wishes to recapture in his last stanza, a music that would inspire the creative spirit to feats of miraculous construction, embodying reconciliation of warring elements in the manner that Sir John Davies pictured when he described Love as the intervening creator in *Orchestra*:

Then did he rarefy the element,
    And in the centre of the ring appear,
The beams that from his forehead spreading went,
    Begot an horror, and religious fear
In all the souls that round about him were;
    Which in their ears attentiveness procures,
    While he, with such like sounds their minds allures.[54]

Davies, also, brings us close to the inner significance of Coleridge's aspiration, which is to achieve the poetry that reconciles warring elements. The ultimate calling of the poet is to become (in Coleridge's own words) one of the 'Gods of Love who tame the Chaos' (*CN*, ii, 2355). Small wonder then, that the last lines have led critics to recall an ancient description of poets who, like 'the priests of Cybele', 'perform not their Dances, while they have the free Use of their Understandings' but who, 'possessed by some Divine Power, are like the Priestesses of Bacchus, who, full of the God, no longer draw Water, but *Honey* and *Milk* out of the Springs and Fountains . . .'. For these are the poets as envisaged in the *Ion*.[55] Behind Spenser and Sir John Davies stands Plato, chief ancient guarantor of the love-lore that we earlier traced out of the poem's mythical symbolism. By way of the Platonic tradition, as revived among the Elizabethans, that idea of a reconciling yet fearful love has lived on into the traditions behind Coleridge's last stanza, where the Elizabethan music that had returned to haunt English Romantic poetry, and the visionary symbolism which he had developed from many mythological sources, find themselves for a moment magically at one.

After-languages

A reader who has accepted the course of the discussion so far and attended to the various languages proposed may by now feel glutted by the richness of the meanings that have emerged. This is likely to be a temporary effect, however. It remains perfectly possible to revert to a reading that treats the poem as a smaller, self-contained artefact, with images and words working on each other more directly. At this level, the results of an investigation such as has been carried out here are simply to help establish a remarkably high degree of common resolution in the presented images – certainly in the first two stanzas, where the element of dialectic between natural creativeness and natural destructiveness is reinforced in all the sources we have examined. The images of the last stanza, equally, are consistently those of a more absolute paradise – though somewhere behind the triumphant conclusiveness of the final cadences lurk intimations of false paradises, still warning the poet that to attempt such absolute creation within the limitations of human life may after all be folly. Just how the elements in that last stanza are weighed will vary from reader to reader. The powerful rhythm assists the sense of triumph, yet to those who attend more delicately to details of language there may seem to be an accompanying distancing and diminishing effect – almost as if the whole scene were about to disappear. In the very depths of the language, I have argued, there lies an irresoluble ambiguity between the language of loss in Milton's *Paradise Lost* and the language of surviving possibility in the Elizabethans and the young Milton. Coleridge is torn both ways and his language reflects the fact.

It would be a pity to rest in a 'simple' reading of the poem, therefore, since *Kubla Khan* provides a many-faceted example of the 'overdetermination' that Freud traced in much dream-work. It is only by degrees that we detect within its apparently simple diction the various voices that are contending together, but as we do so new perspectives of meaning open. The preceding discussion has relied on the assumption that Coleridge was not only a voracious reader but unusually tenacious in remembering passages that impressed him in his favourite authors, and that the peculiar conditions under which *Kubla Khan* was composed brought some of those impressed words and images into an unusual concentration and complexity of patterning. I have spoken of successive 'layers' of language but to do so would be misleading if it suggested that each layer was of the same kind. Although held together in a single linear word-continuum, the different languages of *Kubla Khan* sometimes operate in quite different modes. The poem which contains them cannot, therefore, be reduced to a final fixity, but will constantly be leading the mind in new directions. Among other things it reminds the reader that intense study of a poetic structure can bring one, at one extreme, to the point where it resolves itself into 'music' or, at another, to that where it passes into an intermelting array of visual images. Coleridge's query whether 'that . . . can be called composition in which all the images rose up before him as *things*, with a parallel production of the correspondent expressions, without any sensation or consciousness of effort' (in the most convincing part of his later account (*PW*, I, p. 296)) indicates something of what is at issue. There remains the question of significance, which dances in and out, back and forth, freeing the reader to range between seeing the poem as an attempt at total comprehension of human experience, as a personal document, or, for that matter, as a poem about itself.

The language that mediates most readily between the surface and the hidden layers is that of genius and sensuousness. This was the new way of writing that Coleridge had been most drawn to in the intervening years, and it here emerges into a mode that for those who heard the poem for the first time was startlingly original. While it foreshadows future developments in the Romantic poetry of feeling, as in Byron and Keats, it also at the time of composition formed part of a new departure in Coleridge's poetry which we associate more generally with his poems of the supernatural. I have assumed from the outset that the composition of the poem took place when Coleridge originally said it did, late in 1797. If it was later, Coleridge's creative breakthrough came with *The Ancient Mariner*, conceived in November of that year, and *Kubla Khan* is to be read as one of the results of that breakthrough. On the present evidence, however, it is better to assume that the breakthrough came during the unusual state of semi-conscious composition described in his 1816 preface, and that the precipitation of his speculative themes in the patterning of *Kubla Khan* assisted the gestation of the still more riddling *Ancient Mariner*. In that poem, the themes we have been examining appear, but in a different ordering. The note of fear which was struck from time to time in *Kubla Khan*, to be quelled in the final triumphant cadences, dominates much of the longer poem, as Coleridge explores the paradox that awareness of the esoteric harmony underlying all things might be granted to an ordinary person only under unusual conditions of fear and terror. In this poem visionary knowledge, far from inducing a state of ecstasy, is intermingled with the taking on of guilt. It becomes a cross between curse and blessing.[56]

Another good reason for believing that *Kubla Khan* came first is that by late 1797 Coleridge seems, at least for the time being, to have laid the ghost of Miltonic language in the form in which it had dogged his early poetry. Milton has little part to play in *The Ancient Mariner* (which recalls rather the poetry of Spenser and Sir John Davies)[57] while in *Christabel* the Miltonic echo that sounds momentarily with 'The gate that was ironed within and without, / Where an army in battle array had marched out' suggests that if the castle is Milton's Hell it is simply in its form as a 'world of death'.[58]

Meanwhile some of the words and phrases in *Kubla Khan* continued to enjoy their transformed life in Coleridge's subsequent poetry. In some cases the effect is slight. 'Down to', which entered his poetry for the first time in 'down to a sunless sea', recurs in *The Ancient Mariner* in the Hermit's wood which 'slopes down to the sea', the 'honey-dew' in the voice 'as soft as honey-dew'. Here it is as much as anything a similarity of tone that is being carried over. We may also notice, however, that some of the most vigorous words and images in the poem echo words in the energetic middle section: 'burst', in 'We were the first / That ever burst'; 'flung' in 'It flung the blood into my head'; and the 'bound' of 'rebounded' in 'She made a sudden bound'. The 'chaffy grain' may be echoed very specifically in the 'Like chaff we drove along' of the 1798 version – though here we are aware of the common matrix of speculation that lies behind both poems. The relationship between the flashing eye of the genius in *Kubla Khan* and the 'glittering eye' of the Mariner, for example, may be a conscious one, marking the difference between inspiration in its active and passive forms. So much is suggested by the previous glittering eye of the baby in 'The Nightingale'.

Two verbal formulations in the poem seem to have pleased Coleridge particularly. 'Momently' was used again a year later in a letter to his wife describing his voyage to Germany ('a beautiful white cloud of foam at momently intervals roars & rushes by the side of the Vessel') and re-emerged during the winter of 1799–1800 (*CL*, I, p. 416).[59] Similarly with the 'fast thick pants' of the earth's breathing. Coleridge's nearest approach to the phrase in his previous poetry had been his 'thick and struggling breath' in the 'Ode to the Departing Year', but in 'The Three Graves' the new form occurs more closely: 'But soon they heard his hard quick pants.' A few months later the form has been transmuted into a phrase to describe the nightingale 'That crowds, and hurries, and precipitates / With fast thick warble his delicious notes'. After that the use disperses itself into the language of 'And pleasures flow in so thick and fast' in the conclusion to Part II of *Christabel*.[60] The words associated with music and song also enjoy a vivid afterlife: the Hermit *'singeth loud his goodly hymns'* while the Pilot's boy laughs *'loud and long'*; the Bard in *Christabel* sets out to exorcise the evil spirit 'with music *loud*', 'with *music* strong and saintly *song*'.

For some years the poem enjoyed a limited subterranean life in Coleridge's circle. The Crewe manuscript was apparently sent to Southey, and may have influenced his 'Oriental' writing.[61] The first major reac-

tion in print came from Mary ('Perdita') Robinson, who had once composed a poem in circumstances similar to those described by Coleridge[62]
and who, in her *Lines to S. T. Coleridge Esq.* (written about the end of 1799)
wrote,

> Now by the source, which lab'ring heaves
>   The mystic fountain, bubbling, panting,
> While gossamer its net-work weaves,
>   Adown the blue lawn, slanting!
> I'll mark thy 'sunny dome,' and view
> Thy 'caves of ice,' thy fields of dew![63]

In the same way Collier was to record in his diary for 1811 Coleridge's
recitation of 'some lines he had written many years ago upon the building
of a Dream-palace by Kubla-Khan' (*Sh C*, II, p. 47). Mary Robinson's
reference to the 'mystic fountain' suggests that Coleridge might have ex-
pounded the meaning of the poem to her, but if so he was to give up the
practice. His relationship with Sara Hutchinson failed to fulfil the hopes
created by his intense affection for her, and this must have sapped his faith
in love's paradisal transforming power. In such circumstances the absolute paradise projected in his last stanza turned back into the vulnerable
paradise of his first, and the familiar dialectic between sensuous indulgence and guilt reasserted itself. It is not surprising, then, that his attitude to the poem itself was defensive. By the time he wrote his preface
in 1816 he was offering it as a 'psychological curiosity' – leaving only
the subtitle, *A Vision in a Dream*, to tease an attentive reader with other
possibilities.

The most tantalizing silence on the subject of the poem's meaning is
that of Wordsworth, who was close enough to Coleridge in 1797 to have
known something of the speculations involved, but who is not known to
have even mentioned the poem before 1830, when he discussed it with
some undergraduates at Cambridge.[64] He told them that he thought it
'might very possibly have been composed between sleeping and waking,
or as he expressed it, in a morning sleep; he said some of his own best
thoughts had come to him in that way'. His view is in line with Coleridge's early statement that it was produced in 'a sort of Reverie'; but
the matter does not end there, since there are signs in his own poetry and
prose that he had not only read the poem intently but was aware of its
larger meanings. Elisabeth Schneider has drawn attention to his eloquent
journal letter to Coleridge of late December 1799, describing their visit
to Hardraw Force, where they found themselves in an ice-festooned
cavern, while the stream 'shot from between the rows of icicles in ir-
regular fits of strength and with a body of water that *momently* varied'. He

commented later, 'In the luxury of our imaginations we could not help feeding on the pleasure which in the heat of a July noon this cavern would spread through a frame exquisitely sensible.'[65] On the same journey the ruins by a well and the tale told by a peasant gave him the inspiration for his poem 'Hartleap Well', in which he recorded how a knight, impressed by the leap of a hart which he had been hunting, had commemorated its feat by raising a 'pleasure-house' at the spot, the ruins of which are now all that survive. This mute comment by nature on his presumption is reinforced by the fate of his mansion, 'The finest palace of a hundred realms' of which nothing whatever remains (*WPW*, II, pp. 249–54). Just as *Peter Bell* may be read as Wordsworth's version of *The Ancient Mariner*, so this poem, with its vaunting scheme of pleasure succeeded by an avenging desolation ('More doleful place did never eye survey') seems to be Wordsworth's own version of Coleridge's first two stanzas. Elsewhere the imagery of the opening is echoed in his description of

> Gehol's matchless gardens, in a clime
> Chosen from widest empire, for delight
> Of the Tartarian dynasty composed
> Beyond that mighty wall, not fabulous
> (China's stupendous mound!) by patient skill
> Of myriads, and boon Nature's lavish help:
> Scene linked to scene, and ever-growing change,
> Soft, grand, or gay, with palaces and domes
> Of pleasure spangled over . . .   (1805, VIII, ll. 123–31)

The description continues through many lines, down to 'And all the landscape endlessly enriched / With waters running, falling, or asleep', before Wordsworth turns back to his own 'true' paradise: 'But lovelier far than this the paradise / Where I was reared . . .'. Equally telling, in view of the bodily language that we have traced in the poem, is the reflection, earlier in *The Prelude*,

> Caverns there were within my mind which sun
> Could never penetrate . . .   (1805, III, ll. 246–7)

I have already suggested that the imagery of genius in the poem may have been connected by Coleridge with his sense of Wordsworth's powers, and there is some evidence that the point was not lost on Wordsworth himself. Although he normally took a humble view of himself his language sometimes suggests something more sublime, as when he describes the beatitude that hides the soul in its power,

> like the mighty flood of Nile
> Poured from his fount of *Abyssinian* clouds
> To fertilize the whole Egyptian plain.   (1850, VI, ll. 614–16)

and describes Como as 'a darling bosomed up / In *Abyssinian* privacy'. There is, equally, a touch of the Abyssinian maid in one of his best-known figures, the Solitary Reaper, whose song has such a powerfully vivifying effect in the heart of the hearer; while visionary creation such as that at the end of the poem is reflected in 'The Power of Sound':

> The gift to king Amphion
> That walled a city with its melody
> Was for belief no dream . . .
>
> (ll. 129–31; *WPW*, ii, p. 327)

The most telling reference, however, comes in *The Prelude* when Wordsworth (in lines that recall Cowper's 'lips wet with Castalian dews') thinks of Coleridge in Sicily and remembers him telling how 'bees with honey fed / Divine Comates':

> How with their honey from the fields they came
> And fed him there, alive, from month to month,
> Because the goatherd, blessèd man, had lips
> Wet with the Muse's nectar.   (1805, x, ll. 1023–6)

A few lines later Wordsworth pictures Coleridge searching for the Arethusa fountain and, when he finds one that might have been the original, lingering 'as a gladsome votary'. Such references suggest some intimacy with the 'subtle speculations' and 'toils abstruse / Among . . . Platonic forms / Of wild ideal pageantry' (as Wordsworth called them elsewhere in *The Prelude* (1805, vi, ll. 308–10)) which Coleridge was fond of exploring and which had helped to shape his poem.

Coleridge meanwhile seems to have remained unsure what to do with his work. It was not until Byron heard him recite the lines and responded enthusiastically that he was encouraged to publish them as they stood. (Byron, who can be said to have exploited the vein of genius and sensibility more successfully than anyone else of his generation, himself used the line 'And woman wailing for her demon-lover' as the epigraph for *Heaven and Earth*.)

Mrs Coleridge was driven almost to despair by news of the forthcoming publication ('Oh! when will he ever give his friends anything but pain?'),[66] while Lamb was cautious about its likely reception, describing it as 'a vision' – ' . . . which said vision he repeats so enchantingly that it irradiates & brings Heaven & Elysian bowers into my parlour while he sings or says it, but there is an observation Never tell thy dreams, and I am almost afraid that Kubla Khan is an owl that wont bear day light. I fear lest it shall be discovered by the lantern of typography & clear reducting to letters, no better than nonsense, or no sense' (*LL(M)*, iii, p. 215). In the event the immediate reception was tepid. Hazlitt, taking his cue from Lamb, perhaps, commented that the lines showed how Coleridge could 'write better *nonsense* verses than any man in England', *Kubla Khan* being 'not a poem, but a musical composition'.[67] The most favourable comment, from an anonymous writer in the *Anti-Jacobin*,[68] was that, like 'The Pains of Sleep', the poem was 'not wholly discreditable to the author's talents'.

Soon, however, the tide began to turn. By 1821 Leigh Hunt was describing the poem as 'a voice and a vision, an everlasting tune in our mouths, a dream fit for Cambuscan and all his poets . . . a piece of the invisible world made visible by a sun at midnight and sliding before our eyes'.[69] John Bowring, similarly, commented that he who had ever heard it read well 'without exquisite enjoyment at that time, and a haunting recollection at intervals ever after' certainly had 'no music in his soul'.[70]

With such comments the terms for nineteenth-century appreciation of the poem were set in place, falling in with a growing fashion for 'musical' poetry. It is possible that one or two of Coleridge's contemporaries read the poem symbolically: the 'Indian maid' of Keats's *Endymion*, conceived in the year following its publication, may have owed something to Coleridge's 'Abyssinian maid', for example. But apart from a single intriguing use of 'Mount Abora' in Coventry Patmore's poetry[71] there is little further hint of a search for meaning. Instead the poem was seized upon gratefully as an example of pure music in poetry.

There is of course good reason for this in the poem itself. When we ask where the originality lies in *Kubla Khan* as a whole, we are likely to conclude that it is in the general sense of enchantment that is embodied particularly in the rhythms and cadences. But to limit the poem's effects in this way is not only to accede to those who feel that such poetry is the purest and best, but to miss the degree to which Coleridge's achievement in this mode is like an iridescent veil, lightly screening the reader from conflicts that lie hidden in the very languages that are being used to such effect. Those conflicts themselves are the result of Coleridge's aspirations: aspirations towards psychic integration in the individual and harmonizing social order in the community. In these very quests, also, there is implicit the desire for a version of human knowledge which will answer to the best potentialities of humankind. Meanwhile, however, the languages of the poem are betraying a continual clash between that of Spenser, the Elizabethans and the early Milton at their most lyrical, which suggests that the aspiration for a total harmonizing and paradisal knowledge is attainable, and that of the later Milton, which is built in the sad assurance that for human beings the knowledge of such paradise must always be a knowledge of loss.

Much of Coleridge's later prose work represented a series of continuing attempts to find harmonizing solutions to such problems, which he encountered in himself and in the society about him. Yet as his notebooks and letters record, those aspirations were always shot through with a darker awareness of his own failures of will, suggesting that the moral capabilities of human beings were not powerful enough to sustain any such state, even if it could be temporarily attained. The struggle between the two recognitions seems sometimes to have been subtle and intense enough to thwart the actual production of poetry: to glimpse its more creative existence by way of the languages that run together beneath the gothic sensuousness of *Kubla Khan* is to catch his mind, for once, in its fullest ferment. It may also suggest something important about the problems that have been inherent in making serious poetry during the last two hundred years.

Notes

[1] First described in *TLS* (2 Aug 1934), p. 541 and later reproduced photographically in articles by John Shelton, *Review of English Literature* VII (1966), pp. 32–42, and T. C. Skeat *British Museum Quarterly* XXVI (1962–3), pp. 77–83.

[2] See my essay 'Poems of the Supernatural', in *S. T. Coleridge*, ed. R. L. Brett, 'Writers and their Background' series (1971), pp. 54–60. For my retention of the four stanza division of *Kubla Khan* used by Coleridge in all editions appearing during his lifetime, see my note in the 1970 reprint of *Coleridge the Visionary*, p. 10.

[3] See 'Poems of the Supernatural', p. 60, and D. H. Karrfalt, 'Another Note on "Kubla Khan" and Coleridge's retirement to Ash Farm', *N&Q* CCXI (May 1966), pp. 171–2.

[4] See Joan Cooper, *Culbone: A Spiritual History* (Culbone, 1977), pp. 27–36.

[5] See e.g. Jacob Bryant, *A New System of an Analysis of Ancient Mythology* (1774–6), and the *Mythological, Etymological and Historical Dictionary* derived from it by William Holwell (1793).

[6] Samuel Purchas, *Purchas his Pilgrimage* (1617), p. 472.

[7] See Berkeley's *Siris*, sect. 187, quoted in *Coleridge the Visionary*, pp. 119, 218.

[8] Ibid., p. 211.

[9] Ibid., pp. 216–22.

[10] Ibid., pp. 251–5; 262.

[11] See passages (including Isaiah 7: 15–4) quoted ibid., pp. 265–6.

[12] Richard Gerber, 'Keys to "Kubla Khan"', *English Studies* XLIV (1963), pp. 1–21. Since this appeared, Coleridge's familiarity with Cybele has been confirmed by publication of a description in 1805 of rocks, 'once or twice with a Tower like the Head of Cybele' (*CN*, II, 2690), and his 1818 reflection that 'in the elder world the Infinite was hidden in the Finite – Every Stream had its Naiad – the Earth its Cybele, the Ocean its Neptune'(*CN*, III, 4378, f.3v).

[13] Some typical examples are by R. F. Fleissner, who draws attention to the river meandering for several miles to the sea in *Tom Jones* (*N&Q* CCV

(1960), pp. 103–5); S. C. Harrex, who notices the 'dome where Pleasure holds her midnight reign' in Goldsmith's *Deserted Village* (*N&Q* CCXI (1966), pp. 172–3), and Michael Grosvenor Myer, who notes versions of the ballad *The Daemon Lover* – especially Scott's in 1812 (*N&Q* CCXXVIII (1983), p. 219).

14   See my article 'Influence and Independence in Blake' in *Interpreting Blake*, ed. M. Phillips (Cambridge, 1978), pp. 196–261.

15   See letter to Poole, Oct 1797, *CL*, I, p. 347, letter of 1815, *CL*, IV, p. 606, and my *Coleridge's Poetic Intelligence* (1977), pp. 23–32.

16   *BL*, I, pp. 19–20 – where, however, Coleridge dates the paper a year earlier.

17   The echoes of Erasmus Darwin have been noticed by Lowes in *The Road to Xanadu*, pp. 18f, 35f, 94–9, 189f, 464–5, 473, 495; one or two more have been noted by Norman Fruman, *Coleridge: The Damaged Archangel*, pp. 243 and 253–4. For *Zoönomia* see my *Coleridge's Poetic Intelligence*, pp. 50–7, 74–7.

18   Cf. *The Pleasures of the Imagination* (1757), I, ll. 98–102.

19   *The Pleasures of Imagination*, II, ll. 273–6, 281–8, 292–5, 660–2 (and 175–771 generally).

20   *PW*, I, pp. 45–6 and n. See W. Braekman, 'The Influence of William Collins on Poems Written by Coleridge in 1793', *Revue des Langues Vivantes* (1965), pp. 228–39.

21   John Ower, 'Another Analogue of Coleridge's "Kubla Khan" ', *N&Q*, CCXII, p. 294.

22   'Ode on the Poetical Character', ll. 34–40.

23   *Coleridge the Visionary*, pp. 258–9.

24   'The Passions', ll. 62–8 quoted Lowes, *Road to Xanadu*, pp. 399–400. Lowes also mentions Coleridge's project for editing Gray and Collins (see *CN*, I, 161 (2) and 174 (15)).

25   Dryden, 'Song for St. Cecilia's Day', l. 14; *WPW*, I, p. 259.

26   James Ridley, *Tales of the Genii*, 1766, I, pp. 51–2, 135–6, 77. Cf. my essay 'Poems of the Supernatural', pp. 65–6.

27   A translation of this by Southey is reproduced in my *Coleridge the Visionary*, pp. 297–300.

28   *Tales of the Genii*, I, p. 81.

29   See, e.g., Lawrence Hanson, *Life of Coleridge: The Early Years* (1938), pp. 34–40.

30   Song of Solomon 4: 12–15, 16; 8: 10, quoted in *Coleridge the Visionary*, pp. 270–1.

31   S. Purchas, *Hakluytus Posthumus or Purchas his Pilgrimes* (Glasgow, 1905–7), XI, pp. 208–9. Quoted Lowes, pp. 361–2.

32   For further accounts, with references, see my *Wordsworth in Time* (1979), pp. 43–6, and *Wordsworth and the Human Heart* (1978), pp. 26–36.

33   See Rivers's Speech in *The Borderers*, ll. 1493–6, *PW*, I, p. 187, partly used again *Prelude* (1805), X, ll. 826–9.

34   *Oxford 'Prelude'*, p. 633. See J. Wordsworth, *The Borders of Vision* (Oxford, 1982), pp. 36–8 and nn.

35   For detailed experiments in this field see F. C. Bartlett, *Remembering: A Study in Experiential and Social Psychology* (Cambridge, 1932).

36   R. Lowth, *De Sacra Poesi Hebraeorum*, tr. G. Gregory (1787), I, pp. 148–9. Coleridge borrowed the original Latin edition of 1753 from Bristol Library from 16 to 22 Sept. 1796. *Bristol LB*, p. 123.

37 'I saw Milton in imagination and . . . he wished me to show the falsehood of his doctrine that the pleasures of sex arose from the Fall.' E. J. Morley, *Henry Crabb Robinson on Books and their Writers* (1938), I, p. 330. See also my discussion in *Blake's Humanism* (Manchester, 1968), pp. 31–2.

38 See J. M. Evans, *Paradise Lost and the Genesis Tradition* (Oxford, 1968), pp. 48–50.

39 Line 806. A more likely reference is to the wailing for Thammuz: see *Paradise Lost*, I. ll. 446–57.

40 *Paradise Lost*, IV, l. 239. It is also reinforced when Satan resolves to fold himself in the 'mazy folds' of the serpent; *ibid.*, IX, ll. 161–2. Milton's use of 'mazy' in Book Four was no doubt responsible for the extraordinary popularity of the word in eighteenth-century verse.

41 See *Coleridge the Visionary*, pp. 63, 208, 241, 252f, 342.

42 '"Keys to "Kubla Khan" "', pp. 16–17.

43 To Hazlitt in 1798 he 'spoke of Cowper as the best modern poet': 'My First Acquaintance with Poets', *H Works*, XVII, p. 120.

44 See, e.g., Humphry House, *Coleridge* (1953), pp. 78–9; N. Fruman, *Coleridge the Damaged Archangel* (1971), pp. 305–9.

45 'On the living Poets', *H Works*, V, pp. 165–8.

46 *The Task*, I, l. 165; III, l. 778; 'Anti-Thelypthora', l. 11; *The Task*, III, l. 203; 'Alexander Selkirk', l. 28, 'Hope', l. 749; 'Conversation', l. 467, 'Epistle to Lady Austen', I, l. 60 (also 'decreed'); 'Mutual Forbearance', l. 48, *The Task*, IV, 100 (in both cases the word '*war*' comes later in the line).

47 *Paradise Lost*, I, ll. 192–6; 'Morning of Christ's Nativity', l. 68, 'Comus', l. 861.

48 Dedicatory Sonnet to *Faerie Queene*, VIII, 6; cf. *Amoretti* LXV, 14, 'Virgil's Gnat', l. 135.

49 *Faerie Queene*, II, ix, 45, ll. 1–2. In the Bible the form 'compassed about' is more normally used.

50 *Paradise Lost*, II, l. 862; VII, l. 27.

51 *Midsummer Night's Dream*, V, i, ll. 59–60; *Measure for Measure*, III, i. l. 123; *Richard II*, I, iii, ll. 296–9; *Merchant of Venice*, III, ii, l. 31.

52 *CN*, I, 1725, citing *Paradise Lost*, II, ll. 594–5.

53 *Faerie Queene*, II, xii, 54.1, III, i. 34–6, V, ix, 27–8. (Cf. also V, v, 12.3: 'A miracle of nature's goodly praise'.)

54 Sir John Davies, *Poetical Works* (1733), p. 248.

55 *Ion* 534 (tr. F. Sydenham (1759), pp. 42–4). Cf. E. Schneider, *Coleridge, Opium and 'Kubla Khan'* (1966), pp. 245–6 and P. Adair, *The Waking Dream* (1967), pp. 138–9.

56 See my *Coleridge's Poetic Intelligence*, ch. vii.

57 Cf. the 'great chrystal eye' of the ocean in 'Orchestra', Sir John Davies, *Poetical Works*, p. 155, and the occurrence in the poem of words such as 'eftsoones', 'Kirke', 'swound' and 'clomb', all of which are Spenserian.

58 See my 'Poems of the Supernatural', p. 82.

59 Cf. 'The whole scene moves and bustles momently'; *Piccolomini*, *PW*, II, p. 613.

60 'Departing Year', l. 111; 'Three Graves', l. 520; 'Nightingale', l. 45; *Christabel*, l. 662. *PW*, I, pp. 166, 284, 235.

61 It bears a pencilled note, 'Sent by Mr. Southey, as an autograph of Coleridge'. J. Shelton, *loc. cit.*, p. 33.

62 See her account in *Memoirs of the Late Mrs Robinson, Written by Herself* (1801),

II, pp. 129–32. 'One night after bathing . . . she swallowed . . . near eighty drops of laudanum. Having slept for some hours, she awoke and, calling her daughter, desired her to take a pen and write what she should dictate . . . she repeated, throughout, the admirable poem of The Maniac, much faster than it could be committed to paper.' Quoted Elisabeth Schneider, *Coleridge, Opium and 'Kubla Khan'*, p. 86. Coleridge knew Mrs Robinson during the winter of 1799–1800.

63 The poem is in *The Poetical Works of the late Mrs Mary Robinson* (1806), II, pp. 298–303.

64 F. Alford, *Life, Journals and Letters of Henry Alford* (1873), p. 62.

65 Letter to Coleridge, 24–7 Dec. 1799. *EY*, pp. 279–80. Schneider, *Coleridge, Opium and 'Kubla Khan'*, pp. 184–5, 208.

66 *Minnow among Tritons: Mrs S. T. Coleridge's Letters to Thomas Poole*, ed. S. Potter (1934), p. 13.

67 *The Examiner*, 2 June 1816, pp. 348–9., reptd *Coleridge, the Critical Heritage*, ed. J. R. de J. Jackson (1970) (hereafter *CH*), pp. 205–8.

68 July 1816, I, pp. 632–6, reptd *CH*, pp. 217–21.

69 *The Examiner*, 21 October 1821, pp. 664–7, reptd *CH*, pp. 417–9.

70 *Westminster Review*, January 1830, XII, pp. i-31, reptd *CH*, pp. 525–56.

71 C. Patmore 'The Contract', in *The Unknown Eros* (1877), p. 21. See also my *Coleridge the Visionary*, pp. 292 ff.

Notes on the contributors

* J. ROBERT BARTH, S.J., is Professor of English at the University of Missouri-Columbia, and like most of the contributors to this volume is a regular participant in the Wordsworth Summer Conference held annually at Dove Cottage, Grasmere. His publications include *Coleridge and Christian Doctrine* (1969) and *The Symbolic Imagination: Coleridge and the Romantic Tradition* (1977). He is currently working on an extended study of the theme of love in Coleridge.

* JOHN BEER is Reader in English Literature at the University of Cambridge and a Fellow of Peterhouse. His books include *Coleridge the Visionary*, *The Achievement of E. M. Forster*, *Blake's Humanism*, *Blake's Visionary Universe*, *Coleridge's Poetic Intelligence*, *Wordsworth and the Human Heart* and *Wordsworth in Time*. During 1975 he was a visiting professor at the University of Virginia.

* KRISTINE DUGAS, Assistant Professor of English and Women's Studies at Ohio State University, received her B.A. from the University of Wisconsin in 1977 and her Ph.D. from Cornell University in 1984. She is editing *The White Doe of Rylstone*, volume 13 of the Cornell Wordsworth series.

* DAVID V. ERDMAN teaches Romantic Literature at SUNY Stony Brook, and edits the Bulletin of Research in the Humanities for the New York Public Library. The author of *Blake: Prophet Against Empire*, and editor of numerous volumes of the works of Blake, he has also edited Coleridge's *Essays on his Times* for the Collected Coleridge, and is coordinating editor of the annual *Romantic Movement Bibliography*.

* NORMAN FRUMAN, who is Professor of English at the University of Minnesota, studied at Columbia University and the Sorbonne, and did his first teaching as a prisoner of war. He has published on a wide variety of subjects, and is best known for his *Coleridge, The Damaged Archangel* (1972). His latest work is a new edition of *Biographia Literaria*.

* RICHARD GRAVIL teaches at the College of St Mark & St John, Plymouth, part of which – St Mark's – had Derwent Coleridge as its principal. His publications include casebooks on *The Prelude* and

263

Gulliver's Travels, and essays on Wordsworth, Coleridge, Swift, Lawrence, Conrad, and contemporary British poets. He has taught at the University of Victoria and the University of Lodz.

* ANTHONY JOHN HARDING studied at Manchester and Cambridge before going to Canada in 1974 to teach at the University of Saskatchewan, where he is now Associate Professor of English. His publications include *Coleridge and the Idea of Love* (1974), *Biblical and Poetic Inspiration in Coleridge and His Tradition* (1984), and essays on Thoreau, James Marsh and John Sterling.

* PETER LARKIN has been, since 1970, Assistant Librarian (Humanities) in the University of Warwick Library. He has published articles on Hardy and Wordsworth, and presented papers at the Wordsworth Summer Conferences. A sequence of his prose poetry was published in 1983, and a selection from more recent work in 1984.

* MOLLY LEFEBURE's study of the poet, *Samuel Taylor Coleridge: A Bondage of Opium* (1974), was informed by a close working knowledge of drug addiction and its pathology. She is the author of 'high-brow childrens' novels', and of two works on the history, topography and culture of the Lake District, *Cumberland Heritage* (1970) and *Cumbrian Discovery* (1977). She is soon to publish a biography of Mrs Coleridge, together with unpublished letters.

* THOMAS McFARLAND is Murray Professor of English Literature at Princeton University. His work on Coleridge includes *Coleridge and the Pantheist Tradition* (1969), *Romanticism and the Forms of Ruin: Wordsworth, Coleridge and Modalities of Fragmentation* (1981), and *Originality and Imagination* (1985). Among his forthcoming works are *Shapes of Culture* and *Romantic Cruxes: the English Essayists and the Spirit of the Age*. He is currently editing Coleridge's *Opus Maximum* for the Collected Coleridge.

* LUCY NEWLYN is a lecturer in English at St Edmund Hall, Oxford. Since completing her D.Phil. thesis in 1983 she has held Lectureships at Mansfield College and Christ Church. She has published articles in a number of journals and her book, *Coleridge, Wordsworth and the Language of Allusion* is being published by O.U.P.

* STEPHEN PARRISH is Professor of English at Cornell University. He edited *The Prelude, 1798–1799* for the Cornell Wordsworth Series, of which he is General Editor. His many publications include *The Art of the Lyrical Ballads* (1973), and *Keats and the Bostonians* (with Hyder Rollins). He is also editor of the Cornell Concordances.

* NICHOLAS ROE is Lecturer in English at the Queen's Universi-

ty, Belfast. He read English at Trinity College, Oxford, and remained there to write his D.Phil. thesis on Wordsworth, Coleridge and the French Revolution. He has published a number of articles on the political activities of these poets in the 1790s, and a full length study of these topics in relation to their poetry is in course of publication.

* WILLIAM RUDDICK lectures at the University of Manchester. His publications include an edition of *Peter's Letters to his Kinsfolk* by J. G. Lockhart, articles on Milton, Scott, Byron and Lamb, and (as co-editor) exhibition catalogues on Joseph Farington and Kate Greenaway. He is preparing a book on the early Tours and Guides to the Lake District, up to and including Wordsworth's *Guide*.

* JONATHAN WORDSWORTH is a Fellow of St Catherine's College, Oxford, and University Lecturer in Romantic Studies. He is also Chairman of the Dove Cottage Trust, Grasmere. Publications include *The Music of Humanity* (1969), *Bicentenary Wordsworth Studies* (1970) (as editor and contributor), and *The Borders of Vision* (1983). Editions of Wordsworth to date: *Selections* (1974), *The Prelude* 1799, 1805, 1850 (1979, with collaboration from M. H. Abrams and Stephen Gill), *The Ruined Cottage, The Brothers and Michael* (1984) and *The Pedlar, Tintern Abbey* and *Two-Part Prelude* (1984). He is at present working on a three-volume Cambridge *Wordsworth* and a book on Romantic imagination from Coleridge to Stevens.

Index